THE BETTER PART, GOSPEL OF LUKE

A CHRIST-CENTERED RESOURCE
FOR PERSONAL PRAYER

BY JOHN BARTUNEK, LC, THD

SOPHIA INSTITUTE PRESS
Manchester, NH

Cover image: iStock.com

Imprimi Potest:
Francisco Mateos, LC
Nihil Obstat
Imprimatur
† Most Reverend Henry J. Mansell
Archbishop of Hartford
June 14, 2007

ISBN: 978-1-64413-145-9

First Printing

CONTENTS

INTRODUCTION

The Importance of Personal Prayer

Conscientious Christians pray. Their typical days, weeks, months, and years are seasoned with prayer—traditional prayers, liturgical prayers, spontaneous prayers. They make prayer commitments, giving structure and consistency to their faith journey. Prayer keeps Christians united to the Vine, so their lives can bear the fruit both they and Christ long for.[1]

Among the most basic prayer commitments is one that can have more bearing on your life than any other, because it is more personalized: the daily meditation. Certainly you can't mature as a Christian without the sacramental life, just as crops can't mature without sunlight and soil. And the various devotional and vocal prayers that punctuate your day keep you strong and focused amid the unrelenting blows of the unchristian culture all around you. But, as generations of saints and sinners have found out, that is not enough.

Without the daily renewal and deepening of your personal relationship with Jesus Christ that happens especially through meditation, sooner or later routine sets in. You get into a rut. Your prayers get mechanical, your sacramental life slides into hollow ritualism, and before you know it, your faith gets sidelined and you get dragged back into the rat race in some form or other. The daily meditation keeps your faith, that pearl of great price,[2] lively, supple, and relevant.

It irrigates the soil of your soul, making your sacramental life more fruitful, keeping your other prayer commitments meaningful, and continually opening up new vistas along the path to spiritual maturity.

This is why spiritual writers through the ages have so consistently emphasized the importance of meditation, also known as mental prayer, since it is a deeply interior way of praying. Here is what two doctors of the Church have to say about it:

> He who neglects mental prayer needs not a devil to carry him to hell, but he brings himself there with his own hands. (St. Teresa of Ávila)

> It is morally impossible for him who neglects meditation to live without sin. (St. Alphonsus Ligouri)

> And by experience we see that many persons who recite a great number of vocal prayers, the Office and the Rosary, fall into sin, and continue to live

---

1 "I am the vine, and you are the branches. He who dwells in me, as I dwell in him, bears much fruit; for apart from me you can do nothing" (Jn 15:5).

2 "Again, the kingdom of Heaven is like a merchant looking for fine pearls; when he finds one of great value he goes and sells everything he owns and buys it" (Mt 13:45-46).

> in sin. But he who attends to mental prayer scarcely ever falls into sin, and should he have the misfortune of falling into it, he will hardly continue to live in so miserable a state; he will either give up mental prayer, or renounce sin. Meditation and sin cannot stand together. However abandoned a soul may be, if she perseveres in meditation, God will bring her to salvation. (St. Alphonsus Ligouri)

The daily meditation, in other words, is not an optional extra for super-Christians; it's every Christian's bread and butter. Without it, your Christian identity shrivels. But it's not enough just to do a daily meditation; you need to learn to do it better and better. Maturity in the spiritual life depends to a great extent on constantly going deeper in your personal prayer life. The law of life is growth, so if your capacity for mental prayer isn't growing, your life with Christ is in danger of wasting away.[3]

The Benefits of *The Better Part*

The Better Part is meant to foster and accompany growth in mental prayer. It is not primarily instructional (like a "how-to" book on prayer) and not complete in itself (like ready-made meditations). Rather, *The Better Part* is a companion for your daily meditation, providing enough structure and content to serve as a catalyst for you to learn to pray better as you pray, to make your meditation more personal and personalized, to help you learn to follow the Holy Spirit's lead more readily.

Used well, *The Better Part* helps you discover at least three things:

1. ***HOW YOU PRAY BEST.*** Prayer is similar to walking. To walk, everyone has to follow the same principles of physics—friction, gravity, muscle propulsion, momentum. And yet, even though the principles are the same, everyone's walk is a little bit different. When babies learn to walk, they start out clumsy and awkward, until they develop the rhythm and style proper to their body type, personality, and environment. Meditation follows a similar pattern: the same principles for all, activated uniquely

3 This intensely personal prayer—Christian meditation—contributes significantly to the communal life of the Church. As our personal friendship with Christ develops, we become more mature and fruitful members of his Body, the Church. Therefore, although this book focuses on the personal encounter with Christ in meditation, it does not mean to belittle the ecclesial nature of the Christian vocation. The two aspects are complementary and intertwined.

by each. *The Better Part* can help you wherever you happen to be on the spectrum.

2. ***THE DIMENSIONS OF CHRIST.*** (These include his characteristics, actions, words, and sufferings that speak most profoundly to your soul.) The heart of Christianity is each believer's friendship with Jesus Christ, and friendship is never generic. If you read the lives of the saints, you quickly discover how each one's holiness has its own, unique flavor—St. Francis' friendship with Christ was different than St. Dominic's, because St. Francis and St. Dominic were different. Every person has a unique personality, so each person will relate to Christ uniquely. God created you to know him as only you can know him. *The Better Part* is designed to help you uncover and develop the distinctiveness of your friendship with Christ, without which you will always feel more restless and dissatisfied than you need to.

3. ***THE INESTIMABLE VALUE OF A DEEP PRAYER LIFE.*** Every Christian has a responsibility to become an expert in prayer. Without a mature prayer life, you cannot become a mature Christian, in which case you will never discover the authentic Christian joy, wisdom, and fruitfulness that flow from being fully formed in Christ.[4] This expertise in prayer comes only from the Holy Spirit, who uses two training methods:

   First, he instructs you in prayer through the experience of others. Through the ages, the Church and its saints have produced a whole library of accessible, practical, and inspiring books on prayer. You'll want to read them and study them. All Christians who take their friendship with Christ seriously should regularly read good books (and plenty of good articles) on prayer or the spiritual life.[5] *The Better Part* is not one of these treatises on prayer, but Part I: The Fundamentals of Christian Meditation will serve as a refresher course on the central principles of Christian meditation, something you can refer to in order to keep your meditation in shape.

   Second, the Holy Spirit makes you an expert in prayer when you actually pray. You need to dive into the pool and splash around so that your coach can teach you to swim. Here *The Better Part* is a valuable

---

4 "My dear children, for whom I am again in the pains of childbirth until Christ is formed in you..." (Gal 4:19); "...to build up the Body of Christ, until we all reach unity in faith and knowledge of the Son of God and form the perfect man, fully mature with the fullness of Christ himself. If we live by the truth and in love, we shall grow completely into Christ" (Eph 4:12-13, 15).

5 See Appendix 2 for a list of excellent books on prayer and the spiritual life.

tool. Instead of supplying you with spiritual reflections gleaned from others' experience of God in prayer, as many spiritual books do so well, this is a truly Christ-centered resource, purposely open-ended, but in a strategically structured way. Each unit in *The Better Part* will thus serve as a springboard for your own praying, a way to aid your docility to the Holy Spirit's coaching (Part I: The Fundamentals of Christian Meditation explains more fully how this works.)

And so, if you are just starting out in Christian meditation, *The Better Part* can help you lay a firm foundation. If you are already adept at mental prayer, its open-ended, Christ-centered structure makes it a rich and flexible source of meditation material. It is perhaps most helpful, however, for those who would label themselves neither beginners nor advanced, but somewhere in between.

Many Christians—even committed, well-formed Christians—reach a plateau in their prayer life because their meditation stays at the level of reflective spiritual reading, even when their soul is ready to go higher (this distinction is explained more fully later). *The Better Part*, used rightly, can help foster this move forward.

The rest of this Introduction will explain how *The Better Part* is composed and organized. It will show how to make this book a tool for knowing, loving, and following Christ more wholeheartedly, which is what God is hoping for, your soul is thirsting for, and all prayer is striving for. Then, Part I: The Fundamentals of Christian Meditation will review in detail the fundamental principles, steps, and difficulties of Christian meditation, and it will equip you to do a checkup on your own prayer life. The rest of the book contains the actual meditation units.

Be forewarned—*The Better Part* is not necessarily the easier part. Christ never promised that following him would be easy. In fact, he promised it wouldn't. The spiritual life is full of mystery. You find yourself on unfamiliar ground when you trust God to lead you to richer pastures. Often it is much more comfortable to keep doing what you already know how to do, like Martha, who busied herself in the kitchen when Jesus and the Apostles dropped by for dinner. Her sister Mary put normal activities on hold for a little while instead and sat at Jesus' feet, drinking in his wisdom, his love, and his beauty. When Martha complained that Mary was being lazy and impractical, Jesus smiled at her and said:

"Martha, Martha. You worry and fret about so many things, and yet few are needed, indeed only one. It is Mary who has chosen the better part, and it is not to be taken from her." (Lk 10:41-42)

How to Use *THE BETTER PART*

No book can pray for you. No book can teach you to pray. At most, a book can be a useful tool. *The Better Part* is designed to help you engage more actively in the quest of Christian meditation so you can reap more fruits of spiritual growth.

The Better Part is divided into units. Each unit consists of five parts: a passage from the Gospel according to St. Luke and a four-part commentary based on the same four themes throughout the book: Christ the Lord, Christ the Teacher, Christ the Friend, and Christ in My Life. This structure is substantive, meditative, and flexible.

SUBSTANTIVE: A CHRIST-CENTERED RESOURCE *The Better Part* is substantive because it is eminently Christ-centered. Christ is the "power of God and the wisdom of God" (1 Cor 1:24). The gospel is the good news of the "boundless riches" (Eph 3:8) of Christ. The Christian life consists in knowing, loving, and imitating Christ. He is God made man—"for the sake of our salvation," as the Creed puts it. You will never be able to exhaust the Gospels. They are the heart of the Bible and the privileged place of God's revelation. The Old Testament was a preparation for the revelation of the mystery of Christ, and the rest of the New Testament shows the consequences and flowering of this revelation. The Church has always taught that because Christ is God as well as man, all of his words and actions as recorded in the Gospels are not merely edifying events from the past. Christ spoke and lived them with you in mind, so that they are alive and relevant and addressed to you and the circumstances of your life at every moment: "Jesus Christ is the same yesterday and today and forever" (Heb 13:8).

This eminently Christ-centered approach derives especially from the spirituality characterizing the Legionaries of Christ and the Regnum Christi Movement.[6] This spirituality, one of the many fragrant blossoms in the Church's rich garden of charisms, imbues the entire book.

At times in your spiritual journey you may find other sources more stimulating and helpful for your personal prayer, but after each such sojourn you will feel yourself drawn back to the Gospels, the living Word of God, the life,

---

6 For more information on the Legionaries of Christ and the Regnum Christi Movement, visit www.legionariesofchrist.org and www.regnumchristi.org.

words, actions, passion, death, and resurrection of our Lord and Savior, the inexhaustible fountain of the Christian life:

> In the beginning was the Word. . . . Through him all things were made; without him nothing was made that has been made. In him was life, and that life was the light of men . . . grace and truth came through Jesus Christ. No one has ever seen God. It is God the only Son, who is close to the Father's heart, who has made him known. (Jn 1:1, 3-4, 17-18)

MEDITATIVE: A PRAYER-INDUCING COMMENTARY ON THE GOSPEL *The Better Part* is meditative because the commentaries are drawn from the Gospel passages themselves and point back to them. They do not develop an instructional treatise on the spiritual life, nor do they focus on biblical exegesis or catechetical apologetics. Those themes are addressed only to help the magnificent figure of Christ emerge more clearly.

The four-part commentaries on each Gospel passage follow the same structure, which is based on the faculties of the human soul. Thus, each unit helps bring the whole person into contact with Christ.

- The "Christ the Lord" commentary points out how a particular passage illuminates Christ's mission and qualities as Savior, Redeemer, and Eternal King. It appeals most directly to the will, the faculty by which you make the decisions that direct your life. As you contemplate more and more the grandeur and splendor of Christ the Savior and King, your decision to follow him unconditionally grows firmer and firmer.
- The "Christ the Teacher" commentary draws out the lessons that Christ teaches by word and example, appealing more directly to the intellect. You cannot live out your desire and decision to follow Christ if you don't know the standards and criteria of thought, speech, and behavior that Christ asks of his disciples.
- The "Christ the Friend" commentary brings out the intimate and personal love of Christ's heart. Jesus doesn't want to be a distant Savior and leader; he longs to be your companion and most intimate friend, and he shows this longing over and over again in the Gospels. This commentary appeals to your heart, so that your

discipleship grows in passion, intimacy, and warmth, as well as determination and wisdom.[7]

- The "Christ in My Life" commentary (mostly written in the first person) consists of observations and questions in the form of prayers that help you evaluate how you should follow Christ in light of the passage you are meditating on. This is a safety net: if for some reason your reflections up to that point have stayed too abstract, this section will bring Christ's light to bear on your own life, behavior, and attitudes, provoking a fresh conversion and re-commitment to Christ. This commentary will also help ensure that your spiritual life goes beyond mere feelings and good dispositions to become truly transforming.

The quotations from saints and popes that introduce each chapter of the Gospels and each meditation unit can also spark reflection. They add spice to the commentaries by giving glimpses into the deep experience of Christ had by your older brothers and sisters in the faith.

Each unit in *The Better Part*, then, facilitates bringing your will, mind, heart, and life into contact with Christ, helping you bathe your soul in his truth and his grace. The entire series has only one aim: to help you know, love, and follow Christ more closely by encountering him more deeply and personally in prayer.

FLEXIBLE: THEMES AND VARIATIONS *The Better Part* is flexible because it can be used in so many ways—it is not a book of meditations, but a resource for personal prayer.

At the end of the book (in Appendix 1), you will find a list of Gospel passages in relation to some pivotal virtues of the spiritual life. This resource can be used in numerous ways, depending on your personal needs and preferences.

You may prefer to coordinate your meditations with the needs of your own spiritual life, in accord with your program of spiritual work. For a Christian, growth in virtue never occurs simply through one's own effort; you become more like Christ by contemplating Christ, opening your heart to his grace, loving him more, and being moved to imitate him within the circumstances of your own life. In this case, you can use Appendix 1 to find the theme you are hoping to meditate on and bookmark the units that correspond.

---

7 Sometimes this commentary includes paragraphs written in such a way that Jesus or others are speaking in the first person. This literary technique is designed to stimulate fresh encounters with familiar passages, not to revise Catholic doctrine.

You can also combine *The Better Part* with other meditation material, alternating between Gospel passages and spiritual books, or using a Gospel passage and one of its commentaries from *The Better Part* as the first point of consideration, a paragraph from another source as the second point, and so on.

The Better Part is also a good resource if you have a commitment to do a daily Gospel reflection in addition to a morning meditation.

***MEDITATING WITH* THE BETTER PART** However you choose to arrange your meditation themes (and this is a good topic to discuss with a confessor or spiritual director), always keep in mind the difference between spiritual reading and meditation.

If you were to use *The Better Part* for spiritual reading or a daily Gospel reflection, you would simply read an entire unit or two straight through each day—a helpful and beneficial spiritual exercise.

Meditating on a unit, however, requires a different approach. In this case, each part of the unit is treated separately, like five connected rooms in an art gallery. During the Consider and Converse stages of your meditation, you spend plenty of time in one room before moving on to the next.

Start with the Gospel passage itself. You take enough time to enter into the scene with your imagination, with your mind, searching for whatever God has to say to you in that passage. You may find a word or phrase or characteristic in the Gospel passage itself that is sufficient material for consideration and conversation for the entire meditation. The next day, you begin there again, and you may find that the Holy Spirit wants you to stay with the same point and continue to savor it. This is ideal, because it means that your prayer is intensely personal—direct contact between you and the Gospel, with the Holy Spirit setting the pace.

When you are ready, either in the same meditation or the next day, you move on to the first commentary. You read it and consider it calmly, inquiringly. The main point of the commentary may strike you and become the matter of further conversation and consideration, or a tangential point may pop out at you. The commentary may bring you right back into the Gospel passage, showing you something that you hadn't noticed before. Here again, your search for what Christ has to tell you proceeds at a more meditative pace than spiritual reading—there is no rush; you take your time and seek out what the Holy Spirit has to say to you.

Just one of the commentaries may occupy an entire meditation, or even two or three meditations, or on the other hand, it may take only a minute or two. Whenever you are ready, you move on to the next commentary, into the next room of the gallery, continuing to search for whatever nourishment God has ready for your soul.

If you find yourself regularly spending more than one day with the same unit, try going back to the Gospel passage each day at the start of your meditation, before moving on to the next commentary. Thus, your first point each day is the Gospel passage, then you move on to the first commentary; the next day you start again with the Gospel passage, then move right to the second commentary, and so on. God's Word really is the privileged place for your encounter with him.

Feel free to write in the margins and mark certain passages or units that speak to you in a special way. All Christians should have their favorite Gospel passages, the ones they go back to again and again to feed their souls. In fact, since *The Better Part* is built on the Gospel itself, it is a resource that can be used over and over again, through the years.

As a resource for meditation, then, *The Better Part* affords you both substantive structure (Gospel commentaries directed to your will, intellect, and heart) and flexibility. You should feel no pressure to go at any particular pace. One unit a day is more than enough material for a twenty-minute meditation done well, or even for thirty or sixty minutes. You may find yourself drawn to stay with the same unit for a few days, working through it slowly. Try your best to follow along, however the Holy Spirit guides you. What matters is that your prayer life deepens and your friendship with Christ grows—not that you finish this book in record time.

SMALL-GROUP USE *The Better Part*, though primarily a resource for personal prayer, also can be adapted for use in small groups. It is more spiritual than instructional, but its Christ-centered character can make it rewarding as a change of pace from typical Bible study guides or *Catechism* studies.

A prayer group that meets each week, for instance, may use *The Better Part* throughout a liturgical season (such as Lent or Advent), or for a few weeks before a particular event (a pilgrimage, convention, or local feast day), or when they want to get a Christ-centered perspective on a particular aspect of the spiritual or moral life (following Appendix 1), or as the regular material for their first meeting of every month. It can also be used in this way for breakout activities during retreats or weekend conferences.

In any of these instances, the small group can read through the Gospel passage and commentaries together, a different member reading each paragraph out loud. Then the members of the group can reflect on the passage together, discussing what strikes them and what applications it has to their own lives. To facilitate this type of use, suggested questions for small-group discussion and references to the *Catechism* finish off each unit. These can be skipped when the book is being used by individuals.

Now that you understand the approach and usefulness of *The Better Part*, you can start using the meditation units (Part II) immediately. Eventually, however, you may want to take some time to read over Part I: The Fundamentals of Christian Meditation. If you feel called to go deeper in your personal prayer life, a review of Part I, with its explanation of the fundamentals of Christian prayer and meditation, could be just the kick start you need.

PART I

THE FUNDAMENTALS OF CHRISTIAN MEDITATION

God's Idea of Prayer

What do you picture yourself doing when you start to pray? What image, conscious or not, do you have in mind? Maybe you see yourself merely fulfilling a duty, as when you mechanically recited the Pledge of Allegiance at the start of homeroom in elementary school. Maybe you see prayer as an exercise in self-mastery and self-help, an activity (pseudo-yoga, aerobics, or weightlifting) that keeps you fit. Whatever you think you are doing when you pray affects the way in which you do it. So the more your idea of prayer matches God's, the better.

Prayer at its most basic level is conversation with God. This seems obvious, but it harbors an awesome reality. To converse with someone implies that that someone wants to pay attention to you; otherwise you have a monologue, not a conversation. The mere existence of prayer, then, implies that God is paying attention, that he is interested in spending time with you. Christian prayer is an invitation from God to the one who prays—it starts with God, not with you.

The whole Christian edifice is built on this simple but awe-inspiring reality. The *Catechism* highlights it in its very first numbers: "At every time and in every place, God draws close to man.... God never ceases to draw man to himself" (1, 27). God is always drawing close to you, and he is always drawing you closer to him. That means he is always thinking of you, just like the Good Shepherd who is always thinking of and watching over his sheep. Prayer starts here.

You are the lost and hungry sheep; God is the shepherd who knows what you desire and need and is guiding you to the lush fields and cool, refreshing waters of his Truth and Love. The shepherd sees the big picture, the whole landscape, the weather, the seasons, the dangers and the opportunities; the sheep can only focus on this little patch of grass here, and then that one over there. Prayer is the Good Shepherd, wise and loving, guiding the hungry, shortsighted, and needy sheep.

God is the real protagonist of Christian prayer. Prayer is the soul's response to God's initiative. The essence of Christian prayer is relationship. As the *Catechism* puts it: "'Great is the mystery of the faith!' ... This mystery, then, requires that the faithful believe in it, that they celebrate it, and that they live from it in a vital and personal relationship with the living and true God. *This relationship is prayer*" (2558, emphasis added).

Prayer, then, is more than just a dry religious duty, more than self-centered and self-sufficient self-help techniques; Christian prayer is a friendship with

God in Christ. It's being led by the Good Shepherd to ever richer pastures in the Father's Kingdom.[1]

CHRISTIAN PRAYER: EMINENTLY CHRIST-CENTERED What matters most in prayer, then, is docility to that Good Shepherd, listening honestly, and responding honestly. God is already at work; you have only to hear and heed his voice. So how does he speak to you?

> At various times in the past and in various different ways, God spoke to our ancestors through the prophets; but in our own time, the last days, he has spoken to us through his Son, the Son that he has appointed to inherit everything and through whom he made everything there is. He is the radiant light of God's glory and the perfect copy of his nature, sustaining the universe by his powerful command.... That is why all you who are holy brothers and have had the same heavenly call should *turn your minds to Jesus*, the apostle and the high priest of our religion. (Heb 1:1-3, 3:1, emphasis added)

Christian prayer consists of that "turning your minds to Jesus," the Jesus who comes to us through the revelation of the Gospels, the good news of the "boundless riches" (Eph 3:8) of Christ.

The riches of Christ are boundless because Christ is God-revealing-himself-to-man, and God is infinite. If you want to get to know someone, it is not enough to learn about him from the outside; he has to open his mind and heart to you so that you can really get to know him, his thoughts and desires, his yearnings, his way of seeing things, his concerns. Interpersonal knowledge, the knowledge of friendship, can only come through personal revelation. Christ is God-revealing-himself-to-you, offering you his friendship.

Only Christianity is so bold as to claim that in Christ we can become God's friends, because only Christianity offers a God who becomes man, a Good Shepherd who becomes a lamb in order to win the hearts of his sheep:

> I shall not call you servants any more, because a servant does not know his master's business; I call you friends, because I have made known to you everything I have learnt from my Father. (Jn 15:15)

---

1. This definition of prayer—as an ongoing relationship—doesn't eliminate the need for particular times dedicated to conversing exclusively with God. There's no better way to make a relationship grow cold than by not spending quality time together. As the *Catechism* puts it, "We cannot pray 'at all times' if we do not pray at specific times, consciously willing it" (2697).

True Christian prayer, therefore, is Christ-centered prayer. Above all, it consists in contemplating and conversing with Christ, the "one Mediator" between man and God (1 Tim 2:5). In prayer you sit at the feet of the Master, listening, learning, and loving. Prayer comes before action; the active life, for a Christian, overflows from the contemplative life. Christ taught this clearly when he gently reprimanded the busy and active Martha for resenting her sister Mary's preference for the better part.[2]

CHRISTIAN PRAYER: INTENSELY PERSONAL But Christian prayer is also intensely personal. This friendship that God has struck up with you is unique, because you are unique. Christ is not an abstract concept; he is a real person. Your friendship with him will be different than mine, because your life experience, your personality, your problems and talents and worries and dreams are different from mine, and all those things go into a friendship.

In prayer, the Good Shepherd calls his sheep individually: "One by one he calls his own sheep and leads them out. When he has brought out his flock, he goes ahead of them, and the sheep follow because they know his voice" (Jn 10:3-4).

Prayer is Christ speaking to you in your heart, revealing himself to you in accordance with what he knows you need to discover, to know, to see. At the same time, prayer is your attentive listening to that revelation, your response to what he reveals, and the trusting, reciprocal revelation of your heart—your needs, your hopes, your desires—to him.

In this mysterious, beautiful exchange, the Holy Spirit is the bridge between Christ's heart and yours: "Now instead of the spirit of the world, we have received the Spirit that comes from God, to teach us to understand the gifts that he has given us" (1 Cor 2:12). The Holy Spirit guides you from within, into the arms of Christ, the Good Shepherd of your soul.

If you want to continue to discover and follow God's path for your life, this intensely personal prayer is a necessary element in your spiritual life. While you are here on earth, God always has more he wants to reveal to you and teach you; he has more he wants to do in your soul, making it the masterpiece that he envisioned from the moment of your creation. He also has more work he wants you to do, work that will bear eternal fruit to his glory and to your temporal and everlasting happiness. All of this, however, requires that you grow closer to him, and without a deep, personal prayer life, you simply can't.

---

2 "Martha, Martha, you worry and fret about so many things, and yet few are needed, indeed only one. It is Mary who has chosen **the better part**; it is not to be taken from her" (Lk 10:42, emphasis added).

Types of Prayer

The *Catechism* points out three basic types of personal (as distinct from liturgical) prayer: vocal, meditative, and contemplative, all of which have a place in the life of every Christian.

VOCAL PRAYER Vocal prayer consists in reciting ready-made prayers, either silently or aloud, uniting the intention of your heart to the meaning of the words. This is the kind of prayer recited together before a meal, or the prayers often used each morning to offer the day to God. The words of these prayers help you express your faith, and that conscious expression in turn reinforces and exercises your faith. All Christians should have their favorite vocal prayers, the ones that resonate best with their own experience of Christ, the ones they can go back to in moments of dryness, sickness, or difficulty.

MEDITATIVE PRAYER Meditative prayer is less formulaic. It consists in lifting the heart and mind to God through focused reflection on some truth of God's revelation. It involves the intellect, the imagination, the memory, the emotions—the whole person.

In meditation, as you turn your gaze to God's self-revelation in Christ, you are moved to respond to what you discover there, and you converse with God in the silence of your own heart, using words that flow naturally from your reflection.

Reflecting on the beauty of God's creation, for example, may move your heart to expressions of gratitude, wonder, and praise. Reflecting on the sufferings of Christ during his crucifixion may move your heart to expressions of humility, repentance, or sorrow. The essence of Christian meditation is this exchange between God and the soul, this intimate conversation that can take an infinite variety of forms.

Whatever form it takes, however, meditation puts the soul in contact with the eternal truths, with the love and goodness of God in its myriad manifestations, and thus it nourishes the soul. Just as the body needs food and water, the soul feeds on truth and love. This reality is categorically ignored by today's secularized, materialistic culture, which denies the existence of moral and spiritual truth and reduces love to mere feelings. Meditative prayer, however, only makes sense in light of this reality. Your soul, your intellect, and your will yearn for the true and the good as much as your body yearns for solid food and fresh drink. "Happy are those who hunger and thirst for what is right: they shall be satisfied" (Mt 5:6).

Meditation's loving dialogue between God and you praying in Christ opens your soul to experience the highest, most nourishing truth of all: the total, transforming, unconditional love with which God himself regards you. This experience literally feeds the soul, enlivening its own capacity for love, energizing it, and inspiring it.

Meditative prayer, then, exercises the great Christian virtues of faith, hope, and love, helping the soul that has been wounded by sin, both original and personal, to rehabilitate its capacity to discover, experience, and communicate God's own truth, goodness, and beauty.

Christian meditation differs essentially from transcendental meditation and other New Age centering techniques.[3] Christian meditation is Christ-centered, a loving dialogue between Christ and the soul that deepens your friendship with Christ. It starts with the Holy Spirit urging you to pursue a greater knowledge and love of Christ, and ends with your renewed commitment to follow and imitate Christ in the unique circumstances of your daily life.

Transcendental meditation, on the other hand, is self-centered. Instead of a dialogue with God, an opening of the soul to God, it consists primarily in calming the many passions of the soul, creating a self-induced interior tranquility and focus that overflows in certain types of feelings. The goal of transcendental meditation is to withdraw from the complexities of life in order to experience emotional tranquility; the goal of Christian meditation is to know, love, and follow Jesus Christ more completely, to discover and embrace God's will for you more and more each day.

CONTEMPLATIVE PRAYER Contemplative prayer consists of a more passive (and more sublime) experience of God. If meditation is the soul's inspired quest to discover God, contemplation is God's lifting of the soul into himself, so that it effortlessly basks in the divine light. It is the soul's silent gazing upon the grandeur of God.

---

3 Some Christian spiritualities have tried to adopt so-called centering prayer techniques from non-Christian sources. Although some of these techniques can be incorporated into the first stage of the meditation (Concentrate), they are unnecessary and can often be harmful. They frequently result in becoming ends in themselves; the one praying uses them to create certain higher emotional states, as if those states were the goal of prayer. Christian prayer is interpersonal; centering prayer is really no more than a technique for calming oneself. It originated in the context of Eastern transcendental asceticism, and these techniques are ill-suited for Christian prayer. For a more complete discussion of this issue, see the Pontifical Council for Interreligious Dialogue's document from February 3, 2003, "Jesus Christ: The Bearer of the Water of Life," available on the Vatican website, www.vatican.va.

Often meditation leads to contemplation—the line of demarcation is hazy. When you find yourself lifted into silent contemplation during your meditation, there is no need to fear. The practice of Christian meditation gradually purifies the heart and familiarizes it with the voice and the ways of God, so that little by little the soul is made more docile to the promptings of God, and God can reveal himself more and more completely.

All three types of prayer—vocal, meditative, and contemplative—put the Christian in contact with the grassy pastures and refreshing waters of God's grace. They are the sure paths along which the Good Shepherd faithfully leads his sheep.

Meditation vs. Spiritual Reading

The Better Part is not a book of meditations. Sometimes following ready-made meditations[4] is an excellent way to pray. The structure helps you stay focused, the content is sure to be healthy, and the easy access motivates you to keep up a regular prayer life. But ready-made meditations also have a disadvantage. They can become nothing more than spiritual reading.

Spiritual reading refers to reading texts—books, articles, homilies, essays—that teach you about the spiritual life; it's like taking a class from whoever wrote the book. It enlightens your conscience by helping you see yourself and the world around you from a Christian perspective. As such, it is an essential ingredient for growth as a Christian. Just as historians are always reading about history, and teachers are always informing themselves about developments in pedagogy, so Christians should constantly be refining and expanding their understanding of how to be a follower of Christ.[5]

Christian meditation also involves an effort to better understand Christ and the Christian life, and so it often yields results similar to those of spiritual reading, especially for beginners in the spiritual life. Primarily, though, meditation is a matter of the heart more than the intellect; it's like taking a leisurely walk with Christ, your friend.

The focused reflection at the core of meditation opens the soul to hear not an abstract truth about the Christian life, but a particular word that God, the

---

4 Like those published daily through the Regnum Christi website, www.regnumchristi.org.

5 Regnum Christi members' daily Gospel Reflection falls into this category of spiritual reading. It keeps you constantly in touch with Christ's criteria and example, so that throughout the day you can keep aligning your thoughts, attitudes, and actions with Christ's. It's like rebooting your computer—it clears away the interior clutter that accumulates during the day.

Good Shepherd, wishes to speak to you in the unique here and now of your life. When you tune into this word, this truth, this message from the Holy Spirit, your heart is drawn to stay with it, to consider it, to savor it. Savoring it in turn stirs your heart to express itself and give voice to your most intimate, personal yearnings, hopes, affections, or needs. In this conversation, you are actually exercising the Christian virtues of faith, hope, and love; you are exercising your friendship. In spiritual reading, you are learning, you are gaining knowledge. Both spiritual reading and meditation are useful—indeed, both are necessary for a healthy spiritual life—but it's important not to confuse them.

Although ready-made meditations have many advantages, they also have the disadvantage of easily morphing into spiritual reading. You lead a busy life with little time to prepare your daily meditation. You have committed to doing it, though, so you faithfully gather the daily meditation from the website and read it over in between errands or before speeding off to work. It keeps you in touch with spiritual things, and gives you new insights or renews old ones, but because it's a complete, self-contained meditation, you easily slip into the spiritual-reading mode: instead of using the points of reflection as springboards for focused personal reflection, attentive listening to the Holy Spirit, and intimate, heart-to-heart conversation with Christ, you simply read, understand, agree, and move on.

Spiritual reading is valuable; it will help you grow closer to Christ. The Lord is happy that you make time for him. And yet, unless you learn to go deeper, to personalize your prayer more, you will limit your growth in virtue. God wants to make you into the saint he created you to be, but that requires a more personal, heart-to-heart prayer life. He wants to give you that grace, but he needs you to give him the chance.

The Better Part is a resource designed to help your personal prayer time become more personalized, increasingly deeper, and more transforming. Instead of offering ready-made meditations, it provides a structure for meditation along with Christ-centered commentaries that are more open-ended, more flexible, more personalized than complete meditations.

The 4-Step Structure of Your Meditation

AN OVERVIEW Perhaps you are already familiar with the general meditation structure recommended in *The Better Part*. Drawn from the long-lasting and fruitful traditions of Ignatian and Carmelite spirituality, it follows four steps: *Concentrate*, *Consider*, *Converse*, and *Commit*.

Sometimes a meditation flows easily, following these steps one after another without a hitch. Other times tiredness, distractions, or temptations plague you so persistently that each step demands a heroic effort. Still other times, the steps blend together and your conversation with God happens almost spontaneously. This shows that the four-step method of meditation is not an end in itself, nor is it an arbitrary concoction. Rather, this method sets out the basic elements of any heart-to-heart conversation with God, as gleaned from experience and theology. In so doing, it provides a dependable framework for your personal encounter with God in spite of the persistent and sometimes almost overwhelming obstacles to prayer that surface.

At first you may find it awkward to follow the steps. You may feel tempted to fall back into the less demanding pattern of spiritual reading, but as your prayer life deepens, this simple structure becomes second nature. When kids first learn to play basketball, they have to master the basic skills—dribbling, shooting, passing—one at a time. As they improve, they develop the ability to combine these fundamentals into a smooth, seamless whole. Eventually they are free to really play. Assimilating the structure of your meditation happens a lot like that.

MAKING PROGRESS Keep in mind that growth in the spiritual life and in prayer takes time and consistent effort. Sometimes you may feel that you are making great progress; then suddenly you seem to have a relapse. Other times you may feel that you are making no progress at all, and then you unexpectedly spring forward.

This isn't because God whimsically comes and goes. Rather, he is mysteriously guiding you through a gradual purification of the selfish tendencies deeply embedded in your soul. Points of view, emotional patterns, mental landscapes—all of these, because of original and personal sin, are shot through with myriad forms of self-centeredness that clog the flow of God's grace. Thus, learning to pray better is like turning a wild, overgrown plot of rocky ground into an ordered, fragrant, beautiful garden—God supplies the sunshine, the water, and the soil, but you still have to dig and plant and prune, and then keep on digging and planting and pruning. Think of the four steps of the meditation as your gardening tools.

Understanding the reasons behind each step will help you follow them more peacefully and fruitfully. These steps can also be useful reference points as you discuss your prayer life during spiritual direction. A clear idea of these elements will make your ongoing reading about prayer more fruitful as well. Remember, every Christian should steadily strive to become an expert in prayer, since prayer is that "vital and personal relationship with the living and true God" (CCC, 2558)—the relationship which gives life itself and all of life's components their deepest, most authentic, and most satisfying meaning. Below is an explanation of each step. After the explanation you will find the full text of a real, sample meditation with all the steps identified.

STEP 1: CONCENTRATE

1. This involves drawing your attention away from the exterior activities and practical concerns that tend to monopolize your thoughts, and turning your attention to God, who is already paying full attention to you. You refresh your awareness of God's presence, which tends to be drowned out by the din of the daily grind.
2. Useful in this step are the traditional preparatory acts of faith, hope, and love, wherein you lift your heart and mind to God, tuning your attention to God's wavelength. You can use ready-made texts for your preparatory acts, compose your own, voice them spontaneously, or combine all three methods. *The Better Part* provides some sample preparatory acts. The morning prayers from your prayer book can make for good preparatory acts as well.
3. The most important part of this step is not the actual words you use. Rather, you need to remind yourself of the truths that underlie your relationship with God, reviving your most basic Christian attitudes. The goal of this step is fourfold:
    - Recall that God is truly present, listening to you, paying attention. Remember that God is all-powerful, all-wise, all-loving, and that he knows you intimately and cares for you more than you care for yourself. He deserves your praise, your attention, and your time.
    - Recall that God has something he wants to say to you. He has a word for you today. He knows what you are struggling with, in the short term and the long; he knows what the day will have in store for you; he knows the path he has marked out for your growth in happiness and holiness. He is going to work in your soul while you pray, whether you feel anything or not. Remember, your daily meditation isn't just your idea, it is a prayer commitment linked with your particular vocation in the Church, and your vocation comes from God. You know without a doubt that God has something to say to you during this time, because he made the appointment.
    - Recall that you need to hear that word. You are dependent on God for everything, starting with your existence. You have failed and

sinned many times; the duties and mission you have in life are beyond your own natural capabilities; you are surrounded by morally and spiritually corrupting influences, by a variety of temptations. In short, you are a dependent, created being damaged by sin: you need God's grace.

- Renew your desire to hear that word. You want to follow him. You believe that he is the Lord, your Savior, your Friend, and your Guide. You have committed your life to him; you have put your trust in him.

4. In this context, part of your concentration will consist in asking God for the grace you feel you most need, in accordance with your program of spiritual work. Sometimes this is called the petition or the fruit of the meditation. Asking God for this grace brings all those basic attitudes into play. At the same time, however, you leave the reins in his hands, knowing that he will guide you in hidden ways to the rich pastures he has in store for you.
5. Whether you use your favorite traditional acts of faith, hope, and love to achieve this concentration matters less than simply achieving it. Sometimes it is enough to call to mind your favorite verse or psalm from the Bible to activate all these sentiments; sometimes it's enough to remember the beauties of nature or one of your most powerful experiences of God.
6. As the weeks and months pass by, you may need to vary the way you concentrate, in order to avoid falling into a dry routine where you say all the right words, but in fact fail to turn your heart and mind to God. Without that, without concentrating on God, it will be nearly impossible for you to really enter into conversation with him and hear what he wants to tell you—your prayer will turn into a self-centered monologue or an empty, wordy shell.
7. At times these preparatory acts may launch you directly into a heart-to-heart conversation with the Lord, bypassing Step 2, Consider. When this happens, don't feel obliged to backtrack; the material of your preparatory acts has provided the Holy Spirit with all he needed to lift you right into Step 3, Converse.
8. Concentrating on God doesn't mean ignoring the realities of your life. Your worries and concerns and yearnings and dreams and challenges should all enter into your meditation. But they come into play within the context of your heart-to-heart conversation with the God who loves you. This is the difference between simply worrying and actually praying about something. When you sit down to have a cup of coffee with a

close friend, your worries and dreams don't disappear, but they fall into line behind the attention you give to your friend, and the attention your friend gives to you.

9. Related to Step 1 is your choice of time and place for your daily meditation. These factors affect your ability to Concentrate.
   - The time. Most spiritual writers agree that doing your meditation in the morning helps imbue your coming day's activities with their true Christian meaning. Your mind is fresh, so it's easier to focus. And a morning meditation can give unity and direction to your daily duties by reminding you of your life's mission (to know, love, and follow Christ) and preparing you to meet the day's unexpected (or expected) challenges. With a little effort and creativity, you can usually make room for the morning meditation, whether it's ten, fifteen, twenty minutes, or even half an hour. (If you have any doubts about the proper length of your daily meditation, you should discuss them with a confessor or spiritual director.) If the morning is simply impossible, try to find some space in your day when you know you won't be interrupted—a time when you will be able to give your best to your prayer. Use the same time slot each day as much as possible. Try not to just squeeze it in; give your best time to God.
   - The place. Where you do your meditation should be out of range of interruptions and conducive to your conversation with God. Some people prefer their church or a chapel with the Blessed Sacrament; others prefer a particular room at home. Here again creativity and practical convenience come into play. A businessman in Boston stops at a cemetery on his way to work and does his meditation walking among the tombs and monuments (during the summer)—it's the only place where he can consistently dodge interruptions. Avoid changing places frequently in a vain search for the perfect atmosphere. The place doesn't make the prayer; it is only a means to help.
   - On special days or during certain periods (e.g., vacation, Holy Week), you may find it helpful to change your normal place and time of prayer. Temporary, planned changes can keep you from falling into a dull routine.
10. If you habitually find it hard to concentrate at the start of your meditation, check on the status of your remote and proximate preparation. These terms refer to what you do outside of your meditation that affects what happens during your meditation.

- Remote preparation. You don't meditate in a vacuum. The more you live in God's presence during the rest of day, seeking his will and finding other times here and there to pray (vocal prayers, the Rosary, examination of conscience), the easier it will be for you to turn your heart and soul to God at the start of the meditation. This is your remote preparation.
- Proximate preparation. You will also avoid a plethora of distractions if you get your meditation materials (the book you will be using, your notebook or journal for writing down thoughts) ready the night before. You can even briefly look over the passage you will be meditating on before you go to bed; this too primes the prayer-pump. This is your proximate preparation.

11. Jesus himself explained the step of concentrating simply and vividly: "When you pray, go to your private room and, when you have shut your door, pray to your Father who is in that secret place, and your Father who sees all that is done in secret will reward you" (Mt 6:6). The prophet Elijah discovered this truth when the Lord spoke to him on the mountain:

> Then the Lord himself went by. There came a mighty wind, so strong it tore the mountains and shattered the rocks before the Lord. But the Lord was not in the wind. After the wind came an earthquake. But the Lord was not in the earthquake. After the earthquake came a fire. But the Lord was not in the fire. And after the fire there came the sound of a gentle breeze. (1 Kgs 19:11-12)

12. Concentrate, the first step of your meditation, involves shutting the door on the storms and tumult of daily life for a time, so that you can hear the Lord's still, small voice that whispers in your heart like a gentle breeze.

STEP 2: CONSIDER

1. With life's hustle and bustle in its proper place, you are ready to listen to God's message for you today. Here you take time for focused reflection on God's words, usually as they are found in Scripture—although you can also turn to other spiritual writings, the works of the saints, Church documents, and even sacred art as texts for consideration. Gradually, with the help of your confessor or spiritual director, you will find the kind of material that helps you most, in accordance with your program of spiritual work.

2. During this stage, you slowly and thoughtfully read the text you will be meditating on. You reflect on it, you examine it, you dig into it. You read it again, searching to discover what God is saying to you through it in the here and now of your life. You exercise your whole mind: intellect, imagination, and memory. You involve your emotions, relating the passage to your own life experience.
3. This type of meditative consideration differs from study. The goal of meditation is not necessarily to learn new truths, but to give God a chance to make the truths you need most sink deeper into your mind and heart. Considering a truth involves understanding it more clearly, more deeply. But it also involves savoring it, gazing upon it, basking in it.
4. This step poses a challenge for victims of the media age. The human mind is capable of wonder, contemplation, and reflection, but when the principle source of information is mass media, these capacities can atrophy. Mass media stimulates the surface of the mind, but the constant, rapid flow of images and information militates against going deep. Meditation provides a respite from frenzied mental stimulation and gives the soul a chance to simply love and be loved in the intimacy of a spiritual embrace.
5. Just as it takes the body time to digest food and benefit from its nutrients, so the soul needs time to take in and assimilate the healing, enlightening, and strengthening truths God has revealed through Christ's gospel. Just as it takes long hours in the sun for plants to photosynthesize so they can grow and flourish, so the soul needs extended exposure to the light of Christ in order for God's grace to purify, enliven, and heal it.
6. God knows which truths you need to dwell on; part of the Consider stage is searching for them. God speaks most often in whispers, not storms, and so you have to move forward in your meditation calmly, gently, hunting for the insight God wishes to give you. This is one of the most mysterious aspects of meditation. Christ the Good Shepherd guides you towards the rich pastures and refreshing waters of his truth and grace, sometimes along an easy path and other times along a steep and difficult path. For each day when it is easy to find and savor God's word for you, there is another day when your meditation seems to entail nothing but work.
7. This exercise of seeking out where God is speaking to your soul turns Christian meditation into a quest: "Meditation is a prayerful quest engaging thought, imagination, emotion, and desire" (CCC, 2723). Usually, as you read and reflect on the subject of your meditation, you can detect where the Holy Spirit wants you to stop and consider simply by the reaction of your heart.

8. In a garden full of beautiful flowers and plants, you stay longer in front of one because you find that its beauty resonates more deeply with you. In a gallery of magnificent works of art, you are drawn to one or two of them more powerfully, because they have something to say to you, in the here and now of your life, that the others don't. Likewise with meditation. If you have done your best to focus the powers of your soul on God in the Concentrate step, as you begin to Consider the material for your meditation, one or two things will catch your attention; they will jump out at you, as if they were highlighted. It may be a phrase in the actual text, or an idea that comes to your mind. That highlight is the guiding hand of the Good Shepherd. Thus the Holy Spirit gently leads you to the spiritual food your soul needs most.
9. If nothing strikes you right away, you can intensify your consideration by asking questions.
    - For instance, if you are considering a passage from the Gospel, you can enter into the scene by asking basic, journalistic questions: Who is here? What are they feeling, doing, and saying? When is this event taking place? Where is it happening and what does everything look like? Why is it happening in this way? How is each person reacting? As you enter more deeply into the living Word of God, the Holy Spirit will guide your mind and heart to the point he wants you to consider. When you find it, savor it.
    - Another approach uses less imagination and more reason. You can begin to consider the material of your meditation by asking analytical questions: What strikes me about this passage? What does this mean? What does it tell me about Christ, the Church, the meaning of life? And after having looked at it in the abstract, make it personal—What does it mean for me? What is Christ saying to me in the here and now of my life? How is this truth relevant to my own struggles, my own mission, my own vocation, my own program of spiritual work, my own friendship with Christ, and my own journey of faith?
10. It may take almost the whole time you have set aside for meditation to discover the point God wants you to consider. This is not a cause for discouragement or frustration: during the search, the quest, you are exercising all of the Christian virtues—faith in God, hope in his goodness, love for him, humility, and trust. The more difficult the search, the more these virtues are being exercised; the Holy Spirit is giving you a vigorous spiritual workout. God knows just what you need and how to guide you; he is the Good Shepherd.

11. Sometimes you never seem to find the highlights at all. In these cases, too, God is at work. Never doubt his active presence. When the material you have set aside for consideration doesn't yield any insights worth savoring, you can feel free to turn to your favorite biblical images, your favorite vocal prayers, or your favorite verses—go back to the waters and pastures that have nourished you in the past. All mature Christians gradually discover certain truths of the gospel that can always provide food for their souls.
12. At times you may find so many highlights that you feel overwhelmed. Stay calm. Don't rush. Take one flower, one painting, one highlight at a time and exhaust it, delight in it until your heart is saturated. Only then move on to the next highlight. As long as your consideration continues to move your heart, stay with that point, like a bee extracting nectar from a blossom. Never move on just because you feel like you're supposed to. Prayer is a personal conversation, not a generic connect-the-dots operation.

STEP 3: CONVERSE

1. Precisely because Christian prayer is interpersonal, your consideration of the truths of Christ, your basking in his light, is never only passive. In an embrace, both people receive and both people give. In the embrace of prayer, you receive the truth and grace of God's revelation, and you give your personal response. As soon as the truth you are considering touches your heart, it will stir a response. This is the heart of your meditation.
2. If you are considering the wonders of God's creation, you may be moved to respond with words or sentiments of praise: How great you are, my God! How beautiful you must be if your creation is this awe-inspiring....
3. If you are considering God's mercy, you may be moved to respond with contrition, remorse, and sorrow for your sins: You are so good and generous, so patient; why, Lord, am I so slow to trust you, why am I so selfish? Forgive me, Lord; a thousand times, please forgive me; I know you have, you do, and you will, but still I ask you to forgive me; I am sorry....
4. If you are considering some of the many gifts he has given you, like your faith, your family, or the Eucharist, you may be moved to express gratitude: Thank you, Father, from the bottom of my heart; I really mean it, thank you. Thank you for giving me life, for showing me the meaning of life, and for saving me from so many dangers, so many sins....
5. Whatever you may be considering, sooner or later, like a child in the presence of his benevolent and powerful father, you will probably find

yourself asking for good things from God: O my Lord, how I want to love as you love! How I need your grace to be patient, to see the good side of others and not just the negative. Please teach me to do your will, to be your true disciple.... This asking can also take the form of confusion and complaint, as happens so often in the Book of Psalms: Why, my God, have you forsaken me? Why do you let these things happen? Lord, I don't understand; teach me, enlighten me. Help me to go where you want me to go, because right now I don't feel like going there....

6. As your consideration gives rise to these responses, the response will naturally come to a close and give way to a new consideration, and you will find yourself turning back to the meditation material. You may look again at the same highlight you just considered, or you may move on to something else, until a new consideration sparks a new response and a new topic of conversation. This exchange—this ongoing conversation in which you reflect on God's revelation and respond in your heart, with your own words—is the essence of Christian meditation. This is usually where the soul comes into its most intimate contact with Christ through the action of the Holy Spirit. Consideration is never enough; it must stir the heart to Converse with God.
7. During your meditation, then, you may often find yourself going back and forth between Steps 2 and 3, Consider and Converse. Just because you have considered one point and conversed with Christ about it doesn't mean you can't go back and consider it again from another angle, or consider another point, and then converse about that. The conversation is two-way; you move back and forth between considering (listening) and responding, as much or as little as the Holy Spirit leads you.
8. Sometimes your response will be a torrent of words—so many that they tumble over each other as you struggle to express all that's in your heart. Other times you may find yourself simply repeating a short phrase, or even one word, and it says everything: Lord... Jesus... Sometimes, like the famous peasant of Ars, you will simply find yourself held by God's gaze and gazing back, and words, even in the silence of your heart, will be unnecessary. Whatever its specific form, this third step of your meditation, Converse, consists in letting down the guard around your heart, so that God's word for you today penetrates, regenerates, and inflames the most secret depths of who you are.
9. In this step of the meditation, you may also feel moved to converse with the saints and angels or the Blessed Virgin Mary, speaking with them

about Christ, whom they know much better than you do, contemplating their example of fidelity to Christ, and asking for their intercession.

STEP 4: COMMIT

1. Toward the end of your meditation, it will be time for you to draw this heart-to-heart conversation to a close. There is a need to bring all the sentiments together, to wrap things up. Before you step back into life's hectic activity, you need to renew your commitment to the mission God has given you. In your prayer he has renewed his call, and now you renew your answer, accepting once again the life-project that gives meaning to your existence—that of following him, of imitating Christ by your fidelity to God's will in the big things as well as the small.
2. Usually this desire to renew your adherence to God's will flows naturally and easily out of the consideration and conversation stages. The renewal and deepening of your commitment to Christ and his Kingdom, whether or not it is accompanied by intense feelings, is actually a prayer of adoration, worship, and love: You know how weak I am, my Lord, but you also know how much I want to follow you. You have planted that desire in my heart: I am yours, Lord. Wherever I go, whatever happens, I belong to you. I never want to be separated from you. As hard as it is, I want to do your will, because you are God, my Creator and Redeemer, my Father and my faithful Friend. Thy will be done in my life today, Lord; thy Kingdom come.
3. You may even find yourself responding to your considerations with acts of adoration similar to those during the Converse stage of the meditation—this is fine. It doesn't mean you have to end your meditation right then. If you have time, you can go back and continue the Consider step, or converse with other responses, like praise and gratitude. Then, at the end of the time you have set aside to meditate, you can return to this adoration, to this Commit step.[6]
4. If you can link this recommitment to the concrete tasks of your day, all the better. Most often, the daily meditation has followed themes connected to your program of spiritual work. In that case, you can recommit to following your program, or one particular point of your program, as a specific way of expressing your love for Christ. Sometimes, however, the Holy Spirit will nudge you towards a specific act of charity (i.e.,

---

8 In both the Converse and the Commit steps, then, you find the traditional types, the traditional goals of prayer: Praise, Adoration, Sorrow, Thanksgiving, and Asking—P.A.S.T.A.

visit your colleague who's in the hospital), or of self-governance (i.e., call your brother and apologize). This too can give substance to your recommitment.

5. The meditation itself has glorified God and nourished your soul, regardless of any specific resolution you make in Step 4. The lifeblood of the meditation is your heart-to-heart conversation with the Lord, a conversation that puts you in contact with God and his grace, gradually transforming you into a mature Christian. You have deepened your friendship with Christ through spending this time with him. A new specific resolution may be an appropriate way to express this friendship at the end of the conversation, but often its most sincere expression is simply a renewal of your commitment to Christ and his Kingdom, to the points of spiritual and apostolic work already on your agenda, and to the everyday tasks that are his will for you.
6. This fourth step is the bridge between prayer and action. If you are working on being more courageous about sharing your faith with your coworkers, you may finish your meditation by a commitment to put forth in a natural way the Christian point of view in today's conversations around the water cooler. If God has been leading you towards being a better spouse, you may renew your commitment to Christ by promising to avoid today that particular thing that you know really bothers your wife or husband. If you have been neglecting your prayer life, you may commit to giving your best attention to your daily Rosary in the evening. The specific form your recommitment takes will depend on the overall direction of your spiritual life. It doesn't have to be anything new (although it may be); it just has to be true.
7. Finish up your meditation by renewing your commitment to Christ in your own words. Then take a few moments to write down the lights God sent you during the meditation and thank him for them. Briefly go over how the meditation went. Did you follow the steps? Did anything in particular help you? Was there anything that hindered you? This brief analysis will help you get to know better each day what kind of pray-er you are, so that you can apply this knowledge in subsequent meditations, gradually learning to pray as God created you to pray.
8. It often helps to conclude your meditation with a short vocal prayer like the Our Father, the Hail Mary, the Anima Christi, or another favorite prayer of your own. *The Better Part* provides some possibilities at the end of Part I.

Concentrate, Consider, Converse, and *Commit.* These are the four elements of a Christian meditation. The many books and manuals of prayer that enrich our Christian heritage offer numerous aids to meditation, and you should familiarize yourself with them and take advantage of them, but in the end, the methods and aids all tie in to these four steps of prayer. This tried-and-true structure will give God more room to work in your soul than he would have if you only dedicated yourself to vocal prayer and spiritual reading.

Difficulties in Prayer

You will always face difficulties in prayer. Just accept it. The saints all experienced it, the *Catechism* teaches it, and theology confirms it. The difficulties stem from two sources—two unique qualities of your friendship with Christ.

1. First, this friendship is mediated by faith. You can't just call Jesus on the phone, as you can with your other friends. He is always with you, but your awareness of and access to his presence passes through faith. Faith is a virtue, which means that it can be more or less developed. The less developed it is, the more effort it takes to activate your awareness of God's presence. Many modern Christians have an underdeveloped faith. They have been unwittingly contaminated by the consumer culture's veneration for quantifiable evidence ("I won't believe it unless a scientific study proves it") and its elevation of feelings over reason ("I don't feel in love anymore, so why should I stay married?")—both of which weaken faith. A scrawny faith often makes Jesus look fuzzy and seem distant, just as the sun seems weak and irrelevant when you're wearing dark glasses. Your ability to pray will suffer the consequences. Have you ever noticed how hard it is to be distracted when you watch a good movie? Effortlessly you pay perfect attention to a complex story for two hours. Contrast that with what typically happens during your fifteen minutes of meditation. What's the difference? Contact with God takes faith, "going as we do by faith and not by sight" (2 Cor 5:7). It takes the effort of "all your heart, soul, mind, and strength" (Mk 12:30) to align your fallen nature (which tends to seek fulfillment in the things of this earth) with the sublime truths that God has revealed through the teachings of the Church.
2. Your friendship with Christ is unique not only by its mediation through faith, but also because the two friends are not equals. Christ is not just your friend; he is also your Creator, your Redeemer, and your Lord; he

is all-wise and all-loving, and he's trying to lead you along the steep and narrow path of Christian maturity. So, on your part, your relationship with him requires docility. But docility demands self-denial, which rubs your concupiscence the wrong way. Remember, baptism gave you back God's grace, but it didn't take away your deep-seated tendencies to selfishness (arrogance, independence, vanity, laziness, anger, lust, greed, etc.) that you inherited from original sin. Because of them, docility chafes. Sometimes the Good Shepherd leads you where you would rather not go, or pushes you farther along when you would prefer to sit back and relax, or doesn't let you drink from a stream that looks fine to you. This divergence of wills makes prayer a constant battle.

SLOTH AND DISTRACTIONS The difficulties flowing from this need for faith and docility come in two basic varieties: sloth and distractions.

Sloth is spiritual laziness, distaste, and sluggishness in cultivating your relationship with God: I can't pray before I go to work, because I need that extra few minutes of sleep; I can't go on a retreat, since the playoffs start this weekend and I really want to watch them; I know I committed to begin praying the Rosary again, but I just don't feel like it, I have so much else to do.... Anything but spend time attending to the most important thing: your "vital and personal relationship with the living and true God" (CCC, 2558)—in other words, your life of prayer. That's sloth.

In the meditation itself, sloth can tempt you in numerous ways: procrastinating (I'll do it later; I'll start meditating tomorrow), not getting your material ready ahead of time, giving in to tiredness, rushing through your preparatory acts instead of really concentrating, simply reading for most of the time instead of really engaging in the quest to consider and converse, or finishing with a vague and halfhearted commitment that really has no practical effect at all in your daily life or the pursuit of spiritual maturity. In these and many other ways, sloth slyly undermines the life of prayer.

Sloth drains energy from your spiritual life; distractions, on the other hand, steer that energy away from God. You go to Mass and sincerely want to worship God, but can't take your eyes off that family in the front pew that's making such a ruckus (or maybe you're part of that family); you pray the Rosary every day, but halfway through you realize that you have no idea which decade you're on because you're thinking about the budget presentation you have to make on Tuesday; you desperately try to spend some time every day in personal prayer, in Christian meditation, but you end up thinking about everything except God—family worries, upcoming engagements, temptations, pending bills and phone calls, job interviews, billboards, news stories.... They all violently and unremittingly claw at your attention as soon as you try to quiet your soul and attend to the Lord (more often than not, the devil has a hand in this). And sometimes when you pray, you're just plain bored. Welcome to the world of distractions.

SOLVING THE DIFFICULTIES The best defense against sloth and distractions is a good offense. Following a sound and simple meditation method like the one outlined above both flushes these temptations out of hiding—since you know clearly what you should be doing during your meditation, you catch yourself more easily as soon as you stop doing that—and also gives you a rudder and a lighthouse to navigate through their ambushes. But the method won't resolve the difficulties all by itself. You still have to steer the rudder and look to the lighthouse.

Temptations to sloth or distractions don't damage your prayer life—only giving in to temptations does that. In fact, each temptation is permitted by God because it gives you a chance for spiritual growth.

Take for example a temptation to slothfulness. The alarm clock goes off. Bleary-eyed, I wake up, and the last thing I feel like doing is getting up to pray. If I cut out my fifteen-minute meditation, I can have fifteen minutes more sleep. How sweet that sounds! But wait a minute, why did I set my alarm to get up fifteen minutes earlier than I actually need to? Because I made a commitment; I resolved to start out my day with God because he is the purpose of my life and deserves my praise and because I need his grace. A crisis of the heart has arisen: my feelings and habits of self-indulgence (egged on by the devil) tell me to hit the snooze button, roll over, and doze off again; my faith (animated by my guardian angel) tells me to turn off the alarm, throw back those cozy covers, touch my bare feet down on that cold tile floor, and keep my appointment with God.

If God wanted to, he could resolve the crisis for me: he could push me out of bed, or make the bed disappear, or give me good feelings about prayer and bad feelings about staying in bed. But he doesn't, at least not usually. Rather, he leaves it up to me, nudging my conscience perhaps, but not forcing me either way. Here is where I can exercise the virtues of faith and docility, and in exercising them, strengthen them.

Distractions work the same way. I'm in the Blessed Sacrament chapel doing my daily meditation. Someone else comes through the door and enters the silent, sacred space. He takes a seat not too far away. I can't help noticing that he's wearing brand-new tennis shoes. Are they Nikes or Reeboks? That reminds me about the marketing presentation I have to give this afternoon. My boss will be there. It's a critical account for the company.... Suddenly I realize that my mind is wandering. Up to this point, I haven't been responsible for the distraction, because I wasn't even aware of it, but now I have three options: (1) I keep thinking about the presentation. After all, a lot is hanging on it, and my meditation is a bit dry anyway. (2) I get distracted by my distraction: "There I go again. Why can't I stay focused? I always get distracted. I am such an idiotic Christian, such a hypocrite. I'm so frustrated with myself...." (3) I calmly steer my attention back to my meditation, renewing my conviction that God and his action here matter far more than fruitless worrying about my presentation (which I have already prepared anyway), and that my tendency to get distracted affords me a new opportunity to exercise my faith and docility and turn back once again to my Lord.

Will I choose 1, 2, or 3? If I choose 3, then that distraction, which the devil wants to use to distance me from God, will actually have become an instrument of God's grace, drawing me closer to him and giving him glory. God allows temptations against my communion with him in order to afford me opportunities to deepen that communion.

The more closely you try to follow the 4-step method of meditation outlined above, the more you will get to know how these ubiquitous temptations try to derail your personal prayer life in particular, and the better equipped you will be to stay on track, using them to build up the virtues of faith and docility and become the pray-er God wants you to be.

HOW DO I KNOW IF I'M PRAYING WELL? We all tend to measure our prayer by our feelings: I prayed well if I felt God's presence, if I felt an emotional thrill. That's not the way to evaluate your prayer. Your relationship with Christ is a deep friendship built on faith and love. It goes much deeper than feelings. Feelings and emotions change with the weather, with our biorhythms, with our circumstances—they are often unpredictable and always undependable. Any friendship built on feelings, therefore, is doomed to frustration and failure. Mature Christians don't seek feelings or emotional states in their prayer. If God provides good feelings too, great, but the sincere Christian is after Christ: praising him, knowing him better, discovering what he wants, and renewing and deepening the decision to imitate him and follow him in the nitty-gritty of daily life, no matter the cost. Feelings are frills, but Christ is the core.

The fruit of a healthy prayer life takes time to grow and mature. Ultimately, it shows itself by growth in virtue, as you become more like Christ. Gradually, you grow in self-governance (controlling and channeling your instincts, passions, and basic human desires), prudence (seeing clearly what ought to be done in any particular situation and doing it), love (seeing others as Christ sees them and being able to sacrifice your own preferences for their sake), fortitude (taking on challenging tasks or projects for the sake of Christ's Kingdom, and persevering through difficulties, obstacles, and opposition), and wisdom (detecting and relishing God's presence in all things and circumstances). Growth in these virtues takes place gradually, almost imperceptibly, on a day-to-day basis, just as a child slowly but surely grows into adulthood, or as plants mature in a garden. Meditation supplies much of the spiritual nutrients that cause these virtues to grow.

On any given day, then, measuring whether your meditation went well or badly is not so easy. Your meditation may have been quite pleasing to God and full of grace for your soul even when it was unpleasant and difficult from a strictly emotional perspective. An athlete may have a great practice session even though it was painful and frustrating—likewise with a daily meditation.

You'll find some helpful indicators below. The most important thing, though, is simply to keep striving to pray better. Speak about your prayer life in spiritual direction and confession, and trust that if you are sincerely doing your best, the Holy Spirit will do the rest.

My meditation went badly when I...

- Didn't plan ahead regarding what material I would use, when and where I would meditate, making sure to turn off my cell phone, etc.
- Simply gave in to the many distractions that vied for my attention
- Let myself fall asleep
- Skipped over the first step, Concentrate, or did it sloppily; how can my prayer go well if I am not keenly aware of God's presence?
- Didn't humbly ask God to help me and to give me whatever graces I need to continue growing in my spiritual life
- Spent the whole time reading, thinking, or daydreaming; didn't stop to ask what God was saying to me and then respond from my heart
- Tried to stir up warm, fuzzy feelings and intense emotions instead of conversing heart-to-heart on the level of faith
- Didn't renew my commitment to Christ and his Kingdom at the end of the meditation
- Shortened the time I had committed to without a really important reason

My meditation went well when I...

- Actually fulfilled the commitment I made to spend a certain amount of time in meditation every day

- Faithfully followed the methodology in spite of tiredness, distractions, dryness, or any other difficulty (or if it was impossible to follow the four-step method, did my best to give praise to God in whatever way I could throughout my meditation time)
- Stayed with the points of consideration that struck me most as long as I found material there for reflection and conversation
- Sought only to know and love Christ better, so as to be able to follow him better
- Made sure to speak to Christ from my heart about whatever I was meditating on (or whatever was most on my heart), even when it was hard to find the words
- Was completely honest in my conversation—I didn't say things to God just out of routine or because I wanted to impress him with my eloquence; I told him what was really in my heart
- Made a sincere effort to listen to what God was saying to me throughout the time of prayer, seeking applications for my own life, circumstances, needs, and challenges
- Finished the meditation more firmly convinced of God's goodness and more firmly committed to doing my best to follow him faithfully

A Sample Meditation

The paragraphs below are adapted from a meditation directed by Father Anthony Bannon, LC, and taken with permission from www.vocation.com. Although everyone prays a little bit differently from everyone else, reading through a real meditation from start to finish can help these ideas come into focus. Comments are included in italics.

STEP 1: CONCENTRATE I come into the place where I will be meditating. I remind myself that God is truly present, here and everywhere, that he is watching over me and listening to me, eager to spend this time together; he sees into the depths of my heart. Then I kneel or sit, make the Sign of the Cross, and address him.

I thank you, Father, for the immense love you showed me in creating me and redeeming me, giving me this time with you, spending this time with me, intervening in my life. I know you have something to say to me today. I want to hear it; I need to hear it. I want to love you in a real way, not abstractly or in theory only. I want to love you today, and not only tomorrow. I want to love you here where you have placed me and not somewhere else in my dreams.

I want to love you in your Church. I want to love you in the people that you place in my path.

STEP 2: CONSIDER First, I read the Gospel passage, then I read it again, more slowly, picturing it, paying attention to whichever words jump out at me. Maybe something strikes me right away, and I stay with that, considering it and letting it lead me into a conversation with Christ.

Gospel Passage: Matthew 13:47-50

The Kingdom of Heaven is like a dragnet that is cast into the sea and brings in a haul of all kinds of fish. When it is full, the fishermen haul it ashore. And then sitting down they collect the good ones in baskets and throw away those that are no use. This is how it will be at the end of time. The Angels will appear and separate the wicked from the upright, to throw them into the blazing furnace where there will be weeping and grinding of teeth.

Maybe one thing that strikes you after reading the passage is a consideration like the following:

Unlike the previous parables in this chapter, which described the Kingdom as already present, this one describes the Kingdom as something still to come. Jesus speaks about the relationship between this Kingdom of God and the future life at the end of time. And Jesus seems to want to get across to us one particular message. "The Kingdom is like a dragnet that is cast into the sea and brings in a haul of all kinds of fish." The end of time is just as unexpected for us as a net that drops into the water and is pulled along behind the boat is for the fish it catches. Just as sudden as that…

STEP 3: CONVERSE After making that reflection, you may naturally find yourself wanting to converse with Christ about it, simply and sincerely, as follows, for example:

I know and I believe that the end of the world will come, that you will judge me and everyone. And yet, I really don't think about it very much. You thought about it a lot. You often spoke about it. Lord, you know all things; you are Wisdom itself. I thank you for this reminder that the end will come. You want me to be ready. You want me to keep the end in mind. I want to too. I don't want to live like an animal, interested only in satisfying my momentary desires. No, I want to live in the light of your truth. I believe in the power of your truth. Lord Jesus, enlighten me, guide me, never stop teaching me how you want me to live.

STEP 2 AGAIN: CONSIDER After I have had my say and spoken what is in my heart, I turn my attention back to the Lord's Word to see what else he has to say to me. I have already sought material for reflection and conversation in the passage itself, and I don't seem to find any more. So now I move on to the commentary. I read one section of the commentary, which points out something I may have overlooked. It sparks another personal reflection, so I pause and consider it—what it means, what it tells me about Christ, what it means for me, how it applies to my hopes and struggles:

> Prewritten Commentary
>
> When it is full, the fishermen haul the net ashore. Then they do the all-important thing: they sit down and start sorting out their catch. They keep the good fish and throw away the useless ones. And Jesus said, "This is the way it is going to be at the end of time. The angels will appear and separate the wicked from the upright." At the end of time, the angels won't simply check and see how God has made us and separate us according to the qualities that God has given us. Instead, their criteria will be our own wickedness and uprightness. In other words, we will be judged according to what we have done with those things that God has given us, whether we have used them wickedly (selfishly) or uprightly.

A personal reflection sparked by that commentary could be something like this:

PERSONAL CONSIDERATION OF THE COMMENTARY What do the angels recognize in each one of those people? They recognize which ones are members of Christ's Kingdom; they see signs of that in each person's heart, each person's character, which was formed by the choices they made throughout their lifetime.

I will be one of those fish, one of those people. Will the angels recognize in me the signs of the Kingdom that Jesus has talked about in the previous parables? Will they see in me someone who searched for the fine pearl, recognized its value and beauty, and had the good sense to sell everything else in order to possess it? Will they see me as someone who recognized the treasure in the field and sold everything else in order to buy it? When the angels find me, will they recognize in me the leaven that uplifted the people around me? Will they see in me someone who spent his whole life transforming the world around him, transforming himself as he served those around him, or will they find me no different from those I should have changed? Will they find just the flat dough of the world in my life, unrisen?

STEP 3 AGAIN: CONVERSE At some point while you consider whatever struck you in the commentary, you may find yourself wanting to respond directly to the Lord, to say something in response to what the Holy Spirit has been saying to you through your consideration. If nothing comes spontaneously, as your time for meditation draws to its close, you will need to purposely transition into a conversation. Remember, consideration only matters insofar as it draws you into a heart-to-heart conversation with God. Your response to God that emerges out of the above consideration may look something like this:

Lord Jesus, I thank you for speaking this parable, because so often I get too caught up with the urgent cares of today and the apparent difficulty of following you. I forget that all of this will come to an end, and that you have a bigger plan in mind.

You invite me to look at what is coming in the future life, to be ready for the dragnet. You ask me to look at heaven, which is awaiting me. Lord, I can only live as your faithful disciple, as a member of your Kingdom, with the help of your grace. I can only persevere with your help. Please never let me lose sight of the hopes and expectations that you have for me—you really do have a dream for my life; this parable reminds me that you do. The greatest thing that I can do, the greatest thing I will ever see, will be the joy on your face if you can one day say to me, "Well done, good and faithful servant." Then you will be able to receive me as you want to receive me, among the upright, and bring me into the true Kingdom of heaven.

STEP 4: COMMIT As your meditation time comes to an end, you need to recommit yourself to Christ in light of what the Holy Spirit has been showing you through your considerations and conversation. Most importantly, you want to refocus your most basic attitudes: you are a follower of Christ, and God's will is the path of your life. You can also translate that focused attitude into a concrete commitment—for example, in accordance with your program of spiritual work, or in accordance with a particular circumstance you will be facing today. You also wrap up the meditation itself, thanking God for the graces you have received and asking forgiveness for your distractions and shortcomings. For this meditation, your recommitment may look something like this:

Jesus, you know that I want to live as a true Christian, with my sights set on your Kingdom. Whatever you ask me today, I will do, if you give me the strength I need to do it. I know I will need your strength to be patient with my coworkers and to give myself eagerly to this tedious project at work. If I stay faithful to your will, to my conscience and to these normal duties of my state in life, and if I live your will with love and gratitude in my heart, then I will be ready for the last day, whenever you decide to bring it along. And don't let me hide my faith in my conversation at lunch today. Jesus, they need to know you as much as I do; make me a good messenger. Thy will be done, Lord, not mine.

Thank you, Lord, for being with me in this meditation. Thank you for the good thoughts, the good affections, and the beginnings of good resolutions that you have placed in my heart. I am sorry for the moments I have been distracted, gone off on tangents, been less attentive to your presence. Grant me in some other way any graces that I might have missed. And I also pray for each one of my brothers and sisters: I pray for each one who wants to follow you. Our Father…

Some Possible Preparatory and Concluding Prayers

PREPARATORY PRAYERS These are provided as examples and helps. Sometimes you may need help during Step 1 of your meditation, Concentrate. These small prayers express the attitudes that you need to stir up at the start of your meditation. They can sometimes serve as material for Consider and Converse as well.

1. *ENTERING INTO GOD'S PRESENCE*

My Lord and my God, I firmly believe that you are present here and everywhere, that you are looking upon me and listening to me, and that you see into the very depths of my soul. You are my Creator, my Redeemer, and my Father. I believe in your love for me. You never take your eyes off me. You have something to say to me today. Your love for me never grows weary. You never stop drawing close to me, and drawing me closer to you.

Lord, who am I to place myself in your presence? I am a poor creature unworthy of appearing before you, and yet amid all my misery I adore you devoutly. I ask you to forgive my many sins.

Jesus, teach me to pray. Direct my prayer, so that it may rise to your throne like fragrant incense. Let all the thoughts of my spirit and my heart's inmost sentiments be directed towards serving and praising God in a perfect way. I need to hear your Word for me today, and I long to hear it. You know how much I need you, how much I want to follow you. Grant me in this prayer the grace of knowing you better, loving you more, and becoming more like you. Grant me the grace I most need.

My loving Mother Mary, my holy guardian angel, angels and saints in heaven: intercede for me so that this prayer will help me and all the other people connected to my life.

2. TRADITIONAL ACTS OF FAITH, HOPE, AND LOVE

Act of Faith

My God, I firmly believe all that you have revealed and that the Holy Church puts before us to be believed, for you are the infallible truth, who does not deceive and cannot be deceived. I expressly believe in you, the only true God in three equal and distinct persons, the Father, Son, and Holy Spirit. And I believe in Jesus Christ, Son of God, who took flesh and died for us, and who will give to each one, according to his merits, eternal reward or punishment. I always want to live in accordance with this faith. Lord, increase my faith.

Act of Hope

My God, by virtue of your promises and the merits of Jesus Christ, our Savior, I hope to receive from your goodness eternal life and the necessary grace to merit it with the good deeds I am required and propose to do. Lord, may I be able to delight in you forever.

Act of Love

My God, I love you with all my heart and above all things, because you are infinitely good and our eternal happiness; for your sake I love my neighbor as I love myself, and I forgive the offenses I have received. Lord, grant that I will love you more and more.

Petition

My God, here present now, hear and guide my prayer, and lead me to the verdant pastures and refreshing waters of your Truth and your Love.

3. ENTERING INTO GOD'S PRESENCE THROUGH ACTS OF GRATITUDE AND HUMILITY

My Lord and my God, you are infinitely kind and merciful. I thank you with all my heart for the countless gifts you have given me, especially for creating and redeeming me, for calling me to the Catholic faith and to my vocation, and for freeing me from so many dangers of soul and body.

You have shown me the door that leads to heaven, to being one with you forever. What am I? Mere sand. And so, why have you sought me out, why have you loved me, why have you shown me that door? Why did you become flesh and leave me your Gospel? Because you love me. I want to thank you for everything you did for me and all that you do for me. In this prayer I want to praise and glorify you.

How I need your grace! Please guide me now. Teach me to know, love, and do your will for me. I am nothing without you; I am no one without you, but I know that with you all things are possible.

4. IN THE CONTEXT OF SEEKING GOD'S WILL

My Lord and my God, you are Love itself, and the source of all love and goodness. Out of love you created me to know you, love you, and serve you in a unique way, as no one else can. I believe that you have a plan for my life, that you have a task in your Kingdom reserved just for me. Your plan and your task are far better than any other I might choose: they will glorify you, fulfill the desires of my heart, and save those souls who are depending on my generous response.

Lord, grant me the light I need to see the next step in that plan; grant me the generosity I need to set aside my own plans in favor of yours; and grant me the strength I need to put my hands to your plough and never turn back. You know me better than I know myself, so you know that I am sinful and weak. All the more reason that I need your grace to uphold the good desires you have planted in my heart, O Lord!

Make my prayer today pleasing to you. Show me your will for me, O gentle and eternal God, and help me to say with Mary, "I am the servant of the Lord; let it be done to me according to your word," and to say with Jesus, "Let not my will be done, but yours."

5. RECALLING CHRIST'S PERSONAL LOVE FOR ME

Lord, you wished to create me. I would not exist were it not for your almighty power. You created me because you love me, and I want to love you the way you have loved me. Lord, two thousand years ago mankind walked the earth in darkness, lost by the sin of our first parents. And you, in obedience to the Father and out of love for me, decided to become flesh in the Virgin's womb. You became a man so as to suffer for me, redeem me from my sins, and open the gates of heaven for me. Thank you for your love, Jesus; thank you for being born of the Blessed Virgin. Thank you, dear Mother, for saying yes to God and allowing the Second Person of the Blessed Trinity, Jesus Christ, to become man.

Lord Jesus, you are here with me now. You came into the world to teach me. You left me the path I must take to reach you and possess you forever in the Gospel. Thank you, Jesus, for such love. You truly are almighty God. I am a poor and miserable creature; and yet you loved me and continue to love me, not only in words, but with real love: love shown in works. That is why I know that you are with me now, in my heart, watching over me. Guide my prayer, Lord, cleanse my soul of all my sins and selfishness, and fill it with your light and your love. Grant me the grace I need most, because without you, I can do nothing.

6. FROM THE CHURCH'S RICH LITURGICAL TRADITION

The Te Deum

You are God: we praise you; you are the Lord: we acclaim you; you are the eternal Father: all creation worships you. To you all angels, all the powers of heaven, Cherubim and Seraphim, sing in endless praise: Holy, holy, holy, Lord, God of power and might, heaven and earth are full of your glory. The glorious company of Apostles praises you, the noble fellowship of prophets praises you, the white-robed army of martyrs praises you. Throughout the world the holy Church acclaims you: Father, of majesty unbounded, your true and only Son, worthy of all worship, and the Holy Spirit, advocate and guide. You, Christ, are the King of glory, the eternal Son of the Father. When you became man to set us free, you did not spurn the Virgin's womb. You overcame the sting of death, and opened the Kingdom of heaven to all believers. You are seated at God's right hand in glory. We believe that you will come, and be our judge. Come then, Lord, and help your people, bought with the price of your own blood, and bring us with your saints to glory everlasting. Save your people, Lord, and bless your inheritance. Govern and uphold them now and always. Day by day we bless you. We praise your name forever. Keep us today, Lord, from all sin. Have mercy on us, Lord, have mercy. Lord, show us your love and mercy, for we put our trust in you. In you, Lord, is our hope: and we shall never hope in vain. Lord, hear my prayer, and let my cry reach you.

Prefaces to the Eucharistic Prayer, Sundays in Ordinary Time I

It is truly right and just, our duty and our salvation, always and everywhere to give you thanks, Lord, holy Father, almighty and eternal God, through Christ our Lord. For through his Paschal Mystery, he accomplished the marvelous deed, by which he has freed us from the yoke of sin and death, summoning us to the glory of being now called a chosen race, a royal priesthood, a holy nation, a people for your own possession, to proclaim everywhere your mighty works, for you have called us out of darkness into your own wonderful light.

Preface to the Fourth Eucharistic Prayer

It is truly right to give you thanks, truly just to give you glory, Father, most holy, for you are the one God living and true, existing before all ages and abiding for all eternity, dwelling in unapproachable light; yet you, who alone are good, the source of life, have made all that is, so that you might fill your creatures with blessings and bring joy to many of them by the glory of your light. And so, in your presence are countless hosts of Angels, who serve you day and night and, gazing upon the glory of your face, glorify you without ceasing.

CONCLUDING PRAYERS Once you have renewed your commitment to follow Christ and expressed that in your own words and in a concrete resolution, briefly reviewed how your meditation went, and jotted down the insights God gave you (Step 4, Commit), it often helps to wrap up your meditation with a short, ready-made prayer that sums things up. St. Ignatius of Loyola used to finish with the Our Father, the Hail Mary, and the Glory Be. Here are some other options, in case you still haven't found your personal favorites. It is customary to end the meditation with the Sign of the Cross.

Prayer of Dedication

Lord Jesus,
I give you my hands to do your work.
I give you my feet to follow your way.
I give you my eyes to see as you do.
I give you my tongue to speak your words.
I give you my mind so you can think in me.
I give you my spirit so you can pray in me.
Above all, I give you my heart
So in me you can love your Father and all people.
I give you my whole self so you can grow in me,
Till it is you, Lord Jesus,
Who lives and works and prays in me. Amen.

Prayer to the Holy Spirit

Holy Spirit,
Inspire in me
What I should think,
What I should say,
What I should leave unsaid,
What I should write,

What I should do,
And how I should act
To bring about the good of souls,
The fulfillment of my mission,
And the triumph of the Kingdom of Christ. Amen.

Lead, Kindly Light

Lead, kindly Light, amid the encircling gloom,
Lead thou me on;
The night is dark, and I am far from home,
Lead thou me on.
Keep thou my feet; I do not ask to see
The distant scene; one step enough for me.
    I was not ever thus, nor prayed that thou
Shouldst lead me on;
I loved to choose and see my path; but now
Lead thou me on.
I loved the garish day, and, spite of fears,
Pride ruled my will: remember not past years.
    So long thy power hath blest me, sure it still
Will lead me on.
O'er moor and fen, o'er crag and torrent, till
The night is gone,
And with the morn those Angel faces smile,
Which I have loved long since, and lost awhile.

–Saint J. H. Newman (1801-1890)

From St. Patrick's Breastplate

I bind unto myself today
The strong name of the Trinity:
By invocation of the same,
The Three in One and One in Three
    Christ be with me, Christ within me,
Christ behind me, Christ before me,
Christ beside me, Christ to win me,
Christ to comfort and restore me.
Christ beneath me, Christ above me,
Christ in quiet, Christ in danger,

Christ in hearts of all that love me,
Christ in mouth of friend and stranger.
Praise to the Lord of my salvation—
Salvation is of Christ the Lord!

–Ascribed to St. Patrick of Ireland (circa A.D. 450)

Prayer of Self-Dedication to Jesus Christ

Take, Lord, and receive
all my liberty, my understanding, my whole will,
all I have and all I possess.
You gave it all to me;
To you, Lord, I return it all.
It is all yours: Do with me entirely as you will.
Give me your love and your grace:
This is enough for me. Amen.

–St. Ignatius of Loyola (1491-1556)

Prayer of St. Francis

Lord, make me an instrument of Your peace.
Where there is hatred, let me sow love;
where there is injury, pardon;
where there is doubt, faith;
where there is despair, hope;
where there is darkness, light;
and where there is sadness, joy.
O, Divine Master,
grant that I may not so much seek
to be consoled as to console;
to be understood as to understand;
to be loved as to love;
for it is in giving that we receive;
it is in pardoning that we are pardoned;
and it is in dying that we are born to eternal life. Amen.

–St. Francis of Assisi (1181-1226)

Litany of Humility

This prayer renews one's commitment to follow Christ's summary for Christian living: "Set your hearts on his kingdom first, and on his righteousness, and all these other things will be given you as well" (Mt 6:33). It should be prayed from that perspective.

Jesus, meek and humble of heart, hear me!
From the desire of being esteemed, Lord Jesus, free me!
From the desire of being loved…
From the desire of being acclaimed…
From the desire of being honored…
From the desire of being praised…
From the desire of being preferred…
From the desire of being consulted…
From the desire of being approved…
From the desire of being valued…
From the fear of being humbled, Lord Jesus, free me!
From the fear of being despised…
From the fear of being dismissed…
From the fear of being rejected…
From the fear of being defamed…
From the fear of being forgotten…
From the fear of being ridiculed…
From the fear of being wronged…
From the fear of being suspected…
From resenting that my opinion is not followed…
That others will be more loved than I, Lord Jesus, make this my prayer!
That others will be esteemed more than I…
That others will increase in the opinion of the world while I diminish…
That others will be chosen while I am set aside…
That others will be praised while I am overlooked…
That others will be preferred to me in everything…

Lord Jesus, though you were God, you humbled yourself to the extreme of dying on a cross, to set an enduring example to the shame of my arrogance and vanity. Help me to learn your example and put it into practice so that, by humbling myself in accordance with my lowliness here on earth, you can lift me up to rejoice in you forever in heaven. Amen.

–Cardinal Merry del Val, Secretary of State under Pope St. Pius X (1865-1930)

Mission Prayer

Lord, you have created me to do you some definite service; you have committed some work to me which you have not committed to another. I have my mission—I never may know it in this life, but I shall be told it in the next.

Somehow I am necessary for your purposes, as necessary in my place as an Archangel in his—if, indeed, I fail, you can raise another, as you could make the stones children of Abraham. Yet I have a part in this great work; I am a link in a chain, a bond of connection between persons. You have not created me for naught. I shall do good, I shall do your work; I shall be an angel of peace, a preacher of truth in my own place, while not intending it, if I do but your commandments and serve you in my calling.

Therefore I will trust you. Whatever, wherever I am, I can never be thrown away. If I am in sickness, my sickness may serve you; in perplexity, my perplexity may serve you; if I am in sorrow, my sorrow may serve you. My sickness, or perplexity, or sorrow may be necessary causes of some great end, which is quite beyond me. You do nothing in vain; you may prolong my life, you may shorten it; you know what you are about; you may take away my friends, you may throw me among strangers, you may make me feel desolate, make my spirits sink, hide the future from me—still you know what you are about.

–Adapted from a reflection composed by Saint J.H. Newman (1801-1890)

MORE FROM THE CHURCH'S RICH LITURGICAL TRADITION

The Gloria

Glory to God in the highest, and on earth peace to people of good will.
We praise you, we bless you, we adore you, we glorify you,
we give you thanks,for your great glory,
Lord God, heavenly King, O God, almighty Father.
Lord Jesus Christ, Only Begotten Son,
Lord God, Lamb of God, Son of the Father,
you take away the sins of the world, have mercy on us;
you take away the sins of the world, receive our prayer;
you are seated at the right hand of the Father: have mercy on us.
For you alone are the Holy One, you alone are the Lord,
you alone are the Most High, Jesus Christ, with the Holy Spirit,
in the glory of God the Father. Amen.

The Apostles' Creed

I believe in God, the Father almighty, creator of heaven and earth. I believe in Jesus Christ, his only Son, our Lord, who was conceived by the power of the Holy Spirit and born of the Virgin Mary, suffered under Pontius Pilate, was crucified, died, and was buried. He descended into hell. On the third day he rose again from the dead; he ascended into heaven, and is seated at the right hand of God the Father almighty; from there he will come to judge the living and the dead. I believe in the Holy Spirit, the holy catholic Church, the communion of saints, the forgiveness of sins, the resurrection of the body, and the life everlasting. Amen.

Here is some space where you can write in other prayers that you personally find helpful for wrapping up your meditation and returning to your other daily activities…

PART II

MEDITATION UNIT

The Gospel according to St. Luke

THE GOSPEL OF LUKE
Chapter 1

"The Son of God himself,
who is before all ages,
the invisible, the incomprehensible, the bodiless,
the beginning from the beginning,
the light from the light,
source of life and immortality,
image of the archetype,
immoveable seal,
unchangeable image,
the Father's definition and Word,
he it is who came to his own image and took to himself
flesh for the sake of our flesh."

– ST. GREGORY NAZIANZEN, *Orations*

149. Doing Our Part (Lk 1:1-4)[1]

"The only-begotten Son of God, wishing to enable us to share in his divinity, assumed our nature, so that by becoming man he might make men gods." – St. Thomas Aquinas

LUKE 1:1-4
Seeing that many others have undertaken to draw up accounts of the events that have taken place among us, exactly as these were handed down to us by those who from the outset were eyewitnesses and ministers of the word, I in my turn, after carefully going over the whole story from the beginning, have decided to write an ordered account for you, Theophilus, so that your Excellency may learn how well founded the teaching is that you have received.

CHRIST THE LORD St. Luke is the only non-Jewish author to write part of the New Testament (he wrote both the Gospel of Luke and the Acts of the Apostles). He was a doctor, a scholar (as is evident in his elegant writing style), and an artist who

1 Note: the unit numbering began with the Gospel of Matthew and ends with the Gospel of John.

converted to Christianity during the first wave of evangelization after Jesus' ascension. He accompanied St. Paul on his journeys and during his imprisonment, and he had the chance to meet all the major figures of the early Church. He addresses this manuscript to a high-ranking Roman official (the title "your Excellency" was reserved for such well-positioned men), who may have been financing its publication.

This background information itself speaks volumes about Jesus. He never left Palestine, he died on a cross as a criminal, and only a handful of simple fishermen continued to preach his message after he left this earth. In spite of such star-crossed beginnings, in a matter of just a few years the gospel of Jesus Christ had spread like a storm throughout the Roman Empire. It penetrated the social strata of rich and poor alike, the educated and the ignorant, shedding its saving light into human hearts of every kind.

History can boast of no similar case, unless we count the many instances of saints who brought the gospel to pagan lands. They too started infinitesimally small and soon imbued entire societies and whole cultures with Christ's truth and grace. No greater proof of Christ's universal, saving Lordship can be found than that history of his Church.

CHRIST THE TEACHER Sometimes we mistakenly think that the Bible came right from Christ's lips. Christ established his Church, the living community of his followers gathered around and "built upon the foundation of the apostles and prophets" (Eph 2:20). He commissioned that Church to hand on (the same term that gives the etymological root for "tradition") his message. The Bible followed, as disciples like St. Luke realized a need to record the events and teachings of Christ's life and the early Church for the sake of having common reference points to guide the Church's growth. The Bible truly is the Word of God, a uniquely inspired compendium of God's own self-revelation, but it doesn't exist in a vacuum. It is a sacred text whose full meaning only shines through when read and interpreted in the context of the living Church, which preserves the tradition from which the Bible itself sprang.

That's why the term "biblical Christian" is a misnomer—the Bible is not enough to make a mature Christian. And that's why all Christians need to stay tuned to what the Church is saying; we all need to feed our souls on God's Word as served up by the Church.

CHRIST THE FRIEND St. Luke is about to begin telling the most important, wonderful story in all human history. He obviously feels a need to do so, to write it out in a way that others can understand it and reflect on it. Just so, each Christian should sense a need to hand on the story of Christ.

Did Luke know that the Holy Spirit was inspiring him to write one of the infallible books of the New Testament? Probably not. He just knew that he had to do this, and he had to do it as well as he could—asking all the eyewitnesses, putting things together clearly and truly, doing his homework. He rolled up his sleeves and got to work, and that's what God used in order to achieve his plan for Luke's life, and to reach out through him to millions of thirsty, searching souls.

The Christian life is always like that. The partnership between each Christian and the Holy Spirit is a collaboration between true friends. Jesus doesn't do everything himself, leaving us with some symbolic but useless gesture, like a dad who lets his son follow behind him with a plastic lawnmower. Instead, Jesus has given us the mysterious gift of freedom, and when we join his team, he wants us to put all our creativity, talents, and love into action on his behalf. If we do, the results will far outstrip our natural capacities, but our natural capacities will still be the basis of those results. It's like the bread used at Mass. It's small, flimsy, plain, and weak, but without our giving it to God, Christ's Eucharistic presence would never come to pass.

CHRIST IN MY LIFE Your Church is so human, Lord. Its history can only be explained by your gentle, sure hand guiding and protecting it in every era. Thank you for the Church. Thank you for this Gospel. Thank you for making sure that I would have a chance to hear the Good News of your salvation. Thank you for the gift of faith. Jesus, never let me be separated from you.

So many voices clamor for my attention. Jesus, teach me to tune in to your voice. Show me how to listen to the teachings of the Church, to the advice of the saints. My life is so short! I have so little time! Help me to keep first things first. Teach me to do your will, Lord.

Sometimes it's hard for me to believe that you have made your Kingdom depend in some small way on my efforts. But it's true. You have called me, and you lead and inspire me, as you did with St. Luke, to make my own unique contribution. Make me docile to heed your guidance; strengthen my spirit to persevere in doing your will; inflame my heart with true Christian zeal.

Questions for SMALL-GROUP DISCUSSION

1. What struck you most in this passage? What did you notice that you hadn't noticed before?
2. What do you think might have been the most exciting thing about living in the first Christian communities?

3. Some critics deride the Church because of its many cases of corruption throughout history. How would you respond to someone who made such an argument to you?
4. In general, how can you tell if an inspiration or an idea really comes from God?

Cf. Catechism of the Catholic Church, 4-10 on the nature of handing on the faith; 36-43 on knowing God through the Church and speaking of God within the limits of human language; 106-107 on the inspiration and truth of Sacred Scripture

150. The Time Has Finally Come (Lk 1:5-25)

"When I read the Gospel and find there testimonies from the Law and from the Prophets, I see only Christ." – St. Jerome

LUKE 1:5-25

In the days of King Herod of Judaea there lived a priest called Zechariah who belonged to the Abijah section of the priesthood, and he had a wife, Elizabeth by name, who was a descendant of Aaron. Both were worthy in the sight of God, and scrupulously observed all the commandments and observances of the Lord. But they were childless: Elizabeth was barren and they were both getting on in years. Now it was the turn of Zechariah's section to serve, and he was exercising his priestly office before God when it fell to him by lot, as the ritual custom was, to enter the Lord's sanctuary and burn incense there. And at the hour of incense the whole congregation was outside, praying. Then there appeared to him the angel of the Lord, standing on the right of the altar of incense. The sight disturbed Zechariah and he was overcome with fear. But the angel said to him, "Zechariah, do not be afraid, your prayer has been heard. Your wife Elizabeth is to bear you a son and you must name him John. He will be your joy and delight and many will rejoice at his birth, for he will be great in the sight of the Lord; he must drink no wine, no strong drink. Even from his mother's womb he will be filled with the Holy Spirit, and he will bring back many of the sons of Israel to the Lord their God. With the spirit and power of Elijah, he will go before him to turn the hearts of fathers towards their children and the disobedient back to the wisdom that the virtuous have, preparing for the Lord a people fit for him."

Zechariah said to the angel, "How can I be sure of this? I am an old man and my wife is getting on in years." The angel replied, "I am Gabriel who stand in God's presence, and I have been sent to speak to you and bring you this good news. Listen! Since you have not believed my words, which will come true at their appointed time, you will be silenced and have no power of speech until this has happened." Meanwhile the people were waiting for Zechariah and were surprised that he stayed in the sanctuary so long. When he came out he could not speak to them, and they realised that he had received a vision in the sanctuary. But he could only make signs to them, and remained dumb. When his time of service came to an end he returned home. Some time later his wife Elizabeth conceived, and for five months she kept to herself. "The Lord has done this for me," she said, "now that it has pleased him to take away the humiliation I suffered among men."

CHRIST THE LORD The entire history of the Old Covenant made sense only because it converged on the promised Messiah. John the Baptist, the child promised to Zechariah, is to be the Messiah's first herald, and Israel's last and greatest prophet, the final link in the Old Covenant's chain. So it is highly appropriate that when the moment comes for the Messiah to be announced, the first movement of the Messianic age takes place inside the priests' court of the Temple (where only priests could go), in accordance with the daily rhythm of prayer and sacrifice that the Old Testament had prescribed. The liturgy of the Old Covenant centered on thanking God for his past blessings and imploring him for future blessings, especially the greatest blessing of all, the arrival of the promised Messiah. St. Luke begins his Gospel by plugging the story of Jesus into the very heart of the story of Israel, showing the continuity of God's action throughout the history of salvation.

But St. Luke also provides another context for the beginning of the Messianic era. He provides specific references to rulers and places in the pagan world (in this passage: Herod, the King of Judaea), references that historians have cross-checked and corroborated with nonbiblical sources. In Jesus, then, the age of preparation comes to its conclusion, and the hope offered to Israel is also held out to all nations. Just as Jesus, the Savior and Redeemer, comes to dwell in and among the Jews living in Palestine, so he comes to dwell in and among the Romans, who ruled Palestine and most of the civilized world at the time.

St. Luke is already cluing us in to a key characteristic of the Lord's leadership style: it has a personal, incarnational touch, but a universal extension.

CHRIST THE TEACHER Why did Zechariah hear God's voice inside the Temple during the liturgical ceremony? Why didn't God send him the message in the quiet of his garden at home, while he was meditating in comfort and contemplating the beauty of nature? Why didn't God send the angel while Zechariah was pouring over the Scriptures early in the morning, in his study, by the light of a lantern? God can speak to our hearts at any time and in any place, but he has established some normal channels, and we would be wise to attend to them: they are the various seasons and celebrations of the liturgy.

Ancient Israel had them, and it had a clergy to go along with them. All of that Old Covenant liturgical establishment was a precursor for the Church's liturgy. Just as God prepared the way for Christ through setting aside a Chosen People—an entire nation that served and followed him as a community—so Christ himself established a New Chosen People: the believing community of his Church.

Often, perhaps, we would prefer something more individualistic, something more comfortable and amenable to our personal tastes, but God is a family (the Trinity), and his salvation is administered and experienced through the family of the Church. If we are serious about seeking and fulfilling God's plan for our lives, and coming to full maturity as Christ's followers, then participating deeply in the life of the Church—above all the liturgical life of the Church: the sacraments, the seasons, the Mass—will be among our top priorities. And if it is, we will surely hear God's voice guiding and strengthening us, just as Zechariah did.

CHRIST THE FRIEND Elizabeth and Zechariah were both pure Jews and faithful to God. In fact, St. Luke makes a point of saying they were exemplary in every way. And yet, God had sent them a weighty cross, one that also brought with it a social stigma in ancient Israel: they were childless. This was their great burden. Jews of the time considered it a curse to be without children. How often they must have begged God to give them the blessing of a child; how often they must have shed secret tears at the disdain of their neighbors! How it must have wrung Elizabeth's heart at times to see her neighbor's children! They must have wondered why God didn't answer their prayer. But God had heard their prayer—this is the first thing the angel Gabriel says to Zechariah, that his prayer has been heard. And God's plan was unfolding. Elizabeth's long barrenness and miraculous pregnancy were part of God's plan, just as the couple's suffering had been.

The example of God's dramatic action in their lives should fill us with comfort and confidence even in the midst of our own struggles. Any burden that God permits or sends us is part of his wise, providential plan for our good and the good of his Kingdom. He doesn't ask us to ignore our sufferings, but to bear them with trust and faith, bringing our needs and concerns to him in prayer, confident that his love knows how to work everything out in the end.

CHRIST IN MY LIFE You are the center and goal of all human history, Lord. You are enthroned even now in heaven, ruling over all creation. You are guiding all hearts and nations towards the definitive culmination of the human story. I believe in you, Lord. I believe that history has meaning, and that you forget no one. Help me to be your instrument of grace in my part of the story...

I wish I could hear your voice more clearly. But you are always speaking to my heart, drawing me closer to you, guiding me. I know this. Maybe I look too eagerly for special signs, like the one you gave to Zechariah—but even that didn't convince him. Lord, I want to believe with a fresh, simple, robust faith. Lord Jesus, increase my faith and open my heart to hear your voice...

I beg you, Lord, once and for all, please teach me to recognize your hand in the sufferings and hardships that come my way. You are all-powerful and all-good, all-knowing and all-loving. Nothing is outside of your purview. I trust in you, Lord. Increase my trust. And teach me to bolster my neighbors' trust and help them journey towards you...

Questions for SMALL-GROUP DISCUSSION

1. What struck you most in this passage? What did you notice that you hadn't noticed before?
2. Why do you think Zechariah doubted Gabriel's message, even after seeing the glorious signs of the angel's presence?
3. Two daily liturgical sacrifices were offered in the Temple, one in the morning and one in the evening. Do you think it's significant that God chose to announce John the Baptist's arrival during the evening sacrifice instead of during the one in the morning?
4. Why do you think Gabriel made Zechariah mute as a result of his doubt? Does the "punishment fit the crime," so to speak?

Cf. Catechism of the Catholic Church, 1066-1075 on the nature, role, and importance of the Church's liturgy; 269, 304, and 450 on Christ as the Lord of history; 388 and 1040 on grasping the ultimate meaning of history

151. The Greatest Yes (Lk 1:26-38)

"Therefore, though it is God who takes the initiative of coming to dwell in the midst of men, and he is always the main architect of this plan, it is also true that he does not will to carry it out without our active cooperation." – Pope Benedict XVI

LUKE 1:26-38

In the sixth month the angel Gabriel was sent by God to a town in Galilee called Nazareth, to a virgin betrothed to a man named Joseph, of the House of David; and the virgin's name was Mary. He went in and said to her, "Rejoice, so highly favoured! The Lord is with you." She was deeply disturbed by these words and asked herself what this greeting could mean, but the angel said to her, "Mary, do not be afraid; you have won God's favour. Listen! You are to conceive and bear a son, and you must name him Jesus. He will be great and will be called Son of the Most High. The Lord God will give him the throne of his ancestor David; he will rule over the House of Jacob for ever and his reign will have no end." Mary said to the angel, "But how can this come about, since I am a virgin?" "The Holy Spirit will come upon you," the angel answered, "and the power of the Most High will cover you with its shadow. And so the child will be holy and will be called Son of God. Know this too: your kinswoman Elizabeth has, in her old age, herself conceived a son, and she whom people called barren is now in her sixth month, for nothing is impossible to God." "I am the handmaid of the Lord," said Mary; "let what you have said be done to me." And the angel left her.

CHRIST THE LORD Of whom can it be said, "His reign will have no end"? Only of Jesus Christ, the Son of God and the son of David (from whose descendents the promised Messiah was to be born), and the only man ever born of a virgin. Gabriel's brief announcement to Mary foretells the advent of someone absolutely unique: the Davidic king who will rule over all the nations, the one who would save mankind from their sins ("Jesus" means "God saves"), and the one who would fulfill all the Old Testament prophecies about the reunification of Israel and Judah (the "House of Jacob"). The entire gospel is packed into this Annunciation of the Archangel Gabriel to Mary.

It is a gospel that at times is hard to believe. Sometimes it seems almost too good to be true—too simple, too easy. On the other hand, when the sufferings and tragedies of life and the tumultuous twists and turns of human history oppress us, it seems more like a fairy tale, a pipe dream. For Mary, too, the announcement was almost overwhelming. But her faith and purity sensitized her to God's truth. She accepted the angel's message and all its implications for her own life—a radical, unforeseen change in her plans. She was able to do so because she had long ago assimilated a doctrine we too often ignore, one that Gabriel reminded her of: "Nothing is impossible for God."

CHRIST THE TEACHER Christmas, the part of Christ's life this Gospel passage is connected to, presents us with the mystery of God who became man, but it also includes the mystery of man cooperating in the saving action of God. God sends his messenger to Mary in order to invite her to become the mother of the Savior. She accepted the invitation, and history has never been the same. But it would have been possible for her to reject it. Like the parable Christ tells of the many townspeople who decline the king's invitation to attend his son's wedding feast, Mary could have considered God's intervention just a disruption of her plans, an inconvenience. But she did not.

When God asked her to take on a role in his plan of salvation, she said yes: "I am the handmaid of the Lord, let what you have said be done to me." Her question to the archangel, "But how can this come about, since I am a virgin?" was different than the similar sounding question Zechariah had posed: "How can I be sure of this? I am an old man and my wife is getting on in years." Zechariah was asking for proof that God could do what he promised; Mary was merely asking what God wanted her to do—she had promised her virginity to God, and she wanted to know if God was asking her something else. She didn't doubt God's wisdom or power; she just wanted more instructions. This is why the angel's response to her was generous, while his response to Zechariah was harsh. Zechariah answered God's call by saying, "Prove it to me"; Mary answered saying, "Show me the way to go."

We can learn no greater lesson than how to say yes to God. Mary's "yes" reversed Eve's "no," and paved the way for Christ's undoing of Adam's fall. Likewise, when God disrupts our lives—through the voice of conscience, the normal responsibilities and demands of our state in life, or the indications of Church teaching—our "yes" can echo Mary's and make more room for Christ in this fallen world. But our "no"—or even our "maybe"—can just as easily shut him out.

CHRIST THE FRIEND Many friends exchange gifts, but only Christ has given us his own mother, to be our solace and our refuge as we strive to follow in his footsteps.

As he was dying on the cross, Jesus entrusted his mother to the care of his "beloved disciple," and he entrusted the disciple to her care: "When Jesus saw his mother and the disciple there whom he loved, he said to his mother,

'Woman, behold, your son.' Then he said to the disciple, 'Behold, your mother.' And from that hour the disciple took her into his home" (Jn 19:26-27).

From its earliest days, the Church has interpreted this passage in a deeply spiritual way: since Jesus has desired to have us as his brothers and sisters, he has also desired to share with us his mother, to give us a mother in the order of grace. Through the ages, Christians in all walks of life have been inspired by Mary's example, comforted by her spiritual solicitude, and aided by her heavenly intercession. Wherever one finds true devotion to Mary (which consists primarily in the imitation of her yes to God, not just in pious expressions and pretty pictures), one finds as well a passionate love for Jesus Christ, the Savior. She accompanied him on every step of his earthly sojourn, and she accompanies his little brothers and sisters (that's us) with equal love and concern.

CHRIST IN MY LIFE Thank you for making me a Christian. You are the one Savior, the promised Messiah, and your Kingdom will have no end. You have called me into your Kingdom. What more could I ask for? You have given me your friendship. Lord, teach me to live closer to you, to have the same scale of values that you have, and to see all things with your eyes.

Mary, you were just a girl when God came and invited you to be the mother of the Savior. Even then you knew that God's will was the highest and wisest calling. You didn't fear missing out on all that the world had to offer, because you only wanted to stay close to the world's Creator. Teach me to trust and love Christ, and teach me to give him to others, as you gave him to us.

How strange, Lord, that you made the history of salvation depend not only on your own actions, but also on the free cooperation of your creatures! You waited for Mary to say yes before coming to be our Savior. You wait for each of us to say yes before coming to save us. I renew my yes right now. Teach me to help others say yes too; only what I do for your Kingdom will last forever.

Questions for SMALL-GROUP DISCUSSION

1. What struck you most in this passage? What did you notice that you hadn't noticed before?
2. What can we do to renew our appreciation of the wonderful miracle of Christmas, which we so often take for granted?
3. How can we benefit more from Mary's motherly interest in our Christian discipleship?

4. Christ asked something difficult from Mary. Do you think she ever regretted her answer? Do you know anyone else who has said yes to something difficult that God asked of them?

Cf. Catechism of the Catholic Church, 484-507 on the privileges and role of Mary in Christ's Kingdom; 456-478 on the mission and uniqueness of Jesus Christ, Son of God and man

152. Mary's Song (Lk 1:39-56)

"The Holy Spirit heated, inflamed and melted Mary with love, as fire does iron, so that the flame of the Spirit was seen and nothing was felt but the fire of the love of God." – St. Ildephonsus of Toledo

LUKE 1:39-56

Mary set out at that time and went as quickly as she could to a town in the hill country of Judah. She went into Zechariah's house and greeted Elizabeth. Now as soon as Elizabeth heard Mary's greeting, the child leapt in her womb and Elizabeth was filled with the Holy Spirit. She gave a loud cry and said, "Of all women you are the most blessed, and blessed is the fruit of your womb. Why should I be honoured with a visit from the mother of my Lord? For the moment your greeting reached my ears, the child in my womb leapt for joy. Yes, blessed is she who believed that the promise made her by the Lord would be fulfilled." And Mary said: "My soul proclaims the greatness of the Lord, and my spirit exults in God my saviour; because he has looked upon his lowly handmaid. Yes, from this day forward all generations will call me blessed, for the Almighty has done great things for me. Holy is his name, and his mercy reaches from age to age for those who fear him. He has shown the power of his arm, he has routed the proud of heart. He has pulled down princes from their thrones and exalted the lowly. The hungry he has filled with good things, the rich sent empty away. He has come to the help of Israel his servant, mindful of his mercy—according to the promise he made to our ancestors—of his mercy to Abraham and to his descendants for ever." Mary stayed with Elizabeth about three months and then went back home.

CHRIST THE LORD Elizabeth knows what's going on. After years of infertility, God has seen fit to make her the mother of John the Baptist, the Messiah's herald, whom she is still carrying in her womb. In response to such a privilege she has drawn closer to God, filled as she is with humble gratitude and a new appreciation of his mercy and generosity. Therefore, God begins to fill her with the Holy Spirit, who in turn keeps drawing her deeper into the mysterious and wonderful events taking place through and around her. This intimate union with God enables her to perceive God's presence in Christ, even though he is only an embryo in Mary's womb. And she calls him "my Lord."

Before he ever worked any wonders, before he mesmerized the crowds with his preaching, before he rose from the dead, indeed, from all eternity, Jesus is "the Lord."

CHRIST THE TEACHER It's impossible to tell the story of Christmas without including Mary. As Christ's first and most faithful disciple, the first one to welcome him into the world, she shows all of us how to live every Advent and Christmas season—indeed, every season of our Christian life—with faith. Through her example, Christ teaches us how to respond to God's action in and around us: by believing in him and by trusting that whatever he may be asking of us is the best available option.

Who are we to argue with God, to disobey him? Will he deceive us? Will he lead us astray? Mary, partially enlightened by her heartfelt knowledge of God's plan as revealed in the Old Testament scriptures, could not see clearly how God's plans would work themselves out in the end. Even so, humbly and trustingly she put her faith in them, and for that wise faith she was "blessed among women," as Elizabeth exclaimed. The Lord is constantly hoping that we will put our trust in him in the same way, so that he can shower his blessings upon us as well.

What was Mary's secret? Why was she able to believe so firmly and to fulfill her vocation so magnificently? Why did she succeed where Eve had failed? She reveals her secret in this hymn of praise that bursts from her heart as soon as she greets Elizabeth.

During the whole journey from Nazareth to the hill country outside Jerusalem where Elizabeth and Zechariah lived, she had been joyfully contemplating all that God had done in her life and in the whole history of salvation. When she meets Elizabeth and realizes that God has revealed his plans to her as well, she feels free to give full expression to her thoughts and sentiments. She sings the Magnificat, a prayer that still echoes throughout the world every day through the liturgy of the Church. In its simple words, imbued with the prayers of the Old Testament, we glimpse Mary's vision of reality, in which God rules all things with perfect power and with a wisdom that confounds the vain ambition of men. Humility, a serene recognition of our utter dependence on God, unleashes the power of divine grace in the world. Those who depend on themselves—the rich, the self-satisfied, the proud, the powerful—thwart God's action in and through them. This is Mary's secret—and it is a secret no longer. She teaches it to all who are willing to learn.

CHRIST THE FRIEND God is already caring for us long before we realize it. He has had a plan in mind for us, a particular vocation, a unique role in his Kingdom, from before we were born, before we were ever conceived. In discovering and living out that plan we find our true and lasting joy. Why else is John the Baptist able to "leap for joy" while he is still in his mother's womb? Only because God had made him the herald, the precursor, the one who would announce the imminent manifestation of the Messiah—this was his God-given mission in life, his vocation. Before he is aware of it, he is already fulfilling it.

Likewise, before we hear God's call in our life, he is already preparing us to follow it—and hoping that when the call comes we will respond generously, so that he can make our hearts leap continually with joy until he welcomes us into his heavenly Kingdom.

CHRIST IN MY LIFE Lord, are you still at work in the world the way you were back when these wonderful happenings were unfolding? I know you are. I know that every time Mass is celebrated, it's a new Annunciation, a new Bethlehem, a new Calvary. I know that you never cease drawing us to yourself. Open my eyes, increase my faith! I want to see you at work in all things...

Humility is a mystery to me, Lord. How humble Mary must have been! Unspoiled, uncontaminated by original sin and the slew of selfish tendencies it sets loose in our souls! Mary, my Mother, teach me your secret. Teach me to be truly humble, truly great in God's eyes, so that my life will bear fruit for Christ's Kingdom...

Lord, I know that you really do have something in mind for me. You created me to know you and love you as only I can. My concept of my vocation may not be in perfect sync with yours. But even so, I want to follow you. I want to discover and fulfill your will for me. I want to perceive it and understand it more deeply every day, so that I can embrace it more fully each moment...

Questions for
SMALL-GROUP DISCUSSION

1. What struck you most in this passage? What did you notice that you hadn't noticed before?

2. How can we be more sensitive, like Elizabeth, to the action of God in our lives? How can we cultivate the beautiful virtue of gratitude?
3. What more can we do to discover our true vocation? How can we follow it more energetically?
4. What aspects of popular culture encourage us to think of life in terms of our God-given mission, as God thinks of us? What aspects discourage that?

Cf. Catechism of the Catholic Church, 484-507 on the privileges and role of Mary in Christ's Kingdom; 456-478 on the mission and uniqueness of Jesus Christ, Son of God and man

153. The Fruits of Obedience (Lk 1:57-80)

"After the fullness of time had come, there came too the fullness of the Godhead." – St. Bernard of Clairvaux

LUKE 1:57-80

Meanwhile the time came for Elizabeth to have her child, and she gave birth to a son; and when her neighbours and relations heard that the Lord had shown her so great a kindness, they shared her joy. Now on the eighth day they came to circumcise the child; they were going to call him Zechariah after his father, but his mother spoke up. "No," she said "he is to be called John." They said to her, "But no one in your family has that name," and made signs to his father to find out what he wanted him called. The father asked for a writing-tablet and wrote, "His name is John." And they were all astonished. At that instant his power of speech returned and he spoke and praised God. All their neighbours were filled with awe and the whole affair was talked about throughout the hill country of Judaea. All those who heard of it treasured it in their hearts. "What will this child turn out to be?" they wondered. And indeed the hand of the Lord was with him.

His father Zechariah was filled with the Holy Spirit and spoke this prophecy: "Blessed be the Lord, the God of Israel for he has visited his people, he has come to their rescue and he has raised up for us a power for salvation in the House of his servant David, even as he proclaimed, by the mouth of his holy prophets from ancient times, that he would save us from our enemies and from the hands of all who hate us. Thus he shows mercy to our ancestors, thus he remembers his holy covenant, the oath he swore to our father Abraham that he would grant us, free from fear, to be delivered from the hands of our enemies, to serve him in holiness and virtue in his presence, all our days. And you, little child, you shall be called Prophet of the Most High, for you will go before the Lord to prepare the way for him. To give his people knowledge of salvation through the forgiveness of their sins; this by the tender mercy of our God who from on high will bring the rising Sun to visit us, to give light to those who live in darkness and the shadow of death, and to guide our feet into the way of peace." Meanwhile the child grew up and his spirit matured. And he lived out in the wilderness until the day he appeared openly to Israel.

CHRIST THE LORD Christ the Lord fulfills both God's promises and the human heart's deepest longings.

The beginning of Zechariah's prophecy links his son's mission of announcing the Messiah's arrival with the whole history of Israel. Ever since our first parents fell from grace, God had been preparing the world for a Savior. The events, personalities, and prophesies of the Old Covenant were orchestrated with Christ in mind; they always pointed towards the Redeemer and Savior. Zechariah recognizes this. After his nine months of muteness, during which he had plenty of time to reflect, pray, and listen to God's words (instead of drowning them out with his own idle chatter), he mulled over the marvelous history of Israel, and God was able to give him a clear vision of what the Messianic age consisted in: the fulfillment of God's many-faceted, ancient, and constantly renewed promise of salvation.

The second half of his prophecy takes a different angle on things. It looks into the longings of the human spirit that had been alienated from God and exiled from its true homeland because of sin. The human soul yearns for forgiveness—we long to know that we are loved unconditionally, generously, no matter what. The human mind longs for light—we hunger to know the truth of things, the reason we exist, where we are going, the meaning of life, and the path to fulfillment. And all of us pine above all for peace—the peace that is so much more than a mere absence of war, the peace that is fullness, prosperity, goodness, social harmony, creative expansiveness, and cultural flourishing.

God's Savior comes to bring all of these mighty gifts. He comes, as John the Baptist will announce, to inaugurate a New Creation, a New Covenant that will end in an everlastingly fruitful life.

CHRIST THE TEACHER Elizabeth and Zechariah are put to the test when the time comes to name their child. It was customary to give firstborn boys names that would link them to their families, their fathers, and their fathers' fathers. But this elderly couple chooses a name foreign to their family. They do so because that's what God asked them to do through the angel's message. Fidelity to God's will in this case means causing a stir. It means bucking social convention. It means risking the gossipmongers' epithets. But they do the right thing—and as a result, Zechariah miraculously recovers his speech, and the whole region is thrown into awestruck admiration of God. Elizabeth's and Zechariah's fidelity to God's will in spite of social pressure plants the seeds that John the Baptist will later harvest when he begins his mission of preaching and baptizing.

Whenever God makes his will known to us, through the voice of conscience, Church teaching, or even strong interior motions of the Holy Spirit, he does so for a reason. Our obedience will draw us closer to God personally, but it will also cause a domino effect of grace and blessing to those around us. Trusting obedience to God and his Church is always the best policy.

CHRIST THE FRIEND We take for granted John the Baptist's role in the story of Christ—we are so used to it. But isn't there something strange about it? Was it absolutely necessary to send a herald ahead of the Messiah? Couldn't the Messiah handle the job himself? Probably he could have, but his choice to send a forerunner reveals something essential about his personality.

Jesus never forces his way into our lives. He is too polite, too respectful. He refuses to conquer hearts by compulsion. He acts gently, gradually. He prepares us for the special graces he has in store for us. Since he is always thinking of us, he guides us little by little. The more generously we respond to the many messengers and signs he sends ahead of him, the more he will pick up the pace of his action in our lives. But even then, his grace warms our soul like sunlight: silently, gently, but surely. Such is our Lord, who longs to be our closest friend.

CHRIST IN MY LIFE I believe in you, Lord Jesus. I believe that you are the only Son of the Father, the Savior of all people, the way, the truth, and the life. I believe that you were born of the Virgin Mary, that you came to earth for our salvation, that only in your name can we find salvation. And I believe that you will come again to judge all of us and that your Kingdom will have no end...

I often feel pressure to conform to social patterns instead of being faithful to my call to holiness. How can I love you wholly and still be prudent? Lord, it's so hard to keep the balance. I want to fulfill the life-mission you have given me, but at times I just don't see things clearly. But I trust in you, Lord. You will guide me, in spite of my clumsiness and egoism. You are faithful...

Sometimes I wish you would be less polite with me—force your way into my heart, Lord! I want to love you more and to love others as you love me, but my selfishness clings to my soul and weighs me down. Purify me, Lord. Strip away every stain of egoism and self-absorption so that I can be truly free to live as you created me to live, to fulfill the mission you have given me in life...

Questions for SMALL-GROUP DISCUSSION

1. What struck you most in this passage? What did you notice that you hadn't noticed before?
2. What are the most dependable ways to identify God's will in our lives?
3. Zechariah's song rejoices in the salvation God sends through the Messiah. How should this healthy desire for salvation manifest itself in a Christian's life in our day and age?
4. According to this passage, the Messiah will bring satisfaction to all the longings of the human heart. Where does popular culture claim such satisfaction can be found?

Cf. Catechism of the Catholic Church, 1-3 on God's long-term plan of salvation; 27-30 on the human heart's natural desire for God; 51-53 on God's loving plan of salvation; 54-64 on all the stages of revelation leading up to Christ

THE GOSPEL OF LUKE
Chapter 2

"For this cause he came down upon earth, that by pursuing death he might kill the rebel that slew men. For one underwent the judgment, and myriads were set free. One was buried, and myriads rose again. He is the mediator between God and man. He is the resurrection and salvation of all. He is the guide of the erring, the shepherd of men who have been set free, the life of the dead, the charioteer of the cherubim, and the king of kings, to whom be the glory for ever and ever. Amen."

– ST. ALEXANDER OF ALEXANDRIA

154. THE PROMISE OF PEACE (LK 2:1-14)

"He does not want to overwhelm us with his strength. He takes away our fear of his greatness. He asks for our love: so he makes himself a child." – Pope Benedict XVI

LUKE 2:1-14

Now at this time Caesar Augustus issued a decree for a census of the whole world to be taken. This census—the first—took place while Quirinius was governor of Syria, and everyone went to his own town to be registered. So Joseph set out from the town of Nazareth in Galilee and travelled up to Judaea, to the town of David called Bethlehem, since he was of David's House and line, in order to be registered together with Mary, his betrothed, who was with child. While they were there the time came for her to have her child, and she gave birth to a son, her first born. She wrapped him in swaddling clothes, and laid him in a manger because there was no room for them at the inn. In the countryside close by there were shepherds who lived in the fields and took it in turns to watch their flocks during the night. The angel of the Lord appeared to them and the glory of the Lord shone round them. They were terrified, but the angel said, "Do not be afraid. Listen, I bring you news of great joy, a joy to be shared by the whole people. Today in the town of David a saviour has been born to you; he is Christ the Lord. And here is a sign for you: you will find a baby wrapped in swaddling clothes and lying in a manger." And suddenly with the angel there was a great throng of the heavenly host, praising God and singing: "Glory to God in the highest heaven, and peace to men who enjoy his favour."

CHRIST THE LORD The universe is not a democracy. Rather, it is ruled directly by God, who is a King, and his Kingdom is one of peace—the interior peace that comes from a clean conscience and the knowledge that our heavenly Father loves us, and the exterior peace that comes from communities built on humility, generosity, charity, and solidarity. Just as David (who was also one "anointed" by God) brought peace to ancient Israel, so his descendent, Jesus Christ, born in David's city, will bring universal peace to all mankind. Those who submit to his rule will begin to experience that peace even now, while his Kingdom is still incomplete. Those who rebel against his rule, ignoring or disdaining his wisdom and authority, will never experience the peace they long for—neither in this world, nor in the world to come. Jesus is the Prince of Peace, but the peace he came to give can only be had if we obey him as our wise and loving Lord.

As his followers, we often wonder how we can more effectively communicate this message of peace. Through the mystery of his birth, Jesus teaches us that eloquence in announcing the message comes from obedience in doing God's will. Jesus obeys the divine decision to become a human being, to be born as an infant, unable to utter a word. Yet, at that very moment of his seeming weakness, the angels come and announce the message with a superhuman power and beauty. The Lord is the one who builds his Kingdom; our task is simply to carry out whatever orders he gives us.

CHRIST THE TEACHER We tend to search for elaborate methods to get into contact with God. We often expect to find God in extraordinary circumstances. But we're usually wrong. The shepherds were responsibly fulfilling their normal, unglamorous duties when the angels appeared to them. Joseph and Mary welcomed the Son of God in a poor stable-cave while they were waiting to register for the census. The great lesson of the Incarnation is precisely that God wants to meet us—and befriend us—right where we are. With Christ, the everyday circumstances of the human condition become occasions of divine revelation and grace-filled salvation. St Teresa of Ávila used to say that she found the Lord among the pots and pans; with a simple, childlike faith, we can do the same.

The shepherds were shivering in the cold, watching over their tranquil flocks, gazing at the stars, mulling over their worries. They had no reason to expect that anything special would happen that night. But God finds a way to break through the routine.

Joseph was concerned for his wife, who had to give birth in a grotto used to shelter livestock. How he would have longed to give Jesus a worthier welcome! Yet he had to do the best he could under the circumstances, and God took his best and turned it into the most eloquent story in human history. God throws off his glory and power and wraps himself in humility and poverty, because he wants to walk with his people and lead them home to heaven.

Mary, whose heart had been beating in sync with Christ's Sacred Heart for nine months now—nurturing in her womb the sacred humanity of our Savior and nurturing in her mind the unfathomable love of God—was most likely not distracted at all by the circumstances. Her gaze was fixed entirely on Jesus. Every detail of the night was emblazoned on her memory, and each one spoke to her of God. The hay, the manger, the cave, the cold, the swaddling clothes, the animals, the darkness... Jesus had chosen to be born in their midst, and that was enough of an explanation for one who believed.

CHRIST THE FRIEND God is all-powerful. He is all-knowing. He could have come to us in any way at all, but he chose to do so quietly. He chose to give us a "sign" by becoming an "infant wrapped in swaddling clothes and laid in a manger."

Small, weak, and helpless—that's how our Lord comes to us, because he wants us to welcome him, to let him into our lives. Would we feel drawn to him if he had come in the form of a powerful giant? Probably not. But who can resist the charm of a helpless baby? By making himself weak, in need of constant care and attention, he draws us into a relationship with him, a relationship that God has longed to restore ever since it was shattered in the Garden of Eden. Each Christmas, and each day, when the Bethlehem event is renewed on the altar during Mass, God reissues his gentle invitation. Will we accept? Will we let Christ come into our lives anew, or will we keep him at a distance, afraid to risk our self-sufficiency and comfort for the sake of a helpless, needy child? It's cold in that Bethlehem cave, and he's hoping to be warmed by our embrace.

CHRIST IN MY LIFE I believe in you, and I want to follow you. I don't want to rule you or rule the universe, or even rule my own life and the lives of those around me. I am your ambassador, your servant, your messenger, your soldier. Do with me as you will, Lord. I ask only that you bring your peace to my heart each day, and make me an instrument to bring that same peace to those around me...

Sometimes it's easy for me to find you among the pots and pans, but other times I feel quite alone. How can I see your hand at work in the normal events of my daily life? I want to find you there, to embrace you there, to converse with you there, to obey you and follow you there. Lord, I believe, but help my unbelief…

You are so gentle, so respectful. You never force your way into my heart. Teach me to be like you, Lord: full of strength, but a strength that acts with respect, gentleness, and humility. Teach me to love my neighbors, to treat them with the same sincere and attentive kindness with which you have always treated me. And teach me to love all my neighbors, not just the ones who are easy to love…

Questions for *SMALL-GROUP DISCUSSION*

1. What struck you most in this passage? What did you notice that you hadn't noticed before?
2. How can we live our normal responsibilities with greater fidelity, so that we will be more attuned to God's presence and action in and through them?
3. What evidence should there be in the daily life of Christians that Christ is really the Lord of their life?
4. What can we do to live the liturgical seasons (like Christmas) in a way more pleasing to God, more in accord with the reason for which they exist?

Cf. Catechism of the Catholic Church, 2544-2547 on poverty of heart (which the shepherds had); 525-526 on the Christmas Mystery; 456-463 on why Jesus came to earth in the Incarnation

155. Praising and Pondering (Lk 2:15-21)

"God made himself small so that we could understand him, welcome him, and love him." – Pope Benedict XVI

LUKE 2:15-21

Now when the angels had gone from them into heaven, the shepherds said to one another, "Let us go to Bethlehem and see this thing that has happened which the Lord has made known to us." So they hurried away and found Mary and Joseph, and the baby lying in the manger. When they saw the child they repeated what they had been told about him, and everyone who heard it was astonished at what the shepherds had to say. As for Mary, she treasured all these things and pondered them in her heart.

> And the shepherds went back glorifying and praising God for all they had heard and seen; it was exactly as they had been told. When the eighth day came and the child was to be circumcised, they gave him the name Jesus, the name the angel had given him before his conception.

CHRIST THE LORD When Jesus was born, the angels of heaven could not restrain their joy, so they appeared to some humble shepherds and gave them a Christmas concert they would never forget. The birth of Christ shows that its consequences are unlimited by time and space, and the same goes for his Lordship. This child, this infant, holds the universe in his hands—which is why we sometimes see the infant Jesus depicted as a king, holding a sphere in his left hand (symbolizing the world) and a scepter in his right hand (symbolizing power and authority). Christ is Lord because he is God's Anointed, even when lying in a lowly little manger.

Perhaps the most beautiful thing about this absolute, universal Lordship is that it exists entirely for our sake. St. Luke makes a point of telling us about Christ's circumcision day, the day when he shed his first drop of blood, taking his place among sinners so that he could redeem them. It was traditional to give a boy his name on the same day he was circumcised. And so Mary and Joseph give him the name that God had assigned him through Gabriel's message: Jesus, which means "God saves." Luke reminds us that this name was given to him even before he was conceived in Mary's womb. The Word of God created us because he knew we would like it, and now he comes to redeem us because he knows we need it. Christ's whole life, his whole mission, is for our good, for our salvation.

Jesus' us-centered orientation wasn't an afterthought; we are the reason Jesus came to earth, lived, taught, healed, suffered, died, and rose again. Perhaps this is why saints throughout the ages have found in the simple name of "Jesus" one of their favorite and most fruitful prayers. Merely invoking our Lord, repeating his name over and over again, gives rest to our souls, because that's exactly what he came to do.

CHRIST THE TEACHER How are we to respond to the wonders God has done and is doing in the world and in our own lives? We can respond by following the shepherds' example. First, we should "hurry away" to find Christ, go in haste to seek him out in the midst of his family, the Church, here represented by Mary and Joseph. Second, as the shepherds "repeated what they had been told" about Christ, we should make known the message we have received. Third, we should "glorify and praise" the God who comes to save. We must allow the wonder of God's love to burst into our lives, as the shepherds did. We too must let God's marvelous works amaze us, never falling into a blasé attitude, a routine, been-there-done-that Christian mediocrity. Children get excited every Christmas, so why shouldn't we—who know so much more about the real meaning of the story—let it fill us with spiritual enthusiasm every single day?

We should also respond as Mary did: "Mary treasured all these things, and pondered them in her heart." God did not tell Mary his entire plan. We know much more than she did about how everything was going to work out. She had to walk in the dim light of faith, one step at a time, trusting in God, witnessing his action, and seconding it whenever she could. But she paid attention. She knew that the life and mission of Christ eclipsed in importance any other concern or event that might surface. She pondered in her heart all of God's gifts to her, all of his words, all of his actions and plans... She was truly a woman of the Kingdom. We need to learn this lesson as well, to be men and women who "seek first the Kingdom," and let everything else fall comfortably (and properly) into second place (cf. Mt 6:33).

CHRIST THE FRIEND God wants to give us the fullness of life. And he can give it to us—as a matter of fact, he is the only one who can give it to us. The problem is that we tend not to pay attention to him. His love, however, is determined. So he came up with a radical solution: he became a little baby, a helpless infant. Everyone pays attention to babies. So now we will look at him, even if only to see how cute he is. That's a start. Let's not belittle this reality! Coming to the baby Jesus and letting ourselves be charmed by his simplicity and innocence should be a frequent practice of our spiritual life—not something reserved exclusively to the Christmas season. We should, like the shepherds, gather around the manger with Mary and Joseph, and bask in the warm light of God's love radiating out from the infant Lord.

CHRIST IN MY LIFE You have revealed your name to me, because you want to stay close to me. Whenever I speak your name from my heart, you turn your attention to me. When I call you, you always come to me. You want to be available, to be close, to stay near. Why don't I call you more often? Why do I let the hustle and bustle of life drown you out? Jesus, please walk with me...

More than half the people in this world still don't know you or believe in you. I am one of the privileged minority who has received the Good News. Teach me, Lord, to be full of joy and generosity, like the shepherds, full of wonder and contemplation, like Mary, and full of the eager desire to spread the word...

How odd this Christmas story really is! The Creator and Sustainer of the universe becoming a little infant! No other religion has such a strange event. Dear Jesus, let me hold you in my arms. You are so small, so helpless. Let me take care of you. I adore you, Lord. I will never leave you; I will never abandon you. You are my life and my joy. You are safe with me, and you know that I love you. You can trust me, my Child; I love you, and I will watch over you…

Questions for SMALL-GROUP DISCUSSION

1. What struck you in this passage? What did you notice that you hadn't noticed before?
2. Why aren't we as eager as the shepherds to share with others our knowledge and experience of Christ?
3. How can we encourage each other to better imitate the Blessed Virgin in her prayerful spirit, "pondering all these things" in our hearts?
4. What do you think St. Joseph's reaction to these events was?

Cf. Catechism of the Catholic Church, 2673-2679 on praying the way Mary prayed; 2544-2547 on poverty of heart (which the shepherds had); 525-526 on the Christmas Mystery

156. The First Christian Homily (Lk 2:22-40)

"The patriarchs and prophets longed and prayed and yearned with all their hearts for this time. That just man Simeon at long last saw this time and his joy was boundless." – St. Charles Borromeo

LUKE 2: 22-40

And when the day came for them to be purified as laid down by the Law of Moses, they took him up to Jerusalem to present him to the Lord—observing what stands written in the Law of the Lord: Every first-born male must be consecrated to the Lord—and also to offer in sacrifice, in accordance with what is said in the Law of the Lord, a pair of turtledoves or two young pigeons.

Now in Jerusalem there was a man named Simeon. He was an upright and devout man; he looked forward to Israel's comforting and the Holy Spirit rested on him. It had been revealed to him by the Holy Spirit that he would not see death until he had set eyes on the Christ of the Lord. Prompted by the Spirit he came to the Temple and when the parents brought in the child Jesus to do for him what the Law required, he took him into his arms and blessed God; and he said: "Now, Master, you can let your servant go in peace, just as you promised; because my eyes have seen the salvation which you have prepared for all the nations to see, a light to enlighten the pagans and the glory of your people Israel." As the child's father and mother stood there wondering at the things that were being said about him, Simeon blessed them and said to Mary his mother, "You see this child: he is destined for the fall and for the rising of many in Israel, destined to be a sign that is rejected—and a sword will pierce your own soul too—so that the secret thoughts of many may be laid bare."

There was a prophetess also, Anna the daughter of Phanuel, of the tribe of Asher. She was well on in years. Her days of girlhood over, she had been married for seven years before becoming a widow. She was now eighty-four years old and never left the Temple, serving God night and day with fasting and prayer. She came by just at that moment and began to praise God; and she spoke of the child to all who looked forward to the deliverance of Jerusalem. When they had done everything the Law of the Lord required, they went back to Galilee, to their own town of Nazareth. Meanwhile the child grew to maturity, and he was filled with wisdom; and God's favour was with him.

CHRIST THE LORD Under the influence of the Holy Spirit, Simeon joyfully explains who this newborn child really is. Christ is "God's salvation": God had long ago promised to save fallen mankind (thus he is a "light for revelation to the Gentiles"; i.e., the non-Jews), and he had promised to save a remnant from unfaithful Israel (thus he is "glory for your people Israel").

But Christ is also a sign of contradiction. God will not save us against our will. Many respond to Christ with humility and gladness, pushing aside their selfishness to follow him. Yet others respond with suspicion and disdain; they prefer to clutch their own little kingdoms instead of submitting to the true King. Throughout the Gospels, we see both reactions, and in the world today we also see them. Even in our own hearts we often vacillate between rising up to follow the Lord and falling away from his friendship. The only constant in this equation is Christ himself, the everlasting Lord; we can always count on him.

CHRIST THE TEACHER Mary and Joseph are obliged to follow the dictates of Jewish law in regards to their firstborn son. Because children are a gift from God, ultimately they belong to God. The Jewish law prescribed a ritual by which the parents could acknowledge this truth: they would offer God a gift in symbolic exchange for their child. This is what St. Luke refers to when he writes that Mary and Joseph "consecrated" Jesus to God. (This ritual is also related to the Passover, when God slew the firstborn sons of Egypt, but spared those of Israel.)

After giving birth, women were required by Jewish law to wait for a specified amount of time before they could appear in the Temple or participate in any religious ritual. Once the time had elapsed, they rejoined community worship by offering two sacrifices (this is what the "pair of turtledoves" was for). This requirement reflects the religious value that God's people have always put upon human life, a way of acknowledging the sacredness of life. When a woman gave birth, she was participating intimately in a mystery that touched God directly, since he was the creator and sustainer of all life (most especially human life, since the Jews believed that all men and women were created "in the image of God"). So it was appropriate that she remain segregated from normal activities immediately afterwards.

Christ's submission to these religious laws shows that he verifies the reverential view of human life that they reflect. Every child, every human life, is a gift from God, a participation in the mystery of God's infinite power and unwearied love. We cannot own, nor govern the life of, an individual person, even those of our own children. Jesus is pro-life, because he is the author and protector of life—of each of our lives.

CHRIST THE FRIEND Mary offers two pigeons instead of the normal combination of a lamb and a pigeon. A stipulation of the Jewish law allowed this for those families too poor to afford a lamb (pigeons cost much less than lambs).

Jesus Christ, King of the universe, not only became man, but he became a member of a normal, humble, working-class family. Mary, Queen of heaven and earth, lived her incomparably holy life as a wife and mother in a poor family. Joseph, patron of the universal Church and greatest of all Patriarchs, worked hard just to keep enough bread on the table. Such a normal family, such an ordinary life… God wants us to know that his Kingdom is within us; we can find him in the midst of our normal occupations, where he wants to be with us as our friend. Though we may be ordinary people, by letting Christ into our lives we can end up doing extraordinary things.

Jesus: You don't need as much as you think you need to be happy. True happiness comes from a kind of wealth that no one sees, the wealth of a heart set on knowing and loving me. If I had come among you as a worldly prince, surrounded by luxury and comfort, I would have given you reason to believe that such things bring meaning and happiness. But I didn't. Have you thought deeply about my poverty? Do material things have too tight a hold on your heart? Look at me, look at my example. Come and live with me in Nazareth, and I will show you the path to lasting happiness.

CHRIST IN MY LIFE It's a good thing you are patient with me, Lord; I am so inconsistent. Every day is a little war between my selfishness and my faith. You know that I wish the war were over, but I know that it's part of your plan. Somehow, my efforts to follow you in spite of my selfish tendencies give you glory, extend your Kingdom, and make my soul grow and mature. And you never leave me to fight alone...

You despise no human life because you see every person as they truly are: unique reflections of infinite beauty. You died for every person. Your love has no exceptions. Am I following your example? Is my heart open to all people? You know I have a tendency to play favorites, but I want to love as you love, because that's what you made me for. Teach me to love, Lord...

Wealth, pleasure, and luxury items are always attracting me, and yet you chose to live in poverty and simplicity. You could have chosen any lifestyle, yet you and your family lived simply, detached from the beautiful things of this world. Teach me to follow in your footsteps. Have mercy on the countless people who idolize money. Make me a good steward of your gifts...

Questions for *SMALL-GROUP DISCUSSION*

1. What struck you most in this passage? What did you notice that you hadn't noticed before?
2. What can we do to live more fully the Church's uniquely fruitful and beautiful teaching on family life?
3. How can we increase our sincere reverence for God's gift of life to us and to those around us, instead of taking it so much for granted?
4. How have you let Christ enter more into the nitty-gritty of your most mundane struggles and joys, instead of reserving him just for the times when you go to Church or when you're really in trouble?

Cf. Catechism of the Catholic Church, 2201-2206 on the Family in God's Plan; 527-530 on the meaning of Christ's infancy

157. The Secrets of Nazareth (Lk 2:41-52)

"By giving us his Son whom, in order to spare us he did not spare, he gave us everything: grace, love, heaven; for all these indeed are less than his Son." – St. Alphonsus Liguori

LUKE 2:41-52
Every year his parents used to go to Jerusalem for the feast of the Passover. When he was twelve years old, they went up for the feast as usual. When they were on their way home after the feast, the boy Jesus stayed behind in Jerusalem without his parents knowing it. They assumed he was with the caravan, and it was only after a day's journey that they went to look for him among their relations and acquaintances. When they failed to find him they went back to Jerusalem looking for him everywhere. Three days later, they found him in the Temple, sitting among the doctors, listening to them, and asking them questions; and all those who heard him were astounded at his intelligence and his replies. They were overcome when they saw him, and his mother said to him, "My child, why have you done this to us? See how worried your father and I have been, looking for you." "Why were you looking for me?" he replied. "Did you not know that I must be busy with my Father's affairs?" But they did not understand what he meant. He then went down with them and came to Nazareth and lived under their authority. His mother stored up all these things in her heart. And Jesus increased in wisdom, in stature, and in favour with God and men.

CHRIST THE LORD At the age of twelve Jewish boys took their place in their community as young men. Up till then, they were not strictly under the law, but upon coming of age, they were expected to carry their own weight religiously and begin to do so socially and economically. Thus this trip to Jerusalem for the Passover was probably Jesus' first; previously he would have stayed at home with the other young children. Certainly the throngs of pilgrims, the glory of the big city, and the pageantry of the religious ritual fascinated him (especially because of his unique mission and identity), inducing him to stay behind when the caravan from Nazareth headed home—the women traveling ahead of the men, which is why Joseph probably thought Jesus was with Mary, and vice versa.

During the Passover festival, the Jewish leaders (members of the Sanhedrin) gave open lectures and led public discussions in the Temple precincts. Jesus participated in these, his unusual interest and uncanny intuition making a dramatic impression upon the other youngsters as well as the rabbis.

What was on Jesus' mind as he spent these three days alone in the City of David? St. Luke gives us a clue. When Joseph and Mary finally catch up to him,

Mary says, "Your father and I have been looking for you..." and Jesus answers, "I must be in my Father's house." At some point in his young life, Jesus the human boy, the son of Joseph the carpenter, must have begun to understand who he was as Jesus the Son of God. And even if he had known it long before, now that he had officially come of age, it was high time that he begin to act in accordance with it.

Once again, we see that Christ's Lordship is not an exterior tag, a romantic title tacked on to a great philosopher by sycophant disciples. He is Lord of men because he is God become man, come to live with us and establish his eternal Kingdom.

CHRIST THE TEACHER For thirty of his thirty-three years of earthly life, Jesus "was obedient to" his parents in Nazareth. In other words, he lived the most normal, unglamorous life that can be imagined: he worked in a carpenter's shop in a small town on the edge of the Roman Empire. He did chores, he studied his lessons, he went to the synagogue on Saturdays, he played with his cousins, he helped his mother fetch the water... for thirty years. He did nothing miraculous or spectacular... for thirty years. Is he trying to teach us something? Isn't he showing us that to be a Christian, to be a saint, begins with the faithful fulfillment of the normal responsibilities of life? God created us to be human, and he expects us to reach our potential by living fully human lives. A Christian should be a model son, daughter, father, mother, student, carpenter, athlete, bricklayer, statesman, marketing director—whatever our situation in life, we should live it deeply, conscious that by taking upon himself our human nature, Christ sanctified the human condition. He made the ordinary activities and duties of life into channels of divine grace.

CHRIST THE FRIEND Often we are afraid to be honest in our prayer. We feel that our everyday struggles, needs, questions, and frustrations are too petty for God. But Christ proves that attitude wrong. He grew up in a family—a poor family, in fact—and he did not magically protect them from all the mundane concerns that buffet the daily struggle of such families. Mary and Joseph didn't understand what he was saying; they were worried sick when they couldn't find him—they reacted the way any healthy parents would react to a crisis situation. It is precisely in the midst of these seemingly petty experiences that God can work in our souls, on one condition: that we, like Mary, "store up all these things" and ponder them in our hearts. God is always drawing close to us, drawing us closer to himself—we need only make an effort to detect his action, and his action will be able to take its effect.

Joseph: I really never knew what was going to happen next. Most days followed the same pattern of work and rest. Mary made our home the brightest and neatest in the town, and Jesus was the most energetic, healthiest, and most helpful boy you could imagine. Our little place was always buzzing with activity. Everyone who needed help or comfort came by, knowing that Mary would find a solution—and that kept me busy too. They were both docile, always finding ways to make me happy. Yet, this normal, strenuous, beautiful life was lit up every once in a while by flashes of the extraordinary, like when we lost Jesus in the Temple. I knew I was part of a bigger story, and God kept reminding me of it. I always felt that it was something far beyond what I could understand. I listened to the Lord; I did every task as best I could, and I simply had to trust that he would work everything out in the end.

CHRIST IN MY LIFE Thank you for coming to be my Savior, Lord. Thank you for becoming Mary's child, so that I could become a child of God. When I take time to think of all that you have done and all that you are doing, my worries and concerns shrink down to their proper size. You are busy about your Father's work—teach me to be busy doing your will in my life...

I think I have lost some of my ability to enjoy the simple pleasures and challenges of life. I think I have fallen into the trap of consumerism—always needing new toys to feel stimulated and happy. Purify me, Lord. You were happy amid the work and suffering of Nazareth. Blessed be Nazareth, blessed be your holy name...

Mary, how were you able to keep believing the words of the angel when for thirty years you saw no advances of your son to claim his Kingship.... Teach me to live with faith. I always want so badly to understand everything. Did you want that too? You bore Wisdom himself in your womb, and you raised him and taught him and loved him. He clung to you and depended on you. Mary, teach me to live with Jesus, to learn from him...

Questions for *SMALL-GROUP DISCUSSION*

1. What struck you most in this passage? What did you notice that you hadn't noticed before?
2. Jesus was eager to hear the rabbis' teaching and learn all that the experts in the Law had to say. How should a similar eagerness manifest itself in the life of today's Christian?
3. How should we be living out the Fourth Commandment ("Honor your father and mother") in the particular circumstances of our lives?
4. How can we make our prayer life more sincere?

Cf. Catechism of the Catholic Church, 564 on life in the Holy Family; 1655 on the Holy Family as a prototype of the Church; 531-534 on the mysteries of Jesus' hidden life in Nazareth

THE GOSPEL OF LUKE
Chapter 3

"How privileged is water in the sight of God and of his Christ, that it should so bring out the meaning of Baptism! Christ made use of it constantly. He himself was baptized in the Jordan, and when invited to a wedding, it was by means of water that he inaugurated his miracles. Does he preach the word? He calls upon those who are thirsty to drink of his eternal water. Does he speak of charity? He recognizes as a work of love the cup of water given to a neighbor. Near a well, he rested. He walked on the water. He washed the feet of his apostles with water. This witness in favor of Baptism is found even in his Passion; at his condemnation, Pilate washed his hands in water. When his side was pierced with a lance, water flowed from his side with blood."

– TERTULLIAN, *On Baptism*

158. Preparing the Way (Lk 3:1-6)

"For Jesus Christ reigns over the minds of individuals by his teachings, in their hearts by his love, in each one's life by the living according to his law and the imitating of his example." – Pope Pius XI

LUKE 3:1-6

In the fifteenth year of Tiberius Caesar's reign, when Pontius Pilate was governor of Judaea, Herod tetrarch of Galilee, his brother Philip tetrarch of the lands of Ituraea and Trachonitis, Lysanias tetrarch of Abilene, during the pontificate of Annas and Caiaphas the word of God came to John son of Zechariah, in the wilderness. He went through the whole Jordan district proclaiming a baptism of repentance for the forgiveness of sins, as it is written in the book of the sayings of the prophet Isaiah: A voice cries in the wilderness: Prepare a way for the Lord, make his paths straight. Every valley will be filled in, every mountain and hill be laid low, winding ways will be straightened and rough roads made smooth. And all mankind shall see the salvation of God.

CHRIST THE LORD Great personages announce their official visits ahead of time. This provides people with an opportunity to prepare for the visit, so as to be able to be ready for it. John the Baptist is Christ's precursor, the one sent to announce his coming and get people ready to welcome him. He plays a central role in the liturgy of Advent, the season during which the Church recalls Christ's first coming, readies itself to welcome him at his new, spiritual coming each Christmas, and looks forward to his definitive, second coming at the end of history (*Advent* derives from the Latin for "coming toward"). Luke emphasizes the incomparable importance of Christ's coming by pointing out how Isaiah had prophesied not only the arrival of Jesus but even the appearance of the precursor, John. God had long been preparing this pivotal moment in the world's history, and wanted to do everything possible to alert his people of its imminence.

Although Christ has come to the earth, and although he has come to dwell in many human hearts and societies, many more have still not heard of him or welcomed him. The Lord has his eye on those and is planning advents for each one of them. With each person, he continues to use this same methodology: he sends his heralds ahead of him. We are those heralds. Every Christian is another John the Baptist, boldly drawing others' attention to the truth and grace of Christ with his words, deeds, and example. Among the many responsibilities each of us has, none is greater or more rewarding than teaming up with the Holy Spirit to prepare hearts for the Lord.

CHRIST THE TEACHER Isaiah's prophecy, which summarizes John's message, offers us two lessons. First it tells us what to do in order to get ready for Christ's comings in our lives and those around us. We are to "prepare the way," filling in valleys, leveling hills, straightening crooked roads, and smoothing out rough paths. The imagery comes from a typical scene in the ancient world (before concrete and asphalt highways). Roads were notoriously unreliable in Isaiah's time, long before the establishment and spread of the Roman Empire. When a king or emperor made the rounds of his territories, his officials would travel ahead of him, making sure that the roads were safe and in good condition so that he wouldn't be delayed and would be less vulnerable to enemy ambushes. Likewise, we are called to examine our own souls on a regular basis, especially in the penitential seasons of Advent and Lent, to see where selfishness has encroached upon our relationships with God and with other people, and where laziness and self-indulgence have worn away our self-discipline. We may need to fill in some spiritual potholes or clear away some unwelcome debris, so that the graces God has in store for us during each season of our lives will be able to stream unhindered into our hearts.

Second, Isaiah tells us why we should prepare our hearts for Christ's comings: "All flesh shall see the salvation of God." He reminds us that we (the entire human family, as well as each of us individually) need God's grace. The peace, meaning, and joy that we thirst for above all else is out of our sinful reach; we need someone to bring it us, to search us out in this desert of our earthly exile and give us the waters of eternal life. Christ is the one to do this. He always wants to bring us closer to God, closer to the fullness of life that we long for. But he won't force his way in; we need to ready ourselves to welcome him.

CHRIST THE FRIEND St. Luke begins this chapter of his Gospel curiously: with a list of names and places that seem irrelevant at first glance. Twenty centuries after the fact, we are interested in Jesus, not in tetrarchs and obsolete geography. But these details reveal something crucial about Jesus: he is not an abstract God. He weaves his action and presence into the fabric of our day-to-day lives; he takes up his stance on the crossroads of everyone's personal history and addresses us there. And he does it because he wants to. Jesus Christ is a God who is our friend, not a faceless, aloof divine architect.

Jesus: I know where you were born and when. I remember every moment of your childhood, every one of your experiences growing up. I have been with you through it all. I will continue to be with you. Nothing about you is indifferent to me; all the circumstances of your life matter, and I am using them all to draw you closer to me, to show you your mission and guide you to its fulfillment. If you look for me, you will always find me, right there beside you.

CHRIST IN MY LIFE Am I a good messenger, Lord? Do my words stir up noble sentiments? Do my actions clear the way for your grace? Does my manner point people to the goodness of Christ? Do I even try to help bring others a step closer to you? Life is so busy, Lord. Can I be your ambassador in the midst of my busy-ness? Of course I can, if you will show me the way...

I know that my fears and self-centered habits obstruct your action in my life. I want to be free of them. Thank you for always being ready to forgive me and supply me with your grace. I want to take advantage of your generosity, to make use of confession and all the other ways you give me to grow, little by little but surely and constantly, into the saint you created me to be...

You teach me so clearly that the drama of salvation history is played out in the mundane reality of my life and the lives of those around me. Tune me in to this drama. Open my eyes. I want to see you in every event and every person. I want to detect and seize every opportunity to love you and make you known. You are my hope, my light, my Lord...

Questions for
SMALL-GROUP DISCUSSION

1. What struck you most in this passage? What did you notice that you hadn't noticed before?
2. Who were the "John the Baptists" in your own story of becoming a disciple of Christ, and how did they do their job of bringing Jesus into your life?
3. How can we take more seriously the Church's continual call to prepare ourselves for Christ's coming?
4. What can we do to foster the kind of intimate, personal relationship with Christ that God wants us to have (and avoid a distant, abstract, impersonal religiosity)?

Cf. Catechism of the Catholic Church, 717-720 on the role of John the Baptist in the mystery of salvation; 1430-1433 on interior penance; 2566-2567 on the mysterious mutual desire of man for God and God for man

159. Basic Training (Lk 3:7-20)

"... So far as I am concerned, to die in Jesus Christ is better than to be monarch of earth's widest bounds. He who died for us is all that I seek; he who rose again for us is my whole desire." – St. Ignatius of Antioch

LUKE 3:7-18

He said, therefore, to the crowds who came to be baptised by him, "Brood of vipers, who warned you to fly from the retribution that is coming? But if you are repentant, produce the appropriate fruits, and do not think of telling yourselves, We have Abraham for our father because, I tell you, God can raise children for Abraham from these stones. Yes, even now the axe is laid to the roots of the trees, so that any tree which fails to produce good fruit will be cut down and thrown on the fire." When all the people asked him, "What must we do, then?" he answered, "If anyone has two tunics he must share with the man who has none, and the one with something to eat must do the same." There were tax collectors too who came for baptism, and these said to him, "Master, what must we do?" He said to them, "Exact no more than your rate." Some soldiers asked him in their turn, "What about us? What must we do?" He said to them, "No intimidation! No extortion! Be content with your pay!" A feeling of expectancy had grown among the people, who were beginning to think that John might be the

Christ, so John declared before them all, "I baptise you with water, but someone is coming, someone who is more powerful than I am, and I am not fit to undo the strap of his sandals; he will baptise you with the Holy Spirit and fire. His winnowing-fan is in his hand to clear his threshing-floor and to gather the wheat into his barn; but the chaff he will burn in a fire that will never go out." As well as this, there were many other things he said to exhort the people and to announce the Good News to them. But Herod the tetrarch, whom he criticised for his relations with his brother's wife Herodias and for all the other crimes Herod had committed, added a further crime to all the rest by shutting John up in prison.

CHRIST THE LORD Many great teachers and leaders have come and gone throughout human history, but there is only one Jesus Christ. Even John the Baptist, whom Jesus later called "more than a prophet… the greatest of those born of women," can only "baptize with water." In other words, he can only work with souls on a natural level, strengthening them in virtue and helping them understand the requirements of a good life, but that pales in comparison with what Christ does. Jesus "baptizes with the Holy Spirit and fire." In him, we come into contact with God himself, and we are completely transformed (as the saints testify), just as fire completely transforms whatever it burns. This is why he is the Messiah, the "anointed one" sent to fill the breach that sin opened between God and man. No one else can be the Messiah, because no one else can bridge that infinite gap. His coming into our midst is an utterly unique event. St. Luke wants to make that clear—over and over again—so that we stop taking it for granted.

CHRIST THE TEACHER Often John the Baptist is depicted as an ill-tempered, fire-and-brimstone preacher who scared the people into repentance. First of all, such a conception fails to explain how he was able to attract such huge crowds and win over so many hearts. And secondly, it neglects the main point of his message: that salvation is at hand. Salvation, friendship with God, the fullness and security of living in communion with our Creator and Redeemer, of being "gathered into the barns" of his eternal and sublime Kingdom… this is John the Baptist's true message.

John teaches his listeners how to please Christ, how to live in communion with the God who wants to save us. His lesson is nothing new (though his personal integrity gives it new weight); he merely applies the Ten Commandments to the particular situations of his hearers. He appeals to the demands of justice and the demands of humility—we are not to take undue advantage of anyone, and we are to help those in need. How different the world would be if everyone followed these simple directives! And how open our souls would be to God's grace if we would combat our selfishness in these apparently trivial ways! Often people reject Christianity not because its theology is too difficult to comprehend, but because its moral demands are too basic. Isn't it much more romantic and titillating to perform esoteric rituals and commune with invisible forces through crystals and spells than to be honest and hardworking? And yet, the glitz of pseudo-religion can't nourish the soul. The real path that leads to life is steep and narrow, as Christ himself would put it later, but why would we want to take any other?

CHRIST THE FRIEND The human heart longs for a purpose and a joy that no earthly experience can supply; John brings the Good News that Christ is on his way, and that he can provide our hearts with everything they yearn for if we will accept his offer of friendship. Indeed, it is in our ongoing, growing, changing, maturing, personal relationship with Jesus that our yearning souls will find what they seek. The Christian life is a journey with Christ. The Christian answer to the human heart's search for happiness isn't a drug or a pill you take once in order to enter into an altered state of bliss. The human heart is made for greater things, and the adventure of friendship with Christ will gradually show us what they are.

The heart of this adventure consists in following Christ's example of self-giving, of emptying ourselves, of putting ourselves at the service of Christ and our neighbors. When it becomes our way of life, this Christian charity, this giving away our tunics and sharing our food, leads us to discover the meaning and joy that Christ came to give, which only experience can describe.

CHRIST IN MY LIFE Why is my life not as fruitful as the lives of the saints? I know you have called me to real holiness, and I believe that the fulfillment I long for will only be found there. But something is still holding me back. I want to see your glory, Lord. I want to experience your love and your greatness so thoroughly that my whole life is polarized around your Kingdom, and all my pettiness and selfishness falls away...

Okay, Lord, I believe in you—you know I do. And so I believe the lesson of this Gospel, that I can fulfill your dream for my life simply by living out my normal activities with responsibility, generosity, and faith. Help me to take my sights off some abstract, pie-in-the-sky holiness. I want to love you in the here and now of my life. I know I am not worthy even to untie your sandal strap, but you have given me a chance to serve you by doing all things as you would have me...

If I found myself completely alone, I wouldn't quit, because I would still have you. If I found myself kidnapped and thrown into prison, I wouldn't panic, because you would still be with me. If I found myself drowning in failure and rejection or submerged in endless pain, I wouldn't despair, because even there your friendship would be my meaning and salvation...

Questions for
SMALL-GROUP DISCUSSION

1. What struck you most in this passage? What did you notice that you hadn't noticed before?
2. How does the daily life of someone who really believes in the uniqueness of Christ differ from that of someone who doesn't?
3. John the Baptist knew about the gospel, and he made sure that everyone around him found about it as well. We know about the gospel, but are we being as effective as John in making sure others know about it? If not, why not?
4. How can we keep our hearts filled with fresh joy and the hope of the "good news" of Jesus Christ? In other words, how can we keep ourselves from falling into routine, from becoming "used to" the saving message of Christ?

Cf. Catechism of the Catholic Church, 410, 436-445, 453, and 547 on the meaning of Christ as the "Messiah"; 524 on John the Baptist as a model for Advent living; 1803-1845 on the virtues

160. Son of God, Son of Man (Lk 3:21-38)

"The promise of a Redeemer brightens the first page of the history of mankind, and the confident hope aroused by this promise softened the keen regret for a paradise which had been lost." – Pope Pius XI

LUKE 3:21-38

Now when all the people had been baptised and while Jesus after his own baptism was at prayer, heaven opened and the Holy Spirit descended on him in bodily shape, like a dove. And a voice came from heaven, "You are my Son, the Beloved; my favour rests on you."

When he started to teach, Jesus was about thirty years old, being the son, as it was thought, of Joseph son of Heli, son of Matthat, son of Levi, son of Melchi, son of Jannai, son of Joseph, son of Mattathias, son of Amos, son of Nahum, son of Esli, son of Naggai, son of Maath, son of Mattathias, son of Semein, son of Josech, son of Joda, son of Joanan, son of Rhesa, son of Zerubbabel, son of Shealtiel, son of Neri, son of Melchi, son of Addi, son of Cosam, son of Elmadam, son of Er, son of Joshua, son of Joshua, son of Eliezer, son of Jorim, son of Matthat, son of Levi, son of Symeon, son of Judah, son of Joseph, son of Jonam, son of Eliakim, son of Melea, son of Menna, son of Mattatha, son of Nathan, son of David, son of Jesse, son of Obed, son of Boaz, son of Sala, son of Nahshon, son of Amminadab, son of Admin, son of Arni, son of Hezron, son of Perez, son of Judah, son of Jacob, son of Isaac, son of Abraham, son of Terah, son of Nahor, son of Serug, son of Reu, son of Peleg, son of Eber, son of Shelah, son of Cainan, son of Arphaxad, son of Shem, son of Noah, son of Lamech, son of Methuselah, son of Enoch, son of Jared, son of Mahalaleel, son of Cainan, son of Enos, son of Seth, son of Adam, son of God.

CHRIST THE LORD At the time of Jesus' baptism, which marked the beginning of his public ministry, the people were filled with expectation (cf. Lk 3:15) for two reasons. First, rumor had it that according to the prophecies of Daniel, the first century AD (although they didn't call it that at the time) was to witness the arrival of the promised Messiah, the King anointed by God to restore the Davidic kingdom. The identifying marks of that Messiah were much disputed among scholars of the time, but a sense that the time had come was widespread. Second, no true prophet had arisen in Israel in more than two centuries. Therefore, when John the Baptist came onto the scene, they knew something big was afoot; many hoped that he himself was the Messiah.

God certainly supplied plenty of signs to indicate the coming of Jesus. Even so, Christ found a welcome in only a few hearts; the others gave him up to be crucified. We need to ask ourselves why, lest we make the same mistake. Could it be that the people of Israel were expecting one kind of Lord, and God wanted to give them another? We often fall into the same trap; we know clearly the things we want, but God sends us something else, and we resent it. If Christ is truly the Lord, however, and the greatest prophet of all time was not even worthy to "loosen the thongs of his sandals" (Lk 3:16—this was a slave's job, because ancient roads were nothing but dirt, mud, and animal manure, and the condition of one's sandals often proved it), why do we expect him to do things our way? And why do we expect them to fit our schedule? Isn't it possible that he knows better?

CHRIST THE TEACHER What God the Father tells Jesus is what he wants to say to each one of us: "You are my son, today I have fathered you." Jesus came to earth in order to call forth God's pleasure on sinful mankind, to lift us back into membership in God's family. Adam is described here as the "Son of God" yet our rebellion against God in the Garden of Eden made it impossible for us to continue to be members of his family. Jesus, through his loving obedience to the Father's will, even to the point of accepting death on a cross, reversed that rebellion. Now, by uniting ourselves to Christ, we can become God's beloved children and live in communion with him.

How do we unite ourselves to Christ? By taking three steps: knowing him, loving him, and imitating him. (The prerequisite, of course, is baptism, which unites us to God as branches are united to the vine, making our friendship with Christ possible.) The more fully we come to know Christ, especially through prayerful reading of the Gospels and time spent with him in the Eucharist, the more we will come to love him. And the more we love him, the more we will want to follow him and imitate him, especially in his perfect fulfillment of the Father's will and his tireless love for all people. If we let these three motifs set the rhythm for our daily living, we too can please the heart of God and be filled with his life-giving love.

CHRIST THE FRIEND John was baptizing "all the people" as a way to help them prepare their hearts to welcome Christ. Their hearts needed preparing, because they were full of selfishness, doubt, arrogance, greed, etc. Christ's heart, however, was pure; he did not need to be baptized. And yet, he got in line with the rest of the sinners and submitted to the ritual.

Jesus: I came to earth to be Emmanuel, God with you. I eagerly desired to reunite you with the Father, and so I became your brother–just as human as anyone else, whether Jew or Gentile, as the list of my ancestors shows. Do you see how deeply I long for your friendship? I knew how hard it was for you to accept my offer and give me your friendship. So I decided to come and walk beside you along the rough and dangerous paths of life, to be your strength in times of struggle, to meet your glance, and assure you that I will never forsake you. I took your place in the waters of baptism, and I took your place on the wood of the cross. What more could I have done to gain your trust?

CHRIST IN MY LIFE I want to do things your way, but it seems so hard! Lord, why does my nature rebel against your will? Have mercy on me, Lord. Your faithfulness is as firm as the mountains. Send your wisdom and your grace into my soul to help me follow you as both you and I want. Come to my aid, Lord. I can do nothing without you...

The world doesn't understand you. I want to understand you, to seek you, to know you, to love you. I believe that you are the Creator and the Savior of the world, and that all the urgent and absorbing cares that tend to overwhelm me are only secondary. You are primary; your Kingdom is what matters most. Make me a true Christian, a true ambassador of that Kingdom...

Thank you for coming to take my part and be my companion. I want to walk with you, to follow you, to learn from you. But Jesus, I know many people who are trying to journey through life alone, on their own strength. Don't you want to walk with them too? Please come to them, as you came to me. Make me your messenger, your instrument...

Questions for *SMALL-GROUP DISCUSSION*

1. What struck you most in this passage? What did you notice that you hadn't noticed before?
2. How can we make a constant effort to know Christ better every day? Why should we?
3. How can we help one another to know, love, and imitate Christ better?
4. Each of us should evaluate frequently the status of our friendship with Christ —what kind of a friend we are being toward Jesus. The following question may help: If the friend I love most treated me the way I treat Christ, would I be pleased or saddened?

Cf. Catechism of the Catholic Church, 535-537 on the meaning of Christ's baptism; 456-460 on why Christ came among us; 430-451 on the names of Jesus and how they incite us to know, love, and imitate him

THE GOSPEL OF LUKE
Chapter 4

"Come, Holy Spirit. May the union of the Father and the will of the Son come to us. You, Spirit of truth, are the reward of the saints, the refreshment of souls, light in darkness, the riches of the poor, the treasury of lovers, the satisfaction of the hungry, the consolation of the pilgrim Church; you are he in whom all treasures are contained. Come, you who, descending into Mary, caused the Word to take flesh: effect in us by grace what you accomplished in her by grace and nature. Come, you who are the nourishment of all chaste thoughts, the fountain of all clemency, the summit of all purity. Come, and take away from us all that hinders us from being absorbed in you."

– ST. MARY MAGDALENE OF PAZZI

161. First Victory (Lk 4:1-13)

"When temptation comes, turn straight to God, and he will help you." – St. Leonard of Port Maurice

LUKE 4:1-13

Filled with the Holy Spirit, Jesus left the Jordan and was led by the Spirit through the wilderness, being tempted there by the devil for forty days. During that time he ate nothing and at the end he was hungry. Then the devil said to him, "If you are the Son of God, tell this stone to turn into a loaf." But Jesus replied, "Scripture says: Man does not live on bread alone." Then leading him to a height, the devil showed him in a moment of time all the kingdoms of the world and said to him, "I will give you all this power and the glory of these kingdoms, for it has been committed to me and I give it to anyone I choose. Worship me, then, and it shall all be yours." But Jesus answered him, "Scripture says: You must worship the Lord your God, and serve him alone." Then he led him to Jerusalem and made him stand on the parapet of the Temple. "If you are the Son of God," he said to him, "throw yourself down from here, for scripture says: He will put his angels in charge of you to guard you, and again: They will hold you up on their hands in case you hurt your foot against a stone." But Jesus answered him, "It has been said: You must not put the Lord your God to the test." Having exhausted all these ways of tempting him, the devil left him, to return at the appointed time.

CHRIST THE LORD Jesus' temptation in the desert, which the liturgy locates in the first Sunday of Lent, vividly reminds us that Christ came "to destroy the works of the devil" (1 Jn 3:8). Since the dawn of time, the devil had mastered the human heart, leading every man and woman more or less into the tangle of selfishness and sin, encouraging them to use power to procure pleasure, to compromise principles for the sake of popularity, and to disobey the voice of conscience in favor of convenience. But Christ was too much for him. In this first combat, the devil tried "every way of putting him to the test," but they glanced off Jesus like so many plastic darts. The almost irresistible lure of temptation that causes such anguish and struggle in us has no power over our Lord. Staying close to him, therefore, leaning on him and filled with his grace, we can experience the victory over sin. In him we can attain freedom from slavery to our own evil tendencies. Christ indeed is the Lord, and he has come to conquer. If we follow him, we will share the spoils.

CHRIST THE TEACHER By letting himself be tempted, Jesus teaches us how the devil works and how to overcome him. The devil appeals to our selfish tendencies in order to draw us away from God. We all desire physical pleasure and comfort ("Tell this stone to turn into a loaf"), but sometimes we need to subordinate that desire to a higher ideal ("Man lives not on bread alone"). We all desire to be self-sufficient, to have power to do whatever we want whenever we want, free from natural limitations ("I shall give you all this power"), but only God is self-sufficient. Our existence depends on him—we need him to sustain and guide us ("God alone you must serve"). We all desire recognition, popularity, and praise (a swan dive from the Temple parapet would have won Jesus instant fame), but these are no substitute for the true meaning and happiness given by humble friendship with God; it's not worth risking the latter to gain the former ("You must not put the Lord your God to the test"). The devil wants us to keep "self" in the center of our lives, so that we feed our egoism and eventually become a moral black hole. But as long as we keep God at the center, "seeking first the Kingdom," we will be safe from his wiles.

The devil doesn't change his agenda of temptations as the years go by, because he knows that human nature stays the same. For the same reason, the three great Christian virtues of poverty, obedience, and chastity (lived most fully by those called to the religious or consecrated life) are always in season as antidotes to the tempter's poison.

CHRIST THE FRIEND Jesus Christ was tempted, and so he redeemed temptation. What a relief! Now we know that our own temptations can give glory to God. We know that feeling the attraction of evil and the tug of selfishness is no cause for despair; rather it provides an opportunity to exercise our love. Every time we resist a temptation, we extend the Kingdom of God, winning back territory from the devil. Christ didn't come to exempt us from spiritual combat, but to give us strength to fight valiantly for his cause. He is the great champion, and he invites us to battle at his side, sharing in his sufferings and his triumphs. He has become one of us, so as to make us just like him.

CHRIST IN MY LIFE You conquered sin and evil. You want to extend your conquest into every human heart. I intercede for all those hearts that resist you. Lord, convince them of your goodness! Make them trust in you! Wash them in your mercy, and make my life a billboard for the power of your love...

What interests you most is what happens in my heart. The world and other people see only appearances; I can fool them. You see the decisions that determine my character and the direction of my moral journey. You are interested in that, because you want me to choose to spend eternity in your palace in heaven, with Mary and all the saints, on the everlasting adventure...

Mary, you know that sometimes I get tired of the battle and simply want to rest. I know you humbled yourself every day, conquering sin with the grace you had received and living solely for Christ in spite of discomfort, obstacles, and opposition. You are the school of every virtue. Teach me to persevere in my mission, as you did, until the very end.... And doing so, you showed me that life on earth is not meant to be a cakewalk, but a mission. Thy will be done, Lord; you can count on me...

Questions for SMALL-GROUP DISCUSSION

1. What struck you most in this passage? What did you notice that you hadn't noticed before?
2. The season of Lent lasts for forty days, just as long as Christ's temptation in the desert, the rains that led to Noah's flood, and the years Israel spent wandering in the desert. How would you explain the relationship between these events?

3. The devil quoted the Bible in order to tempt Jesus. Is there a lesson in that for us?
4. How can we get and keep our conscience "in shape," able to recognize easily the difference between an innocent desire, a temptation, and a sin?

Cf. Catechism of the Catholic Church, 391-395 on Satan and the other fallen angels; 538-542 on Jesus' temptations and his first sermon; 1427-1433 on Jesus' call to repentance and on our need for constant conversion

162. More Than a Human Mission (Lk 4:14-21)

"As there are many kinds of persecution, so there are many forms of martyrdom. You are a witness to Christ every day." – St. Ambrose

LUKE 4:14-21

Jesus, with the power of the Spirit in him, returned to Galilee; and his reputation spread throughout the countryside. He taught in their synagogues and everyone praised him. He came to Nazara, where he had been brought up, and went into the synagogue on the sabbath day as he usually did. He stood up to read and they handed him the scroll of the prophet Isaiah. Unrolling the scroll he found the place where it is written: "The spirit of the Lord has been given to me, for he has anointed me. He has sent me to bring the good news to the poor, to proclaim liberty to captives and to the blind new sight, to set the downtrodden free, to proclaim the Lord's year of favour." He then rolled up the scroll, gave it back to the assistant and sat down. And all eyes in the synagogue were fixed on him. Then he began to speak to them, "This text is being fulfilled today even as you listen."

CHRIST THE LORD Here we have Jesus' first sermon. He reads a passage from the Old Testament that refers to the Messiah, to the descendent of David whom God promised to raise up to establish a Kingdom of justice and peace that would never end. When he finishes reading it, he sits down (the recognized posture for official teaching in Jewish culture at the time) and pauses, meeting the expectant gazes of everyone gathered in the synagogue. Probably he had read the scripture passage with a force of expression that they had never heard before, and so their attention was riveted on what he was going to say. He looks at them, and speaks: "This passage is fulfilled today, right now: I am that Messiah, that promised Savior, that King whose Kingdom will never end." If they had difficulty believing it (and they did), and if others throughout the centuries would have the same difficulty (and they would), at least Jesus made clear what exactly it was he wanted them to believe—that he is the Lord.

It is a worthy spiritual exercise every once in a while to examine our faith in Jesus as Lord. Often we get so caught up in our efforts to follow him, to fulfill our responsibilities, to imitate his virtues, and to spread the faith that we forget about the majesty and nobility of our God. Jesus is King of the universe. He is the promised Messiah God had promised to send since the beginning of salvation history. He will come again to judge all people, living and dead, and bring this fallen world to an end, resolving once and for all the struggle between good and evil. Reflecting on this bigger picture can do wonders for putting our little pictures in proper perspective—the Lord's perspective.

CHRIST THE TEACHER Here St. Luke begins his description of Jesus' public ministry. Jesus will spend the coming two or three years traveling throughout Palestine, teaching, healing, and gathering his twelve apostles, whom he will put in charge of the Church after his passion, resurrection, and ascension. His itinerant career is a pattern for every Christian life, in a sense, and for the Church as a whole. He is the light of the world, and through his disciples—through their words, actions, and example—he brings that light to shine in all the sin-darkened corners of the globe. He wants to bring his truth (what he taught) and his grace (that which heals both body and soul) to every human heart, of every epoch and to every nation. This is his mission; this is our mission.

But notice how Jesus set up this pattern of Church life. St. Luke points out that Jesus entered Galilee "with the power of the Spirit in him, and the first line of the prophecy he quotes is "the Spirit of the Lord is upon me," Jesus' mission was more than a merely human mission, and so is ours. We received that very same Spirit in baptism, and we received a further outpouring of the Spirit in confirmation. Our mission in life, in the Church, and in the world is one that we must carry out depending on God's supernatural grace and following his supernatural lead. Much of the frustrations, conflicts, and discouragements that Christians experience come from forgetting this fact. We are instruments, foot soldiers, and ambassadors, but the Holy Spirit is coordinating all of our efforts. If each of us is docile to him, when the last battle comes to its close, we will be amazed at the hidden progress that blossoms forth in the definitive establishment of Christ's Kingdom. The most fundamental lesson the active Christian needs to learn is to see all things with eyes enlightened by the Spirit.

CHRIST THE FRIEND Jesus came to bring "good news" to those who suffer, to free captives, and to cure the blind—he came because we needed him to come. We suffer the moral agony of incurable selfishness; we are shackled by our strong tendencies to sin; we are blinded by the sparkling allure of temptation. He came to be our Savior. And when we truly contemplate him, he attracts us with a force that leaves all other material realities far behind. If we want to experience life as God means it to be lived, all we need to do is call upon the name of Jesus and follow where he leads; he is all for us, the perfect friend, the one we can trust without limits.

CHRIST IN MY LIFE Many people consider you to be just one more great philosopher. I know better, Lord. You have given me the gift of faith. I know that you are God-made-man, the source of all existence, and you come to dwell among your creatures. You stay with us in the Tabernacle; you feed us in Holy Communion. You are all-powerful and all-loving. Never let me be separated from you…

Teach me to lean on you, to listen for your instructions, to pay attention to the teachings and directives of the pope, to live, as you lived, "by the power of the Spirit." Why do I fear failure when I know you can bring glory out of grime? Why do I fear loneliness when I know you have made me a Temple of the Holy Spirit? Reign fully in me, Lord, for the glory of your name…

I need your grace. What can I do on my own? You know what happens when I try to follow you and build your Kingdom and be faithful to your teaching depending on my own strength alone. I don't even want to think about it. I am glad to admit that I need you. Without you, I wouldn't even exist. I would simply disappear, be obliterated. Be my light and my refuge, Lord…

Questions for *SMALL-GROUP DISCUSSION*

1. What struck you most in this passage? What did you notice that you hadn't noticed before?
2. What evidence should there be in our daily living that we believe Christ's Kingdom "will have no end"?
3. How can we foster a more responsible and reverential love for Scripture and for the Church?
4. How can we develop the confidence in God that we need in order to be sincere with him in prayer, instead of vainly putting on a show?

Cf. Catechism of the Catholic Church, 430-440 on who Christ is; 456-460 on why Christ came; 74-95 on the transmission of divine revelation

163. Troubles at Home (Lk 4:22-30)

If you search for the reason why a man loves God, you will find no other reason at all, save that God first loved him. – St. Augustine

LUKE 4:22-30

And he won the approval of all, and they were astonished by the gracious words that came from his lips. They said, "This is Joseph"s son, surely?" But he replied, "No doubt you will quote me the saying, 'Physician, heal yourself' and tell me, 'We have heard all that happened in Capernaum, do the same here in your own countryside.'" And he went on, "I tell you solemnly, no prophet is ever accepted in his own country. There were many widows in Israel, I can assure you, in Elijah's day, when heaven remained shut for three years and six months and a great famine raged throughout the land, but Elijah was not sent to any one of these: he was sent to a widow at Zarephath, a Sidonian town. And in the prophet Elisha's time there were many lepers in Israel, but none of these was cured, except the Syrian, Naaman." When they heard this everyone in the synagogue was enraged. They sprang to their feet and hustled him out of the town; and they took him up to the brow of the hill their town was built on, intending to throw him down the cliff, but he slipped through the crowd and walked away.

CHRIST THE LORD In the sermon Jesus has just finished giving to the hometown synagogue-crowd he explained that he was the Messiah. He identifies himself with the Savior that the prophets foretold would come to restore Israel's greatness and fulfill God's promise of an everlasting Kingdom under the rule of David's son. Unfortunately, the people of Nazareth were expecting something a bit more dramatic from the Messiah. They were hoping for military might and political glory, not wisdom from the lips of a carpenter's son. And so they reject his claim. It is a pattern that history will repeat countless times. Few people question Jesus' claim to be the Lord, but many reject him because they find his Lordship uncomfortable. They don't want him to be their Lord.

We need to ask ourselves continually: am I satisfied with Jesus' style of leadership? Am I willing to accept his way of saving humanity and making me a saint—the way of patience, mercy, self-giving, and suffering? Unless we consciously keep the Lord's criteria in mind, especially through prayer and study, we may easily fall prey to devilish whispers that encourage us to branch out on our own instead of banking on the one Lord of life and history, who loved us and gave himself for our happiness, both here on earth and forever in heaven.

CHRIST THE TEACHER To receive God's grace we need to be open to it. One of the great obstacles to that openness is routine and familiarity. The people of Israel became so accustomed to the remarkable favors that God showered upon them (like parting the Red Sea and feeding them with manna in the desert), that they began to take him for granted. Foreigners (like Naaman the Syrian and the widow of Zarephath), however, were not used to experiencing God's miracles and did not take the supernatural for granted. Consequently, they were open to the action of God; their humility and faith allowed his grace to work.

The citizens of Jesus' hometown made the same mistake Israel had made. They refused to believe that God could work among them through one of their own; they had become so used to Christ that they became incapable of putting supernatural faith in him, even when he showed by his words and miracles that he was worthy of such faith.

We can also make this mistake. We can take God's truly marvelous actions for granted, closing ourselves off from the grace they afford. It takes effort on our part not to fall into routine and boredom at Mass—the most remarkable event that takes place in the world today. It takes faith and humility to appreciate the gift of the Church and its Magisterium, a sure guide through the oppressive moral fog of our times. It takes childlike trust to find God supernaturally at work in the simple symbols of the sacraments and in the people his providence has put alongside us—a spouse, a spiritual director, a boss.... The more we fall into a merely superficial, going-through-the-motions type of faith, without concentrating and putting our whole mind and strength into it, the more exposed we are to the danger of falling into routine. Only heartfelt prayer and humility will enable us—like Mary—to give Christ a fresh welcome into the hometown of our hearts every day.

CHRIST THE FRIEND *John: I often wondered why Jesus didn't claim his rights. He could have—there were many times when I wanted him to. If he had stayed more aloof in public, perhaps more people would have believed in him—people are funny that way. If he had insulated himself behind hundreds of servants and deputies and courtiers, letting himself be seen and heard only on the rarest of occasions and performing an impressive miracle every once in a while, he would have appealed more readily to the human appetite for sensationalism. But he didn't do it that way. He wanted to walk among his people, to touch and heal their diseases, to hear their stories and speak to them of his Kingdom, to be with them. How he loved to be among people! That was always his desire. He always risked being rejected as ordinary in order to be accepted as* *a friend. When my turn came to go out and spread the good news, I thought to myself: If that's the way our Lord did it, then that's the way his followers should do it as well.*

CHRIST IN MY LIFE To be completely honest, Lord, I have to admit that I am often weighed down by problems—problems in the world, problems in my own life, problems in my family. I know that you have chosen to save us by meeting us in the midst of our problems, but I also know that not all suffering is necessary, healthy, or desired by you. Help me to see the difference, so I can live in your peace...

I never want to fall into an empty routine. I never want my faith to dim or my love to grow cold. Only you can keep my commitment fresh, Lord. And any of your followers who are just going through the motions, or who are giving into selfishness—I pray for them now. Especially your priests and consecrated souls. Keep their love fresh; stir their hearts with your wisdom and zeal...

You have given me such a treasure in my Catholic faith. Show me how to share it. Often I don't know when to speak and when to stay silent. I don't know what others are thinking or suffering. But you do. You know exactly what everyone needs. Guide me; give me courage and simplicity. Make me a channel of your peace...

Questions for SMALL-GROUP DISCUSSION

1. What struck you most in this passage? What did you notice that you hadn't noticed before?
2. How do you think Christ felt at this reaction of his friends and extended family, a reaction so vehement that he had to exercise his messianic powers in order to escape execution?
3. Which of God's gifts do we tend to take most for granted? How can we break out of the routine?
4. How do you think his disciples reacted to this incident?

Cf. Catechism of the Catholic Church, 543-546 on the proclamation of the Kingdom of God; 587-591 on Israel's rejection of Jesus; 150-165 on the nature and necessity of faith

164. Authority and Power (Lk 4:31-44)

"If you seek to know where you are going, stay close to Christ, because he is the truth that we long to reach." –St. Thomas Aquinas

LUKE 4:31-44

He went down to Capernaum, a town in Galilee, and taught them on the sabbath. And his teaching made a deep impression on them because he spoke with authority. In the synagogue there was a man who was possessed by the spirit of an unclean devil, and it shouted at the top of its voice, "Ha! What do you want with us, Jesus of Nazareth? Have you come to destroy us? I know who you are: the Holy One of God." But Jesus said sharply, "Be quiet! Come out of him!" And the devil, throwing the man down in front of everyone, went out of him without hurting him at all. Astonishment seized them and they were all saying to one another, "What teaching! He gives orders to unclean spirits with authority and power and they come out." And reports of him went all through the surrounding countryside. Leaving the synagogue he went to Simon's house. Now Simon's mother-in-law was suffering from a high fever and they asked him to do something for her. Leaning over her he rebuked the fever and it left her. And she immediately got up and began to wait on them. At sunset all those who had friends suffering from diseases of one kind or another brought them to him, and laying his hands on each he cured them. Devils too came out of many people, howling, "You are the Son of God." But he rebuked them and would not allow them to speak because they knew that he was the Christ. When daylight came he left the house and made his way to a lonely place. The crowds went to look for him, and when they had caught up with him they wanted to prevent him leaving them, but he answered, "I must proclaim the Good News of the kingdom of God to the other towns too, because that is what I was sent to do." And he continued his preaching in the synagogues of Judaea.

CHRIST THE LORD In this brief passage, St. Luke describes a flurry of activity that sets the tone for the rest of Jesus' public ministry. He also profiles Christ's qualifications as Redeemer, as the second Adam who came to restore and renew the fallen world. Adam's sin had caused the human family to fall under the influence of ignorance, sickness and death, and the devil. Jesus proves his Lordship by overcoming all three of those curses. His teaching makes a deep impression on normal people who are usually full of doubts, questions, and conflicting opinions, because his grasp of the truth is firm and complete. He cures the sick and diseased with a simple word or gesture. The demons flee his very presence, recognizing in him a unique closeness to God and an unassailable spiritual strength (theologians differ on whether the devil knew that Jesus was the incarnate Second Person of the Holy Trinity—the titles

"Holy One of God" and "Son of God" could refer, in the Semitic mindset, to a merely human Messiah).

What comes across in these encounters is Christ's authority. Where even strong and intelligent men have to guess and labor, Jesus simply acts. The same fearlessness and effectiveness are exhibited throughout the centuries in the lives of the Church's many saints. He is truly a King, and his Kingdom is already well advanced.

CHRIST THE TEACHER Jesus has had great success in his first appearances at Capernaum. Yet he decides to move on. Purely human logic fails to explain such a move, but Jesus leaves behind the adoring crowds and takes his disciples to the next town, because "That is what I was sent to do."

Every Christian shares in Christ's mission. We have all received a commission, something to do in this world to advance Christ's Kingdom. As we make our way through life trying to accomplish it, sometimes we are unsure what the next step should be. Should I move on, or should I stay here? Human logic can shed a bit of light on those decisions, but ultimately, since God is the commander-in-chief who alone has a view of the entire spiritual war, I can only make those decisions wisely if my prayer life is in good shape (and if I make humble use of the advice God sends through his representatives). This is how Jesus discerned when it was time to leave Capernaum: "When daylight came he left the house and made his way to a lonely place." He went off to pray. In the quiet of prayer, he was able to detect his Father's will.

And it wasn't easy to find the time to pray. He had to get up early enough to avoid the crowds, even after what was surely a busy and tiring schedule the day before. He had to find a "lonely place" where he could recollect his spirit and converse peacefully with the Father.

It is possible to picture a faithful Christian who never travels the globe or converts thousands or builds cathedrals—indeed, plenty of saints have lived outwardly normal and unspectacular lives. But it is not possible to picture a faithful Christian who doesn't give God the time he deserves every day in prayer. If Christ needed it, we all need it.

CHRIST THE FRIEND Simon Peter's mother-in-law knew what it meant to be Christ's friend. As soon as he healed her, she "immediately got up and began to wait on them." She learned from Jesus, who came to serve. When we experience his saving power in our lives, the most natural way to respond is to stand up and join his team, loving and serving others as Jesus has loved and served us.

Friendship is, among other things, a kind of partnership. Jesus has a mission to win over hearts for his Kingdom, to bring lost and frustrated souls back into communion with God. When he offers us his friendship, he also offers us a share in his work. He wants us to experience the joy of loving as he loves, because that's what he created us to do. Simon Peter's mother-in-law got the picture; Jesus hopes that we get it too.

CHRIST IN MY LIFE Sometimes I think that if I could just see you and hear your voice, my life would take on an entirely different sheen. But that's not true. It's not lack of knowledge that hinders my discipleship—in fact, you are always speaking to me—it's my persistent selfish tendencies. They weaken my confidence in you and make me deaf to your words. Give me the strength to rein in my self-centeredness, so you can work more freely in and through my life...

Thank you for the gift of prayer. It's something I take for granted. At any time, at any place, I can turn to you and know for certain that you hear me and pay attention to me. No busy numbers, no voicemails, no crammed inboxes—you are always attentive and eager to hear and answer me. I have a direct line. Teach me to pray, Lord. Teach me to live always in the light of your truth and love...

I can't imagine what life would be like without your friendship. What hope would I have? Where would I go to repent of my sins, to get the light and strength I need for my life's mission, to restore my soul? And what would I look forward to after death? But many, many people haven't accepted your offer of friendship. Make me an instrument of your grace...

Questions for *SMALL-GROUP DISCUSSION*

1. What struck you most in this passage? What did you notice that you hadn't noticed before?
2. How do you think the disciples might have reacted when Jesus said it was time to move on to another town?
3. Why do you think Jesus ordered the demons to stay quiet about his identity as Messiah?
4. Many people don't believe in the devil, but the Gospels clearly show the reality of demonic action and presence in the world. How would you explain the devil's existence to a skeptical, agnostic friend?

Cf. Catechism of the Catholic Church, 397, 413, 1707, 2583, and 2851 on the devil as the origin of evil; 394-395, 398, and 2851-2852 on the works of the devil; 547-550 on the signs of the Kingdom of God

THE GOSPEL OF LUKE
Chapter 5

"Jesus Christ, our God and our Redeemer, is rich in the fullest and perfect possession of all things: we, on the other hand, are so poor and needy that we have nothing of our own to offer him as a gift. But yet, in his infinite goodness and love, he in no way objects to our giving and consecrating to him what is already his, as if it were really our own; nay, far from refusing such an offering, he positively desires it and asks for it: 'My son, give me your heart' (Prv 23:26). We are, therefore, able to be pleasing to him by the good will and the affection of our soul. For by consecrating ourselves to him we not only declare our open and free acknowledgment and acceptance of his authority over us, but we also testify that if what we offer as a gift were really our own, we would still offer it with our whole heart."

– POPE LEO XIII, *Annum Sacrum, 149*

165. Catching Fish and Leaving Boats (Lk 5:1-11)

"Christ is the light and the lamp stand is Peter." – St. Ephraem

LUKE 5:1-11

Now he was standing one day by the Lake of Gennesaret, with the crowd pressing round him listening to the word of God, when he caught sight of two boats close to the bank. The fishermen had gone out of them and were washing their nets. He got into one of the boats—it was Simon's—and asked him to put out a little from the shore. Then he sat down and taught the crowds from the boat. When he had finished speaking he said to Simon, "Put out into deep water and pay out your nets for a catch." "Master," Simon replied, "we worked hard all night long and caught nothing, but if you say so, I will pay out the nets." And when they had done this they netted such a huge number of fish that their nets began to tear, so they signalled to their companions in the other boat to come and help them; when these came, they filled the two boats to sinking point. When Simon Peter saw this he fell at the knees of Jesus saying, "Leave me, Lord; I am a sinful man." For he and all his companions were completely overcome by

> the catch they had made; so also were James and John, sons of Zebedee, who were Simon's partners. But Jesus said to Simon, "Do not be afraid; from now on it is men you will catch." Then, bringing their boats back to land, they left everything and followed him.

CHRIST THE LORD Jesus shows his mastery over the hearts of men (the crowd was "pressing round" him to hear him speak) and over the forces of nature (they caught a "huge number of fish"). Yet when he asks Peter to "put out into deep water and pay out your nets for a catch," the future Apostle complains before he obeys. However many times God shows himself worthy of our trust (creation, the Incarnation, the Passion, the Resurrection, the sacraments—what more could he have done to win us over?), we still hesitate to do things his way. We need to acknowledge him as Lord not only with our lips, but with our hearts as well, and with our decisions. Like Peter, we need to apply all our natural effort (they had been fishing all night), but then take the extra step of faith: "Master… if you say so, I will…"

This applies to our apostolic endeavors, but it also applies to our moral lives. Many times the Church's teaching on controversial moral issues (for example, artificial and assisted reproduction, contraception, divorce and remarriage) is hard to understand on a merely natural level, especially when the prevailing culture bombards us with contrary views. In those moments especially, we need to realize that the life we are called to live surpasses our natural capacities. Jesus could never have proved to Peter beforehand that he would take in a miraculous catch in the middle of broad daylight, but that's what the Lord had in store for his disciple. To experience the wonderful action of God's grace in our lives, we have to bolster our natural understanding with supernatural faith (we need both faith and reason—either one without the other is not Christianity), and then we, like Peter, will draw in a wondrous catch.

CHRIST THE TEACHER Whenever we trust Jesus sufficiently to admit the limits of our merely human judgment, God rewards us in multiple ways. He gives us a greater experience of his goodness (the enormous catch of fish); he gives us a deeper knowledge of ourselves (in the wake of the miracle Peter sees clearly, maybe for the first time in his life, how arrogant and headstrong he really is: "I am a sinful man…"); he brings us closer to him, giving us a more intimate knowledge of him and the mission he has entrusted to us ("from now on you will be catching men… they left everything and followed him…").

Whenever God asks anything of us, it is always for our good and for the good of his Kingdom. This is the experience of all the saints—as soon as they launch themselves into the enterprises of God, life takes on an entirely new and indescribable dimension. On the other hand, when we hesitate, or demand proofs, or measure God by the undersized standards of human reason, we inhibit him from showing forth his goodness and love. But when we make an act of trust in God, obeying his will even when our human nature resists, God rewards us beyond our wildest imaginations.

CHRIST THE FRIEND God doesn't want to do everything by himself; he wants us to help him. He wants it so much that he makes himself weak in order to actually need our help. In this passage, he asks Peter to take him out from the shore so he can more effectively address the crowds—God enlists the help of a fisherman to make his voice heard! Since that moment, the advance of Christ's cause has been linked to an unbroken chain of men and women generous enough to lend their boats to the Lord, just as Peter did—or even to dock their boats, to "leave everything, and follow" him. He doesn't want to impose his Kingdom from above; he wants us to enter freely into it, and help others to do the same, walking right beside him.

Andrew: It was mid-morning, my least favorite time of day. We were fixing our nets on the shore—my least favorite task. Everyone was tired and surly. As Jesus came by with the crowds I didn't even look up, I was in such a rotten humor. But he came over to us. I could tell Simon didn't want to oblige the Master, but sometimes it was simply impossible to say no to Jesus. We rowed out a little way. You should have seen the faces of the people as they listened to Jesus. They didn't miss a syllable. You could see their souls in their eyes, begging him for solace. I was barely listening to him. I couldn't look away from the crowd. Some of their faces were full of joy and enthusiasm. Others were yearning for something. Others were trying to hide, but unable to pull themselves away. When Jesus asked us to put out for a catch, I was still thinking about all those people. And then, when we drew in the overflowing nets, and when he told Simon that he would make us into fishers of men, it all came together. The fish were like the crowd of people; the boat was like his Kingdom. From then on I wanted only one thing: to go wherever Jesus went.

CHRIST IN MY LIFE I believe in you, Lord, and I believe in your Church. You continue to teach and guide the human family in every era and in every place through the living Magisterium of your Church. I want to follow you, and I want to experience the life you created me to live, and so I commit myself once again to be a faithful child of the Church, your chosen sacrament of salvation...

I am impressed by Peter's faith. He resisted at first, but when he saw the light in your eyes, he did what you asked him. And he did it only because it was you who were asking. I want to be like that. I want to see the light in your eyes and obey your every command, your every indication. You are the Lord; you are my Savior; Thy will be done...

Take my boat, Lord; enter into my life and use it to preach your saving message. I will go wherever you ask me. I will do whatever you require of me. Give me the strength to persevere in your will, no matter how dull or how painful it may become. You alone have the words of eternal life; turn my life into an amplifier that will make them resound to the ends of the earth...

Questions for SMALL-GROUP DISCUSSION

1. What struck you most in this passage? What did you notice that you hadn't noticed before?
2. Why do you think Christ told Peter, "Do not be afraid"?
3. Why do you think Christ decided to give the men a miraculous catch of fish?
4. Is Christ asking us (or youpersonally) to "put out in the deep" in any way? If so, is he pleased with our (your) response?

Cf. Catechism of the Catholic Church, 547-550 on the signs of the Kingdom; 551-553 on the primacy of Peter (from whose boat Jesus taught) among the apostles

166. Hints of a Storm (Lk 5:12-26)

"There are many who study humanity and the natural world; few who study the Son of God." – Pope Leo XIII

LUKE 5:12-26

Now Jesus was in one of the towns when a man appeared, covered with leprosy. Seeing Jesus he fell on his face and implored him. "Sir," he said "if you want to, you can cure me." Jesus stretched out his hand, touched him and said, "Of course I want to! Be cured!" And the leprosy left him at once. He ordered him to tell no one, "But go and show yourself to the priest and make the offering for your healing as Moses prescribed it, as evidence for them." His reputation continued to grow, and large crowds would gather to hear him and to have their sickness cured, but he would always go off to some place where he could be alone and pray.

Now he was teaching one day, and among the audience there were Pharisees and doctors of the Law who had come from every village in Galilee, from Judaea and from Jerusalem. And the Power of the Lord was behind his works of healing. Then some men appeared, carrying on a bed a paralysed man whom they were trying to bring in and lay down in front of him. But as the crowd made it impossible to find a way of getting him in, they went up on to the flat roof and lowered him and his stretcher down through the tiles into the middle of the gathering, in front of Jesus. Seeing their faith he said, "My friend, your sins are forgiven you." The scribes and the Pharisees began to think this over. "Who is this man talking blasphemy? Who can forgive sins but God alone?" But Jesus, aware of their thoughts, made them this reply, "What are these thoughts you have in your hearts? Which of these is easier: to say, "Your sins are forgiven you" or to say, "Get up and walk?" But to prove to you that the Son of Man has authority on earth to forgive sins,"—he said to the paralysed man—"I order you: get up, and pick up your stretcher and go home." And immediately before their very eyes he got up, picked up what he had been lying on and went home praising God. They were all astounded and praised God, and were filled with awe, saying, "We have seen strange things today."

CHRIST THE LORD This passage marks a turning point in the Gospel. Luke explains that Jesus' teaching and miracles were drawing huge crowds, and his reputation was spreading like wildfire. But even so, Jesus himself continues to carefully circumscribe his work. He heals the leper, a social and religious outcast, but he orders him to keep the miracle quiet and respectfully follow all the normal Jewish rules surrounding cures from leprosy. And although massive throngs gather around him, he still makes a point of going off to be alone to pray when he is finished teaching them and healing the sick. In other words, Jesus is not stirring up some kind of political revolution. He is not trying to gather an army to execute a coup d'état against the Pharisees, the Scribes, the Sadducees, and the Elders who made up Israel's ruling body, the Sanhedrin. Jesus is not instigating conflict.

Immediately after making this clear, however, St. Luke points out that while Jesus is teaching one day, representatives of those ruling parties were in the crowd, listening to him and judging him. His work had sparked their interest, because they saw in him a rival for the people's allegiance. Then, in the course of his teaching, Jesus makes claims to forgive the paralytic's sins—something that, in the Old Covenant, could only be done through the proper Temple sacrifices carried out by the Levitical priests. Immediately these rulers of the status quo grumble in opposition. A conflict begins to brew. But Jesus recognizes their disquiet, and so right away he sets out to allay their suspicions. For the Jews, physical suffering was a result of sin. So Jesus knows that if he demonstrates enough power to cure this man's paralysis, it will be a clear indication that he also had the authority to forgive sins. And that's precisely what he does. This clear and obvious sign, however, won't be sufficient for many Pharisees and other Jewish leaders. Unfortunately, they are more interested in maintaining their influence than discovering the truth of Christ's identity.

This first inkling of the coming storm illustrates a pattern that the whole history of the Church will follow. Christ's faithful disciples will not seek out conflict with worldly rulers, but their fidelity to Christ's teaching and mission will inevitably challenge the powers that be, since those powers all too often seek self-aggrandizement in the place of truth and justice, and from that tacit challenge conflict will ensue. In the end, there can be only one Lord, and anyone unwilling to accept his rule will perish in their vain, but violent, attempts to crush it. A mature Christian is never surprised at opposition.

CHRIST THE TEACHER Christ was both active and contemplative. He spent his days teaching, preaching, and healing, but he spent his nights and mornings in prayer.

Every Christian is called to be another Christ. And so every Christian must also be active and contemplative. We find it hard to keep the balance. Everybody has a natural affinity for one or the other, which creates a tendency to overemphasize the one we naturally like. A central component, therefore, of every Christian's cross is keeping the balance between prayer and action. Without filling our souls with God's grace and light in prayer, we have nothing worthwhile to offer our neighbors. But without bringing Christ to our neighbors, our own spiritual lives stultify, like noxious swamps that have no outlet. The Master prayed and the Master worked, and where the Master is, there too his disciples will be found.

CHRIST THE FRIEND Lepers were unfortunate victims of a virus that gradually and inexorably rotted the diseased person's flesh. Leprosy was highly contagious, so lepers were not permitted to come even within a hundred yards of uninfected people. Besides the sickness itself, then, lepers suffered the agony of social ostracism and isolation. When this leper comes up to Jesus to beg for a miracle, he breaks all the rules, so desperate is he for a cure. And Jesus not only saves him from the disease, but he reaches out and touches him, ending his exile from human companionship. Jesus knew that the man was suffering in his body, but also in his soul, and he is interested in both.

The same thing happens with the paralyzed man. According to the understanding of the times, this man would have considered his illness to be punishment for some sin. When his friends bring him to Jesus for healing, Jesus sees right away that the man's deepest suffering comes from the consciousness of this sin. The Lord sees his repentance and rewards the faith of the whole group of friends by offering God's forgiveness. Only then does he heal the man's body.

Jesus always knows what we need. The more we get to know him, the more his saving grace will heal us where we truly need to be healed, a place we may not even know about ourselves. Over and over again the Gospels show Jesus performing his miracles as ways of displaying God's goodness to suffering individuals. He is no showman out for applause; he is a loving shepherd tending his needy sheep.

CHRIST IN MY LIFE Why can't building your Kingdom in this world be a peaceful affair? Why must there always be opposition, conflict, and misunderstanding? Your patience astounds me, Lord. You put up with all our petty squabbles and wasteful, self-righteous arguments. Teach me to leave them all behind and be just like you, forging ahead and spreading your truth and love...

I want to do something for your Kingdom, but I also simply want to know you better. I want to learn to contemplate your greatness and majesty in the midst of life's hustle and bustle, and I want to learn to conquer dying hearts with your grace. I want to follow in your footsteps, Lord. Teach me to pray, and teach me to build your Kingdom...

You told us to learn from you, because you are meek and humble of heart. Can I love those around me as you love me? You banished the leper's loneliness and set the paralytic's conscience at ease. Give my heart the wisdom and gentleness of your heart, so I can detect and help meet the real, interior needs of my neighbors and not just live on the surface...

Questions for SMALL-GROUP DISCUSSION

1. What struck you most in this passage? What did you notice that you hadn't noticed before?
2. Surely Jesus was praying at all times, but St. Luke explicitly and repeatedly mentions that he also went off to places where he could be alone to pray. What are some of the common obstacles to a healthy prayer life, and how can we overcome them?
3. St. Luke tells us that Jesus forgave the paralytic when he saw "their" faith, the faith of the whole group of friends. What lesson can we learn from this detail?

4. The four men who brought in the paralytic had to go to quite a bit of trouble to do so. What are some common excuses we make in order to avoid going out of our way to bring others closer to Christ? How do they hold up in light of this Gospel passage?

Cf. Catechism of the Catholic Church, 514-521 on Christ's whole life as mystery; 574-576 on Jesus and Israel; 1440-1449 on how God forgives sin in the New Covenant

167. Making All Things New (Lk 5:27-39)

"As the tree is known by its fruits, so they who claim to belong to Christ are known by their actions; for this work of ours does not consist in just making professions, but in a faith that is both practical and lasting." – St. Ignatius of Antioch

LUKE 5:27-39
When he went out after this, he noticed a tax collector, Levi by name, sitting by the customs house, and said to him, "Follow me." And leaving everything he got up and followed him. In his honour Levi held a great reception in his house, and with them at table was a large gathering of tax collectors and others. The Pharisees and their scribes complained to his disciples and said, "Why do you eat and drink with tax collectors and sinners?" Jesus said to them in reply, "It is not those who are well who need the doctor, but the sick. I have not come to call the virtuous, but sinners to repentance." They then said to him, "John's disciples are always fasting and saying prayers, and the disciples of the Pharisees too, but yours go on eating and drinking." Jesus replied, "Surely you cannot make the bridegroom's attendants fast while the bridegroom is still with them? But the time will come, the time for the bridegroom to be taken away from them; that will be the time when they will fast." He also told them this parable, "No one tears a piece from a new cloak to put it on an old cloak; if he does, not only will he have torn the new one, but the piece taken from the new will not match the old. And nobody puts new wine into old skins; if he does, the new wine will burst the skins and then run out, and the skins will be lost. No; new wine must be put into fresh skins. And nobody who has been drinking old wine wants new. The old is good,' he says."

CHRIST THE LORD Christ's invitation to Levi (aka Matthew) is odd. In fact, the word "invitation" doesn't describe it very well. It's more like a command. Jesus doesn't say, "Levi, would you like to join my band of disciples?" or "Levi, how would you feel about taking some time off work to come and learn how to save your soul?" Instead, he simply looks at Levi and orders him, with no explanation, to follow him: "Follow me."

Jesus is either a megalomaniac or the Lord. Who else would issue such a definitive, personal command? This is no cajoling philosopher; this is a King exercising his rights over his beloved subjects. And Levi makes the right response: when your King sends for you, you come. He is our King too, and he is daily sending for us—how he hopes that we will have the same courage and love that Levi had, so he can make us too into the saints he created each one of us to be.

CHRIST THE TEACHER Following Jesus involves change. Levi the tax collector makes himself into a living parable of this fundamental Christian truth—Jesus called him, and Levi responded the way everyone must respond if they want to enter Christ's Kingdom. First, St. Luke tells us that Levi's response required "leaving everything." Jesus is not a TV show that you can turn on and off when you feel like it, or a website you can visit at your leisure and forget about the rest of the time. Jesus is God. To make room in one's life for his voice, his action, means taking a huge risk. We have to be willing to give up whatever Jesus demands that we give up. Second, St. Luke mentions that Levi "got up" and followed the Lord. He had to step out of his comfort zone. Christ teaches us that life on earth is a mission, not a vacation—a journey, not a destination. Jesus is constantly demanding more from his followers, constantly upsetting their plans and their ease, because love does that: it settles only for the very best, which means inciting continual growth in virtue and wisdom (along with the required growing pains).

Levi's response is a living parable about what the Christian life involves, but to make sure the lesson sticks, Jesus complements Levi's example with some normal parables. Old clothes are comfortable; old, familiar wine is pleasant. When Christ comes into our lives, he brings new clothes and new wine, and responding generously to his call means making an uncomfortable and at first unpleasant adjustment. And as our friendship with Christ grows, he continues to surprise us with another set of new clothes, with another new batch of wine. Earth is not heaven, so while we are on earth making our way to heaven, we can never rest on our laurels. The authentic Christian never conforms to what he has already accomplished, because Christ always has more for us to learn, to do, and to become.

CHRIST THE FRIEND St. Luke paints a vivid picture of the encounter between Jesus and Levi. Jesus is walking downtown, probably with his disciples, and sees Levi there at his office. Luke says that Jesus "noticed a tax collector, Levi by name." Isn't it just like Jesus to notice someone—what a torrent of instruction rushes out of that one little verb! It means that the Lord is always on the lookout. It means that Jesus is thinking not of himself, but of us and of our needs. It means that Jesus recognizes the needs and desires and yearnings of our hearts. Jesus notices this unhappy tax collector, a social pariah, and calls him, renews his life, and gives him a mission and a meaning.

That's what Jesus does. He is the doctor of every soul; he detects our every need and hope, and he prescribes the perfect medicine. He is the bridegroom of every heart; he gazes on us with personal, determined love and leads us into the everlasting adventure of indescribable intimacy and communion with God. Jesus is a friend, true—but what a friend he is, and what great friends he teaches us to be!

CHRIST IN MY LIFE You deserve my whole allegiance and my unconditional obedience. You created me. You placed me on this wonderful, mysterious earth. You gave me faith and showed me the purpose of my life: to know you and love you, and to help build up your Kingdom. I don't need to know anything else, Lord. Your word is enough for me. Thy will be done in every corner of my life...

Lord, sometimes I wonder why you keep asking me for more, why you keep sending me more crosses, more missions. Why can't we relax and take it easy? I know the answer: because you love me too much, and you love every person too much—you suffered and died to win us grace, and you want that grace to fill us and lead us to true meaning and lasting happiness. Lord Jesus, I trust in you...

I remember the first time I heard your voice in my heart. I was like Levi, living an average life, wanting more but not knowing where to find it. And you noticed me. You notice me every day, every moment. Give me a heart like yours, one that responds like Levi to your every wish, and in turn reaches out to others as you have reached out to me. Teach me, Lord...

Questions for
SMALL-GROUP DISCUSSION

1. What struck you most in this passage? What did you notice that you hadn't noticed before?

2. What have been some of the more difficult changes Christ has asked of you in your life?
3. Levi followed Jesus generously and enthusiastically. What can inhibit us from doing the same?
4. How can we reach out to sinners who need Christ without falling into their sins?

Cf. Catechism of the Catholic Church, 1500-1513 on Christ the physician; 545 and 588 on the universality of Christ's mercy; 796 on Christ as the bridegroom of the Church

THE GOSPEL OF LUKE

Chapter 6

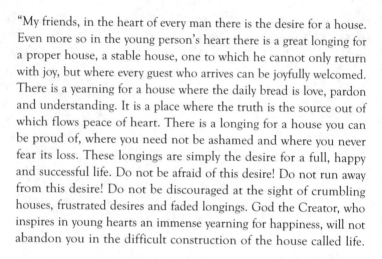

"My friends, in the heart of every man there is the desire for a house. Even more so in the young person's heart there is a great longing for a proper house, a stable house, one to which he cannot only return with joy, but where every guest who arrives can be joyfully welcomed. There is a yearning for a house where the daily bread is love, pardon and understanding. It is a place where the truth is the source out of which flows peace of heart. There is a longing for a house you can be proud of, where you need not be ashamed and where you never fear its loss. These longings are simply the desire for a full, happy and successful life. Do not be afraid of this desire! Do not run away from this desire! Do not be discouraged at the sight of crumbling houses, frustrated desires and faded longings. God the Creator, who inspires in young hearts an immense yearning for happiness, will not abandon you in the difficult construction of the house called life.

"My friends, this brings about a question: 'How do we build this house?' Jesus... encourages us to build on the rock... Building on rock means first of all to build on Christ and with Christ... In short, building on Christ means basing all your desires, aspirations, dreams, ambitions and plans on his will. It means saying to yourself, to your family, to your friends, to the whole world and, above all to Christ: "Lord, in life I wish to do nothing against you, because you know what is best for me. Only you have the words of eternal life" (cf. Jn 6:68). My friends, do not be afraid to lean on Christ! Long for Christ, as the foundation of your life! Enkindle within you the desire to build your life on him and for him! Because no one who depends on the crucified love of the Incarnate Word can ever lose."

– *POPE BENEDICT XVI*

168. The Changing of the Guard (Lk 6:1-16)

"For we can have no life apart from Jesus Christ; and as he represents the mind of the Father, so our bishops, even those who are stationed in the remotest parts of the world, represent the mind of Jesus Christ." – St. Ignatius of Antioch

LUKE 6:1-16

Now one sabbath he happened to be taking a walk through the cornfields, and his disciples were picking ears of corn, rubbing them in their hands and eating them. Some of the Pharisees said, "Why are you doing something that is forbidden on the sabbath day?" Jesus answered them, "So you have not read what David did when he and his followers were hungry—how he went into the house of God, took the loaves of offering and ate them and gave them to his followers, loaves which only the priests are allowed to eat?" And he said to them, "The Son of Man is master of the sabbath." Now on another sabbath he went into the synagogue and began to teach, and a man was there whose right hand was withered. The scribes and the Pharisees were watching him to see if he would cure a man on the sabbath, hoping to find something to use against him. But he knew their thoughts; and he said to the man with the withered hand, "Stand up! Come out into the middle." And he came out and stood there. Then Jesus said to them, "I put it to you: is it against the law on the sabbath to do good, or to do evil; to save life, or to destroy it?" Then he looked round at them all and said to the man, "Stretch out your hand." He did so, and his hand was better. But they were furious, and began to discuss the best way of dealing with Jesus. Now it was about this time that he went out into the hills to pray; and he spent the whole night in prayer to God. When day came he summoned his disciples and picked out twelve of them; he called them "apostles": Simon whom he called Peter, and his brother Andrew; James, John, Philip, Bartholomew, Matthew, Thomas, James son of Alphaeus, Simon called the Zealot, Judas son of James, and Judas Iscariot who became a traitor.

CHRIST THE LORD Jesus is Lord, but he exercises his Lordship through normal human channels. For the duration of the Old Covenant, he governed his Chosen People through prophets, judges, and kings—through flesh and blood human beings. He established his Covenant with Israel through Abraham; he sent them the Law through Moses; he led them into the Promised Land through Joshua; he made them into a Kingdom through Samuel, Saul, and David. God most often sends his grace into human lives through human instruments.

At this point in his ministry, however, Jesus is seeing that the current religious leaders of Israel, who were supposed to be acting as those instruments for that generation, were closing themselves off to his teaching. He answers their objection to the disciples' picking and eating corn on the Sabbath; he explains why their conception of Sabbath regulations is wrong (they have forgotten the reason behind it) and proves the validity of his explanation and his claim to be Lord of the Sabbath by a dramatic miracle. But in spite of these and other proofs and arguments, the Pharisees and Scribes become outraged and harden their minds and hearts even more to the Messiah.

So Jesus goes off to pray. And in his prayer he sees that the time has come to prepare a new generation of leaders who will be his instruments of grace for the New Covenant. The leaders of the Old Covenant have relinquished their roles by rejecting Jesus, who will now name a new generation of shepherds. When his night vigil comes to a close, he chooses twelve of his disciples to be his special envoys, and the apostolic college, the first bishops of the Church, is established. The Lord changes the Covenant, but he doesn't change his methodology: in the New People of God, just as in the Old People of God, he will administer his grace and his salvation through human instruments. He likes to treat us like the people we are.

CHRIST THE TEACHER The Pharisees had become obsessed with their appearance of holiness. They were convinced that external formalities sufficed; if they followed all the rules, that was all that mattered. But in truth they were missing the very point of the rules. The Law of the Old Covenant was a gift of God to his Chosen People. It was aimed at helping them learn to love God and their neighbors better. At the time of Christ, the Pharisees, the experts in interpreting this Law and in carrying it out to the minutest external detail, had forgotten this essential purpose. And so, when Jesus performs a work of mercy (a miraculous work that could only have been performed with God's direct intervention) that contradicts the Sabbath rules (you could heal mortal wounds on the Sabbath, but not illnesses or wounds that weren't putting one's life in immediate danger), the Pharisees become violently indignant, "furious" St. Luke tells us. Their self-righteousness had blinded them completely to God's action, God's presence, and the real needs of their neighbors.

It is easy to point fingers at these Pharisees. It is easy to see how foolish and hard-hearted they were. But the Gospels don't remind us of them just so we can shake our heads in disdain. We too can fall into the exact same trap. How many divisions in the Church happen because we are so attached to appearances (to our appearance) that we neglect the substance! How many times arguments drive divisions deeper just because we are concerned about keeping up vain appearances!

The human heart easily gets too attached to its own practices and preferences, so that other practices and preferences are looked upon not simply as different, but as inferior. Does it please Christ when we break into cliques and quarreling camps? Didn't he give us the papacy to guarantee unity by identifying and protecting what must be maintained and held by all his followers and to determine where variety is allowed? The ancient Pharisees destroyed Christ; modern Pharisees continue, tragically, to wound his Body.

CHRIST THE FRIEND Jesus spends the whole night in prayer. It's clear that he is praying about his next day's choice of the twelve apostles. He chooses carefully, purposely—not randomly. He chooses each one by name.

Christianity is the most personal of religions. True, Christians become members of Christ's Body, of the family of the Church, but their individuality is not destroyed—it is liberated. Jesus knows each of his followers by name. That list of names that St. Luke records assures us that in God's eyes none of us is a mere statistic. None of us is overlooked or chosen by mistake. God is the God of the entire universe, but he knows each of us through and through, and he calls each one of us to follow him individually. We are not generic soldiers in a zombie army. Christ's followers are, first and foremost, his personal friends.

CHRIST IN MY LIFE Sometimes I think that it would be more convenient if I could follow you without the Church, in a purely one-on-one religion. I wouldn't have to bother with other people, many who rub me the wrong way. But you want to send your grace through human instruments. Teach me why, Lord, so that I can love as you love...

The law of your Kingdom is self-giving, not self-assertion. The Pharisees didn't understand that. Lord, I am afraid of becoming like those Pharisees. I see that I too have a tendency toward self-righteousness, a tendency to think I am always right, a tendency to get stuck in my opinions. Keep me humble, Lord. Teach me to love my neighbor as you have loved me. Never let me be separated from you...

You know my name, and you have told me yours. How much peace this should give me! You call me by name! You have gone to heaven to prepare a place there just for me, with my name on it. No one else can love you or know you in quite the same way as I can. Thank you, Lord. Teach me to live in the peace of your love and leave behind the pressure of merely keeping up appearances...

Questions for SMALL-GROUP DISCUSSION

1. What struck you most in this passage? What did you notice that you hadn't noticed before?
2. In all the lists of apostles that appear in the New Testament, Peter is always put first and Judas last. Do you think that arrangement is significant?
3. Once again we see Jesus going off to pray, all by himself. What is the biggest obstacle in your prayer life? What has been the biggest help?
4. If a non-Catholic Christian friend asked you why you don't just "go right to God" instead of "going through a priest or the pope," how would you respond?

Cf. Catechism of the Catholic Church, 857-865 on the Apostolicity of the Church; 758-769 on the Church's origin and mission; 587-591 on the conflict between Jesus and the Pharisees

169. The Way to Go (Lk 6:17-26)

"The more one contemplates him with sincere and unprejudiced mind, the clearer does it become that there can be nothing more salutary than his law, more divine than his teaching." – Pope Leo XIII

LUKE 6:17-26

He then came down with them and stopped at a piece of level ground where there was a large gathering of his disciples with a great crowd of people from all parts of Judaea and from Jerusalem and from the coastal region of Tyre and Sidon who had come to hear him and to be cured of their diseases. People tormented by unclean spirits were also cured, and everyone in the crowd was trying to touch him because power came out of him that cured them all. Then fixing his eyes on his disciples he said: "How happy are you who are poor: yours is the kingdom of God. Happy you who are hungry now: you shall be satisfied. Happy you who weep now: you shall laugh. Happy are you when people hate you, drive you out, abuse you, denounce your name as criminal, on account of the Son of Man. Rejoice when that day comes and dance for joy, for then your reward will be great in heaven. This was the way their ancestors treated the prophets. But alas for you who are rich: you are having your consolation now. Alas for you who have your fill now: you shall go hungry. Alas for you who laugh now: you shall mourn and weep. Alas for you when the world speaks well of you! This was the way their ancestors treated the false prophets."

CHRIST THE LORD We have reached a turning point in the Lord's career. He has just been up on the mountaintop, where he spent the whole night in prayer. When morning dawned, he gathered his disciples and chose twelve of them to be his intimate coworkers, his apostles. Now, with them, he descends to the crowds below and takes his place on a wide plain, where St. Luke locates his first open air sermon, a summary of his new and spiritually revolutionary doctrine.

The picture Luke paints reminds us of Moses, who went up to the top of Mt. Sinai to be with God and to receive the divine law, which he then taught to the people of Israel in the plain below; it is a picture of God-given authority, of someone who teaches with power. Luke also gives inklings of the universality, the definitiveness of Christ's authority: the crowds hail not only from Judea and Jerusalem (the territory of the Jews), but also from Tyre and Sidon (pagan lands and Gentile territories). Christ's law, unlike Moses' law, will extend God's covenant to all people. Finally, Luke provides a detail that turns these "statements" of Jesus into challenges, into commands: "And raising his eyes toward his disciples...." Christ presents his doctrine while looking us right in the eye—this is no mere professor, no theoretician; this is One who comes to conquer, this is the Lord. When we read these familiar words with that in mind, it makes all the difference.

CHRIST THE TEACHER In this context "blessed" means truly happy, filled with lasting joy. In a shocking reversal of ordinary standards, Jesus links true happiness with struggle and hardship, suffering and opposition. Those who set their sights merely on what this world has to offer and pursue it with all their heart, soul, mind, and strength will attain it, but that is all they will attain—and it won't be enough to satisfy them. Those who are full now will be hungry later; those who make merry now will be sad later; those who are popular now will experience rejection later. In other words, the human spirit was made to find its fulfillment by living in communion with God, and that can only happen if we use created realities in order to bring us closer to God. If, on the other hand, we set our hearts on the gifts of God in and of themselves (all the pleasures of the created world), we will certainly find enjoyment in them, but we will miss the point; our reservoir of happiness will eventually run dry, because we will have cut ourselves off from their source.

This lesson has to be relearned continually. Because of our fallen nature, we always tend to think we can find heaven on earth by putting together just the right combination of possessions, esteem, and power. But since we can't, as our Lord makes perfectly clear, the mature Christian will always need to avoid the temptation to put his faith and his virtue on cruise control. There is no such amenity in the spiritual life. We are members of the Church militant for as long as we journey here on earth, and that means we need to keep our armor on and our supply lines protected, lest we fall into the enemy's traps.

CHRIST THE FRIEND In Christ's coming down from the mountain, looking his disciples in the eye, and telling them the secret to a meaningful and fulfilling life, we are presented with the entire pattern of salvation history in miniature. In becoming man, God descended from heaven to enter into the realities of our daily life. He did this in order to bring the light and grace of heaven into the darkness of a fallen earth. Why did he do it? Only out of love. He longs to look into our eyes, to catch our attention, and to convince us to join him in the adventure of eternal life. Is it not possible that when Jesus "lifted his eyes to his disciples" there was more than fire burning in them, more than determination and authority? Is it not possible that his power and certainty were softened with a rush of tenderness, with the hint of a knowing smile? If so, it was the smile of one who would be our friend—if we'll accept him.

CHRIST IN MY LIFE I believe in you, Lord, and I believe in all that you teach through your Scriptures and your Church. I have to admit that sometimes your teaching makes me uncomfortable, but because I know that your wisdom is always one and the same as your love, I gladly welcome it. I want to follow your path, and I want to help everyone I can to follow it too. Jesus, I trust in you…

Teach me to put all of the good things of this world in their proper place. Teach me to avoid making any created thing—money, pleasure, praise, success, influence, feelings—into an idol. You alone are the Lord, and you created this world to teach me about you and to give me an arena to exercise love. Thank you, Lord! Blessed be your name throughout the world…

Come again down into my life. Come again into my heart with your grace and into my mind with your truth. Never fail to come to me, never abandon me, Lord; never leave me to walk alone. I have put all my trust in you. I need you to teach me how to love, how to endure, how to understand. Thank you for coming to save me and befriend me; make my heart like yours…

Questions for SMALL-GROUP DISCUSSION

1. What struck you most in this passage? What did you notice that you hadn't noticed before?

2. How could we translate these lessons of Christ (the Beatitudes) into language that would apply to our specific situation? In other words, if he were to explain the Beatitudes to us right here and now, applying their principles to our lives, what would he say?
3. Where does popular culture encourage us to look for happiness? How does that compare with where Christ tells us to look for it?
4. If someone in your life situation were 100 percent committed to Christ's plan of life, how would their weekly schedule differ from the average, non-believer's weekly schedule in the same life situation?

Cf. Catechism of the Catholic Church, 1716-1729 on the Beatitudes and the secret to Christian happiness

170. Love, Give, and Live (Lk 6:27-38)

"The measure of love is to love without measure." – St. Augustine

LUKE 6:27-38

"But I say this to you who are listening: Love your enemies, do good to those who hate you, bless those who curse you, pray for those who treat you badly. To the man who slaps you on one cheek, present the other cheek too; to the man who takes your cloak from you, do not refuse your tunic. Give to everyone who asks you, and do not ask for your property back from the man who robs you. Treat others as you would like them to treat you. If you love those who love you, what thanks can you expect? Even sinners love those who love them. And if you do good to those who do good to you, what thanks can you expect? For even sinners do that much. And if you lend to those from whom you hope to receive, what thanks can you expect? Even sinners lend to sinners to get back the same amount. Instead, love your enemies and do good, and lend without any hope of return. You will have a great reward, and you will be sons of the Most High, for he himself is kind to the ungrateful and the wicked. Be compassionate as your Father is compassionate. Do not judge, and you will not be judged yourselves; do not condemn, and you will not be condemned yourselves; grant pardon, and you will be pardoned. Give, and there will be gifts for you: a full measure, pressed down, shaken together, and running over, will be poured into your lap; because the amount you measure out is the amount you will be given back."

CHRIST THE LORD In this portrait of a true Christian, Jesus indirectly gives us a portrait of himself. He shows us what kind of Lord he really is: a lavish one. Nothing limits his generosity—not ingratitude, not opposition, not concern for himself—nothing. Only because he is unlimited in his generosity can he demand that his followers follow suit. If we truly know him, we will delight in serving such a Lord, and we will go out of our way to be worthy of him.

In the midst of this portrait, Jesus also teaches us one of the most basic laws of his Kingdom: the amount we measure out is the amount we will be given back. The more generous we are to others, the better we learn the art of self-giving, of self-forgetful love, the more intensely we will experience the fulfilled and fulfilling life we long for. The reason for this is simple. We are created in God's image, and God is love; his very divine nature is all about self-giving. So the more we develop our capacity for love—authentic, self-forgetful love—the more we mature into what God created us to be. And just as a mature, healthy apple tree bears abundant fruit, so a mature, healthy human soul overflows with the spiritual fruits of profound joy, peace, and enthusiasm. This is the number one reason heaven will not be boring (contrary to what the devil does his best to make us think)—there's just too much overflowing life and love to leave even a tiny nook or cranny for boredom to creep in!

CHRIST THE TEACHER Through baptism, Christians become members of the body of Christ, brothers of the Lord, and children of God. In our journey through life we either stay faithful to that vocation or abandon it (and sometimes we go back and forth). In this passage, Christ gives us the touchstone of our fidelity, the sign by which we can know that we are living up to our vocation. It isn't vast theological knowledge, nor is it personal charm or professional success. Neither is it having ecstasies in prayer or taking on extreme penances. Rather, the identifying mark of a Christian is treating others—all others—the way God does, the way God treats us. God is kind and merciful "even to the ungrateful and the wicked." If we are his children, his followers, we will be kind and merciful too. We will be quick to forgive, quick to make excuses for others, quick to avoid judging and condemning them. We will think well of others, speak well of them, and treat them like the children of God (and thus our brothers and sisters) that they truly are.

God never holds back his love, and neither should we. God is like the sun, tirelessly emanating the goodness of love as the sun radiates light and heat. When we were baptized, he came to dwell within us, so that he could emanate his goodness to the world through us. Unfortunately, our pettiness, selfishness, and partiality often obscure his light instead of transmitting it. Learning to let his love and light shine more and more, in every moment and in every relationship, is the only task that really matters—the only lesson that Christ is hoping we will learn (with plenty of his help) perfectly.

CHRIST THE FRIEND Jesus presents us with a new way of living so that our "reward will be great" and "there will be gifts" for us. Sometimes we mistakenly think that a Christian ought somehow to be indifferent to the human desire for happiness, as if wanting to be happy were some kind of sin. The truth is much more realistic: the desire for happiness is a gift from God, a homing device that impels us towards God, the only source of true and lasting happiness. If Christ demands sacrifice and generosity, if his way of life seems hard, if the cross is painful, it's only a temporary pain, like that of someone recovering from reconstructive surgery: the doctor demands a long and arduous rehabilitation program so that the patient can once again enjoy a healthy, active, and happy life. Christ is the doctor of our fallen, selfish souls, and he eagerly looks forward to the day when we will join him on the tennis courts in heaven.

CHRIST IN MY LIFE You want me to be truly happy. You will never be satisfied with the counterfeit happiness this world offers, the kind I sometimes would prefer. You love me too much. I believe in you, Lord, but it's hard to follow your path. I need your grace. You know I do. You will never hoard your help. Thank you, Lord. Teach me to do your will…

Your standard of love is much too high for me. So if you want me to live that way, you are going to have to come and be my light and my strength. Send your Holy Spirit into my soul and into the souls of all the members of your Church. Grant us a renewal of authentic Christian charity. You are all-powerful, Lord—you can do it! Come Holy Spirit, enkindle in me the fire of your love…

Dear Lord, a strange opinion about life is circulating out there. People seem to think it is dishonorable to follow you in order to be happy. But that's not what you teach. You came precisely because you wanted to show us—and open up for us—the path to true human fulfillment, both here on earth and forever in eternity. I trust you, Lord; teach me to spread your truth…

Questions for SMALL-GROUP DISCUSSION

1. What struck you most in this passage? What did you notice that you hadn't noticed before?

2. What one thing has most hindered you from living Christian charity (treating others "as I would have them treat me," as God would have you treat them)? What one thing has most helped?
3. In what ways can we better imbue our community with the ethic of Christian charity?
4. Clearly, the world would be a better place if every one followed Christ's commandment to "Do unto others as you would have them do unto you." So why doesn't everyone follow it?

Cf. Catechism of the Catholic Church, 1-3 and 26-29 on God's sheer goodness (unconditional love) as expressed in his plan of salvation; 1822-1829 and 1844 on the primacy and nature of Christian charity

171. Surviving Life's Storm (Lk 6:39-49)

"To build on the rock means to build on Christ and with Christ, who is the rock."
– Pope Benedict XVI

LUKE 6:39-49

He also told a parable to them, "Can one blind man guide another? Surely both will fall into a pit? The disciple is not superior to his teacher; the fully trained disciple will always be like his teacher. Why do you observe the splinter in your brother's eye and never notice the plank in your own? How can you say to your brother, Brother, let me take out the splinter that is in your eye, when you cannot see the plank in your own? Hypocrite! Take the plank out of your own eye first, and then you will see clearly enough to take out the splinter that is in your brother's eye. There is no sound tree that produces rotten fruit, nor again a rotten tree that produces sound fruit. For every tree can be told by its own fruit: people do not pick figs from thorns, nor gather grapes from brambles. A good man draws what is good from the store of goodness in his heart; a bad man draws what is bad from the store of badness. For a man's words flow out of what fills his heart. Why do you call me, Lord, Lord and not do what I say? Everyone who comes to me and listens to my words and acts on them—I will show you what he is like. He is like the man who when he built his house dug, and dug deep, and laid the foundations on rock; when the river was in flood it bore down on that house but could not shake it, it was so well built. But the one who listens and does nothing is like the man who built his house on soil, with no foundations: as soon as the river bore down on it, it collapsed; and what a ruin that house became!"

CHRIST THE LORD By applying Jesus' parable to himself, we can better understand the nature of his Kingdom. What kind of fruit has his tree produced? Saints. Those who have followed Christ and his teaching are the saints, the men and women who have given a moral compass to the world, who have filled the world with hope, light, and enthusiasm. And the culture that was nourished on the love and sacrifice of the saints has given the world much of what it treasures most: hospitals (even the initial idea of hospitals), public education, equal rights, freedom from slavery, universities, technological progress.... These and many other institutions and values have flourished only in the wake of the gospel. To judge our Lord by his fruits, we would have to conclude that his Lordship is incomparable. And if we come to that conclusion, we will want to do all we can to live under his Lordship ourselves and extend it to as many others as possible.

Some critics often point to the sins of Christians as a way to discredit Christianity. Some Christians have sinned and caused as much destruction in the world as some non-Christians, they claim, which shows that Christianity is a pleasant but unsubstantial myth, like every other religion. This argument is shockingly illogical (revealing that those who purport it are being irrational—some other motive really lies behind their vehement opposition to God). Jesus warned his followers that if they heard his teaching and didn't put it into practice, their lives would collapse like a house built on sand collapses in a flood, damaging itself and ruining everyone in it. On the other hand, those disciples who hear and heed his teaching will stand solidly when the storm comes, providing shelter and stability. Discarding his doctrine because some hypocritical disciples proved that sand-grounded houses will indeed collapse in a flood is simply foolish and nonsensical. In the same way, accepting his doctrine because of the fruitfulness and happiness exemplified in the lives of thousands of saints is wise and commonsensical.

CHRIST THE TEACHER St. Luke links four different lessons together in this brief speech. First, Jesus points out that disciples become like their teachers. Consequently, we need to choose our teachers well. (Of course, the obvious conclusion is to become a disciple of Christ—the greatest teacher of all). Second, he warns us about the inanity of useless criticism. We are all flawed and ignorant, so we have no prerogative to go around passing judgment on others for their flaws and ignorance. When we do, we make ourselves out to be fools. (Picture in your mind how foolish a man with a plank in his eye would look trying to remove a speck from his friend's eye—that's what we are like when we take on a "holier-than-thou" type of attitude, which we so easily tend to do.)

Third, we must be careful to be Christians who not only talk the talk, but also walk the walk. The world has plenty of preachers, but precious few saints. If we really want to bring others into the Kingdom, to lead others to Christ, words will not be enough; our lives have to bear the irresistible fruit of real virtue. Finally, Jesus points out that we give ourselves away by what we say. If we really want to know the state of our souls, all we have to do is pay attention to the words that come out of our mouths—especially when we are speaking spontaneously; what we say reveals what we care about. If we really want to improve the state of our souls, we should start by practicing self-control in our speech. In fact, merely starting to pay attention to the loose comments that stream out of our mouths will mark a big step in the right direction.

Any one of these lessons is enough to build a life around; unfortunately, few of us really bear down and study any of them well. We hear them, approve of them, and complain when the people around us don't follow them, but is our effort to learn and implement them as concerted as our effort to learn the ins and outs of our favorite hobby? It's so easy to look at other people and conclude that they are shamefully building on sand. But judging by these standards, wouldn't they be tempted to say the same thing about us?

CHRIST THE FRIEND Try to imagine the tone of Christ's voice as he spoke to the gathering on the plain. Was it like a professor expostulating in a classroom, enamored of his own voice? Was it brittle and fierce, like a harsh taskmaster? Or was it perhaps warm, eager, and exuberant? Most likely the latter—Jesus did not come to earth to flatter himself or to flex his divine muscles; he came to win our hearts back to God, and that's still the one item on his to-do list.

Jesus: You need a solid foundation, a firm anchor, a dependable, unchanging reference point. You need a rock on which to build your life. I have given you your life, along with the desires for meaning, fruitfulness, and adventure that go with it. And I have come to be your rock. The world is full of shifting sands. Opinions change, friends are unfaithful, circumstances take you where you would never have chosen to go—but through it all, I never leave you. My words, my example, my presence, my Church.... You can count on them all. Listen to me, walk with me, confide in me, and follow me. How could I ever lead you astray, when I gave my life for you?

CHRIST IN MY LIFE The fruits you are looking for in my life are the fruits of virtue. It is the heart that interests you most: what I desire in my heart and what I seek with my actions based on those desires. You know that in the very core of my being I want your friendship to be my highest priority. I want to reflect your goodness, your saving goodness, in everything I think, say, and do...

I think it's odd that you didn't teach us about political and economic systems. That's all we think about these days. But you brought us salvation and the secret to happiness, and you never talked about either one of them. Instead, you talked about how to love God and neighbor. That's the rock-solid foundation of a meaningful life, and of any political or economic system. I believe in you, Jesus, and I trust in you...

Jesus, I need you so much. When I am honest with myself, I see that in my heart and in my words I am still very far from following your teaching. I criticize, I judge, I look down on others, I am closed to their points of view. You know this. You can change me. You already have. Stay with me, Jesus. Keep teaching me to do your will...

Questions for SMALL-GROUP DISCUSSION

1. What struck you most in this passage? What did you notice that you hadn't noticed before?
2. In what ways do Christ's four lessons in this passage apply to us? Which lesson is particularly applicable to you?
3. When Jesus first began to preach in public, he drew huge crowds. Do his words still attract? Why or why not?
4. Everyone chooses to follow someone, some teacher, in life. Who are some of the most revered "teachers" according to popular culture? How can a person know if he has really chosen Christ to be his teacher?

Cf. Catechism of the Catholic Church, 1691-1698 *on Life in Christ;* 1701-1724 *on human nature and our vocation to happiness;* 2464-2503 *on the proper use of words and communication*

THE GOSPEL OF LUKE
Chapter 7

"Come here, then, my soul, and tell me—in God's name, I ask you—what hinders you from following wholly after God with all your strength? What do you love if not God, your spouse? Why don't you have great love for him who has so greatly loved you? Had he nothing else to do on earth except to give himself up for you? And seek your benefit even to his own hurt? What is there for you to do on earth except to love the King of heaven? Don't you see that all these things must come to an end? What do you see? What do you hear? What do you touch? Taste? Handle? Don't you see that all these things are but a spider's web that can never clothe you or keep you from the cold? Where are you when you are not in Jesus Christ? What do you think about? What do you value? What do you seek beyond the one perfect good? Let us rise, my soul, and put an end to this evil dream. Let us awaken, for it is day, and Jesus Christ, who is the light, has come."

- ST. JOHN OF ÁVILA

172. Trusting the Lord (Lk 7:1-10)

"Hold fast to the rudder of faith, that you may not be shaken by the heavy storms of this world." – St. Ambrose

LUKE 7:1-10

When he had come to the end of all he wanted the people to hear, he went into Capernaum. A centurion there had a servant, a favourite of his, who was sick and near death. Having heard about Jesus he sent some Jewish elders to him to ask him to come and heal his servant. When they came to Jesus they pleaded earnestly with him. "He deserves this of you," they said, "because he is friendly towards our people; in fact, he is the one who built the synagogue." So Jesus went with them, and was not very far from the house when the centurion sent word to him by some friends: "Sir," he said, "do not put yourself to trouble; because I am not worthy to have you under my roof; and for this same reason I did not presume to come to you myself; but give the word and let my servant be cured. For I am under authority myself, and have soldiers under me; and I say to one man: Go, and he goes; to another: Come here, and he comes; to my servant: Do this, and he does it." When Jesus heard these words he was astonished at him and, turning round, said to the crowd following him, "I tell you, not even in Israel have I found faith like this." And when the messengers got back to the house they found the servant in perfect health.

CHRIST THE LORD Implicit in the title "lord" is superiority. Lords deserve to be obeyed. In human society, this obedience is based on a person's position, not on his intrinsic worth. With Christ it is different. He deserves to be obeyed because he is the Lord; he actually possesses within his very nature as God the authority that commands all things: "God said, 'Let there be light,' and there was light" (Gn 1:3). And yet, Jesus refuses to force people to obey him; his power is wedded to love, and his love seeks a heartfelt, joyful obedience, not one that's compelled or robotic. The centurion recognizes both of these characteristics. Because he has come to believe in Christ's true Lordship, he knows that all forces in the universe will obey him, and because he has perceived Christ's love, he knows that Jesus will gladly use his power to cure this slave who was so valuable to him. Christ is a Lord both incomparably powerful and inestimably loving, and when we approach him with this in mind, he will work wonders for us.

Whenever we are given authority over others, we should keep Christ's example as our standard. Christ always uses his power for serving others; his followers should do the same.

CHRIST THE TEACHER It is possible to amaze Jesus. The centurion did it by having more faith in him than those who should have had the most faith of all. This brief incident instructs us about one of life's greatest mysteries: human freedom. Certainly God knows all things, but not because he directly determines them. He knows what we will do tomorrow only because for him there is no tomorrow; every "tomorrow" is present to him. We have difficulty understanding this, just as a blind man has difficulty understanding color, but our difficulty doesn't alter the fact: God's omnipotence and omniscience respect our freedom. In the core of our being we remain free to accept or reject God's action in our lives—and to accept or reject it more or less intensely. God wants us to accept him with all our "heart, soul, mind, and strength"—in other words, as intensely as possible. But he also knows that we are burdened with selfishness and beset by the devil, so it will take a great effort on our part to correspond to his grace. When the centurion, who had no prior contact with Jesus and no tangible reasons to put his faith in him, shows that he has made that effort, Jesus is amazed—and, most likely, immensely gratified. If we can learn from the centurion, we too can amaze and please our Lord.

Sometimes we put too much distance between faith and daily life. The centurion was facing the kind of crisis that happens only once in awhile, but we can imitate his faith even in normal situations. Every time our conscience nudges us to refrain from sharing or tolerating that little bit of gossip, every time we feel a tug in our hearts to say a prayer or give a little more effort, every time we detect an opportunity to do a hidden act of kindness to someone in need, we are faced with an opportunity to please the Lord by putting our faith in his will.

CHRIST THE FRIEND The words of the centurion have echoed down through the centuries as few others—"Lord, I am not worthy to receive you, but only say the word and I shall be healed" has been repeated in every Mass on every continent for almost two thousand years. In putting them on our lips before we receive Holy Communion, the Church helps us to come to Christ with both reverence and confidence: reverence, because he is God and we have rebelled against God, and confidence, because instead of punishing our rebellion, he wants to come and win back our friendship.

We should be grateful for Christ's willingness to come into our lives, as the centurion was surely grateful for all Jesus had done for him. But having received Christ, having become his brothers and sisters, his ambassadors, we should also imitate his example. The people around us who don't know Jesus should find in us an advertisement for following him. The centurion sensed Christ's divinity and his goodness without ever having met him personally—he knew Jesus only from hearing about others' experience of him and seeing the lives that Jesus had changed. Would that we were such effective messengers to the centurions all around us! Our Friend deserves that we at least give it our best shot—he'll take it from there.

CHRIST IN MY LIFE When I take time to reflect on the beauties of the world around me, I can't help but marvel at your power and your wisdom. All of this came forth from your heart and your hands. You are the Creator and Sustainer of all things, and yet you deign to dwell with us in the humble silence of the Eucharist. Come and reside in my heart, come to rule me gently…

I do believe in you, Lord. I have put my trust in you. You know I have. But my faith is scrawny. I know you have wonderful things you want to do in my life and through my life. You have called me to be a saint, an oasis of virtue and fruitfulness in this fallen world. You just need me to trust you more. Increase my faith, Lord; teach me to follow you and do your will…

How many needy hearts are yearning for your light, your grace, and your forgiveness! You long to hear everyone express a firm and simple faith like the centurion's. When I repeat his words before receiving Holy Communion, let me speak them with a vibrant faith. And make me an instrument through which you can stir up faith in hardened hearts…

Questions for SMALL-GROUP DISCUSSION

1. What struck you most in this passage? What did you notice that you hadn't noticed before?
2. Did Christ grant the centurion's miracle for the same reasons the Jewish leaders used to persuade him to do so? If not, why did he grant it?
3. What practical things can we do to increase our faith?
4. How can we approach Holy Communion with more reverence and confidence? How can we help others do so as well?

Cf. Catechism of the Catholic Church, 142-165 on the nature and necessity of faith; 547-550 on the meaning of Christ's miracles

173. Love Conquers Death (Lk 7:11-17)

"He was indeed the true God and hence brought it about that the blind saw, the lame walked, the deaf heard, he cleansed those afflicted with leprosy, and by a simple command called the dead back to life." – St. Gregory Agrigentinus

LUKE 7:11-17

Now soon afterwards he went to a town called Nain, accompanied by his disciples and a great number of people. When he was near the gate of the town it happened that a dead man was being carried out for burial, the only son of his mother, and she was a widow. And a considerable number of the townspeople were with her. When the Lord saw her he felt sorry for her. "Do not cry," he said. Then he went up and put his hand on the bier and the bearers stood still, and he said, "Young man, I tell you to get up." And the dead man sat up and began to talk, and Jesus gave him to his mother. Everyone was filled with awe and praised God saying, "A great prophet has appeared among us; God has visited his people." And this opinion of him spread throughout Judaea and all over the countryside.

CHRIST THE LORD Jesus commands a dead man to rise, and he is obeyed. He shows that he is the Lord of life. And yet, when he commands us, "Do unto others as you would have them do unto you," or "Do not worry about tomorrow," or "Follow me," we resist. Does his Lordship work only on the dead? Hardly. Rather, he refuses to force his way into our hearts; he is Lord, but he is also Love. He makes his Lordship known, and then he invites us to fight under his banner—but there are no mercenaries in his army, only friends who serve the Lord of Love out of love for the Lord.

When he asks us something difficult, we should remember this passage. The same power which raised this dead man to life is at work in his commands to us. In baptism, this power floods our soul with grace through the words of the priest and the sign of water. In confession, this same power cleanses and renews our souls. Every word that Jesus speaks to us has the power to raise us up, to lift us into the kind of life we long to live.

CHRIST THE TEACHER The lesson is so simple that we may miss it: God cares. "Do not cry," he tells the woman, as if to say, "I can't bear to see you suffer. Let me help." No one asked him to perform this miracle—not even his disciples, who should have. The same motive behind his journey from heaven to earth through the Incarnation moves him to comfort this lonely widow. And the same motive is behind everything else he did before that moment and everything he accomplished since then: he cares. Such a simple lesson—but one that's so easy to forget!

Another more subtle lesson is hidden in this passage as well. The woman was a widow, like Jesus' own mother, Mary. (Joseph had died, tradition tells us, before Jesus set out on his public ministry.) The woman had only one son, again like Mary. Mary too will watch her only son die and be buried. Jesus' reaching out to this suffering woman reveals one of the most attractive characteristics of his Sacred Heart: his truly filial love for his Mother. How could Mary not have an entirely unique place in the perfect heart of the Redeemer? The Church's ancient practice of invoking Mary's intercession is, in this sense, an act of reverence made to Christ's Incarnation. Only because he shares completely our humanity does he have a mother in the first place, and because faithful sons honor and respect their mothers—all the more so when the son is a perfect King and the mother a wise and selfless Queen—Jesus gives Mary a throne at his side. And just as he couldn't resist the heart's desire of this weeping widow of Nain, how can he resist Mary's heartfelt intercession on our behalf?

CHRIST THE FRIEND We never have to suffer alone. Some time before, the widow had lost her husband, and now she loses her only son; she certainly must have felt as alone as a person can feel, inconsolable in her grief even while surrounded by the crowd. Who can fathom the depths of a mother's love? And yet, she found someone who shared her pain: Jesus. Not only did he perceive her moral agony, her utter loneliness, but he had compassion on her; he suffered with her (which is what the word compassion means). Because of this, he knew how to relieve her suffering; when he came over to her and placed her resurrected son's hand in hers, she was no longer alone.

Sometimes we do feel like we are suffering alone—Christ seems far away; at least he doesn't intervene so dramatically as he did in Nain. But indulging such feelings shows a lack of faith. This poor widow did not know about Calvary; she had never seen a crucifix. The only way Christ had to show her his compassion was to restore her son to life. But we have seen Calvary. We know to what depths God's compassion has gone. And we can always go to the Tabernacle, where we find the Eucharist, the living memorial of Calvary—the revelation of God's unfathomable compassion, his "suffering with" each and every one of us. Truly, we never have to suffer alone. And so, when we choose to do so anyway, we not only increase our own pain, but we double Christ's as well, by turning a blind eye to his cross.

CHRIST IN MY LIFE Lord, I know I have to obey someone in life: either myself, with all my ignorance and limitations, or some other teacher or guru, or the shallow advice of popular culture (which only cares about turning me into a good consumer)—or you. I want to obey you. I choose once again to follow you. Lord Jesus, I believe that you are the way, the truth, and the life…

I know that you are with me in every moment of my life, the good moments and the bad ones. You suffer with me, because you know that having to suffer alone would double my pain. Why do I insist on walking alone? Why do I insist on resisting your compassion and comfort and the soothing balm of your Church's doctrine? Jesus, teach me to bear my cross with you…

Mary, you are my mother as well as Christ's, because my baptism made me a child of God. Teach me to be like Jesus. Teach me to trust in him, to know his goodness and his power so deeply that I never doubt him—so that I never fall back into self-absorption and angry frustration. Teach me to be a bold and faithful ambassador of his Kingdom. Queen of peace, pray for me…

Questions for SMALL-GROUP DISCUSSION

1. What struck you most in this passage? What did you notice that you hadn't noticed before?
2. What evidence should there be in a Christian's day-to-day life that says to other people around him: "God really does care"?
3. What can we do now to learn how to suffer as a Christian, uniting our sufferings to Christ's on the cross, so as to be ready for bigger crosses that will come later?
4. Every committed Christian makes a definitive option to fight under Christ's banner no matter how difficult the battle may get. What aspects of popular culture make it hard to stay true to that decision?

Cf. Catechism of the Catholic Church, 1-3, 27-30, and 50-67 on how much God cares; 901, 1508, and 556 on the role of trials and tribulations in the Christian life

174. It's Up to You (Lk 7:18-35)

"For this reason the Word of God became man and the Son of God became the son of man, in order that man, being mingled with the Word of God and being granted adoption, should become the son of God." – St. Irenaeus

LUKE 7:18-35

The disciples of John gave him all this news, and John, summoning two of his disciples, sent them to the Lord to ask, "Are you the one who is to come, or must we wait for someone else?" When the men reached Jesus they said, "John the Baptist has sent us to you, to ask, Are you the one who is to come or have we to wait for someone else?" It was just then that he cured many people of diseases and afflictions and of evil spirits, and gave the gift of sight to many who were blind. Then he gave the messengers their answer, "Go back and tell John what you have seen and heard: the blind see again, the lame walk, lepers are cleansed, and the deaf hear, the dead are raised to life, the Good News is proclaimed to the poor and happy is the man who does not lose faith in me."

When John's messengers had gone he began to talk to the people about John, "What did you go out into the wilderness to see? A reed swaying in the breeze? No? Then what did you go out to see? A man dressed in fine clothes? Oh no, those who go in for fine clothes and live luxuriously are to be found at court! Then what did you go out to see? A prophet? Yes, I tell you, and much more than a prophet: he is the one of whom scripture says: See, I am going to send my messenger before you; he will prepare the way before you. "I tell you, of all the children born of women, there is no one greater than John; yet the least in the kingdom of God is greater than he is." All the people who heard him, and the tax collectors too, acknowledged God's plan by accepting baptism from John; but by refusing baptism from him the Pharisees and the lawyers had thwarted what God had in mind for them. "What description, then, can I find for the men of this generation? What are they like? They are like children shouting to one another while they sit in the market place: 'We played the pipes for you, and you wouldn't dance; we sang dirges, and you wouldn't cry.' "For John the Baptist comes, not eating bread, not drinking wine, and you say, He is possessed. The Son of Man comes, eating and drinking, and you say, 'Look, a glutton and a drunkard, a friend of tax collectors and sinners.' Yet Wisdom has been proved right by all her children."

CHRIST THE LORD John the Baptist has already recognized and acknowledged Jesus as the promised Messiah. But some of his disciples are still not convinced. Nothing John tells them can shake their doubt, so he sends them to ask Jesus directly, point blank, whether he is the Messiah. Jesus' answer seems evasive; he doesn't simply say, "Yes, I am." In fact, however, the answer is much more convincing than such a direct statement would be.

St. Luke has just described all the remarkable healings and exorcisms that Jesus was performing at this time. So Jesus invites John's disciples to simply look around them and see the evidence: the prophets all announced that the Messianic era would be marked by giving the blind their sight, the deaf their hearing, the lame their health, the imprisoned freedom, and the dead new life (e.g., Is 35:4-6, 61:1). These are the exact signs that Jesus is performing. Jesus lets his actions speak for themselves and leaves it up to his questioners to accept or reject his claim. And he does the same thing today.

CHRIST THE TEACHER This passage teaches a harrowing lesson. St. Luke points out that the sinners who believed in John the Baptist's preaching have also come to believe in Christ; they have "acknowledged God's plan" for salvation and for their own lives. As a result, God's plan is unfolding itself for them. But the apparently pious and religious people, the Pharisees and scribes, "thwarted what God had in mind for them," and so found themselves excluded from the Kingdom. Jesus himself gives a portrait of those resistant souls. They are like immature children who care only about satisfying their whims, regardless of how much God tries to accommodate them.

The lesson is clear, but so frightening that we can easily miss it: it is possible for a human person—for me—to thwart God's purpose for my life. We can, by abusing our freedom through self-indulgence and arrogance, shut out God's grace from our lives. When we live focused on our feelings, our petty desires, and our whims, we blind ourselves to God's will (which always demands self-mastery and self-sacrifice), and we frustrate his glorious plan and beautiful hopes for us. The scariest part of this lesson, however, isn't merely the fact of this possibility; it's the fact that the Pharisees, who had fallen into just such a state, truly thought they were doing the right thing by rejecting John and Jesus. They were so full of self-importance that they were literally blinded to the truth. May God save us from such a tragedy!

CHRIST THE FRIEND Jesus explains that, although John was the greatest of prophets, "the least in the Kingdom of God is greater than he is."

Jesus: This shows how much I want to give you. I not only want you to become citizens of my everlasting Kingdom, but I want to be your brother. I want you to dwell with me forever—not just as guests, but as members of my family; I came to make that possible. If you truly understand this generosity, this desire of my heart, you will begin to grasp how much I really love you. And knowing that will set you free from your fears and from your self-imposed (and unnecessary) pressure to try and earn my love. It also equips you to love others on a whole new level, since you are able to give them something that has everlasting value—you are able to help them come into the Kingdom.

CHRIST IN MY LIFE All of history was leading up to your appearance, Lord, and now all of history points to your final victory. I believe in you, Lord; I believe you are the Messiah sent by God to atone for our sins and to teach us the way to go. I believe that you govern all things with your providential wisdom and love. I believe that you will come again. Thy Kingdom come, thy will be done…

It scares me to think that I could become so self-absorbed as to be completely deaf to your voice. Never let me be separated from you, Lord. Many times your teaching and your will go against my whims and personal preferences, but these are just opportunities to show you that I love you and trust you. Hold me close to your side, Lord; keep me on the path of life…

Grant me, Lord, a clearer vision of your dream for my life. Sometimes I just don't know what to do with all the yearnings that I find in my heart. But you put them all there. They have their true object in you and your Kingdom.

Help me to live entirely for my true vocation, and help me help those I love find theirs...

Questions for SMALL-GROUP DISCUSSION

1. What struck you most in this passage? What did you notice that you hadn't noticed before?
2. In what ways does popular culture encourage us to give first priority to our passing whims and fancies, like the immature children Jesus uses in his parable?
3. If you had to explain "the Kingdom of God" to a non-believing friend, how would you do it?
4. Jesus performed many signs that indicated he was the Messiah. Why do you think it was so hard for John's disciples to accept him?

Cf. Catechism of the Catholic Church, 456-460 *on why the Word became flesh;* 436-440 *on Jesus as the "Christ" or "Messiah";* 547-550, 560, 670, *and* 1505 *on the signs of the Kingdom of God*

175. Humble Pie (Lk 7:36-50)

"There will be no defense left to you on the day of judgement, when you will be judged according to the sentence you passed on others and you will be dealt with as you have dealt with others." – St. Cyprian

LUKE 7:36-50

One of the Pharisees invited him to a meal. When he arrived at the Pharisee's house and took his place at table, a woman came in, who had a bad name in the town. She had heard he was dining with the Pharisee and had brought with her an alabaster jar of ointment. She waited behind him at his feet, weeping, and her tears fell on his feet, and she wiped them away with her hair; then she covered his feet with kisses and anointed them with the ointment. When the Pharisee who had invited him saw this, he said to himself, "If this man were a prophet, he would know who this woman is that is touching him and what a bad name she has." Then Jesus took him up and said, "Simon, I have something to say to you." "Speak, Master," was the reply. "There was once a creditor who had two men in his debt; one owed him five hundred denarii, the other fifty. They were unable to pay, so he pardoned them both. Which of them will love him more?" "The one who was pardoned more, I suppose," answered Simon. Jesus said, "You are right." Then he turned to the woman. "Simon," he said, "you see this woman? I came into your house, and you poured no water over my feet, but she has poured out her tears over my feet and wiped them away with her hair. You gave me no kiss, but she has been covering my feet with kisses ever since I came in. You did not anoint my head with oil, but she has anointed my feet with ointment. For this reason I tell you that her sins, her many sins, must have been forgiven her, or she would not have shown such great love. It is the man who is forgiven little who shows little love." Then he said to her, "Your sins are forgiven." Those who were with him at table began to say to themselves, "Who is this man, that he even forgives sins?" But he said to the woman, "Your faith has saved you; go in peace."

CHRIST THE LORD How did this woman enter the dining room? Sheepishly? If she were self-conscious, she wouldn't have come at all. She might have swept into the room, searching the faces with an alarming intensity, until she saw Jesus. Then her eyes might have lit up, her frown might have relaxed into a smile, and she rushed to his feet. He had given her something she had long been searching for. We don't know how she had met him. Maybe she had only seen him from a distance and listened to his teaching. However it happened, the power of his grace had reached through the layers of self-protection that she had erected around her heart and touched her soul. She had finally found someone who truly knew her, who truly valued her the way she had yearned to be valued, and who wanted nothing from her except trust and friendship. She had been searching for her self—her true self, her true worth—all these years, in all the wrong places. Now Jesus had shown her the way.

Jesus also reveals himself in this encounter. He shows his full identity in response to this woman's humble love and faith. No longer could people simply call him a great teacher, or a mighty prophet, or a wonderworker. No, he had publicly forgiven this woman's sins, something that God alone can do. Now the die was definitively tossed: either Jesus was the divine Messiah, or he was a lunatic pretending to be God. There is no evidence at all for lunacy, so we must conclude that he is, indeed, the Lord.

How much confidence and peace this conviction would give to our souls if we would simply let it sink in! Jesus is the Lord. He is Lord of history, of life, of good, of circumstances, hopes, and obstacles. And he is my Lord. His Lordship is exercised on my behalf, for the sake of my salvation, to free me from my sins and set me on the path of true love and joy—a path so fulfilling that this fashionable and pleasure-loving woman wept for happiness when she found herself upon it.

CHRIST THE TEACHER Jesus teaches us how he wants to forgive our sins: through real words spoken with a real, audible voice: "Your sins are forgiven." Just as this incomprehensibly mundane and human way of administering divine forgiveness shocked and scandalized Simon and his fellow Pharisees, so it continues to shock people today. If God has chosen to send his forgiveness through the tangible ministry of the sacrament of confession, he must have his reasons (and you can probably think of plenty). Of course, that doesn't make it any easier to go to confession. The sinful woman was doubly shamed, having to lay bare her guilt and repentance not only to her Lord (whom she trusted), but to everyone there at the table with him. We can feel the same shame and humiliation when we have to honestly tell our sins to the priest in the confessional. But Jesus wants to give us that chance. He wants to make it possible for us to confess our sins and our repentance in a physical, tangible way—that's why he became man in the first place. And he also wants us to be able to receive his forgiveness in a physical, tangible way. Christ's final words, "Your sins are forgiven... Your faith has saved you, go in peace" are quoted almost verbatim in the sacrament of confession. And just as we can imagine how deeply pleased he was at this encounter, so is his heart filled with joy whenever we give him a chance to shower us with his love in the confessional.

One thing that often keeps us away from this precious sacrament is the same thing that kept Simon from understanding why Jesus let this woman bathe his feet: we think we don't need God's forgiveness. We belittle our sin and selfish tendencies; we trust in our own strength to keep us on track; we readily admit others' weaknesses, but purposely ignore our own. Regular and frequent confession is one the surest signs of spiritual growth—skipping it is usually an equally trustworthy sign of spiritual stagnation.

CHRIST THE FRIEND How gently Jesus rebukes and teaches Simon the Pharisee! He doesn't yell or humiliate him; instead, he simply asks a couple of questions that quietly light up his conscience. And it had its effect. Many spiritual writers identify this Simon with the Simon who later threw a banquet for Jesus in Bethany just before his passion (it was common for the wealthy to have more than one house in Palestine). We know that by the time of the second banquet this Simon believed in Jesus and honored him. But even if the two Simons are different, the example of Christ's eagerness to win souls over to his Kingdom and the sweet meekness of his manner remains. St. Francis de Sales used to say that one drop of honey will attract more flies than a whole barrel of vinegar. Jesus is dripping honey all over the place in the Gospels—which shows that he is more concerned about our good than his own vanity (patience, gentleness, and mercy aren't typical ways to assert one's self-esteem).

This is how Jesus dealt with Simon, and this is how he deals with us. Just recall how he has acted in your life up to now—steadily, surely, but very gently and respectfully. And if he does so with us, showing himself to be a true friend, shouldn't we do the same with the Simons we run across?

CHRIST IN MY LIFE You know I believe in you, but you also know how shaky my faith can be. Jesus, convince me of your wisdom, your nearness, your greatness. Help me to see your hand at work in all things. Pour your Holy Spirit upon me again, with his gifts of understanding and knowledge. My mind is so caked with the mud of this fallen world! Lord Jesus, be my light...

I don't know why it's still hard for me to go to confession. Shouldn't I be used to it by now? I'm glad I'm not. I'm glad I feel humiliated at confessing my petty selfishness and tantrums of self-indulgence—I should feel humiliated by such things. And what better way to become humble than to exercise humility? Thank you, Lord for your wise and mysterious mercy...

Jesus, you told me to learn from you because you are meek and humble of heart. I want to be a faithful ambassador of your Kingdom. And that means reaching out to those around me with the same gentleness and humility that you always showed. But I need your grace to control my temper, my tendency to arrogance, and my impatience. Lord Jesus, help me...

Questions for *SMALL-GROUP DISCUSSION*

1. What struck you most in this passage? What did you notice that you hadn't noticed before?
2. How do you think Christ feels when we make a good confession? How do you think he feels when we systematically avoid or put off confession?
3. What aspects of popular culture encourage us to be like the sinful woman (recognizing our sins and our need for God), and which aspects encourage us to be like Simon the Pharisee (oblivious of our sins and full of self-righteousness and arrogance)?
4. When Christ comes to us in Holy Communion, how can we better welcome him with the love and attention of the sinful woman instead of the cold aloofness of Simon the Pharisee?

Cf. Catechism of the Catholic Church, 1420-1484 on the sacrament of confession; 3, 863-865 on the need God has of our collaboration to extend his Kingdom

THE GOSPEL OF LUKE
Chapter 8

"We live in an age of inventions. We need no longer climb laboriously up flights of stairs. And I was determined to find an elevator to carry me to Jesus, for I was too small to climb the steep stairs of perfection. So I sought in Holy Scripture some idea of what this lift I wanted would be, and I read, 'Whoever is a little one, let him come to me' (Lk 8:16). I also wanted to know how God would deal with a "little one," so I searched and found: 'You shall be carried in her arms and fondled in her lap; as a mother comforts her son…' (Is 66:12-13). It is your arms, Jesus, which are the elevator to carry me to heaven. So there is no need for me to grow up. In fact: just the opposite. I must become less and less."

– ST. THÉRÈSE OF LISIEUX

176. In Partnership with Grace (Lk 8:1-15)

"Obedience is the backbone of faith." – St. Francis of Paola

LUKE 8:1-15

Now after this he made his way through towns and villages preaching, and proclaiming the Good News of the kingdom of God. With him went the Twelve, as well as certain women who had been cured of evil spirits and ailments: Mary surnamed the Magdalene, from whom seven demons had gone out, Joanna the wife of Herod's steward Chuza, Susanna, and several others who provided for them out of their own resources.

With a large crowd gathering and people from every town finding their way to him, he used this parable: "A sower went out to sow his seed. As he sowed, some fell on the edge of the path and was trampled on; and the birds of the air ate it up. Some seed fell on rock, and when it came up it withered away, having no moisture. Some seed fell amongst thorns and the thorns grew with it and choked it. And some seed fell into rich soil and grew and produced its crop a hundredfold." Saying this he cried, "Listen, anyone who has ears to hear!" His disciples asked him what this parable might mean, and he said, "The mysteries of the kingdom of God are revealed to you; for the rest there are only parables, so that they may see

> but not perceive, listen but not understand. This, then, is what the parable means: the seed is the word of God. Those on the edge of the path are people who have heard it, and then the devil comes and carries away the word from their hearts in case they should believe and be saved. Those on the rock are people who, when they first hear it, welcome the word with joy. But these have no root; they believe for a while, and in time of trial they give up. As for the part that fell into thorns, this is people who have heard, but as they go on their way they are choked by the worries and riches and pleasures of life and do not reach maturity. As for the part in the rich soil, this is people with a noble and generous heart who have heard the word and take it to themselves and yield a harvest through their perseverance."

CHRIST THE LORD Jesus is humble. He has all knowledge and all power, and he wants to give us a share for our happiness and salvation, but he constantly shows an attentive respect for our freedom. The passage illustrates this characteristic respect in two ways.

First, St. Luke has Jesus start using parables. A parable presents a truth in brilliant clarity, but leaves it up to the listener to apply that truth to his own life. Jesus wants us to do this, saying, "Listen, anyone who has ears to hear!" At the same time, he knows that many who hear him are so attached to their own ideas and way of living that they are not really looking for wisdom, and so they will not search the parable for how it applies to their lives—"They may see but not perceive, listen but not understand..." If Jesus had taught more directly, those who were eager to learn would have assimilated it less completely—because when we have to make an effort to understand, we learn more deeply—and those who were just hanging around to see the show would have been immediately turned off, losing even the small chance they had of getting hit by a stray spark of grace.

Second, the parable itself reveals God's astonishing methodology of salvation. His grace is the seed, and our souls are the soil. Without the soil, the seed is completely useless. But without the seed, the soil is utterly barren. Each is made for each other. God's grace cannot work in our lives unless we receive it with a "noble and generous heart," unless we recognize our need for God, even if only in a vague and partial way, and seek his guidance. But no matter how intensely we may be seeking answers and wisdom and meaning, unless God intervenes with his grace, we will remain completely in the dark, like the barren blackness of a lifeless field.

How humble the Lord is to enter into an equal partnership with the very sinners who banished his grace from their souls!

CHRIST THE TEACHER God always supplies his grace. He always does his part in our spiritual lives. We can count on it. But we don't always do our part. Our attitude towards God's will determines the fate of his grace. If we are "noble and generous," his grace will have plenty of room to fill our lives with the fruits of holiness and happiness. If we give up when God's will requires us to persevere through tough times, his grace will wither. If we try to two-time God and the world, as if the cares and pleasures of life on earth were on an equal footing with our friendship with Christ, his grace will be sterile. Unless we make God's will—especially as discerned in our conscience and through Church teaching—our highest priority, we aren't really letting God be God, and so he can't make our life what he created it to be.

But the parable has yet another lesson. The first obstacle to God's grace appears to be the devil—represented by the birds that pick the seed up off the path. Actually, however, the occasion that gives the devil a chance to get in there is, once again, due to the quality of the soil, the attitudes of our soul. The soil on the path is hardened. The seed can't sink in. This is the superficial soul, the person who never takes time to reflect, to pray, to think deeply, the person who lets himself be "distracted from distractions by distractions," as T.S. Eliot put it. In a culture more and more dominated by information and mass media, this is perhaps the greatest danger of all. The constant flow of images, ideas, opinions, advertisements, chats, noise, music, entertainment, news, and everything else can, if we let it, create such a quantity of traffic in our minds that we become unable to savor truth, even on the off chance that we recognize it amidst the din. The same mind we use all day long, the one we fill with idle chatter and sensationalized news and everything else—that's the same mind we bring to prayer. Unless we put a fence around what we attend to in our minds, unless we practice self-mastery and discipline in our thoughts, the graces God constantly sends us will bounce onto the top of the beaten track and sit there, easy pickings for the devil.

CHRIST THE FRIEND *Susanna: Many things were different about Jesus. His words, his miracles, his presence.... But from the very first time I met him, what struck me most was how he treated women. He had no fear of us, and he put on no airs of superiority or false dignity. He treated us as equals. He knew us. He respected us. He let us help him and take care of him. With Jesus we were colleagues; we shared in his projects, in his work. And we were also friends, because we shared his needs. He depended on us. He chose to need us. In him, I learned that real friendship with God is possible. All distances collapsed. Much later, after he had risen from the dead and gone back to his Father, some of the disciples were frightened and, well, confused and hesitant. Mary* *told us then that we should be afraid of nothing; he left us with a mission, because he wanted to continue in our friendship. He left his Kingdom in our hands because he wanted to continue needing us. He gave us the most precious gift he could think of: he entrusted to us the task of leading others into eternal life. For Jesus, everyone mattered; everyone was worthy.*

CHRIST IN MY LIFE I want to kneel down and thank you for being so patient with me. You want to save me, but not at the cost of obliterating my humanity. How wise you are, Lord! But how slow and distracted I am in response to your wisdom! Teach me, Jesus; I want to learn the secrets of your Kingdom. I have ears, and I want to hear you, but I need you to take me by the hand, every day...

Once and for all, Lord, I want to take control of how I use the mass media. My spiritual progress depends on it. Help me, guide me, teach me, somehow show me the way to make good use of these wonderful inventions, which you surely want to be put at the service of our good, but which are so easy to abuse. Give me the strength of will and mind to guard the soil of my heart...

Thank you for coming into my life. Lord, I think of the thousands, maybe millions, of people who don't know you, who don't know that they can be friends with God and sharers in your incomparable mission. Send messengers to bring them your truth and grace! Send me! I want to want what you want, to do what you want, to want what you do...

Questions for SMALL-GROUP DISCUSSION

1. What struck you most in this passage? What did you notice that you hadn't noticed before?
2. We all have all three of the bad types of soil in our souls, but one of them predominates. How can we discover which one?
3. What tactics can we come up with to make good use of mass media in our lives, so we can make sure that the media culture doesn't devour us?
4. Is there anything we can do for the people who really seem to have no interest at all in discovering transcendent meaning in life?

Cf. Catechism of the Catholic Church, 683-686 on God's action in our souls; 164 on temptations and difficulties on the path of faith; 412, 679, and 1861 on the refusal and privation of grace; 2729-2733 on humble vigilance of heart

177. Fearless Faith (Lk 8:16-25)

"Christ has dominion over all creatures, a dominion not seized by violence nor usurped, but his by essence and by nature." – St. Cyril of Alexandria

LUKE 8:16-25

"No one lights a lamp to cover it with a bowl or to put it under a bed. No, he puts it on a lamp-stand so that people may see the light when they come in. For nothing is hidden but it will be made clear, nothing secret but it will be known and brought to light. So take care how you hear; for anyone who has will be given more; from anyone who has not, even what he thinks he has will be taken away."

His mother and his brothers came looking for him, but they could not get to him because of the crowd. He was told, "Your mother and brothers are standing outside and want to see you." But he said in answer, "My mother and my brothers are those who hear the word of God and put it into practice." One day, he got into a boat with his disciples and said to them, "Let us cross over to the other side of the lake." So they put to sea, and as they sailed he fell asleep. When a squall came down on the lake the boat started taking in water and they found themselves in danger. So they went to rouse him saying, "Master! Master! We are going down!" Then he woke up and rebuked the wind and the rough water; and they subsided and it was calm again. He said to them, "Where is your faith?" They were awestruck and astonished and said to one another, "Who can this be, that gives orders even to winds and waves and they obey him?"

CHRIST THE LORD Imagine how the disciples would have remembered this event. It must have left a particularly deep impression on them. So many of them were fishermen, experts in working a boat and navigating rough waters. And yet in the face of this squall, they panic. It must have been a terrible storm. It must have been humbling for them to admit that their experience and skill failed them, but fail they did.

We are all fragile and small, no matter how much success we may have experienced in life. Sooner or later we have to face this truth, and when we do, we should follow the example of the apostles. They did the right thing when their resources ran out—they went to the Master. He is always near, even if he seems asleep. And no storm is too great for his calming touch. In fact, the most elemental and uncontrollable powers of nature, in the face of which even modern technology has to bow its proud head, meekly obey the word of the Lord.

Some spiritual writers see in this passage a prequel to the Resurrection. Jesus asleep in the boat anticipates his sleep of death in the tomb. The storm corresponds to the fears and doubts that beset the scattered disciples after the tragedy of the cross. Jesus waking up and calming the wind and water is his Resurrection on the third day, which renews the apostles' confidence. In the face of our own storms, we should make a point of keeping the Lord's resurrection in mind—it's our lifetime warranty and everlasting guarantee.

CHRIST THE TEACHER The light of Christ's doctrine, which is only penetrating the apostles' hearts bit by bit as they have a chance to question him in private about his parables and teachings, will one day shine out for the whole world to see, through the work of the Church. And throughout the epoch of the Church, Christ's disciples are called to boldly spread that light. He has given it to us for our own good, but also so that we in turn will light up the whole household of mankind.

Jesus related this parable of the lamp because he knew we would be tempted to keep what we have received to ourselves. We hide things under bowls and under beds when we are afraid that other people will see them. When it comes to our Christian beliefs, fear of mockery, disdain, and rejection often make us hesitate when we should speak forth. The possibility of persecution throws us into a panic, just as the storm on the lake threw the apostles into a panic. The solution for our cowardice is the same as the solution Christ gave the apostles—faith: "Where is your faith?" God has given us more than enough reasons to believe in him and trust in him—now we just have to exercise the little faith we already have, and it will soon grow into a robust, joyful, and fruitful virtue: "Anyone who has will be given more." Otherwise, hiding the lamp under a bowl may protect the lamp, but it will snuff out the flame; our timorous efforts to avoid ridicule and persecution will have deprived even our own lives of Christ's saving light: "From anyone who has not, even what he thinks he has will be taken away."

CHRIST THE FRIEND In this passage, Jesus reiterates his Kingdom's fundamental law of generosity, the only law that makes sense in a Kingdom where all the King's subjects are also his friends, brothers, and sisters. He states this law in a slightly different way than he has before by saying, "Anyone who has will be given more"—a little trust and obedience can quickly grow into an abundant harvest of all the virtues. Then he points to a living illustration: Mary, his mother. She and some of his relatives have come looking for him, and Jesus makes the most of the opportunity to remind his listeners of what he really wants for them. He came to earth to atone for our sins and win us a place inside God's family. If only we trust him enough to fulfill God's will, to live as Jesus teaches we should live, "hearing the word of God and putting it into practice," then we will become his very brothers and sisters and mothers.

This is exactly what had happened with Mary. She trusted in God; she lived with the consciousness of being "the handmaid of the Lord" (Lk 1:38). And because of her faith, God was able to give her much more; he made her into the mother of the Lord. From handmaid to mother, from village girl to Queen of the Universe—this is the "anyone who has will be given more" rule at its best, and Jesus wants us to give him a chance to apply it in our lives as well.

CHRIST IN MY LIFE I wonder why I don't think about your Resurrection more often. Why doesn't that victory make a bigger difference in my attitudes and reactions? You rose from the dead. You showed your power over the wind and the sea, and over death itself. You are the same Lord who comes to me in Holy Communion, who waits for me patiently in the Tabernacle. Lord, increase my faith…

I know I am supposed to trust you in the midst of the storms, but Lord, it's not easy. The storms come and I often cave in. Where is my faith in those moments? You asked your apostles that question, but I ask you: Why don't I believe more firmly? Why don't I trust more easily? Why, Lord, do I advance so slowly? Have mercy on me, Lord. Teach me. I trust in you, I really do…

Mary, you learned perfectly the most important lesson—the path to true happiness: to hear God's word and put it into practice. Teach me what you learned. That's all I want to do. In my work, to work as he would have me; in my family, to be patient and selfless as he would have me; in my prayer, to be humble; in my relationships, helpful, kind, and forgiving. Mary, Seat of Wisdom, make me wise…

Questions for *SMALL-GROUP DISCUSSION*

1. What struck you most in this passage? What did you notice that you hadn't noticed before?
2. Have you ever been "awestruck and astonished" at something God did in your life or the life of someone you know?
3. What are some common fears we have to overcome in order to share our faith? What has helped you most to overcome them in particular situations?

4. In one sense, following Christ is so simple: "Hear the word of God and put it into practice." Why do think so many people refuse to do so?

Cf. Catechism of the Catholic Church, 148, 490, and 494 on Mary's assent; 2030 on Mary as the exemplar of holiness; 257, 1077, and 2009 on our filial adoption in Christ

178. Cold Reception (Lk 8:26-39)

"We proclaim the Crucified, and the devils quake. So don't be ashamed of the cross of Christ." – St. Cyril of Jerusalem

LUKE 8:26-39

They came to land in the country of the Gerasenes which is opposite Galilee. He was stepping ashore when a man from the town who was possessed by devils came towards him; for a long time the man had worn no clothes, nor did he live in a house, but in the tombs. Catching sight of Jesus he gave a shout, fell at his feet and cried out at the top of his voice, "What do you want with me, Jesus, son of the Most High God? I implore you, do not torture me." For Jesus had been telling the unclean spirit to come out of the man. It was a devil that had seized on him a great many times, and then they used to secure him with chains and fetters to restrain him, but he would always break the fastenings, and the devil would drive him out into the wilds. "What is your name?" Jesus asked. "Legion," he said—because many devils had gone into him. And these pleaded with him not to order them to depart into the Abyss. Now there was a large herd of pigs feeding there on the mountain, and the devils pleaded with him to let them go into these. So he gave them leave. The devils came out of the man and went into the pigs, and the herd charged down the cliff into the lake and were drowned. When the swineherds saw what had happened they ran off and told their story in the town and in the country round about; and the people went out to see what had happened. When they came to Jesus they found the man from whom the devils had gone out sitting at the feet of Jesus, clothed and in his full senses; and they were afraid. Those who had witnessed it told them how the man who had been possessed came to be healed. The entire population of the Gerasene territory was in a state of panic and asked Jesus to leave them. So he got into the boat and went back. The man from whom the devils had gone out asked to be allowed to stay with him, but he sent him away. "Go back home," he said, "and report all that God has done for you." So the man went off and spread throughout the town all that Jesus had done for him.

CHRIST THE LORD The people's response to Christ's action is odd. He performs a miracle of staggering proportions, restoring one of their townspeople to full health and ridding the region of a violent and dangerous demonic presence. You would think the townspeople would honor him and ask him to become their king, or at least bring him the rest of their sick and demon-possessed confreres. But instead, "they were afraid... in a state of panic, and they asked Jesus to leave..."

These people were Gentiles. They didn't have the privilege of knowing the one true God, the Creator and Redeemer. Their idea of divine power was the pagan idea, in which the gods have no genuine concern for mankind at all. When they do interact with puny humans, it's only to their own advantage. Jesus' demonstration of power makes them realize, rightly, that one of these unpredictable (to their minds) divinities is at work in him—only a divine power could have cast the demon out of the raving man and into the tranquil herd of pigs, which in turn began raving to the point of self-destruction. Word of the supernatural deed spreads. The people gather around Jesus and the restored man. Knowing (so they think) that the gods have nothing good in store for men, they are scared out of their wits. They don't know what to expect from this man-god who is so powerful that he can cast out mighty demons with only a word. As he shows no sign of aggression, some of the more bold townspeople hesitantly, tremulously ask him to spare their town from divine destruction, to simply pass them by. Jesus obliges them, and gets back into the boat with his apostles.

How it must have pained Christ's heart when they asked him to go away! But at the same time, how it must have inflamed him with renewed zeal to accomplish his mission! This is what fallen humanity had come to—they lived in a state of helpless terror in their relationship with God, instead of in one of loving intimacy. Satan's reign and the widespread contagion of sin had so distorted men's understanding of God that they actually feared their Father and Creator, like an orphaned child that has been so abused that he shrinks even from the loving touch of a genuine benefactress.

Jesus came precisely to rectify the fallen human family's mistaken notion of God, to reestablish communion between God and man. He can't wait to get started, so he sends the man he saved to spread the word among those pagans who aren't quite ready for the Good News from his own lips. The restored man goes off on the first missionary trip to Gentile territory, enthusiastically announcing: "God loves us and wants to fill us with abundant life; I know it for a fact, because he saved me from the tortures of a thousand devils—we need not fear any longer!"

CHRIST THE TEACHER Many times we experience a similar rejection in our apostolic endeavors. We think we are bringing something great to a community or an institution. We start out enthusiastically and see a flurry of progress. And then, all of a sudden, someone balks, and our work is cut short. Just so, the people of this region had seen with their own eyes Christ's transforming power, and then they asked him to leave. At such times we have to trust in God. He has his plan, and human freedom is part of it. Ours is simply to obey God's call in our lives as best we can, stay humble, and never tire of finding new ways to express our love for Jesus Christ.

CHRIST THE FRIEND Jesus tells the man he cured to "report all that God has done for you." He tells us the same thing. And so, unless we have experienced deeply the love God has for us, we will have little to say. Our effectiveness as disciples, as Christ's ambassadors in the world around us and to whomever Providence puts in our path, depends entirely on our personal experience of Christ. Our friendship with him, our relationship with him has to be far and away the most important priority of our lives. Our hearts were made for him, so we will only find meaning and fulfillment in knowing and loving him. Our life-mission is to spread his Kingdom, which means "reporting all God has done" for us, but unless we let him transform our lives, we'll simply have nothing to report, and our mission will never be accomplished.

The healed demoniac: I spent the rest of my life telling people about Jesus. Some people laughed at me. Others shook their heads in disbelief. But many wanted to hear more. At first I was surprised—the more I spoke about him, the more I seemed to know of him. Only much later did I come to know that he was truly divine, and then I understood that he was accompanying me and speaking through me, and that's why people listened. When I told them about him, many of them opened their hearts. I discovered that many, many people—many more than I ever would have imagined—had their own demons that they were battling with. They had been wounded and maltreated and oppressed in ways that only they knew. The more I learned, the more my heart went out to them. I saw these wounds heal in his name. He had freed me from my imprisonment, and then he sent me to free others. He had given me a fresh start, and he showed me the way to make the most of it.

CHRIST IN MY LIFE The world is in dire need of your truth and your grace. I know this, and you know it. Lord, don't abandon us to our ignorance and egoism. Send your light among us, raise up apostles and missionaries who will boldly report all that you have done and wish to do in people's lives. Cast out our fears, cast out our sins, cast out the devil who never tires of tempting us…

Nothing matters but your will, Lord. I can't control other people's hearts. Even you were rejected by many of the people you came to save, many of the people who heard you speak and saw your miracles. Can I expect anything less? Many friends, relatives, and other Christians don't understand my relationship to you or why I follow you. Jesus, help me to seek first your Kingdom…

What was it like to walk with you along the roads of Galilee and Judea, to hear your voice and see the look in your eyes? I want to know you more intimately, Lord. What do you think about all the time? What do you think about world events? What do you want for me? What do you want from me? Teach me, Lord, to know you and to follow you…

Questions for SMALL-GROUP DISCUSSION

1. What struck you most in this passage? What did you notice that you hadn't noticed before?
2. How do you think the disciples might have reacted to the cold welcome the people gave to Jesus?
3. If a non-believing friend of yours came up to you and said that the devil doesn't exist, how would you respond?
4. What does popular culture say about the existence and cause of evil? How does that compare with the Christian view?

Cf. Catechism of the Catholic Church, 2850-2854 on deliverance from the devil; 2110-2117 on idolatry and recourse to demons; 407-409 on man's struggle against the power of evil; 397, 413, 1707, 2583, and 2851 on the origin of evil

179. Determined Faith (Lk 8:40-56)

"Christ gives us help and strength, never deserts, and is true and sincere in his friendship." – St. Teresa of Ávila

LUKE 8:40-56

On his return Jesus was welcomed by the crowd, for they were all there waiting for him. And now there came a man named Jairus, who was an official of the synagogue. He fell at Jesus' feet and pleaded with him to come to his house, because he had an only daughter about twelve years old, who was dying. And the crowds were almost stifling Jesus as he went. Now there was a woman suffering from a hemorrhage for twelve years, whom no one had been able to cure. She came up behind him and touched the fringe of his cloak; and the hemorrhage stopped at that instant. Jesus said, "Who touched me?" When they all denied that they had, Peter and his companions said, "Master, it is the crowds round you, pushing." But Jesus said, "Somebody touched me. I felt that power had gone out from me." Seeing herself discovered, the woman came forward trembling, and falling at his feet explained in front of all the people why she had touched him and how she had been cured at that very moment. "My daughter," he said "your faith has restored you to health; go in peace." While he was still speaking, someone arrived from the house of the synagogue official to say, "Your daughter has died. Do not trouble the Master any further." But Jesus had heard this, and he spoke to the man, "Do not be afraid, only have faith and she will be safe." When he came to the house he allowed no one to go in with him except Peter and John and James, and the child's father and mother. They were all weeping and mourning for her, but Jesus said, "Stop crying; she is not dead, but asleep." But they laughed at him, knowing she was dead. But taking her by the hand he called to her, "Child, get up." And her spirit returned and she got up at once. Then he told them to give her something to eat. Her parents were astonished, but he ordered them not to tell anyone what had happened.

CHRIST THE LORD St. Luke presents us with the finale in a series of miracles. Earlier in the chapter, Jesus had calmed a storm at sea. Then he exorcised an army of demons from a possessed man. Now he cures a hopeless illness and, finally, brings a dead child back to life. Jesus' résumé is complete: he is Lord of the physical universe, of the powers of evil, of sickness, and even of death. This is Christ. This is the Savior-King who claimed us as his own when we were baptized, who gave us a position in his court when we were confirmed, who dwells in our hearts at all times, who feeds us with his own divine life whenever we receive Holy Communion, and who is always ready to receive us when we call at the Tabernacle.

The Gospel portrait of Christ brings out his majesty and his greatness—we are not surprised to see that he was "welcomed by the crowd" who had been awaiting his return, and that the "crowds were almost stifling Jesus as he went." But it should surprise us that we, having him so close to us and having his teaching so available, sometimes relegate him to a small corner of our day. Why aren't we yet the saints God wants us to be? Because we haven't let the Lord come and rule over every aspect of our lives; we circumscribe his action because, like stubborn adolescents, we still want to do everything our own way. It is time to let the Lord be the Lord.

CHRIST THE TEACHER In these encounters Jesus teaches us how to release his power in our lives. He has the power to heal our wounds, as he did with the woman suffering from the hemorrhage, and he has the power to reach out to those we love through our intercession, as he did with Jairus and his daughter. What permits his saving grace to flow into and through our lives is faith: "Your faith has restored you.... Do not be afraid, only have faith...."

Faith is a mysterious virtue. It is a living thing, hard to pin down and comprehend. The examples in this passage show us two characteristics of faith. First, authentic faith moves us to action. Believing in Christ and his capacity and willingness to intervene in our lives always implies some kind of action. As St. James puts it, "Faith without works is dead" (Jas 2:17). Merely wishing isn't really faith, because it takes no risk. Faith always involves trust, and trust always involves stepping out. So we see the woman with a hemorrhage determined to touch Jesus. She has to fight through the huge crowd that is almost stifling the Lord; she has to get down on her knees maybe, getting shoved and kneed and stepped on and pushed aside—but she does it. She touches his cloak, and she is healed. If our faith in Christ isn't driving us to take concrete steps in the direction we need to go, it's not authentic Christian faith.

Second, faith perseveres when confronted with obstacles. When Jairus' servants come to tell him that his daughter is already dead, his hope vanishes. What can be done? Jesus tells him to believe. At that point, the only reason to believe is Jesus' own command. Rationally speaking, the story is over. But Jairus, seeing the look in Christ's eyes when the Lord tells him, "Do not fear..." decides to bank on Jesus. Imagine the long walk back to his house, walking side by side with Jesus. What was he thinking? How he must have had to battle a rush of doubts and sadness, putting his trust in the word and presence of Christ alone. And his faith in the Lord, in the end, is rewarded.

True believers in Jesus, those who want his power and grace to transform their lives and the lives of those around them, put their faith into action and never give up. These are the people who see God work wonders. A flaccid or pie-in-the-sky piety never actually touches Jesus, so it can never see the beauty of holiness or really plug into his love.

CHRIST THE FRIEND Why did Jesus insist on finding the woman who had touched him? He didn't want to take her to task, although she was afraid he did. According to Jewish law, her hemorrhage made her unclean, so consequently those she touched were also made ritually unclean—and so when Jesus demands to see her, she thinks she's in trouble. And it seems like he didn't want to set her up as an example for everyone else, since he doesn't say anything to that effect. Jesus just wanted to see her and to speak to her. He wanted to assure her of his personal love for her. He doesn't want her to think he is just some kind of magician. Trembling, she falls at his feet. Jesus looks at her and calls her "My daughter...." Then he assures her that she truly is healed because she has believed in him, and he sends her home, saying,"Go in peace." How Jesus' eyes must have shined with tenderness and gladness! So many of his followers and opponents had little or no faith in him, but this woman trusted him completely. And the glance of love and tenderness he gave her must have been indelibly fixed in that woman's memory: "He called me his daughter! He knows me, and he cares for me. He sent me away in peace, healed. How good he is! How glad I am that I made the effort to touch his cloak!"

Jesus continues to act in the same way today. It is not enough for him to do things generically. He himself gives us Holy Communion, one-on-one, through the hands of his chosen priests. He wants to speak the words of absolution out loud to us, so that we leave the confessional assured and relieved, as this woman left the scene of the miracle. In countless ways, God makes that extra effort to personalize our experience of him. He longs to see us, to look us in the eye and speak with us. He is our Creator, who created us to be his everlasting friends.

CHRIST IN MY LIFE You truly are the Lord of life and history. All good things come from you. You showed your lordship in the Gospels, you continue to show it in the Church, and you have shown it countless times in my own life. Jesus, I beg you, please teach me to put everything else in my life in second place, so that I can truly be your disciple, your ambassador, and your companion...

You performed these miracles for my benefit. You were thinking of me when you healed. You are trying to convince me to trust in you more. How can I trust in you when I don't know what to do? So many problems swirl around me, and I am so helpless, so ignorant! But you know everything. You know how much I need you. I do believe; I do trust in you, Lord. Teach me what to say; show me what to do…

I live in a noisy world, Lord. I have to shove my way through crowds and chaos to touch you. I need you to clear the crowd away so I can see you look at me and hear you speak to me. Lord, my heart is longing for your grace, for your love. Please, Lord, let me touch you, let me find you in all things, in all people, in every moment…

Questions for SMALL-GROUP DISCUSSION

1. What struck you most in this passage? What did you notice that you hadn't noticed before?
2. Why do you think Jesus only took his three closest disciples with him into Jarius' house?
3. Does popular culture help or hinder the development of authentic Christian faith? What can we do to grow in this key virtue?
4. If a non-believing friend came up to you and said, "I want to believe in Christ, but I simply can't," what would you say to them?

Cf. Catechism of the Catholic Church, 26 and 144-149 on the nature of faith; 153-165 on the characteristics of faith; 65-67 on Christ as the fullness of God's revelation

THE GOSPEL OF LUKE
Chapter 9

"All who in the whole world bear the name of Christian and truly understand the Christian faith know and believe that St. Peter, the prince of the apostles, is the father of all Christians and their first shepherd after Christ, and that the holy Roman Church is the mother and mistress of all the Churches."

- POPE ST. GREGORY VII

180. A Test of Faith (Lk 9:1-17)

"Christ sent out the apostles as the ministers of his divine will. They were to proclaim that spiritual gospel which runs above natural law and written codes, and to call men to himself." – St. Procopius of Gaza

LUKE 9:1-17

He called the Twelve together and gave them power and authority over all devils and to cure diseases, and he sent them out to proclaim the kingdom of God and to heal. He said to them, "Take nothing for the journey: neither staff, nor haversack, nor bread, nor money; and let none of you take a spare tunic. Whatever house you enter, stay there; and when you leave, let it be from there. As for those who do not welcome you, when you leave their town shake the dust from your feet as a sign to them." So they set out and went from village to village proclaiming the Good News and healing everywhere. Meanwhile Herod the tetrarch had heard about all that was going on; and he was puzzled, because some people were saying that John had risen from the dead, others that Elijah had reappeared, still others that one of the ancient prophets had come back to life. But Herod said, "John? I beheaded him. So who is this I hear such reports about?" And he was anxious to see him.

On their return the apostles gave him an account of all they had done. Then he took them with him and withdrew to a town called Bethsaida where they could be by themselves. But the crowds got to know and they went after him. He made them welcome and talked to them about the kingdom of God; and he cured those who were in need of healing. It was late afternoon when the Twelve came to him and said, "Send the people away, and they can go to the villages and farms round about to find lodging and food; for we are in a lonely place here." He replied, "Give them something to eat yourselves." But they said, "We have no more than five loaves and two fish, unless we are to go ourselves and buy food for all these people." For there were about five thousand men. But he said to his disciples, "Get them to sit down in parties of about fifty." They did so and made them all sit down. Then he took the five loaves and the two fish, raised his eyes to heaven, and said the blessing over them; then he broke them and handed them to his disciples to distribute among the crowd. They all ate as much as they wanted, and when the scraps remaining were collected they filled twelve baskets.

CHRIST THE LORD Imagine the apostles' impression as Jesus sent them out on their first missionary journey. He hands them over a share of his own divine power, instructing them to cast out demons, perform miracles, and preach to the crowds. Which of the Twelve was naturally qualified for that kind of an assignment? And just to make sure they don't get cocky, Jesus tells them to travel without supplies—they are to depend entirely on God's providence. You can picture them furrowing their brows in consternation as they set out, eager but nervous. Even bold Peter must have been shaking a little bit the first time he took on a demon all by himself. But the apostles obey and trust, and the results are substantial—even King Herod hears about their goings on.

Then, imagine the apostles' reaction when Jesus commanded them to feed dinner to those thousands of people. They utter a whimpering protest, pointing out that they don't have nearly enough food for that many people. But when Jesus tells them to have the crowds sit down in groups, they do it. What must have been going through their minds? Jesus just keeps stretching their faith. And then he takes their loaves and fish and miraculously multiplies them.

More than our brilliant minds, rich personalities, and fabulous organizational skills, God needs us to give him our trust and our faith. With those, he can expand our small efforts and ideas into miraculous proportions, extending his Kingdom to thousands of souls—many more than we could have reached by trusting merely in our paltry human qualities. He is the Lord; we are only his ambassadors.

CHRIST THE TEACHER Sometimes we are afraid of giving ourselves completely to God because we think we won't have anything left for ourselves.

When he asks us to give up the things that we think make us the happiest, we hesitate. Jesus knows that we struggle with this. In the multiplication of the loaves, he teaches us a lesson to allay those fears.

The apostles were no doubt hungry after a long day of ministry. They had little enough food for themselves (five large loaves and two fish would hardly satisfy a dozen brawny men). Jesus asks them to give it all away. They probably handed them over reluctantly, mouths watering. But Jesus took the food, blessed it, broke it, and gave it back to the disciples to distribute to the crowds (the same four verbs used in the consecration of the bread during the Mass). And at the end, each disciple had an entire basket full of food for his own little feast.

Christ will never, never be outdone in generosity. The more we give to him, the more we will receive. As St. Luke put it in another passage of his Gospel, Jesus said: "Give, and there will be gifts for you: a full measure, pressed down, shaken together, and running over, will be poured into your lap; because the amount you measure out is the amount you will be given back" (Lk 6:38). When God asks us to empty ourselves, it's only so he can have room to fill us up with something better.

CHRIST THE FRIEND When Jesus walked the dusty trails of Palestine, he did so for the sake of the people who lived there. He "talked to them about the kingdom," he "healed those who needed to be cured," and he fed them when they were hungry. His whole life was for others. The mere fact that he came to earth at all tells us that much. The fact that he has remained with us not only in the Holy Scriptures, not only in the living Church, not only in the examples of the saints, but even under the humble and silent appearances of bread and wine in the Eucharist, only makes it that much clearer. Christ came for us! He lived for us, died for us, and rose for us, and he is still here with us, for our sakes. He has not changed since the day he multiplied the loaves for the hungry crowds. He has not all of a sudden become selfish, harsh, and unforgiving. And yet, we often act as if he has. We keep ourselves at a distance; we let doubts and hesitations mar our friendship with him; we leave him alone in the Tabernacle, not even dropping by to say hello. What more could he have done for us to declare his love?

CHRIST IN MY LIFE I wonder how many times my small-mindedness has inhibited your action in and through my life. I get tangled up in complicated considerations and excuses that simply don't take into account the primacy of your grace. Lift me out of the swamp of foolish self-sufficiency! You are the general; I am just a soldier on the battlefield. Teach me to trust, obey, and give my all . . .

I want to be generous with you, Lord. Most of the time, when I'm honest with myself, I know what you are asking of me. But many times I am simply afraid to make the sacrifice. I keep thinking that the result will be boring, unpleasant, or uncomfortable. But would you ever ask of me something that wasn't best for me? Jesus, I trust in you...

You are always thinking of me. Teach me to think of you more often. Teach me to live life deeply and wisely, in constant contact with you, talking things over with you, keeping close to you. Lord Jesus, be my refuge and my strength...

Questions for SMALL-GROUP DISCUSSION

1. What struck you most in this passage? What did you notice that you hadn't noticed before?
2. What are the "five loaves and two fish" that Christ is asking us to give him?
3. If Christ himself, his entire being and life, is truly present in the Eucharist and reserved in the tabernacles of all our Catholic Churches, why do so few people spend significant time with him there?
4. When we have an important meeting or event to attend, we usually take plenty of time to prepare ourselves. Why do we generally not take time to prepare ourselves for Mass and Communion? How can we prepare ourselves better?

Cf. Catechism of the Catholic Church, 1322-1340 and 1406-1419 on the Eucharist; 1391-1401 on Holy Communion; 1345-1390 on the Mass

181. Crosses with Christ (Lk 9:18-27)

"The only petition I would have you put forward on my behalf is that I may be given sufficient inward and outward strength to be as resolute in will as in words, and a Christian in reality instead of only in repute." – St. Ignatius of Antioch

LUKE 9:18-27

Now one day when he was praying alone in the presence of his disciples he put this question to them, "Who do the crowds say I am?" And they answered, "John the Baptist; others Elijah; and others say one of the ancient prophets come back to life." "But you," he said, "who do you say I am?" It was Peter who spoke up. "The Christ of God," he said. But he gave them

> strict orders not to tell anyone anything about this. "The Son of Man," he said, "is destined to suffer grievously, to be rejected by the elders and chief priests and scribes and to be put to death, and to be raised up on the third day." Then to all he said, "If anyone wants to be a follower of mine, let him renounce himself and take up his cross every day and follow me. For anyone who wants to save his life will lose it; but anyone who loses his life for my sake, that man will save it. What gain, then, is it for a man to have won the whole world and to have lost or ruined his very self? For if anyone is ashamed of me and of my words, of him the Son of Man will be ashamed when he comes in his own glory and in the glory of the Father and the holy angels. I tell you truly, there are some standing here who will not taste death before they see the kingdom of God."

CHRIST THE LORD "Christ" means "anointed" (and in Hebrew, "Messiah"). The term is used in reference to King David, who was anointed by the prophet Samuel to show that he had been chosen and sent by God to lead his people to peace and prosperity. (Olive oil comes from olives, and the healthy olive tree was always a symbol of peace and prosperity.) The same term is used in reference to God's promise to reestablish the Kingdom of David forever under one of his descendents (the Davidic Kingdom fell after the reign of Solomon, David's son). Jesus is that descendent. He is the one God has chosen and sent to lead all mankind to the spiritual peace and prosperity of life in communion with God, which had been symbolized by the material peace and prosperity of the Davidic Kingdom. Peter and the other disciples recognized this, and when they asserted it, Jesus did not contradict them. Critics still say that Christ was merely "a prophet" or a "great religious teacher," but Jesus himself made it clear that he claimed to be nothing less than the Lord.

CHRIST THE TEACHER Jesus knew that the general public still associated the title "Christ" with an image of political and military victory. After all, David's kingdom was political, and he had established it through force of arms. But Christ's Kingdom was of a different stamp. It was built around the cross, around suffering, sacrifice, and self-denial. True, he was the Messiah, God's anointed, and his Kingdom would stand forever, but he would establish it through obedience to the Father's will, even unto death by crucifixion. And everyone who wished to enter that Kingdom would have to follow the same path—obedience to God's will, no matter how difficult it might be: "If anyone wants to be a follower of mine, let him renounce himself and take up his cross every day and follow me."

So Jesus told his disciples not to use the term Christ for the time being, allowing him a chance to instruct the crowds, to elevate their hopes and adjust their expectations, to explain how it was that an apparently weak, submissive, suffering Jesus could be the Lord of life and history. We also need time to learn this lesson. We need time spent in prayer, contemplating Christ's teachings and example in the Gospel. We need time spent in study, looking into the history of the Church and the lives of the saints. We need to desire Mt. Calvary as much as Mt. Tabor. Only then will this hardest of all lessons—that earth isn't heaven and never will be, that the path to abundant meaning and happiness passes through a daily cross, that unless we are willing to sacrifice our personal preferences and worldly desires we will never reach the goal for which we were created—only then will this lesson be able to seep down into our hearts and spread into every corner of our minds.

CHRIST THE FRIEND True friends tell friends the hard truth; flatterers don't. In this intimate exchange with his chosen disciples, Jesus looks them in the eye and tells them a very hard truth—that their lives will only take on real meaning if they are willing to sacrifice whatever is necessary (dreams, hopes, comfort, plans) in order to follow him. If we don't take the time to learn this lesson, we run the risk of discarding our friendship with Christ when it starts to cost us. Jesus warns us that if we are ashamed of him and our identification with him, if we prefer acceptance by the world and worldly success to being a faithful Christian, then we may, tragically, end up with what we have preferred. In the end, Christ's Kingdom will come in all its glory (now in the Church it is still in embryonic form), and our allegiance to him in spite of suffering and rejection will prove to have been, as he promises us, the wiser course. If Christ had not traveled that path ahead of us, climbing the hill of Calvary and dying on a cross, it would be hard to believe him. But he has, and so it shouldn't be that hard after all.

CHRIST IN MY LIFE And if you were to ask me this question, "Who do you say I am?" how would I answer? I would say the right words: you are the Messiah, the Son of God, the Lord of life and history. But I think you would keep looking at me, because you see beyond words into my heart. And in my heart, Lord, I have still not surrendered completely to your love. Lord Jesus, help me...

You know I am afraid of the cross. I know that I don't have to be. So why don't you take this fear away? I have a crucifix. I see it all the time. Open my eyes, Lord, so that I not only see the cross, but also the crucifix. May I understand with all my being the immensity of your love that the crucifix communicates. If I truly believe in your love for me, no cross will make me hesitate…

What are you asking of me, Lord? Okay, I give it to you. I will follow where you lead. If you went to Calvary for me, I will go there for you. Help me to see everything with faith. If I know it's your will, I can embrace it, but my faith is sometimes so weak that I forget to look for your hand in the circumstances and responsibilities of my life. Lord, increase my faith…

Questions for SMALL-GROUP DISCUSSION

1. What struck you most in this passage? What did you notice that you hadn't noticed before?
2. What does this dialogue reveal to us about the heart of Jesus?
3. How would the agents of popular culture answer the question Jesus puts to his disciples? How would popular culture react to Jesus' doctrine of the cross?
4. What are the most common "crosses" that we need to "take up daily" in our present life situations?

Cf. Catechism of the Catholic Church, 436-440 on the meaning of the term "Messiah"; 409 and 2015 on the necessity of the cross in the life of every Christian

182. Glimpses of Glory (Lk 9:28-36)

"No music soothes the ear, no words so sweet to hear, no memories half so dear, as Jesus, Son of God." – St. Bernard of Clairvaux

LUKE 9:28-36

Now about eight days after this had been said, he took with him Peter and John and James and went up the mountain to pray. As he prayed, the aspect of his face was changed and his clothing became brilliant as lightning. Suddenly there were two men there talking to him; they were Moses and Elijah appearing in glory, and they were speaking of his passing which he was to accomplish in Jerusalem. Peter and his companions were heavy with sleep, but they kept awake and saw his glory and the two men standing with him. As these were leaving him, Peter said to Jesus, "Master, it is wonderful for us to be here; so let us make three tents, one for you, one for Moses and one for Elijah." He did not know what he was saying. As he spoke, a cloud came and covered them with shadow; and when they went into the cloud the disciples were afraid. And a voice came from the cloud saying, "This is my Son, the Chosen One. Listen to him." And after the voice had spoken, Jesus was found alone. The disciples kept silence and, at that time, told no one what they had seen.

CHRIST THE LORD For a brief moment, Christ reveals a smidgeon of his true glory. Gathered on the mountaintop with his closest apostles and with the greatest prophets from the Old Testament, speaking with them about the most important event in history (his coming Passion and death), he lifts the veil cloaking his divinity, and his disciples become "awake" and "afraid." If a passing glimpse of Jesus' splendor fills them with amazement, just imagine how easy it would have been for him to win all of Palestine to his cause if he had fully unveiled his divinity. And yet, he doesn't. He refuses to overpower us into obedience, preferring to win us over with his love and goodness. Christ indeed is the Lord; he is all-powerful, the Father's "Chosen Son," but he wields his power gently, like a shepherd, so that we won't be scared away.

CHRIST THE TEACHER When these three disciples went off to be alone with Jesus and pray, they saw his glory and came to know him better. Here Jesus teaches us how to come closer to him, how to hear the voice of the Father and encounter the glory of God: by taking time to go off and be alone with him in prayer. In such moments of intimacy with God we will find the light and strength we need to convert the world instead of being converted by it. God has something to say to us; he wants us to discover him and his plan for our lives. But if we refuse to go "up the mountain to pray," we won't be able to hear him.

In the liturgy, the Church presents us with this challenge at the beginning of Lent, reminding us that the best way to prepare for Holy Week and the Solemnity of Solemnities (Easter), the commemoration of the most important event in the history of the human race, is by dedicating ourselves more than usual to prayer, to heartfelt conversation with Christ. But the lesson applies equally for our daily preparation for whatever adventures he sends our way as well as our regular preparation for our own participation in his sacrifice during Mass. Christ has so much he wants to tell us—at all times and in so many ways—that all we need to do is "listen to him," which is impossible unless we set aside time to pray.

CHRIST THE FRIEND As always, in this scene Christ shows how personal his love is. Jesus knew what was going to happen on top of the mountain. And he brought three of his apostles with him to witness it—only three. He knew that in the future they would need to draw on this experience to bolster their faith. Of course, they didn't really understand; they just followed along, dozed off in their prayer, made a senseless remark, and then kept quiet about the whole thing. But Jesus is preparing them for the mission they will have to carry out later. His love for each of us is just as personal and just as wise. He knows what we need when we need it. He gives us moments of consolation in prayer to propel us through dark periods of dryness. All he asks is that we follow along, trusting him, even when we don't understand or when we feel clumsy and ignorant. Peter, James, and John didn't become saints overnight, and neither will we. But if we stay close to the Lord, we will eventually—he will make sure of it.

CHRIST IN MY LIFE You are the Good Shepherd. You know exactly what I need. I remember the times I thought things were going badly, but later I realized that your wisdom had been guiding them all along. Your rule is gentle but sure. Teach me to be docile, to trust in you. I know what you want of me: fidelity to my life's mission, my responsibilities, and my conscience. You will take care of the rest…

I want to pray better. It can't be that hard, because prayer is a gift you give to everyone, young and old, smart and not-so-smart, holy and sinful. So teach me to pray, Lord. Teach me to tune in to your voice. Not only during specific prayer commitments, but all throughout the day. Are you not always with me, a faithful friend at my side? Well then, let's talk…

Even now you are preparing me for future tasks. I want to live each current moment to the full, pouring my love into your will, dedicating myself to whatever you ask of me with all my heart, soul, mind, and strength. If I do, I know you will take my efforts and make them fruitful, both for me and for the Church. I may see the results only later—that's okay. All for your glory…

Questions for *SMALL-GROUP DISCUSSION*

1. What struck you most in this passage? What did you notice that you hadn't noticed before?
2. What can we do to live more intensely and fruitfully during the liturgical seasons in general and the particular season we are in right now?
3. Why do you think mountaintops are consistently referred to as preferred places of prayer in the Bible? What can we learn for our own lives from that?
4. Why do you think Christ talked with Elijah and Moses about his "passing"?

Cf. Catechism of the Catholic Church, 444,459, and 554-556 on the meaning of the Transfiguration

183. Back to the Routine (Lk 9:37-50)

"I resolved always to prefer labors to comforts, contempt to honors. And, in particular, if on one side a kingdom were offered and on the other the washing of dishes, I would refuse the kingdom and accept the dishwashing so as to be truly like Christ, who humbled himself." – St. John Berchmans

LUKE 9:37-50

Now on the following day when they were coming down from the mountain a large crowd came to meet him. Suddenly a man in the crowd cried out. "Master," he said "I implore you to look at my son: he is my only child. All at once a spirit will take hold of him, and give a sudden cry and throw the boy into convulsions with foaming at the mouth; it is slow to leave him, but when it does it leaves the boy worn out. I begged your disciples to cast it out, and they could not." "Faithless and perverse generation!" Jesus said in reply "How much longer must I be among you and put up with you? Bring your son here." The boy was still moving towards Jesus when the devil threw him to the ground in convulsions. But Jesus rebuked the unclean spirit and cured the boy and gave him back to his father, and everyone was awestruck by the greatness of God.

At a time when everyone was full of admiration for all he did, he said to his disciples, "For your part, you must have these words constantly in your mind: The Son of Man is going to be handed over into the power of men." But they did not understand him when he said this; it was hidden from them so that they should not see the meaning of it, and they were afraid to ask him about what he had just said. An argument started between them about which of them was the greatest. Jesus knew what thoughts were going through their minds, and he took a little child and set him by his side and then said to them, "Anyone who welcomes this little child in my name welcomes me; and anyone who welcomes me welcomes the one who sent me. For the least among you all, that is the one who is great." John spoke up. "Master," he said, "we saw a man casting out devils in your so name, and because he is not with us we tried to stop him." But Jesus said to him, "You must not stop him: anyone who is not against you is for you."

CHRIST THE LORD Jesus has work to do. He is a King at war, conquering lost and rebellious hearts by renewing them with his love. The era of the Church, before Christ's second coming, is the era of work and conquest. So his apostles are necessarily called to keep moving, building, and spreading the Kingdom. We all need our mountaintop moments, as Jesus gave to Peter, James, and John at his Transfiguration. These come in many forms—insights and consolations that arrive uninvited at the oddest times, retreats and sabbaticals and vacations that revitalize our minds and hearts with fresh experiences of God's love and goodness, even particular liturgies or moments of prayer when God makes his presence felt in especially intense ways.

God sends these experiences to us because we need them, but they are not the goal, at least not as long as we are members of the Church Militant here on earth. There is always "the following day when they were coming down the mountain," when the demands of our daily life and mission clamor once again for attention. When the moments of bliss give way to moments of battle, we can take comfort that for Christ too the mission was demanding, and even at times exasperating: "How much longer must I be among you and put up with you?" The Lord worked and sweated and suffered, and his earthly joys were only vista points on an uphill journey. His ambassadors (that's us!) are on the same track.

CHRIST THE TEACHER As the time of Jesus' ministry in the district of Galilee is drawing to its conclusion, St. Luke explains that Christ's popularity reaches an all-time high: "Everyone was full of admiration for all he did." Precisely at that moment Jesus pulls his disciples aside and reminds them of his coming Passion and death. The apostles still fail to understand what he means; they feel the surge of his popularity and are already looking forward to his victory—in fact, they are arguing who will get which positions of honor once the Lord takes his rightful throne. But Jesus insists: it's not about self-aggrandizement, it's about self-giving. He tells them that they must keep the Passion, the ultimate model of self-giving, "constantly in your mind."

Jesus says the same thing to us. We are continually beset by the temptation that led Adam and Eve to their demise, the one at the root of every sin: trying to make earth into heaven, trying to find satisfaction in life apart from God and his commands. Suffering, opposition, toil, hardship—these are the bread and butter of human life in a fallen world, and we will never avoid them completely. Jesus doesn't save us from them; he saves us through them. He takes the wafers of bread that are made from the grinding and pounding and baking of the wheat, and he turns them into his Body. We are the grains of wheat, and the sufferings of life are the sickle, the millstone, and the oven that make us into hosts with the Host. They turn our lives into other Christs by giving us a chance to rehabilitate our trust in God and develop all the Christian virtues that such trust entails, that make us into fruitful and fulfilling channels of his wisdom and power. Only self-sacrificial, self-forgetful love can give his grace room to work, and that kind of love always involves the cross.

Christians in the Middle Ages had a beautiful phrase that we should all make our own: *per crucem ad lucem*—"through the cross to the light." Deciphering the mystery of human life means keeping those words "constantly in mind."

CHRIST THE FRIEND True friendship can't be earned, it simply happens. Two people discover in each other a soul mate, and that's that. That's what we're like for Jesus. He doesn't choose us because we have certain talents, or because we're popular, useful, or beautiful. He chooses us simply because we are who we are and we delight him. He tries to convince us of this over and over again.

In this passage, while his apostles are arguing about who deserves more recognition and prestige, Jesus puts a little child beside him—in the place of honor. It's as if he is saying, "Look, I didn't choose you because of what you deserve. You are like this little child, who by yourself can do nothing to build my Kingdom except delight the King. I chose you because I delight in you, because I love you. I want you with me. That's the kind of love I have for you, and that's the kind of love that will be the sole law of my Kingdom. If you want to be great in my Kingdom, accept my love and love others like that. Think not of yourself, but think of others—delight in them, and serve them."

CHRIST IN MY LIFE You are all I need, Lord. I only need to know that you are near me and that I'm on the path you want me to be on. With that I am satisfied. At least, I want to live like that. I don't want my joy to depend on external circumstances. I want to experience truly Christian joy, rooted in your unchanging love for me. Teach me to find you in the moments of calm and in the heat of the battle...

I am struck by how often you warned your apostles about the coming drama of the cross, and how little they understood. But then I have to ask myself, have I understood? I react so violently when my will or my plans or my hopes are contradicted. In your cross is my salvation and that of the whole world. Teach me the wisdom of your cross, Lord...

I know that you love me without any strings attached. Even so, at times I'm afraid. I have been wounded so often. I recoil from such love. Don't let me, Lord. Come after me. Convince me, Lord, that you love me just because I exist. Convince me, Lord, that nothing I can do will every increase or decrease the love you have for me right now. Reign in my heart with your peace...

Questions for SMALL-GROUP DISCUSSION

1. What struck you most in this passage? What did you notice that you hadn't noticed before?
2. How can we keep our hopes up in the middle of life's trials and tribulations and daily grind?
3. Why do you think it took the apostles so long to learn the lesson of the cross? How have we learned this lesson in our own lives?
4. What opportunities to exhibit Christian greatness are provided by our daily life situation?

Cf. Catechism of the Catholic Church, 853 and 863 on how to spread Christ's Kingdom; 699, 1244, and 1261 on Jesus and the little children; 607 and 713 on the meaning and necessity of Christ's Passion

184. Bad Excuses (Lk 9:51-62)

"You who have been present at this bloody tragedy, learn that all torments seem as nothing to one who has an everlasting crown before his eyes. Your gods are not gods; renounce their worship. He alone for whom I suffer and die is the true God. To die for him is to live." – Last words of St. Arcadius, fourth-century martyr

LUKE 9:51-62

Now as the time drew near for him to be taken up to heaven, he resolutely took the road for Jerusalem and sent messengers ahead of him. These set out, and they went into a Samaritan village to make preparations for him, but the people would not receive him because he was making for Jerusalem. Seeing this, the disciples James and John said, "Lord, do you want us to call down fire from heaven to burn them up?" But he turned and rebuked them, and they went off to another village. As they travelled along they met a man on the road who said to him, "I will follow you wherever you go." Jesus answered, "Foxes have holes and the birds of the air have nests, but the Son of Man has nowhere to lay his head." Another to whom he said, "Follow me," replied, "Let me go and bury my father first." But he answered, "Leave the dead to bury their dead; your duty is to go and spread the news of the kingdom of God." Another said, "I will follow you, sir, but first let me go and say good-bye to my people at home." Jesus said to him, "Once the hand is laid on the plough, no one who looks back is fit for the kingdom of God."

CHRIST THE LORD Two of Jesus' closest disciples (James and John) still hadn't understood their leader. Even as Jesus "resolutely took" the road to Jerusalem, where he would allow himself to be rejected, humiliated, tortured, and executed, they were eager to defend his Lordship by violence and force. On the one hand, they were right: Jesus was the Lord, and he deserved to be welcomed and treated with the highest respect. Therefore, in rejecting him, the Samaritan village deserved censure. But on the other hand, Christ had repeatedly explained that he was on his way to Jerusalem precisely to accept the people's rejection. Christ reveals God's mercy precisely by not giving his enemies what they deserve, but by patiently bearing with them. Christ's Lordship is real, but it differs from what we tend to expect: for Christ, and thus for the Christian, success means fulfilling God's will, even if that requires suffering, humiliation, rejection, and total failure in the eyes of the world.

CHRIST THE TEACHER These three encounters with these would-be disciples teach us three tough lessons about what it means to follow Christ.

First, we have to give up our security. Christ is trustworthy, but when we follow him, we have to do so one step and one day at a time—he refuses to give us a full outline in advance. Even foxes and birds have the security of their instincts and natural habitats, but Christians are on an unpredictable adventure.

Second, we have to take risks. The words of the Lord to this young man seem harsh, but in the idiom of the time, they probably weren't. The man's father was probably not dead at all. Rather, the young man simply said that he wanted to follow the Lord, to leave behind the spiritually dead environment he lived in, but he would do so once his father had grown old and died. He felt the tug of Christ calling him, but he also felt the pull of his comfortable life, of the relationships, hopes, and projects that he had long been attached to. Christ warns him that he needs to heed God's voice without delay—as risky as it may be.

Finally, we can expect difficulties. Plowing fields by hand was no easy task, and to do it well, to plow a straight and deep furrow, required dedication, perseverance, and just plain hard work. Following Christ is no different. Once we get into it, we discover how demanding it really is, and we are tempted to look back at the ease and comfort of a self-centered life (conveniently forgetting, of course, about the hardships that go along with that too). But if we go back, we lose. Only Christ's Kingdom lasts forever, only God can fill the deepest longings of our hearts—the hard work that fidelity to God's will requires pays for itself with eternal returns.

CHRIST THE FRIEND Christ invites these potential disciples to follow him, just as he invites us to follow him. This is no insignificant detail. If he invites us, it is because he wants us to be with him; he is interested in us, in bringing us into his Kingdom. What we do, whether we follow him or not, matters to him. God really cares about each one of us. As the Catechism (#30) puts it, "[God] never ceases to call every man to seek him, so as to find life and happiness." If we understood how much we matter to him, it would solve an awful lot of our problems.

Jesus: Would you approve of a doctor who ignored his patient's illness? Would you hire a coach who never pushed his players to excel? Then why do you resist when I ask you to leave things behind in order to follow me? Unless you make room in your heart for my grace by emptying it of selfishness, how can you be my follower? Remember, whenever I ask something of you, I am the doctor of your soul, the coach of your pursuit of happiness and holiness.

CHRIST IN MY LIFE Why am I so afraid of failure and rejection? You chose exactly those realities as your path of glory. You only cared about fulfilling the Father's will, so why do I care so much about what others think of me, about performing better than my neighbor? Lord, free my heart from vanity and arrogance and insecurity. Free me to love and give myself as totally and gladly as you did...

I really do want to be your disciple. You know my limits and my circumstances, and you know my possibilities—much better than I do. So teach me to trust in you and your will more than in my own judgment. Teach me to find the balance between sensibility (I know you don't want me to abandon common sense, since you invented it) and courage...

Since you are God, you think unceasingly of those you love. And since you love me, you must think of me unceasingly. Lord, help me to believe that! Help me to live knowing that you are always surrounding me with your wise, merciful, and loving providence. Inspire me with your love, so I will be generous and courageous in spreading the treasures of your truth and grace...

Questions for
SMALL-GROUP DISCUSSION

1. What struck you most in this passage? What did you notice that you hadn't noticed before?
2. In what circumstances are we tempted to react to others' rejection of Christ (or of Church teaching) as James and John did? How can we learn to be more Christlike in those situations?
3. How does popular culture encourage us to react to the demands and difficulties involved in following Christ? How does Christ want us to react?
4. How can we deepen our appreciation and awareness of God's personal interest in each of us? How can we transmit it to those who have no awareness of it all?

Cf. Catechism of the Catholic Church, 2340, 1734, and 2015 on the need for effort in following Christ; 1846-1848 and 218-221 on God's mercy and love

THE GOSPEL OF LUKE
Chapter 10

"Adapt yourself with gracious and charitable compliance to all your neighbor's weaknesses. In particular, make a rule to hide your feelings in many inconsequential matters. Give up all bitterness toward your neighbor, no matter what. And be convinced that your neighbor is in everything better than you. This will not be difficult if you keep even a little aware of yourself. It will give you the ability to overcome your feelings of resentment. Each day look for every possible opportunity to do a kindness for those you do not like. After examining yourselves on this matter every morning, decide what you are going to do, and do it faithfully with kindness and humility."

– ST. JOHN BAPTIST DE LA SALLE

185. Working for the Lord (Lk 10:1-12)

"I am convinced that there is a great need for the whole Church to rediscover the joy of evangelization, to become a community inspired with missionary zeal to make Jesus better known and loved." – Pope Benedict XVI

LUKE 10:1–12

After this the Lord appointed seventy-two others and sent them out ahead of him, in pairs, to all the towns and places he himself was to visit. He said to them, "The harvest is rich but the labourers are few, so ask the Lord of the harvest to send labourers to his harvest. Start off now, but remember, I am sending you out like lambs among wolves. Carry no purse, no haversack, no sandals. Salute no one on the road. Whatever house you go into, let your first words be, 'Peace to this house!' And if a man of peace lives there, your peace will go and rest on him; if not, it will come back to you. Stay in the same house, taking what food and drink they have to offer, for the labourer deserves his wages; do not move from house to house. Whenever you go into a town where they make you welcome, eat what is set before you. Cure those in it who are sick, and say, 'The kingdom of God is very near to you.' But whenever you enter a town and they do not make you welcome, go out into its streets and say, 'We wipe off the very dust of your town that clings to our feet, and leave it with you. Yet be sure of this: the kingdom of God is very near.' I tell you, on that day it will not go as hard with Sodom as with that town."

CHRIST THE LORD Appointing seventy-two disciples to be collaborators in his mission is an action with deep biblical significance. When Moses was leading the people of Israel into the Promised Land, God had him bring seventy elders to the door of the Tabernacle (the tent where the Ark of the Covenant was kept, and where Moses used to meet with God), so that they could receive the spirit of Moses and become his assistants. Later the Sanhedrin, the ruling body of post-exilic Israel, was made up of seventy-one elders. By following this pattern, Christ once again shows that he is bringing the Old Covenant to its fulfillment. The number seventy-two may even have yet another level of meaning. The Book of Genesis described the division of the non-Jewish world into seventy nations. So Jesus' choice of seventy-two disciples includes those seventy Gentile nations, the nation of Israel, and, perhaps, his Church, the new People of God. In any case, the allusion is clear. Christ is the new Moses; he is bringing a New Covenant and extending it to a new Israel, the Church.

We also see in this passage Jesus' insistence on his methodology of mediation. He had chosen his twelve closest companions, the apostles, the forerunners of the bishops. He had already sent them out on their first missionary journey. Now that their training has advanced, he gathers another group of assistants and sends them out on a similar mission. The structure of the New People of God is already taking shape, and it is even now hierarchical. Jesus is at the top of the pyramid, his twelve apostles come next, and beneath them there is another rung of ministers. Each of these in turn would reach out to others and engage them in building the Kingdom. The Lord came not only to announce the Good News, but to set up the ecclesial structure that would insure its ongoing announcement to the ends of the earth until the end of time, setting a pattern for apostleship that brings the principles of effectiveness and multiplication onto center stage.

CHRIST THE TEACHER Among the many lessons Jesus teaches in this lecture on how to be a Christian apostle, the last one is too often overlooked. He tells his disciples how to react when they are rejected, when their efforts appear to bear no fruit, when they run into opposition, and when they seem to fail in their attempts to win people over to Christ. When that happens, they are simply to shake the dust from their feet and move on.

Everyone remains free to accept or reject God's grace. If Christ himself suffered seeming failures in the apostolate (the Pharisees weren't exactly pushovers), should we expect anything more? The greatest danger for an apostle is discouragement. But discouragement comes from unfulfilled expectations. To avoid discouragement, therefore, Jesus points out what our expectations need to be. If we seek only to please the Lord, the Lord will indeed be pleased, even if no one else is.

CHRIST THE FRIEND "The harvest is abundant, but the laborers are few." Imagine the emotion behind those words. They express a sense of urgency, a burning desire to reach out to all the men and women who so desperately need direction, meaning, and true love in their lives, and to lead them into the Kingdom. So many needs, so many souls ripe for the Good News! And yet, so few of Christ's followers are willing to go out and gather them in. The true friends of Christ, the ones he can really count on, will let his yearning love echo in their hearts, and reverberate in their actions.

Priests share this mission in a special way, and Christ therefore allows them to share his yearning love more closely. They are the extension in time and space of Christ himself, who in his wisdom has chosen to work through them to infuse sacramental grace into the Church. Friendship with Christ, then, includes a supernatural appreciation for his priests, an attitude of respect and cooperation, and an eagerness to help those whom Christ is calling hear and heed him.

CHRIST IN MY LIFE You want your saving message to reach every human heart and society. But you also desire to spread that message through the words and actions of your disciples. I am a bit puzzled by your confidence in us, but even so, Lord, I renew my willingness to go wherever you want me to go and do whatever you want me to do to build your Kingdom. Teach me to do your will...

I tend to measure my Christian life in non-Christian terms, as if I could earn more of your love by showing more results in my efforts to build your Kingdom. I know you want the contrary: you want me to work for your Kingdom out of love for you, not in order to earn your love. But my heart is infected with the upside-down insecurity of this fallen world. Heal me with your love...

Your heart is burning with love. Why else would you have left heaven in order to come and suffer and die on earth? You eagerly desire the friendship of people just like me. Jesus, I can do nothing greater for my neighbors—the ones I know well and the ones I barely know at all—than to bring them deeper into your friendship. With the zeal of your heart, inflame my heart...

Questions for
SMALL-GROUP DISCUSSION

1. What struck you most in this passage? What did you notice that you hadn't noticed before?
2. How do the guidelines that Christ gave the seventy-two apply to us today?
3. What are the biggest obstacles we face in trying to spread Christ's Kingdom and what would Christ say about them?
4. If Christ asked me to give my life completely to "gathering the harvest," would I be willing to? If not, why not?

Cf. Catechism of the Catholic Church, 857-865 on the apostolic nature of the Church; 3 and 1267-1270 on the responsibility of each Christian to spread the Kingdom

186. Joy and Hope (Lk 10:13-24)

"What more do we want than to have at our side a friend so loyal that he will never desert us when we are in trouble or in difficulties, as worldly friends do?" – St. Teresa of Ávila

LUKE 10:13-24

"Alas for you, Chorazin! Alas for you, Bethsaida! For if the miracles done in you had been done in Tyre and Sidon, they would have repented long ago, sitting in sackcloth and ashes. And still, it will not go as hard with Tyre and Sidon at the Judgement as with you. And as for you, Capernaum, did you want to be exalted high as heaven? You shall be thrown down to hell. Anyone who listens to you listens to me; anyone who rejects you rejects me, and those who reject me reject the one who sent me."

The seventy-two came back rejoicing. "Lord," they said, "even the devils submit to us when we use your name." He said to them, "I watched Satan fall like lightning from heaven. Yes, I have given you power to tread underfoot serpents and scorpions and the whole strength of the enemy; nothing shall ever hurt you. Yet do not rejoice that the spirits submit to you; rejoice rather that your names are written in heaven." It was then that, filled with joy by the Holy Spirit, he said, "I bless you, Father, Lord of heaven and of earth, for hiding these things from the learned and the clever and revealing them to mere children. Yes, Father, for that is what it pleased you to do. Everything has been entrusted to me by my Father; and no one knows who the Son is except the Father, and who the Father is except the Son and those to whom the Son chooses to reveal him." Then

stay humble

turning to his disciples he spoke to them in private, "Happy the eyes that see what you see, for I tell you that many prophets and kings wanted to see what you see, and never saw it; to hear what you hear, and never heard it."

CHRIST THE LORD Jesus identifies himself with his chosen missionaries. To demonstrate what a high privilege that is, St. Luke records some of the boldest claims that Jesus ever made.

First, we hear him reprimand the towns that refused to accept his teaching and apply it to their lives. His reaction to their rejection is passionate and dramatic; he prophesies that their cold reception will lead to their demise on the Day of Judgment. The implication is clear: Jesus is the One sent by the Father, and the way we treat Jesus is the way we treat God, for good or for ill.

Second, he exults in the faith-filled welcome the seventy-two gave to his grace, which enabled them to push back Satan's conquests and advance Christ's eternal Kingdom. In the course of that exultation he actually identifies himself with the Father; he explains that although they are two separate persons, they are completely united in the knowledge and love they share—knowledge and love being the two characteristics that bring persons into communion with each other. Here we have a protolesson on the Blessed Trinity.

Third, after celebrating the return of the seventy-two, Jesus speaks alone with his apostles. We can picture his eyes shining with an eager light, his gladness at the seventy-two's faith still overflowing in his countenance. And then it overflows again in his words as he explains that his mission, his presence in Israel, and the establishment of his Church are what all human history and all salvation history had been looking forward to. He is the "center of the universe and of history."[2]

CHRIST THE TEACHER Commentators vary on their interpretation of the striking phrase, "I watched Satan fall like lightning from heaven." Some read it as if Jesus were smiling and affirming the reports from the seventy-two disciples that the devils submitted to them. It would be like Jesus saying, "Yes, while you were preaching and healing, I was here and I saw Satan's rule rolling back wherever you spread the Good News." Others read the saying as a preface to the rest of his mini-discourse, as a warning against unhealthy pride, which was the cause of Satan's original fall from grace. In this case, the phrase would mean, "Well, it's good that you have experienced the power of my salvation, but be careful. If you forget that this power comes not from yourselves but from

---

2 Pope John Paul II, *Redemptor Hominis,* 1.

on high, you may fall into the tragic trap that the devil fell into, thinking that you are on par with God."

In either case, the lesson of his conversation with the returning disciples remains the same. Those who trust in God and obey his call in their lives, as did the seventy-two, will experience God's power acting in and through their lives, and that is exactly what Christ is hoping for. And as long as they remember that their fruitfulness and effectiveness is based on God's initiative and grace working in them, thus staying humble and trusting like "mere children," all will be well. But if they begin to think too highly of themselves, as if their own greatness were yielding these remarkable results, thus considering themselves "the learned and the clever," they will self-destruct.

How easy it is, even for those who have spent long years working faithfully in the Lord's vineyard, to become dangerously proud and self-satisfied! The secret to perseverance in friendship with Christ is to draw our satisfaction not primarily from what we do, but from what God has done for us, and that requires the daily mental discipline of directing our thoughts again and again to God's goodness, cultivating an attitude of gratitude. After all, what can give us greater happiness than knowing that our "names are written in heaven," just as the names of citizens in the Greek cities at the time of Christ were carefully kept on regularly updated lists?

CHRIST THE FRIEND The disciples come back "rejoicing." Jesus catches their spirit, and his acclamation of praise to the Father is given while he is "filled with joy by the Holy Spirit." The Lord rejoices in our joys, just as much as he sorrows in our sorrows. We have a hard time understanding how deeply interested he is in our lives, but the fact remains, as this passage makes clear—he is deeply interested. This is one of Christianity's great differences. The God of the Bible cares passionately about every single human soul. Was Jesus' reaction to Bethsaida and Capernaum's failure to repent one of indifference? Hardly—it was as full of pathos as his reaction to the successful mission of the seventy-two was full of joy. Christ's heart beats with our hearts, because it is one with ours, because it came to earth and started beating in the first place in order to save our hearts from loneliness, frustration, and despair. He is the Friend beyond all imagining.

Philip: I will never forget that day when everyone came back from the second mission trip. We were all exhausted but overflowing with enthusiasm. Everyone wanted to tell Jesus about all the wonderful things that had happened. Everyone had some remarkable stories. As we came together, I was thinking to myself that Jesus wouldn't be as eager to hear our stories as we were to tell them. After all, his own miracles were far beyond the scope of anything we were doing. But I was wrong. As we approached him he came out towards us. It was as if he had been waiting for us. His eyes were full of welcome – and questions. He wanted to know everything. No detail was too slight for him. It made a lasting impression on me. I remembered it frequently in later years, when we had all gone out to spread the Church. When I prayed, I would remember how eagerly he had listened to the seventy-two, and I would tell him everything, absolutely everything that was going on. He would always answer me, somehow. That's the way I stayed close to him.

CHRIST IN MY LIFE You have given me the universe. All that I see around me, Lord, is mine, because it is yours. You have given me your very self, and you continue to give me yourself every time I receive Holy Communion. You hold me in the palm of your hand. You, the all-powerful, all-knowing God, shower me with gifts. Thank you, Lord. Blessed be your name through all the earth…

I bear your name, and you have anointed my forehead with the sign of the cross. You have given me a mission in life, just as you gave one to the seventy-two. I am to bring the sweet aroma of your truth and love into the world where I live and work. Make me your faithful disciple, Lord, so that I can experience the joy of your victory, and so bring joy to your heart…

Why do I insist on walking alone through life? You are always thinking of me, like a lover in the full, fresh bloom of love. You are interested in me, wanting to teach and guide me in all my responsibilities, activities, and relationships. You are on the edge of your seat, waiting to see how I will respond to all the blessings and opportunities for growth that you send me. Thank you, Lord…

Questions for SMALL-GROUP DISCUSSION

1. What struck you most in this passage? What did you notice that you hadn't noticed before?
2. How does Christ expect us to build his Kingdom in our current life situation? What can help us do it more effectively? Christ the Teacher
3. Christ promises to protect those who trust him and strive to do his work. Have you ever felt that protection? Do the examples of the martyrs contradict Jesus' promise that "nothing shall ever hurt you"?
4. What does popular culture encourage us to "rejoice" in? What would Christ say about that?

Cf. Catechism of the Catholic Church, 27, 30, 384, 1028, 1035, and 1723 on how God gives happiness; 774-776 on the Church as the sacrament of salvation; 1554-1571 on the three degrees of holy orders

187. The Good Life (Lk 10:25-37)

"Remember that the Christian life is one of action, not of speech and daydreams. Let there be few words and many deeds and let them be done well." – St. Vincent Pallotti

LUKE 10:25-37

There was a lawyer who, to disconcert him, stood up and said to him, "Master, what must I do to inherit eternal life?" He said to him, "What is written in the Law? What do you read there?" He replied, "You must love the Lord your God with all your heart, with all your soul, with all your strength, and with all your mind, and your neighbour as yourself." "You have answered right," said Jesus, "do this and life is yours." But the man was anxious to justify himself and said to Jesus, "And who is my neighbour?" Jesus replied, "A man was once on his way down from Jerusalem to Jericho and fell into the hands of brigands; they took all he had, beat him and then made off, leaving him half dead. Now a priest happened to be travelling down the same road, but when he saw the man, he passed by on the other side. In the same way a Levite who came to the place saw him, and passed by on the other side. But a Samaritan traveller who came upon him was moved with compassion when he saw him. He went up and bandaged his wounds, pouring oil and wine on them. He then lifted him on to his own mount, carried him to the inn and looked after him. Next day, he took out two denarii and handed them to the innkeeper. 'Look after him,' he said, 'and on my way back I will make good any extra expense you have.' Which of these three, do you think, proved himself a neighbour to the man who fell into the brigands' hands?" "The one who took pity on him," he replied. Jesus said to him, "Go, and do the same yourself."

CHRIST THE LORD This parable is so familiar to us that we often see only one of its dimensions. Certainly it presents a model for us to follow—"Go and do the same yourself"—but it also presents us with a self-portrait of Christ; it reveals what kind of a Lord he is. Each of us has been robbed of our original holiness by original sin. Our own selfishness and sins (and the sins of others) have deeply wounded our souls. We lay on the side of life's path in need of a Savior. We have been bruised and broken and wounded; the Lord kneels down and lifts us up with his healing touch. Christ is the Good Samaritan, the merciful Lord who heals and restores us with the balm of his sacraments, who pays for our salvation with the boundless riches of his grace, poured out generously on Calvary's cross and entrusted to the innkeeper of the Church, who watches over our convalescence until he comes again. He is the Lord, yes, but the truly noble Lord, who cares enough to come meet us in our need and carry us safely to his Father's inn.

CHRIST THE TEACHER Christ's lesson is so simple! "Love God with all your heart and love your neighbor as yourself, and you will live." It is within everyone's reach to live out this simple lesson, even within the reach of a Samaritan, who according to local customs of the time was not supposed to have anything to do with Jews. It summarizes the entire gospel, the entire meaning of life. But we are not satisfied with simplicity. We pester him for clarifications, "Yes, but who actually is my neighbor? . . . " And he obliges us with further explanations, with the explanation given by the words and examples of thousands of saints, by the teaching of the Church in every age, by the nudges of our own conscience. . . . And still we find it hard to learn the lesson. One would venture to think that perhaps we don't really want to learn it. What holds us back from deciding once and for all to make Christ's standard our own? The complicated shadows of self-absorption have become too comfortable; the simple, bright light of Christ's truth hurts our eyes. But in our hearts we know what we should do. The time has come to pack up our books and leave the classroom behind; the lesson of how to live only makes sense when we let it change the course of our life.

CHRIST THE FRIEND The Good Samaritan put himself out to save the half-dead traveler. First of all, it was risky: playing dead was a popular ploy of Palestine's experienced brigands. Second, it was costly: he had to expend his own oil and wine, and he had to leave money with the innkeeper. Third, it was inconvenient: certainly the Samaritan was on the road for business, maybe very important business, and stopping at the scene of the accident and then taking the fellow to a place of safety would delay his trip. The whole thing was really a bad investment, practically speaking. But friends do that; they put themselves out for their friends, they take risks for them and make sacrifices for them. That's what Christ did for us (just look at a crucifix), to prove what kind of friend he is. And if we value his friendship, and want to be his friend, we will "go and do the same."

Jesus: Life is so short. It is so easy to forget that. It is so easy for you to get caught up in the stream of activities that seem so urgent but in fact are secondary. Your primary task, the mission I have given you, is to follow in my footsteps. Open your eyes and your heart to the people around you. See their needs and reach out to them as I have seen yours and reached out to you. If this is hard for you, if the stream of urgencies keeps sweeping you away, don't worry. Keep contemplating my example, keep thinking of the love I have for you and all that I have done and still do for you. Little by little the weight of my love will give you stability, strength, and peace. My wisdom will be the balm that heals your anxiety.

CHRIST IN MY LIFE Jesus, thank you for coming to earth, paying the price of my sins, and inviting me to your heavenly banquet. I don't thank you enough for all you have done for me. You didn't pass me by when you saw me in need. You never do. You are always with me, no matter how hard life may get. Keep me faithful to you, Lord, just as you are always faithful to me...

How I yearn for clarity of mind! Life seems so complicated sometimes, Lord. I know it's because I'm too self-absorbed. Help me, teach me, send me the wisdom of your Spirit, clean out the junk drawer of my soul. I want to be completely free to live life as you created me to live it. I love you, Lord; teach me to do your will...

Being a Good Samaritan at times seems too hard, too demanding. But I know, even from my own experience, that it's really not so hard at all—once I decide to do it. Help me to be courageous in those critical moments of decision. If I can resist the temptation to self-centeredness right when a chance to love presents itself, the rest will be smooth sailing...

Questions for
SMALL-GROUP DISCUSSION

1. What struck you most in this passage? What did you notice that you hadn't noticed before?
2. What can we do to increase our reverence for and appreciation of Christ?
3. When we have moral or religious questions, as did this scholar, where should we go with them?
4. What would the "Good Samaritan" be doing if he were in our place today?

Cf. Catechism of the Catholic Church, 1822-1829 on charity; 1846-1848 on mercy; 1939-1942 on human solidarity

188. Choosing the Better Part (Lk 10:38-42)

"From the top of a hill the rain flows down to the valley. Just as more water collects at the bottom of the hill, so Mary, sitting in a low place at the feet of Jesus, listening to his words, receives more than Martha, standing and serving the temporal needs of her

Master. Mary, loving Jesus, the one thing needed, is in port. Martha, occupying herself about many things, is still at sea." – St. Augustine

LUKE 10:38-42
In the course of their journey he came to a village, and a woman named Martha welcomed him into her house. She had a sister called Mary, who sat down at the Lord's feet and listened to him speaking. Now Martha who was distracted with all the serving said, "Lord, do you not care that my sister is leaving me to do the serving all by myself? Please tell her to help me." But the Lord answered: "Martha, Martha," he said, "you worry and fret about so many things, and yet few are needed, indeed only one. It is Mary who has chosen the better part; it is not to be taken from her."

CHRIST THE LORD If Christ truly is the one Lord of life and history, the one Savior, the one Way, Truth, and Life (and he is), then it is certain that "only one" thing is needed for a fulfilling, meaningful, and fruitful life: to stay as close to him as possible at all times. When we address Christ from our hearts as Lord, we acknowledge our conviction that he truly is our one thing necessary, and he will be as pleased with us for doing so as he was with Mary.

The Lord already is the one thing needed. Our task is to choose to shape our lives accordingly. Jesus doesn't congratulate Mary because she won the spiritual lottery or had received a particularly beautiful soul from God. He praises her because she has "chosen the better part." She chooses it. She chooses to submit to the Lord, to let him be for her what he in truth is for everyone—that one needed thing.

Once again, we are confronted with this amazing truth about Christ's Kingship: he offers the benefits of his rule to all people, but he leaves each person supremely free to accept or reject them. And the offer is not a one-time affair. Martha had chosen to busy herself with her own plans on this occasion, but you can bet she adjusted her behavior the next time the Lord came around. Mary had chosen to adore the Lord this time, but she would still be free to make the same or a different choice the next time. Each and every time we choose to give Christ and his will priority in our lives, we are pleasing him and extending the borders of his Kingdom in our lives. And every time we bring his message to others, we give them a chance to do the same.

CHRIST THE TEACHER We shouldn't berate Martha too much—she also is a saint, and she was also much loved by the Lord. But she needed to learn a lesson. She needed to learn that what we do for Christ has to flow out of what we are for him—his true and devoted friends. It is easy to overload our agenda with so many activities and commitments—good and beneficial as they may be—that we lose sight of our goal: to know, love, and imitate Christ more each day. Only that will give meaning to our lives; only that will equip us to help others find meaning; only that will fill us with the joy we long for. If we are separated from the vine, we cannot bear fruit (cf. Jn 15:5), but if we seek first the Kingdom, everything else will fall into place (cf. Mt 6:33).

The crucial sign that we may be following Martha's footsteps a little too closely is a waning life of prayer. When we skimp on our prayer life, on that precious time that we spend, as Mary did, "at the Lord's feet listening to him speaking," we need to stop and check our spiritual vital signs. Maybe we have allowed ourselves to become so "distracted with all the serving" that we have forgotten why we should be serving in the first place.

CHRIST THE FRIEND Christ was glad to be served, but he was even gladder to be loved. He yearns for our love. When we come before him at the final judgment, he will be less interested in our résumé of achievements than in the love with which we achieved them. He was happy that Mary wanted to listen to him, wanted to sit beside him and spend time with him. That is why he became man in the first place—to make himself available, to offer his friendship. This desire was so strong that he invented a way to extend his Real Presence to all times and places through the sacrament of the Eucharist. In every tabernacle throughout the world, he is available 24/7, just for us, just because he loves us.

CHRIST IN MY LIFE I want to choose the better part every day—every moment of every day. I believe in you completely; I want to live wholly for you. Whose kingdom could I possibly prefer? My own? Save me from that! Someone else's? But who is as wise as you? Who is as powerful as you? Who is as loving as you? Thy Kingdom come, Lord, thy will be done…

I want to build your Kingdom, fulfill my apostolate, and win souls over to your friendship. I want to do so much for you! But I know that my heart is not yet completely pure. The infection of egoism is still there, albeit on the wane because of your grace. So keep me humble, Lord. Keep me focused on you and your Kingdom—not on myself and my achievements…

Thank you for staying with me in the Eucharist. Now I always have a chance to sit at your feet and listen to your words and your heartbeats. I need that. I need a real place, a real presence. Thank you, Lord. Never let me take this great gift for granted. With the love of your heart, inflame my heart…

Questions for
SMALL-GROUP DISCUSSION

1. What struck you most in this passage? What did you notice that you hadn't noticed before?
2. Why do you think Martha had enough confidence to issue such a mundane complaint to Jesus about her sister? What does this tell us about her relationship with Jesus?
3. What substitutes do people come up with for the "one thing needed" when they don't have Christ?
4. What are some tactics that have helped you regularly make time in your busy schedule to sit at the Lord's feet and listen to him? What keeps us from being more like Mary?

Cf. Catechism of the Catholic Church, 2558-2567 on the importance and nature of prayer; 2709-2719 on contemplative prayer; 1373-1381 on Christ's prayer in the Eucharist

THE GOSPEL OF LUKE
Chapter 11

"The man who prays looks above to the goods of heaven whereon he meditates and which he desires; his whole being is plunged in the contemplation of the marvelous order established by God, which knows not the frenzy of earthly successes nor the futile competitions of ever increasing speed; and thus automatically, as it were, will be reestablished that equilibrium between work and rest, whose entire absence from society today is responsible for grave dangers to life physical, economic, and moral."

– POPE PIUS XI

189. Prayer School (Lk 11:1-13)

"One can always enter into inner prayer, independently of the conditions of health, work, or emotional state. The heart is the place of this conquest and encounter, in poverty and in faith." – Catechism of the Catholic Church, 2710

LUKE 11:1-13
Now once he was in a certain place praying, and when he had finished one of his disciples said, "Lord, teach us to pray, just as John taught his disciples." He said to them, "Say this when you pray: Father, may your name be held holy, your kingdom come; give us each day our daily bread, and forgive us our sins, for we ourselves forgive each one who is in debt to us. And do not put us to the test." He also said to them, "Suppose one of you has a friend and goes to him in the middle of the night to say, My friend, lend me three loaves, because a friend of mine on his travels has just arrived at my house and I have nothing to offer him; and the man answers from inside the house, 'Do not bother me. The door is bolted now, and my children and I are in bed; I cannot get up to give it you.' I tell you, if the man does not get up and give it him for friendship's sake, persistence will be enough to make him get up and give his friend all he wants. So I say to you: Ask, and it will be given to you; search, and you will find; knock, and the door will be opened to you. For the one who asks always receives; the

one who searches always finds; the one who knocks will always have the door opened to him. What father among you would hand his son a stone when he asked for bread? Or hand him a snake instead of a fish? Or hand him a scorpion if he asked for an egg? If you then, who are evil, know how to give your children what is good, how much more will the heavenly Father give the Holy Spirit to those who ask him!"

CHRIST THE LORD We, though we tend to be selfish, are still eager to give good things to those we love. God, who is unhampered by even the slightest smidgeon of selfishness, is certainly more eager than we can imagine to give good things to us, whom he loves tirelessly and without measure. Just as Christ answered his disciples' request to teach them how to pray, so he will hear every request we ask of him and answer it even more generously than we could have hoped for. He is a lavish Lord, abounding in every good thing—most especially in forgiveness and faithfulness, the two deepest needs of the human heart—and ready to pour them out upon us, if only we really want him to.

In a sense, the history of salvation is a history of God answering the prayers of his people. The Old Testament is a litany of answered prayers: Moses repeatedly intercedes for the Israelites, and God delivers; the Lord answers their pleas for deliverance by sending them judges and prophets and finally a king; Hannah is granted a son; Judith and Esther are granted victory in the face of overpowering enemies through their heartfelt prayers, and the list goes on. Certainly, God is the initiator of salvation. He created us and guides us through the labyrinth of life, but he guides us in accordance with our nature, and that means respecting our freedom and listening to our entreaties. He is not a Dictator, but an all-powerful Father.

CHRIST THE TEACHER The words of the Our Father, abridged here in St. Luke's version, are God's own instructions on prayer. Each phrase is a gushing stream of grace and wisdom; if we spend our lives tuning our hearts to their inexhaustible meaning (and not just mindlessly rattling them off), we will discover every secret of peace and happiness. They show us how God wants us to approach him and be with him.

In addition to fostering the attitudes and desires woven into the Our Father, however, Jesus teaches us two other qualities of Christian prayer: persistence and confidence. In the Garden of Eden, Adam and Eve failed the Lord by letting the devil trick them out of these two attitudes. Instead of having confidence in God's command not to eat the forbidden fruit, they let their trust in the Creator die in their hearts; and instead of turning to God in their moment of trial and hardship, they depended solely on their own wits. Though baptism has overcome in our souls the alienation from God inherited from original sin, the weakness, the tendency to distrust God and give up on him, remains. God allows it to remain because he wants to give us a share in the all-important work of building up his Kingdom, which is an interior kingdom of the heart. Our prayer life is a privileged place to accomplish that work. By exercising these attitudes in our prayer, we have a chance to rehabilitate our persistent confidence in the Lord, so that we can return to intimacy with him.

CHRIST THE FRIEND "Search and you will find; ask, and it will be given to you." The funny thing about friendship is that it can't be forced. As much as God wants to regain our friendship and deepen it day after day, he can only do so if we share (at least a little bit) that same desire, if we yearn for his friendship as he yearns for ours. He does everything he can to stir it up within us (even descending from heaven to become man and live among us), but ultimately, because he will settle for nothing less than true friendship, he willingly limits his own freedom in order to respect ours.

Jesus: Prayer is much simpler than you think. I am always with you, always at your side and in your heart. I am always paying attention to you, thinking of you. I am always interested in what you are going through and what is on your mind and heart. Remember this, believe it, and prayer will become as natural as breathing. You never have to be alone. I am the one who knows you wholly and loves you no matter what. Live in the awareness of my presence; let me be your life's companion.

CHRIST IN MY LIFE I trust in you, Lord. Send me the gifts of your Holy Spirit. Fill my soul with your light and your peace; wipe away all the stains of selfishness. I want to live each new day with the freshness of your everlasting love. I want to live with the joy of the simple child and the wisdom of old age. I want my life to be a window, clear and spotless, that faces the vista of your Sacred Heart...

Teach me to pray, Lord. I believe in the necessity and importance of prayer. I thank you for the gift of prayer. I want to learn to search for you in prayer, so that I can find you. I want to learn to pray at all times, so that I can always know what's best to do, what's the most effective way to build your Kingdom in my life and my neighbors' lives...

Lord, I still want to follow you. I want you to be Lord of my life, just as you are Lord of history. Thank you for offering me your friendship. But what about all those other people who haven't accepted the offer? Have mercy on them, as you had mercy on me, and move their hearts to trust in you. And teach me what to say and do to bring them closer to your Kingdom...

Questions for SMALL-GROUP DISCUSSION

1. What struck you most in this passage? What did you notice that you hadn't noticed before?
2. St. Luke tells us, "Jesus was praying in a certain place." Many times throughout his Gospel he shows Jesus at prayer. If Christ was God, why did he need to pray? What does this teach us about our own need for personal prayer?
3. What are the most common difficulties facing Christians today who want to have a healthy prayer life? How can Christ's lessons in this passage help us overcome them?
4. How do you think the disciples reacted when Jesus said to them, "If you then, who are evil, know how to give your children what is good..."? Those same words are meant for each of us; how do you react to them? How do you think Christ wants you to react to them?

Cf. Catechism of the Catholic Church, 2759-2865 on the deep meaning of the Our Father; 2734-2745 on trust and persistence in prayer

190. A Closer Look at the Devil (Lk 11:14-26)

"To choose rightly it is necessary to concentrate on the end for which I am created, that is, for the praise of God and for the salvation of my soul." – St. Ignatius of Loyola

LUKE 11:14-26

He was casting out a devil and it was dumb; but when the devil had gone out the dumb man spoke, and the people were amazed. But some of them said, "It is through Beelzebul, the prince of devils, that he casts out devils." Others asked him, as a test, for a sign from heaven; but, knowing what they were thinking, he said to them, "Every kingdom divided against itself is heading for ruin, and a household divided against itself collapses. So too with Satan: if he is divided against himself, how can his kingdom stand?—Since you assert that it is through Beelzebul that I cast out devils. Now if it is through Beelzebul that I cast out devils, through whom do your own experts cast them out? Let them be your judges then. But if it is through the finger of God that I cast out devils, then know that the kingdom of God has overtaken you. So long as a strong man fully armed guards his own palace, his goods are undisturbed; but when someone stronger than he is attacks and defeats him, the stronger man takes away all the weapons he relied on and shares out his spoil. He who is not with me is against me; and he who does not gather with me scatters. When an unclean spirit goes out of a man it wanders through waterless country looking for a place to rest, and not finding one it says, I will go back to the home I came from. But on arrival, finding it swept and tidied, it then goes off and brings seven other spirits more wicked than itself, and they go in and set up house there, so that the man ends up by being worse than he was before."

CHRIST THE LORD The crowds around Jesus ask him to show them an additional sign to disprove the critics who say he is in league with the devil. Jesus shows how superficial that question is. The devil's goal is to enslave men and make them suffer, to keep them from believing in, trusting, and obeying God. Demonic possession is one way of working towards this goal. What could the devil possibly gain from pretending to be his own enemy? Jesus sends the devils out of possessed people as a way of reducing their suffering and restoring their freedom. Doing so inspires people to believe his teaching, which is all about trusting and obeying God. Therefore, no sincere observer could mistake his actions as a deceitful plot of the devil. Those who accuse him of being on the devil's side are obviously not sincere observers, and those who are asking for more signs do so vainly; if they can't rightly interpret the signs Jesus has already given, they won't be able to interpret any sign.

Anyone who looks honestly at the figure of Christ in the Gospels and in the lives of those saints throughout history who have faithfully followed his teachings and example is forced to admit that in him the Kingdom of righteousness (the "stronger man") has overcome the kingdom of evil (the "strong man"). But not everyone takes that honest look. It is the Christian's job to give wavering believers and non-believers countless chances to do so. The Lord will take care of the rest.

CHRIST THE TEACHER Jesus is involved in a spiritual battle. The devil and his minions play an important part in the history of salvation and in the Gospels, as uncomfortable as that may make us feel. In fact, "This was the purpose of the appearing of the Son of God, to undo the work of the devil" (1 Jn 3:8). In our struggles to grow in Christian virtue and build up Christ's Kingdom, we have to always keep this in mind. We are not fighting only against natural obstacles. We are not working in a vacuum. "For it is not against human enemies that we have to struggle, but against the principalities and the ruling forces who are masters of the darkness in this world, the spirits of evil in the heavens" (Eph 6:12).

The most important theater of this war, as Jesus makes clear in his parable, is the human heart, the place where we make decisions. Each day we make thousands of decisions. Every decision is based on a criterion, a goal. If the criteria and goals are in harmony with the true goal of human existence and with Christ's Kingdom, those decisions will be good and thus will contribute to individual and social well-being. The devil wants to stir up selfish motives and self-centered attitudes, so that our decisions will be made as if we were God and everything depended only on ourselves. Christ, through his teaching and his grace, through our conscience and the inspirations of the Holy Spirit, wants to stir up noble and true motives. But neither the devil nor Christ will make our decisions for us. We can make the most of Christ's grace (especially through prayer and the sacraments) to obtain forgiveness and be strengthened in virtue, but as long as we remain on this earth, we will still have to make our own decisions, and we will still be influenced by temptation as well as grace. Life on earth is a mission and an adventure, but it's also an ongoing battle.

CHRIST THE FRIEND Jesus is willing to discuss things with his enemies and with those who doubt, just as the Church is always ready to explain her teachings and listen to the problems and complaints of her children and inquirers. Jesus has been facing opposition since the beginning of his life, but he never loses patience, just as the Church is always willing to receive repentant sinners, no matter how many times they need to repent. Jesus teaches, forgives, invites, and sometimes warns, but he never closes the door to salvation. His love won't let him. Even on the cross itself, as his enemies taunt and deride him, he still showers them with his patient and forgiving love: "Father, forgive them, they do not know what they are doing" (Lk 23:34). His whole life is one huge billboard: "You can trust in me no matter what."

We need to relearn this lesson every day. And we need to do all we can so that our lives continue that same advertising campaign—the salvation of souls depends on it.

CHRIST IN MY LIFE Sometimes I hem and haw about what you are asking me. I ask for signs because I don't want to accept what I know your will is. I don't know how you put up with me, Lord. Teach me humility and docility. Teach me the strength and courage to follow you through thick and thin, trusting all the way...

I know that life is a battle between good and evil, but in the rush of everyday life I forget about it. I don't want to live life on the surface! Save me from skimming along on fashionable and passing preoccupations. I want to go deeper. I want to discover and spread your wisdom, your goodness, and your love...

Patience is so hard for me. But you are perfect in your patience, remaining in the Tabernacle day after day. And you nourish me with your own life, feeding my soul with your virtues in Holy Communion. Activate in my heart the strength of your virtue, so that all I do and say will draw others closer to you instead of pushing them away...

Questions for SMALL-GROUP DISCUSSION

1. What struck you most in this passage? What did you notice that you hadn't noticed before?
2. Why do people continue to resist Christ's teaching so vehemently?
3. What's the difference between temptation and sin?
4. What does popular culture say about spiritual warfare? How does that fit into Christ's teaching?

Cf. Catechism of the Catholic Church, 2087-2094 on faith, hope, and love and the sins against them; 2115-2117 on divination and magic

191. The Most Precious Secret (Lk 11:27-36)

"Man has a noble task: that of prayer and love. To pray and to love, that is the happiness of man on earth." – St. John Vianney

LUKE 11:27-36

Now as he was speaking, a woman in the crowd raised her voice and said, "Happy the womb that bore you and the breasts you sucked!" But he replied, "Still happier those who hear the word of God and keep it!" The crowds got even bigger and he addressed them, "This is a wicked generation; it is asking for a sign. The only sign it will be given is the sign of Jonah. For just as Jonah became a sign to the Ninevites, so will the Son of Man be to this generation. On Judgement day the Queen of the South will rise up with the men of this generation and condemn them, because she came from the ends of the earth to hear the wisdom of Solomon; and there is something greater than Solomon here. On Judgement day the men of Nineveh will stand up with this generation and condemn it, because when Jonah preached they repented; and there is something greater than Jonah here. No one lights a lamp and puts it in some hidden place or under a tub, but on the lamp-stand so that people may see the light when they come in. The lamp of your body is your eye. When your eye is sound, your whole body too is filled with light; but when it is diseased your body too will be all darkness. See to it then that the light inside you is not darkness. If, therefore, your whole body is filled with light, and no trace of darkness, it will be light entirely, as when the lamp shines on you with its rays."

CHRIST THE LORD Jonah's preaching to the Gentile Ninevites led to their repentance and salvation. Solomon's wisdom attracted the Gentile Queen of Sheba and made her into a believer in the one true God. Jesus' preaching and wisdom is far superior to either of theirs, and yet many (and many of the most influential) of his contemporary Jews simply refused to accept him.

The particular greatness of these two Old Testament prophets was that they both brought God's salvation even to non-Jews. In declaring his superiority to both of them, Jesus makes it clear that in him the Messianic era has come; in him the Kingdom of God will be established in such a way so as to fulfill the promise to Abraham that all peoples would be blessed through his descendants. It is possible to become so used to Jesus Christ, that we forget the utter extravagance of his claim. He is the King of all times and places. If we let that truth sink in a bit more thoroughly every day, our lives as his followers and friends will take on a whole new perspective.

CHRIST THE TEACHER Jesus uses an image he has already used—that of the lamp. But he expands on its meaning. Lamps are not meant to be hidden away; they ought to spread light. Just so, each person's life should be full of goodness and generosity, shining with the light of virtue. This is what we were created for—to be full of light ourselves and spread that light around us. But our lives, unlike physical lamps, can fail to achieve their purpose. Instead of being full to overflowing with selfless virtue, we can become full to overflowing with selfish vice. How? What makes the difference?

Jesus makes the answer clear. It depends on our eye. The eye is the organ by which we see. As such, it is a metaphor for our desires, for what we seek—we can only desire what we see. If we desire to love God and love our neighbors, then our eye is bright; if we desire or seek our own self-indulgence and exaltation, then our eye is dark. Our hearts, the seat of our desires and decisions, determine the state of our souls and the fruitfulness of our lives on earth. Jesus is trying to convince us to desire to give, to be like the sun, instead of desiring only to receive, which makes us like a black hole.

CHRIST THE FRIEND It must have warmed Christ's heart to hear the cheer this woman let loose in the middle of his homily. She had detected his goodness and his beauty and couldn't hold back her praise. What a contrast with the many self-righteous intellectuals who sneered at the humble rabbi from Nazareth! But Jesus doesn't luxuriate in the compliment. He seizes the opportunity to reveal the secret that mankind had been seeking since before history began: what makes for a happy life.

The human heart was made to find its true, lasting satisfaction only by living in communion with God, by knowing God and loving God—hearing and heeding God's word. The blessedness that comes from that outstrips even the most profound and worthy natural delights, like that of being parent to a great and wise rabbi. Jesus came to once again make that kind of happiness possible. Whoever trusts in him, follows his teachings, and stays close to him will experience it, just as the example of his closest friend of all time—his mother Mary, whose moral and spiritual beauty he subtly complements in his response to the cheer—eloquently attests to.

CHRIST IN MY LIFE When I take time to think about who you really are, Creator and Redeemer of all things, the infinite One, the all-powerful and all-loving and all-knowing God, I am filled with wonder. And to think that you want to walk with me, to guide my life. You suffered every kind of sorrow and humiliation in order to be able to prepare me a place in your Kingdom. Blessed be your name…

The pace of life often carries me away, and I forget to keep you in my sights. I have to admit, the seductions of pleasure, wealth, popularity, power—they still attract me. Part of me still reaches out to those things. But my eye, the eye of my soul, recognizes that only you and your will can give lasting meaning and fruitfulness. I want you, Lord. Teach me to do your will…

Mary, you treasured in your heart every word of God that came into your life. You sought only to discern and fulfill his will. You are the Queen of all saints and the Seat of Wisdom. Pray for me, and pray for all those people who have been entrusted to my care, in however small a way. Thank you for being our mother and nursing us into the image of Christ. Queen of peace, pray for us…

Questions for *SMALL-GROUP DISCUSSION*

1. What struck you most in this passage? What did you notice that you hadn't noticed before?
2. Where does popular culture indicate happiness can be found? How does that square with what Christ says?
3. If a non-believing but sincerely open friend asked you how he could discover what God was saying to him, how would you respond?
4. Where can we hear God's word, and how can we prepare ourselves better to heed it once we do hear it?

Cf. Catechism of the Catholic Church, 1697, 1718, and 2546 on the path to happiness; on the human desire for happiness; 27, 30, 384, 1028, 1035, and 1723 on happiness coming from God

192. The Pharisees' Failure (Lk 11:37-54)

"And even if I would not confess to you, what could be hidden in me, O Lord, from you to whose eyes the deepest depth of man's conscience lies bare? I should only be hiding you from myself, not myself from you." – St. Augustine

LUKE 11:37-54

He had just finished speaking when a Pharisee invited him to dine at his house. He went in and sat down at the table. The Pharisee saw this and was surprised that he had not first washed before the meal. But the Lord said to him, "Oh, you Pharisees! You clean the outside of cup and plate, while inside yourselves you are filled with extortion and wickedness. Fools! Did not he who made the outside make the inside too? Instead, give alms from what you have and then indeed everything will be clean for you. But alas for you Pharisees! You who pay your tithe of mint and rue and all sorts of garden herbs and overlook justice and the love of God! These you should have practiced, without leaving the others undone. Alas for you Pharisees who like taking the seats of honor in the synagogues and being greeted obsequiously in the market squares! Alas for you, because you are like the unmarked tombs that men walk on without knowing it!"

A lawyer then spoke up. "Master," he said, "when you speak like this you insult us too." "Alas for you lawyers also," he replied, "because you load on men burdens that are unendurable, burdens that you yourselves do not move a finger to lift. Alas for you who build the tombs of the prophets, the men your ancestors killed! In this way you both witness what your ancestors did and approve it; they did the killing, you do the building. And that is why the Wisdom of God said, I will send them prophets and apostles; some they will slaughter and persecute, so that this generation will have to answer for every prophet's blood that has been shed since the foundation of the world, from the blood of Abel to the blood of Zechariah, who was murdered between the altar and the sanctuary. Yes, I tell you, this generation will have to answer for it all. Alas for you lawyers who have taken away the key of knowledge! You have not gone in yourselves, and have prevented others going in who wanted to." When he left the house, the scribes and the Pharisees began a furious attack on him and tried to force answers from him on innumerable questions, setting traps to catch him out in something he might say.

CHRIST THE LORD Jesus seems to treat his host and the other guests harshly. Their furious reaction seems perfectly reasonable. Was our Lord disrespectful and out of place in this diatribe? Not at all.

In the first place, Jesus is now reaching the end of his public ministry, and still the Pharisees, scribes, and other leading Jews of the time, in spite of being perfectly aware of Jesus' impeccable selflessness, his incomparable wisdom and knowledge of the Scriptures, and his truly divine power (he has healed every kind of disease, raised people from the dead, commanded the forces of nature, and sent scores of demons scuttling back to hell)—in spite of being witnesses of all this, many of the Jewish leaders still refuse to believe in him. Time is running short. Jesus knows that to win over any of them who aren't yet believers, he must change tactics. No longer the patient argument and indirect evidence; the time has come to rattle their self-confidence. He will shake them up and make them face their own consciences. His harsh critique flows from his determined love, not from a self-indulgent loss of composure.

In the second place, St. Luke informs us that the conversation took place in a Pharisee's private residence. Jesus levels his criticisms to his opponents' faces. He confronts them head-on, not by launching attacks through third parties or public declarations. To the end, Christ tempers his Lordship with the tact and respect shown only by the most faithful of friends, even to those (including us) who resist his rule and who don't really deserve his friendship.

CHRIST THE TEACHER The Pharisees and the scribes (called "lawyers" here) were the religious leaders of ancient Palestine. The scribes dedicated themselves to studying the scriptures (the law of Moses and the prophets). They knew them backwards and forwards, and through the centuries they had derived an elaborate code of conduct that applied those scriptures to every possible permutation of daily living. For instance, it was forbidden to lift and carry items on the Sabbath. But what if you were to lift just a feather, or lift some food to your mouth? Or what if you were to carry something on the back of your hand instead of in your hand? The scribes' expertise could cover every scenario. And the Pharisees carried out what the scribes taught. The immense code of religious rituals that had accumulated through the ages was too demanding for most normal people to fulfill, but the Pharisees (their name means "the separated ones") were zealously dedicated to being exemplary in every detail.

Together, then, the Pharisees and scribes were supposed to inspire and guide the Jews in Palestine, bringing them closer to God and maintaining religious fervor among the people. But, as is clear from Jesus' description, they had utterly failed to do so. The scribes had turned their intellectual expertise inside out by weaving loopholes into every corner of the law, loopholes that only they could understand and take advantage of. The Pharisees had become so obsessed by their minute attention to externals that they had emptied their religion of its essence: "to act justly, to love tenderly and to walk humbly with your God" (Mi 6:8). They condemned the great bulk of the population that tried to love God and neighbor but couldn't keep up with the morass of external regulations. Thus these leaders were like "unmarked tombs"—by law touching such a tomb, even if you didn't know it, would make you ritually unclean. (Tombs were usually next to major roads, so it was easy to come into contact with old, overgrown ones.) Just so, the majority of Jews at the time who came into contact with the Pharisees and scribes thought they were learning from them the principles of true religion, but in fact they were being poisoned with false ideas about God. An important lesson for us is to learn to live more out of love than by the law, looking seriously into our own lives before condemning the Pharisees and scribes, lest we unknowingly condemn ourselves with them.

CHRIST THE FRIEND A Pharisee: *When I first heard this young rabbi excoriate us, I was deeply offended. But something about his words and manner struck me. He was gaining nothing for himself by laying bare our hypocrisy. The light that flashed from his eyes as he spoke was the light of righteousness, but not self-righteousness. Although his lesson was bitter, it was true. Throughout our history, many of Israel's mainstream leaders rejected, disobeyed, and even murdered the prophets God sent to guide them. There was no denying this. We had tried to make up for it by honoring those previously rejected prophets. We even decorated their tombs, just as he said. Yet, John the Baptist spoke and lived as a prophet, and we turned up our noses at him. Jesus himself, as ordinary and unschooled as he seemed to be, performed works that only someone with God's favor could perform, but* *we never tired of looking for ways to discredit him. It occurred to me then that maybe he was right—maybe we were following the example of the wrong ancestors in rejecting him. Subsequent events proved that this was indeed the case. Our rejection was even graver than the previous ones, since Jesus was the Lord himself and not merely the Lord's ambassador. It also had a greater repercussion: the end of the Old Covenant, the destruction of the Temple, and the scattering of the Jews in a new Diaspora. Repeatedly he tried to show us, but our arrogance blinded us. He offered us a friendship that would last forever, but we preferred the passing glory of popularity and earthly power.*

CHRIST IN MY LIFE I don't think I am like the Pharisees. But maybe I am. I am quick to judge people who have a different idea of what it means to follow you. I am quick to pay attention to other people's faults so that my own good points stand out. And that's not what you want from me. With the love of your heart, Lord, inflame my heart…

Sometimes I don't know whether to speak out or keep quiet. Sometimes I can't tell whether my anger is righteous or disordered. I need your guidance, Lord! I want to be courageous, but prudent. I want to be sincere, but respectful. I want to be coherent, but kind. This is what you were like, and I just want to follow in your footsteps. Teach me to do your will…

I am afraid that I am not hearing your voice, Lord, just as the Pharisees didn't hear it. Is my arrogance making me deaf? Are you correcting and guiding me through the words of my spiritual guide, my spouse, my boss, my teachers? You are all-powerful, Lord. You can break through my barriers. Teach me to be docile, to hear your word, no matter how much it hurts…

Questions for *SMALL-GROUP DISCUSSION*

1. What struck you most in this passage? What did you notice that you hadn't noticed before?
2. Jesus' critique shows that he understood these men inside and out. Why do we tend to judge others without first striving to know them as best as we can?
3. Everything Jesus said about the Pharisees and scribes was true. Why do you think they reacted by attacking him instead of by repenting?
4. In what situations are we most frequently tempted to react to Christ as the Pharisees did?

Cf. Catechism of the Catholic Church, 1581-1589 on a portrait of Church ministers; 2546 on humility of heart

THE GOSPEL OF LUKE
Chapter 12

"... I went across the garden one afternoon and stopped on the shore of the lake; I stood there for a long time, contemplating my surroundings. Suddenly, I saw the Lord Jesus near me, and he graciously said to me, 'All this I created for you, my spouse; and know that all this beauty is nothing compared to what I have prepared for you in eternity.' My soul was inundated with such consolation that I stayed there until evening, and it seemed to me like a brief moment."

- ST. FAUSTINA KOWALSKA

193. Courage and Confidence (Lk 12:1-12)

"God does not expect us to be successful but to be faithful." – St. Teresa of Calcutta

LUKE 12:1-12

Meanwhile the people had gathered in their thousands so that they were treading on one another. And he began to speak, first of all to his disciples. "Be on your guard against the yeast of the Pharisees—that is, their hypocrisy. Everything that is now covered will be uncovered, and everything now hidden will be made clear. For this reason, whatever you have said in the dark will be heard in the daylight, and what you have whispered in hidden places will be proclaimed on the housetops.

"To you my friends I say: Do not be afraid of those who kill the body and after that can do no more. I will tell you whom to fear: fear him who, after he has killed, has the power to cast into hell. Yes, I tell you, fear him. Can you not buy five sparrows for two pennies? And yet not one is forgotten in God's sight. Why, every hair on your head has been counted. There is no need to be afraid: you are worth more than hundreds of sparrows. I tell you, if anyone openly declares himself for me in the presence of men, the Son of Man will declare himself for him in the presence of God's angels. But the man who disowns me in the presence of men will be disowned in the presence of God's angels. Everyone who says a word against the Son of Man will be forgiven, but he who blasphemes against the Holy Spirit will not be forgiven. When they take you before synagogues and magistrates and authorities, do not worry about how to defend yourselves or what to say, because when the time comes, the Holy Spirit will teach you what you must say."

CHRIST THE LORD As Jesus makes his way to Jerusalem for his final showdown and the consummation of his mission, St. Luke takes pains to show us the gradual but substantial increase in the number of people following him. In the previous chapter, St. Luke wrote, "The crowds got even bigger..." (11:29)—implying that the already huge gathering was still growing. Now the massive audience is stadium-sized or bigger (the Greek term translated here as "thousands" literally means "tens of thousands"), so much so that "they were treading on one another."

With such a following, Jesus could have easily organized a revolt and usurped power from the corrupt Sanhedrin and maybe even from the Roman procurator (no more than two legions of soldiers, 12,000 men, were stationed throughout the entire province of Palestine). But his Kingdom is not of this world, and so he wields his Lordship in a different way. He continues to instruct his apostles privately, still training them for their future mission as leaders of the Church. And he continues teaching the crowds publicly, making sure that they learn how to set their sights on eternal life. This Lord's weapons are truth and love, not bullets, bombs, and bludgeons. We who are his ambassadors should take careful note.

CHRIST THE TEACHER The lesson Jesus gives his apostles at the beginning of this passage should instill a healthy fear in every Christian heart. He tells them to beware of the leaven of the Pharisees (with whom he has just had another verbal tussle)—i.e., their hypocrisy. The Pharisees were posers. They cared only about the external appearance of religion and what people thought and said about them, not about the state of their souls, the virtue in their hearts, or the truth in their minds. That much is clear, but why warn the apostles about it—why warn those who believe in him? Because the apostles too were called by God to be leaders, to be the little bit of leaven that affects the whole loaf for good or ill. And the great temptation of anyone in a position of leadership, however small the position may be, is hypocrisy.

The power and esteem that goes with leadership can be intoxicating. It can lead to a reversal of values: instead of using one's influence strictly for the good of others, you begin to care more about simply staying in power. Then the truth—and the true good—inevitably takes a backseat to expediency. And the worst aspect of all is that it's almost irreversible. The Pharisees had completely lost touch with what was right, because they were completely fixated on what was useful to themselves. Every leader, including the leaders of Christ's Church, must be on their guard "against the leaven of the Pharisees," because in the end, the truth will come out.

CHRIST THE FRIEND Jesus' message to the vast crowd is different. He exhorts them to confidence and courage. Our confidence in the face of life's trials should be unlimited, because God cares more about us than we can possibly imagine, numbering even the hairs on our heads. If he keeps an eye even on the fifth sparrow that's thrown into the bag without charge when a person pays enough for four—a sparrow worth absolutely nothing—how could he not keep his watchful, loving eye on each one of us, for whom he went to such trouble in order to save? And our courage should be unflinching. If we are in friendship with God, and if we boldly bear witness to that friendship in word and deed, then what could we possibly have to fear? Will God's loyalty be outmatched by man's hostility? Even if at times it seems so, in the end God's fidelity will shine forth like the sun.

"Do not be afraid… There is no need to fear… Do not worry…." If anyone else were to repeat this comforting injunction so insistently, we would do well to be skeptical. But when the Lord is the one making the point, we don't have to hesitate at all. He is in charge of our lives. However much responsibility or influence we wield, we will always be at peace and never go astray if we always keep that simple fact in mind. Humble courage and unshakable confidence are par for the course when we're at the side of this Friend.

CHRIST IN MY LIFE You are so familiar to me. I go to Mass with humdrum regularity; I receive Holy Communion so mechanically; I open the Bible so casually. Remind me, Lord, of your majesty, your greatness, and your infinite attraction. I need to be reminded, not because I want to live my life based on fickle feelings, but because I am weak and self-absorbed and forget. Lord, increase my faith…

I could become a hypocrite, a Pharisee. It's true. How can I be on my guard? I never want to become so attached to my personal preferences that I completely drown out your voice. And yet, you warn me that I can. Lord, let's make a deal right now: I will always say yes to whatever you ask of me, and you promise never to abandon me…

There's something that seems too good to be true about the sparrows and the numbering of each hair on my head. And yet I know that the truth is even more magnificent, more marvelous! Your love is beyond my wildest imagining, and it's personal. You know my name, you think of me unceasingly, and you guide me untiringly. I believe in you, Lord; I love you…

Questions for SMALL-GROUP DISCUSSION

1. What struck you most in this passage? What did you notice that you hadn't noticed before?
2. In what situations is it particularly hard to bear witness to Christ? How can we do better in those situations?
3. Why is it so hard to accept that Christ's love for each of us is total and unconditional? And if we accept it, why do we not always obey his will manifested through the Church and through our conscience?
4. If an agnostic friend of yours came up to you and asked how he could know that God loves him, how would you respond?

Cf. Catechism of the Catholic Church, 1805, and 1808 on fortitude as a cardinal virtue; 712, 1303, 1831, and 2846 on fortitude and courage as gifts of the Holy Spirit; 1864 on blasphemy against the Holy Spirit

194. Not of This World (Lk 12:13-21)

"All Christians, rich or poor, must keep their eye fixed on heaven, remembering that 'we have not here a lasting city, but we seek one that is to come' (Heb 13:14)." – Pope Pius XI

LUKE 12:13-21

A man in the crowd said to him, "Master, tell my brother to give me a share of our inheritance." "My friend," he replied—"who appointed me your judge, or the arbitrator of your claims?" Then he said to them, "Watch, and be on your guard against avarice of any kind, for a man's life is not made secure by what he owns, even when he has more than he needs." Then he told them a parable: "There was once a rich man who, having had a good harvest from his land, thought to himself, What am I to do? I have not enough room to store my crops. Then he said, This is what I will do: I will pull down my barns and build bigger ones, and store all my grain and my goods in them, and I will say to my soul: 'My soul, you have plenty of good things laid by for many years to come; take things easy, eat, drink, have a good time.' But God said to him, 'Fool! This very night the demand will be made for your soul; and this hoard of yours, whose will it be then?' So it is when a man stores up treasure for himself in place of making himself rich in the sight of God."

CHRIST THE LORD At the end of his earthly life, Jesus will point out to Pontius Pilate, "My Kingdom is not of this world." He gives the same answer to this man's request for probate justice—he refuses to usurp the normal functions of earthly, human justice. Christ came not to take over the world, but to imbue it with a new spirit, to redeem it from within through grace. Jesus came to establish a Kingdom—a heavenly Kingdom, a Kingdom unlike any other kingdom of this world. This was his mission, and through the Church, it remains his mission.

By refusing to arbitrate this man's legal complaint, Jesus exemplifies the kind of mission-centered mindset that all of his disciples should share. Jesus refuses to be sidetracked. He knows exactly what his task in life is, and he dedicates himself to it with unwavering love and total focus. He directs all his words and actions to laying the foundations of his eternal Kingdom. The more closely we follow Christ and imitate his example, the more focused our own lives will be. We too are called to make the eternal Kingdom our first priority (cf. Mt 6:33). If we do, the rest of our lives will fall into place; we will be able to navigate more surely through shoals and straits of our earthly pilgrimage. If we know clearly where we are headed (our heavenly destination), we will be better equipped to make decisions at every juncture along the way. Either we follow the Lord, or we wander aimlessly through an empty life.

CHRIST THE TEACHER Perhaps this inquirer was sincerely interested in justice, and his brother was being unfair, or perhaps he was just being greedy. In either case, Jesus makes the most of this encounter to teach one of the most basic (though not the most popular) Christian lessons: "Man's life is not made secure by what he owns"—our lives do not consist in having possessions.

Earlier in the Gospel, Jesus had put this lesson into action in order to resist the devil's temptation, when he averred, "Man does not live on bread alone" (Lk 4:4). We can almost hear a pleading tone in Christ's response to this man: "Watch, and be on your guard against avarice of all kind. . . ." He knows how easily we tend to equate happiness with things and security with wealth. But he also knows, better than anyone, how wrong we are when we do. We are pilgrims on this earth, travelers. This life is a preparation for heaven, an opportunity to discover the beauty of God and opt for it. But our hearts will be ever restless here on earth until they rest completely in him (cf. St. Augustine's

Confessions, 1:1), which will never happen if we keep them too firmly attached to other things.

We need possessions and material things of all kinds in order to live, and it is certainly no sin to enjoy them, but if we strive after them to the exclusion or neglect of our relationship with God, the Church, and our neighbors, we will come to a tragic end, just like the rich man in the parable. The way to true fulfillment and stability is to make oneself "rich in the sight of God."

CHRIST THE FRIEND Jesus calls his interlocutor "My friend," and then proceeds to refuse his request. Was he just being polite by saying "friend"? Maybe. But maybe he was saying exactly what he meant: "I have come to be the true Friend and Savior of your soul, which doesn't always include managing your bank account for you. You can count on me to give you light, guidance, and strength, and to walk with you along life's path, but you still must walk."

Sometimes we doubt God's love because he doesn't remove all the obstacles along our way, but does a truly loving father take the easy way out and spoil his children? God seeks the true good of his children, and that often differs from what appears to us to be our immediate good. Jesus saw that this man was too attached to material things, and his refusal to resolve the difficulty helps spur the man to reorder his priorities. Christ is our Friend precisely because he never loses sight of our real goal—communion with God starting now and finishing in heaven—and because he never tires of leading us closer to it.

CHRIST IN MY LIFE I get sidetracked too easily. Sometimes I feel like the salvation of the whole world, the resolution of every conflict, the righting of every wrong is up to me. But it's not—it's up to you. And you give me a share of your work. Help me to be as serenely and energetically focused on my mission as you were on yours. Teach me to do your will…

What should I think about money, Lord? In this world, I can't do much without it. But whether I have it or not, it's constantly trying to take hold of me. Teach me to be responsible and smart. Save me from slavery to wealth and the things it can buy. I became your soldier on the day of my confirmation. Help me to persevere every day in fighting for the Kingdom that does not end…

How many times I have been like this man, who wanted you to resolve all his difficulties! But you will never do that. My difficulties are opportunities to get to know myself, to exercise virtue, and to grow in my discipleship. Others' difficulties are my opportunities to show them your goodness and build your Kingdom. Instead of getting discouraged in the face of difficulties, help me to turn to you who will always be there to show me the path and the way to follow it...

Questions for SMALL-GROUP DISCUSSION

1. What struck you most in this passage? What did you notice that you hadn't noticed before?
2. What can we do to become more aware of our mission in life, and how can we stick to it with the same focus and dedication that Christ had?
3. What is popular culture's view of material wealth? (Try to think of some examples.) What would Christ say about it?
4. What are the most common difficulties we face in living out our faith? To what extent do they stem from objective hardship and to what extent do they stem from immature expectations?

Cf. Catechism of the Catholic Church, 2401-2418 on a Christian view of material possessions; 1854-1869 on the gravity and proliferation of sin

195. Setting Our Hearts Straight (Lk 12:22-31)

"Through love for man he created all these things, so that all those creatures should serve man, and that man in gratitude for so many gifts should return love for love to his Creator." – St. Alphonsus Liguori

LUKE 12:22-31

Then he said to his disciples, "That is why I am telling you not to worry about your life and what you are to eat, nor about your body and how you are to clothe it. For life means more than food, and the body more than clothing. Think of the ravens. They do not sow or reap; they have no storehouses and no barns; yet God feeds them. And how much more are you worth than the birds! Can any of you, for all his worrying, add a single cubit to his span of life? If the smallest things, therefore, are outside your control, why worry about the rest? Think of the flowers; they never have to spin or weave; yet, I assure you, not even Solomon in all his regalia was robed like one of these. Now if that is how God clothes the grass in the field which is there today and thrown into the furnace tomorrow, how much more will he look after you, you men of little faith! But you, you must not set your hearts on things to eat and things to drink; nor must you worry. It is the pagans of this world who set their hearts on all these things. Your Father well knows you need them. No; set your hearts on his kingdom, and these other things will be given you as well."

CHRIST THE LORD Jesus is still speaking to the enormous crowds that have gathered around him as he makes his way to Jerusalem. In this part of his discourse, he wants to tell them about God. The people listening to him already believed in God, and they were even familiar with God's self-revelation in the Old Testament, but judging from Christ's words here, they had yet to grasp God's most important quality.

Our idea of God affects how we relate to God. That idea has been played upon by myriad influences, many of them bad. Unless we constantly purify and rectify our idea of God, we will simply never flourish the way he wants us to, because our relationship with him will never be able to mature. At this point in the Gospel, Jesus has proven his privileged relationship with the Father. And by his own actions and manner, he has made God's goodness visible, tangible to everyone who has seen him. But still the idea of a distant, harsh taskmaster lingers. So now Jesus complements his actions with these words. We have heard them many times, but we can never get enough of them. To follow the Lord as he wants to be followed, we have constantly to renew our vision of his utter goodness.

CHRIST THE TEACHER Jesus understands the Father as sheer, ever-present goodness. Christ himself, by the way he treated others and the way he carried out his mission, imaged the sheer part of that goodness—totally unconditional, a pure outpouring of generosity; that's what God is. But creation, often called "the first book of revelation" by the Church Fathers, illustrates the ever-present part. Jesus turns his listeners' gazes to the simple realities of nature—flowers, birds, growth—and unveils their real meaning: God is the one who upholds every atom of it. He does so effortlessly, wisely, generously, not looking for anything in return. The beauty and fruitfulness of nature—which are completely outside our control—flow directly from the power and love of God. If the Father is so attentive to the rest of creation, which will all pass away, how much more attentive will he be to his own children, who will live forever—us!

Having made the concept clear—God's goodness is sheer, endless, attentive, all-powerful, ever-present—Jesus then goes on to apply this point of doctrine to our lives. If God is upholding and guarding and guiding us in each moment, then why do we give in to worries and anxieties? Every worry, every anxiety about the material things of life—health, sickness, money, food, success, reputation—stems from a lack of trust in God. These things are all passing, and if we are faithful to our normal responsibilities, God will provide whatever we need for our life's mission. Instead of living as if the meaning of life were to be found in such things, Jesus invites us—in fact, he commands us—to live with our hearts "set on his Kingdom." Our first and sole concern in life, according to Christ, should be to know and follow him better, to discover, embrace, and fulfill his will. And if he commands this of us, then it must be possible. In this lies the entire spiritual life: training ourselves under the guidance and grace of the Holy Spirit to pay more and more attention to loving God and our neighbors and focusing less and less attention on our natural tantrums of self-absorption.

CHRIST THE FRIEND Jesus simplifies everything with this discourse. He brings the whole complicated, intimidating, impenetrable mystery of the human predicament into perfect focus. All we need to do on our journey through life is let God be God and follow where he leads. But Jesus is never satisfied with mere book lessons. His incarnation, the example he gives by his life, ministry, death, and Resurrection, reveals what "setting your hearts on the Kingdom" looks like in practice. And just in case that wasn't enough, he decided to establish his Church so that his teaching could be kept intact even as historical and cultural conditions changed through time. But even that left him unsatisfied, so he stayed with us in the Tabernacle. With just a little bit of faith, then, we can make good use of all these gifts in order to delight our Savior and become what he has always hoped we would be.

CHRIST IN MY LIFE At times the beauty of your creation overwhelms me. It shows your majesty and your delicacy—mountains and mockingbirds. And you who made and uphold that immense menagerie, you care about me too. In fact, because your love is divine, you care about me as if I were the only one here. Help this truth sink in, Lord, so that I can live freely and love as you love…

What worries me most often and most intensely? And what do you think about that? It should be enough that I do what I can do and leave the rest to you. Aren't my worries, sometimes at least, a subtle type of self-indulgence? Jesus, I don't understand myself. I put myself at your service. Lord Jesus, I believe that you are the Lord of life and history—and of my life and history…

How can I love you more than simply trusting in you at all times? Is that not the best expression of my love for you? Why do I still seek to love you by my achievements when I can't even add an inch to my height or a minute to my life? I want to love you, and I want to trust you. Your love and goodness have no end. Jesus, I trust in you…

Questions for *SMALL-GROUP DISCUSSION*

1. What struck you most in this passage? What did you notice that you hadn't noticed before?
2. Why do we tend to worry about things we have no control over?
3. How can we learn to benefit more from "the first book of God's revelation," his creation?
4. If God is our Father who takes care of all our needs, why are there so many natural disasters and privations in the world (starvation, war, drought…)? How could he possibly be loving us even in and through these? 324, 4 Catechism

Cf. Catechism of the Catholic Church, 313-314 and 322 on God's providence; 396-401 on the role of trust in original sin; 222-231 on the implications of having "faith in one God"; 2544-2550 on the secret to happiness.

When Bad Things Happen to Good People Kushner

196. True Treasure (Lk 12:32-48)

"To become what the martyrs, the apostles, what even Christ himself was, means immense labor–but what a reward!" –St. Jerome

LUKE 12:32-48

"There is no need to be afraid, little flock, for it has pleased your Father to give you the kingdom. Sell your possessions and give alms. Get yourselves purses that do not wear out, treasure that will not fail you, in heaven where no thief can reach it and no moth destroy it. For where your treasure is, there will your heart be also. See that you are dressed for action and have your lamps lit. Be like men waiting for their master to return from the wedding feast, ready to open the door as soon as he comes and knocks. Happy those servants whom the master finds awake when he comes. I tell you solemnly, he will put on an apron, sit them down at table and wait on them. It may be in the second watch he comes, or in the third, but happy those servants if he finds them ready. You may be quite sure of this, that if the householder had known at what hour the burglar would come, he would not have let anyone break through the wall of his house. You too must stand ready, because the Son of Man is coming at an hour you do not expect."

Peter said, "Lord, do you mean this parable for us, or for everyone?" The Lord replied, "What sort of steward, then, is faithful and wise enough for the master to place him over his household to give them their allowance of food at the proper time? Happy that servant if his master's arrival finds him at this employment. I tell you truly, he will place him over everything he owns. But as for the servant who says to himself, 'My master is taking his time coming,' and sets about beating the menservants and the maids, and eating and drinking and getting drunk, his master will come on a day he does not expect and at an hour he does not know. The master will cut him off and send him to the same fate as the unfaithful. The servant who knows what his master wants, but has not even started to carry out those wishes, will receive very many strokes of the lash. The one who did not know, but deserves to be beaten for what he has done, will receive fewer strokes. When a man has had a great deal given him, a great deal will be demanded of him; when a man has had a great deal given him on trust, even more will be expected of him."

CHRIST THE LORD In these parables, Christ portrays himself as the master of the house, his apostles as the stewards (the head servants), and his other disciples as the servants. Even when the master is absent (as during the age of the Church, when Christ delegates his authority to the successors of his apostles), he is still in charge, and he expects his servants to be faithful. He wants to return to his estate and see them working hard, full of joy and enthusiasm as they strive not only to keep the estate going, but to make it thrive. He didn't have to go away. He could have stayed and taken care of things himself, but he wanted to share his responsibility with us. He wants us to be his responsible followers, freely and energetically putting our talents at the service of something that will last forever.

Although he gives us real responsibility as his coworkers, he still remains the Lord. Christ's Kingdom is truly a Kingdom, with an authoritative King—not an elected president. His Church is the seed of this Kingdom in history, and so it too is hierarchical, with real authority. When we call ourselves Christians, we acknowledge ourselves as followers of Christ, trusting that he knows how and where to lead.

We can easily forget that being entrusted with work in Christ's Kingdom is a blessing and a grace. As in the case of the first apostles, the mission of building up the Church gives our ordinary, earthly lives an extraordinary, heavenly dimension. Being a servant in the Kingdom of Christ is such a precious gift that the Queen of Heaven herself glories in being called "the handmaid of the Lord" (Lk 1:38).

CHRIST THE TEACHER This part of Jesus' discourse balances out what he said a few verses earlier about not worrying. He instructed his listeners not to fret about worldly concerns, but lest they take that as an excuse for irresponsible and hedonistic living, he now shows the other side of the coin.

"You too must stand ready," is the first lesson of this passage. You can't cram for life's final exam. If we want to live in communion with God forever, we need to start cultivating that friendship now, making it our first priority. After all, what could be more important than our friendship with God? The good things of this earthly life, its pleasures, challenges, and occupations, will come to an end. To live as if they won't, therefore, is foolish. Christ wants to make sure we don't act like fools.

"When a man has had a great deal given him, a great deal will be demanded of him; when a man has had a great deal given him on trust, even more will be expected of him." Each human life has a task, a mission to know, love, and serve God in a particular way. Our lives will take on their true meaning to the extent that we carry out that task and fulfill that mission—to the extent that our "treasure" (what we value and desire) consists of that task and mission. We are responsible for making good use of the gifts we have received from God (our lives, our talents, our education) in order to accomplish our mission. Christ's view of the universe doesn't include reincarnation—a concept which takes away all personal responsibility, since everyone is just recycled over and over again until they have no choice but to hit on the right combination of circumstances and decisions. The Christian view involves responsibility, and this enables us to love, because love means freely choosing to put oneself and one's talents at the service of another's good. That's what God created us for, and that's how we image God. If, on the other hand, we squander our time, talents, and gifts in self-indulgence and egoism, we will miss out on what Christ wants to give us.

CHRIST THE FRIEND "There is no need to be afraid, little flock...." Jesus came to bring us back into communion with God, to plug us in to heaven, so that even now we can begin to taste the joy and peace that will never end. But he doesn't force us to receive this gift of the Kingdom that it has pleased the Father to give us. We need to let go of the false idols that can't give us the happiness we seek ("sell your possessions and give alms") and realign our hearts so that they lean more consistently towards God. If we store up our hopes (our "treasure") in the heart of Christ, we will certainly not be disappointed; if we store them up anywhere else, we certainly will.

Jesus: In my eyes, the Church is still a little flock, my little flock. Though it includes millions of members throughout the world, and millions more if you include past and future centuries, my heart is big enough to love each one of you personally, intimately. You are my little flock. You have nothing to fear. I am your shepherd, and I am leading you to the grassy pastures and cool, refreshing streams around my Father's house.

CHRIST IN MY LIFE Bless the pope, Lord, and all the bishops and priests. Calm the winds of infidelity and disobedience and pour out the Spirit of wisdom and piety on your Church. I want to be faithful to you and to the friendship you offer me, and I know that means being faithful to your Church. Make me a builder of your Kingdom, Lord, not a nitpicker and complainer…

You have given me a mission in life, and you have given me the freedom to put all my talents and gifts at the service of fulfilling that mission. I am not a squirrel, which isn't free to abandon its little mission. You have given me your greatest gift, the capacity to love. Lord Jesus, with the love of your heart, inflame my heart…

What is holding me back from being all that you created me to be? Is it an unrestrained selfish desire, maybe one I don't even recognize? Is it a self-indulgent relationship? Is it a continuous refusal to give you something you are asking me? Shed light into my heart and conscience, Lord, so that I don't deceive myself and squander this wonderful life you have given me…

Questions for *SMALL-GROUP DISCUSSION*

1. What struck you most in this passage? What did you notice that you hadn't noticed before?
2. Where does popular culture advise us to "store up our treasure"?
3. Why do you think the "master of the house" goes away for a while, leaving his household in charge of the stewards and servants?
4. What is the "great deal" that we have been given, and how can we insure that it yields what the Giver is expecting?

Cf. Catechism of the Catholic Church, 1038-1050 on the Last Judgment and the New Heaven and the New Earth; 1020-1022 on death and the particular judgment; 1023-1037 on heaven, hell, and purgatory ↑pg. 266

197. Reading the Signs (Lk 12:49-59)

"Very many out there fail to become Christians simply because there is nobody available to make them Christian." – St. Francis Xavier

LUKE 12:49-59

"I have come to bring fire to the earth, and how I wish it were blazing already! There is a baptism I must still receive, and how great is my distress till it is over! Do you suppose that I am here to bring peace on earth? No, I tell you, but rather division. For from now on a household of five will be divided: three against two and two against three; the father divided against the son, son against father, mother against daughter, daughter against mother, mother-in-law against daughter-in-law, daughter-in-law against mother-in-law." He said again to the crowds, "When you see a cloud looming up in the west you say at once that rain is coming, and so it does. And when the wind is from the south you say it will be hot, and it is. Hypocrites! You know how to interpret the face of the earth and the sky. How is it you do not know how to interpret these times? Why not judge for yourselves what is right? For example: when you go to court with your opponent, try to settle with him on the way, or he may drag you before the judge and the judge hand you over to the bailiff and the bailiff have you thrown into prison. I tell you, you will not get out till you have paid the very last penny."

CHRIST THE LORD From the vantage point of twenty centuries of the Church's growth, it is easy for us to understand what Christ meant when he said he came "to set the earth on fire." He was speaking of the fire of Christian charity that will bring souls back into communion with God and gradually build up the civilization of justice and love. But imagine the reaction of the apostles and the other disciples—they must have been perplexed, perhaps frightened, maybe energized by such a claim. Though the fire has spread since it first appeared, the whole earth has certainly not yet been set ablaze. So the same zeal to extend his Kingdom that animated him then still animates him now, and if we truly love our Lord, it will burn in our hearts too.

We find it easy to criticize the people of Christ's day for not recognizing more readily the signs of God's action—John the Baptist's preaching, Christ's own ministry. Yet the same Christ is unceasingly at work in our little worlds each day, and we still continue to put off those decisions that will give his grace free rein in our lives. We truly are like that man walking to court with his opponent, because we are journeying through the world to heaven, where we will discover, to our dismay, all the opportunities for doing good that we casually passed by, overly preoccupied as we were with the sports page, the latest fashion trends, the stock index, and any number of other worthy but secondary realities. If we think it's easy to spot the blindness of Christ's contemporaries, just imagine what the saints in heaven think of us as we amble through life satisfied with spiritual mediocrity.

CHRIST THE TEACHER Nothing is more important than our friendship with Christ. When he calls us, when he makes his will known, not even the closest natural ties (like those we have with our mother and father) are worthy constrainers. The peace that comes with following Christ is the peace of a heart in communion with God and of a conscience cleansed of all self-deprecation. If we expect some other, exterior peace—a smooth ride through life, for instance—we are in for a shock. The demands of Christ are so absolute that they will necessarily bring us into conflict with the demands of the fallen world, of other people, and even of our own sin-struck nature. This conflict of interests is built into the heart of Christianity; it appears on the cross itself, which is an intersection of the vertical and the horizontal, the heavenly and the earthly, God's will and my will. Of course, if we are faithful to him, he will be faithful to us, and what we thought we had lost for his sake we will receive back a hundredfold.

CHRIST THE FRIEND The word "baptize" comes from the Greek word for dip or submerge (it also has other uses, such as to wash), and it was often used to refer to a tribulation or a trial through which one had to pass. Christ's choice of the term shows us what he felt about his journey to Calvary and the cross—it was not going to be easy. The thought of it was always with him: "... how great is my distress till it is over..." Although we will never be able fully to understand the depth of suffering that our Lord has endured for our sake, we can acknowledge the fact that he has endured it and welcome the love this fact implies.

Yet, his self-sacrifice on our behalf is more than a sign of his love and more than an example to follow. In a mysterious way, his fidelity actually becomes our fidelity. Because he has been our faithful Friend, we can be his faithful friend. The grace we receive through the sacraments nourishes our souls with Christ's very life. He is faithful, and in him we can be faithful too.

CHRIST IN MY LIFE Why is it so hard for me to read the "signs of the times" in my own life? I know they are there, and I know you are always wanting to guide me and teach me and show me the way to go. I believe that. So why don't I see them more clearly? Maybe I'm looking for the wrong kind of signs. Teach me, Lord, to be simple, like a child, satisfied with knowing your will for me each moment...

It's hard for me to disregard what others think and say of me. I still hope for the kind of peace that I mistakenly think will satisfy me—relief from all opposition, discomfort, and suffering. Fill my heart so full of love for you, Lord, that I jump at every chance to show that love, thinking less and less of my comfort zone, and more and more of your Kingdom...

You came to earth for me. You left heaven behind and worked and toiled and sweat for thirty years, just so you could be close to me. And then, to make sure I would never doubt your unconditional love for me, you freely accepted the indescribable suffering of Good Friday. Thank you, Lord. I believe in you. Jesus, I trust in you...

Questions for *SMALL-GROUP DISCUSSION*

1. What struck you most in this passage? What did you notice that you hadn't noticed before?
2. What can we do to more deeply share Christ's zeal for the salvation of souls and the extension of his Kingdom?
3. What "divisions" have you experienced as a result of following Christ? What would be the hardest thing for you to give up in order to remain faithful to him?
4. Why do you think Christ spoke so openly about his "wish" and his "distress"? Why did St. Luke consider it important enough to include in his Gospel?

Cf. Catechism of the Catholic Church, 456-460 on the mission of Jesus; 606-618 on the "baptism" of Jesus

THE GOSPEL OF LUKE
Chapter 13

"Wake up, O man—it was for you that God was made man! Awake, O sleeper, and arise from the dead, and Christ shall give you light. For you, I say, was God made man. Eternal death would have awaited you had he not been born in time. Never would you be freed from your sinful flesh, had he not taken to himself the likeness of sinful flesh. Everlasting would be your misery, had he not performed this act of mercy. You would not have come to life again, had he not come to die your death. You would have broken down, had he not come to help you. You would have perished, had he not come. Let us joyfully celebrate the coming of our salvation and redemption."

- ST. AUGUSTINE

198. The Meaning of Disaster (Lk 13:1-9)

"What dignity, what security to leave this life with joy, triumphant over trials and tortures, one moment to close those eyes with which we used to gaze on men and on the world, the next to open them to see God and Christ!" – St. Cyprian

LUKE 13:1-9

It was just about this time that some people arrived and told him about the Galileans whose blood Pilate had mingled with that of their sacrifices. At this he said to them, "Do you suppose these Galileans who suffered like that were greater sinners than any other Galileans? They were not, I tell you. No; but unless you repent you will all perish as they did. Or those eighteen on whom the tower at Siloam fell and killed them? Do you suppose that they were more guilty than all the other people living in Jerusalem? They were not, I tell you. No; but unless you repent you will all perish as they did." He told this parable: "A man had a fig tree planted in his vineyard, and he came looking for fruit on it but found none. He said to the man who looked after the vineyard, 'Look here, for three years now I have been coming to look for fruit on this fig tree and finding none. Cut it down: why should it be taking up the ground?' 'Sir,' the man replied, 'leave it one more year and give me time to dig round it and manure it: it may bear fruit next year; if not, then you can cut it down.'"

CHRIST THE LORD Christ spoke with authority not only about heavenly things, but also about the true meaning of earthly events. His Lordship, after all, is universal. Thus he gives the definitive interpretation of these two tragic events, and he points out the real meaning behind them. When Christ decided to exercise his Lordship through the ministry of his Church, he delegated the authority to continue announcing the meaning behind earthly events. No voice in the world speaks so frequently and directly about the critical issues of every age as the Magisterium of the Catholic Church. Just as Jesus himself was "the light of the world" when he walked the dusty roads of Palestine, so through his Church he remains a beacon of truth shining brightly amid the dark fog of the world's confusion.

Unfortunately, however, not everyone heeded his voice back then, and not everyone heeds his voice today. The world is always seeking the fruits of justice, peace, and prosperity. Individuals are always seeking happiness. Without digging into human hearts and fertilizing them with the truth about who we are and what we were created for, however, society will be barren of these most valuable fruits. Imagine how different the world community would be if everyone simply followed the Ten Commandments. The global culture would flourish in every way. Our Lord knows the way to fulfillment and fruitfulness. As his disciples, we know it too, and we should strive to make it known.

CHRIST THE TEACHER An influential school of Jewish thought at the time of Christ drew a direct line of causality from people's sufferings back to their personal sins. The more someone sinned, supposedly, the more they suffered. By this logic, the Galileans who were killed by Pilate's soldiers must have deserved it because of their sins. (Scholars are not in agreement about the incident being referred to. Many think, however, that it was Pilate's violent suppression of a demonstration in Jerusalem. Demonstrators had gathered in the Temple area to protest Pilate's use of Temple money to construct new aqueducts. Pilate then sent armed soldiers among them in disguise. At a signal, the soldiers dispersed the mob with clubs, killing many more than Pilate had anticipated.) Likewise, those who were killed in the construction accident in Siloam (some scholars think the tower being constructed was a part of those same aqueducts), so it was thought, were paying the penalty for their sins.

The Church has often pointed out, however, that personal suffering is not necessarily a result of personal sin (if it were, how could we explain Christ's

Passion and death?) and that suffering is often a sign of God's blessing ("Those whom I love, I reprove and chastise"—Rev 3:19). But Christ's lesson in the passage stands: everyone who refuses to repent (the barren fig tree symbolizes someone who lacks the fruits of repentance) will stay separated from God, and if they die in such a state of alienation (and death can come at any time), they will continue in it for all eternity. Even if the consequences of our actions do not always make themselves completely felt in this life, they will do so eventually—both for good and for ill; earthly tragedies should remind us of the passing nature and relative meaning of earthly life. It is a hard truth, but one that the Church wants us to consider deeply, especially during the penitential season of Lent, when this passage is read in the Sunday liturgy.

CHRIST THE FRIEND God is not indifferent to our lives. He wants them to bear fruit; he wants us to live fully. As our Creator, he has a right to expect us to live as he intended us to, just as the owner of the orchard has a right to expect his fig tree to grow figs. And yet, he doesn't demand his rights. Rather, he sends his Son to "cultivate the ground" of our hearts, to fertilize it with his love, his doctrine, and his sacraments. He does everything he possibly can to convince us to live in friendship with God, a friendship that will yield the lasting fruits of meaning and happiness. In the end, however, he leaves the decision up to us. After all, a forced friendship is no friendship at all.

CHRIST IN MY LIFE Thank you for making your voice resound even into my lifetime through the teachings of your Church. You are present in your ministers, your liturgy, and your Word. You want to point out to me what things mean. You want me to adjust my choices and priorities to the true scale of values. Thank you for thinking of me and staying with me...

No one likes to talk about Judgment Day. But you spoke often about it, and you inspired the Gospel writers to record what you said. I love this world, with all its wonder and beauty, but it is passing away. The struggles and sufferings that you permit should remind me of that. Help me to think as you think and see all things as you see them...

Thank you for your patience. You never give up on me; you keep working with me so I will bear the fruit you created me to bear. Teach me to do the same with those around me. They too are called to bear eternal fruit. How can I fertilize and trim and tend them, how can I help them discover and follow your will for their lives? Teach me to do your will...

Questions for
SMALL-GROUP DISCUSSION

1. What struck you most in this passage? What did you notice that you hadn't noticed before?
2. God instituted the sacrament of confession because he knew that we would need to repent again and again. How can we better take advantage of this sacrament?
3. How can we pay more attention to the Church's voice in national and world affairs?
4. What do you think Christ would say if someone were to ask him about today's world crises? What do you say when you are asked about them?

Cf. Catechism of the Catholic Church, 214, and 218-221 on God's mercy; 888-892 on the teaching office of the Church (the Magisterium); 1033-1037 on the consequences of not repenting from sin

199. The Lord's Day, the Lord's Way (Lk 13:10-21)

"This divine heart is an ocean full of all good things wherein poor souls can cast all their needs; it is an ocean full of joy to drown all our sadness, an ocean of humility to overwhelm our folly, an ocean of mercy for those in distress, an ocean of love in which to submerge our poverty." – *St. Margaret Mary Alocoque*

LUKE 13:10-21

One sabbath day he was teaching in one of the synagogues, and a woman was there who for eighteen years had been possessed by a spirit that left her enfeebled; she was bent double and quite unable to stand upright. When Jesus saw her he called her over and said, "Woman, you are rid of your infirmity," and he laid his hands on her. And at once she straightened up, and she glorified God. But the synagogue official was indignant because Jesus had healed on the sabbath, and he addressed the people present. "There are six days," he said, "when work is to be done. Come and be healed on one of those days and not on the sabbath." But the Lord answered him. "Hypocrites!" he said. "Is there one of you who does not untie his ox or his donkey from the manger on the sabbath and take it out for watering? And this woman, a daughter of Abraham whom Satan has held bound these eighteen years—was it not right to untie her bonds on the sabbath day?" When he said this, all his adversaries were covered with confusion, and all the people were overjoyed at all the wonders he worked. He went on to say,

> "What is the kingdom of God like? What shall I compare it with? It is like a mustard seed which a man took and threw into his garden: it grew and became a tree, and the birds of the air sheltered in its branches." Another thing he said, "What shall I compare the kingdom of God with? It is like the yeast a woman took and mixed in with three measures of flour till it was leavened all through."

CHRIST THE LORD The Sabbath is the Lord's Day. In the Old Covenant, it echoed the seventh day of Creation, the day when God's work was finished. As such, it also pointed towards the fulfillment of God's promise to lead Israel into a future age of prosperity, freeing them from toil and suffering. In Jesus that promise is fulfilled. He is the Lord; wherever he is, the Lord's Day is too. His healing of this crippled woman exemplifies this. On the Sabbath, he takes away her burden and restores her to communion with God. The opposition this miracle stirs up shows once again that Jesus' adversaries have lost their perspective. To them, the Sabbath was an end in itself, and so the complicated rules about what work could be performed on the Sabbath were followed rigidly. They had forgotten the purpose of the Lord's Day: to renew Israel's faith and trust in God, and to refresh their hope in the deliverance he promised them.

When we find ourselves spouting criticism and self-righteous complaints, like the synagogue official, it may be that we too have lost our perspective. In Christ's Kingdom, the only rule that matters is the rule of love, the rule of self-giving. Everything else exists for the sake of enabling us to love God and our neighbor better and better, and thus following more closely the Lord.

CHRIST THE TEACHER Besides reminding the crowd and the leaders about the true meaning of the Old Covenant's Sabbath (and therefore, by association, of the whole body of Old Covenant law), Jesus also teaches them about the New Covenant. He likens it to a mustard seed and a bit of yeast. The comparisons emphasize the contrast between small beginnings and big results. It aptly follows up his lesson about the Sabbath.

The code of conduct that through the centuries Israel had extrapolated from the Law of Moses was big, complex, and highly visible—and the Sabbath regulations formed an important part of it. Those who followed it most closely, the Pharisees, were almost entirely focused on its flamboyant visibility. They made sure that all their religious practices were seen and appreciated. Jesus advocates a different type of religiosity. He focuses on the interior attitude of self-forgetful love for God and neighbor. The Christian way is the way of the heart. But who can see the heart? No one—only oneself and God. This law of love and self-giving, therefore, is like the mustard seed and the leaven: barely perceptible to anyone at the beginning, but magnificent when it matures.

The parables remind us of another image Jesus used when talking about the law of his Kingdom: "Unless a wheat grain falls on the ground and dies, it remains only a single grain; but if it dies, it yields a rich harvest" (Jn 12:24). The Pharisees cared about their appearances, and their lives were barren. Christians should care about the heart, even if it means self-mastery and abnegation. If they do, their lives will flourish.

CHRIST THE FRIEND Friends go beyond the narrow call of duty; they take the initiative to help and please their friends. Jesus did this with the crippled woman. St. Luke makes no mention of anyone asking Jesus for a cure. Jesus simply sees the woman, knows how long she has suffered, and can't hold himself back from showing her the power and the love of God. He reaches out to her as soon as he becomes aware of her need. After eighteen years of walking bowed, looking only at the ground, she can now look once again to the heavens.

He did the same thing with us. When Adam and Eve sinned, they didn't go looking for God so they could set things straight; it was God who came looking for them, to save them. Ever since, it has been God who constantly invites and guides us. Every good thing is a gift from him, a message written by his love. If he had limited himself to his strict duty, we would never have been created in the first place—he had no need or obligation to make the universe—and we would certainly never have been given the hope of redemption (we were the ones who rebelled, not him). When Christ becomes man, our centuries of crippled, earthly existence are over, and we can rise once again to our heavenly vocation.

We can evaluate the status of our friendship with Christ by this standard. The closer we are to him, the more we will treat others the way he has treated us—taking the initiative to come to their aid.

CHRIST IN MY LIFE I am glad I exist. I am glad you created me and invited me to become a citizen of your Kingdom. Thank you, Lord. You have already taken away so many of my burdens—the guilt of my sins, the weight of ignorance and anxiety, the insecurity of wondering what life is all about. I believe in you, Lord, and I am looking forward to the day when I will see you face to face...

Sometimes I get too caught up in the nonessentials; sometimes they look flashier than the essentials. But I want to stay focused, Lord. I want to love as you love, and to build your Kingdom in my heart and in those around me. To love you, to love my neighbor, to love by forgetting myself—this is the mustard seed; plant it firmly in my heart...

It is hard for me to step out of my comfort zone for the sake of my neighbor, even in little things. I want to please you; feed the good desires in my heart. I need you to strengthen me, to push me, to fire my heart with your love. With the zeal of your heart, set my heart on fire…

Questions for SMALL-GROUP DISCUSSION

1. What struck you most in this passage? What did you notice that you hadn't noticed before?
2. Why do you think the reaction of the people to this miracle was so different than the reaction of Jesus' adversaries? After all, everybody saw the same thing….
3. What can we do to celebrate the Lord's Day better, more the way Jesus wants us to?
4. What are some commonly overlooked opportunities to live out the law of Christian charity in our life situations?

Cf. Catechism of the Catholic Church, 577-582 on Jesus and the Law; 2816-2821 on the coming of the Kingdom; 1694 and 2013 on the call to charity; 1844 and 1973 on charity as the perfection of Christian life

200. Heavenly Feast or Hellish Isolation (Lk 13:22-35)

"No misfortune should distract us from this happiness and deep joy; for if anyone is anxious to reach a destination, the roughness of the road will not make him change his mind." – Pope St. Gregory the Great

LUKE 13:22-35

Through towns and villages he went teaching, making his way to Jerusalem. Someone said to him, "Sir, will there be only a few saved?" He said to them, "Try your best to enter by the narrow door, because, I tell you, many will try to enter and will not succeed. Once the master of the house has got up and locked the door, you may find yourself knocking on the door, saying, 'Lord, open to us,' but he will answer, 'I do not know where you come from.' Then you will find yourself saying, 'We once ate and drank in your company; you taught in our streets,' but he will reply, 'I do not know where you come from. Away from me, all you wicked men!' Then there will be weeping and grinding of teeth, when you see Abraham and Isaac and Jacob and all the prophets in the kingdom of God, and yourselves turned outside. And men from east and west, from north and south, will come to take their places at the feast in the kingdom of God. Yes, there are those now last who will be first, and those now first who will be last."

Just at this time some Pharisees came up. "Go away," they said. "Leave this place, because Herod means to kill you." He replied, "You may go and give that fox this message: Learn that today and tomorrow I cast out devils and on the third day attain my end. But for today and tomorrow and the next day I must go on, since it would not be right for a prophet to die outside Jerusalem. Jerusalem, Jerusalem, you that kill the prophets and stone those who are sent to you! How often have I longed to gather your children, as a hen gathers her brood under her wings, and you refused! So be it! Your house will be left to you. Yes, I promise you, you shall not see me till the time comes when you say: Blessings on him who comes in the name of the Lord!"

CHRIST THE LORD Christ alone is the Lord of life and history. There is only one eternal banquet, only one eternal Kingdom, and it is his. He came to earth in order to tell us about it and to blaze a trail that would lead us to it. And he doesn't want to leave anyone out of it—which is why he speaks so vehemently about its importance in passages like this—but neither will he force us into it. He is the Lord, and he invites us to follow him, but he will respect our response to his invitation. This is why we should respond with great care.

Christ himself is the way to salvation and fulfillment. Salvation comes from actually following him, from striving to know him better and from obeying his teaching. This is the narrow door, because he is demanding. It is possible to be labeled a Christian on the outside without really making an effort to follow the Christian way in our hearts or to go to Church and be seen frequently at the parish without ever really entering into a committed, life-changing, personal relationship with Christ. It may be comfortable for awhile, but in the end only those who have followed the Lord will be welcomed to the banquet.

CHRIST THE TEACHER This innocent question, "Will only a few people be saved?" afforded Christ the perfect opportunity to tell everyone, "Relax—all you have to do is be a good guy, more or less, and you'll get to heaven." But he didn't. He told us to "try your best" to enter into his Kingdom, because "many will try to enter and will not succeed." Certainly, the Church teaches that without the help of divine grace no one can live in eternal friendship with God, but Jesus is emphasizing here that we each must do our part as well. If we settle for a comfortable, self-satisfying Christianity, we may be deceiving ourselves. Instead of building up God's Kingdom, we may in fact be erecting an idolatrous house of cards. The spiritual life is a battle, as the Church never tires of telling us, and we are not to take victory for granted. The entrance door is "narrow," and the Lord will refuse entry altogether to "wicked men"—even those who thought they were good. Bottom line: Salvation matters, and it's not just a consolation prize.

CHRIST THE FRIEND Because Christ is a true friend, he sees the heart. Many times those who seem great or holy by the world's standards are filled with selfishness and arrogance, while those whom the world despises are filled with humility and wisdom. But Jesus will correct this injustice: "There are those now last who will be first, and those now first who will be last." Christ sees each of us as we truly are, and he warns us not to trust in appearances—neither our own appearance of righteousness, nor others' appearance of dishonor. If we trust only in Christ, in his goodness and love, we will learn to see as he sees, and when judgment day comes, we won't have to worry about any surprises.

But Jesus knows that many will indeed reject him, including the leaders of Jerusalem who fear losing their privilege and power. His expression of how much their rejection pains him shows his yearning for our friendship. We can picture him looking towards Jerusalem, the earthly center of God's saving action for so many centuries, soon to become the stage of the Atonement itself (Christ's Passion and Resurrection). Then a sigh of yearning escapes him, "Jerusalem, Jerusalem... How often I have longed...!" When we look at our own lives and our often tepid or even rebellious responses to God's invitations, we can see him sighing in the same way over us. Just as a hen cannot help gathering her brood—it's built into the very fiber of her being—so God cannot help desiring our companionship. But if we refuse it, we too will be left on our own, and just as the unwelcoming earthly Jerusalem will soon be completely destroyed, so those without God will lose even the little happiness they think they have—not because God shut the door, but because they chose not to go through it when they could.

CHRIST IN MY LIFE I want to be with you for your eternal banquet, and I know you want me to be there too. You want everyone to be there! What more can I do to bring others into your friendship? What can I do to deepen my friendship with you? Teach me to try my best to enter the narrow door. In the end, nothing else matters...

Why do people think and talk so little about what is sure to happen to us all, death and judgment? Why do people think it's a sign of weakness to look forward to heaven and to live on earth in such as way as to prepare for heaven? I know that earth is not heaven, and I know I need you to lead me to the fulfillment I long for. Never let me be separated from you, Lord...

It should bother me more that so many people reject you. Lord, my heart is still contracted and selfish. Pour your Spirit into my soul and fill me with your love. Real love, deep love, self-forgetting love—that's what you lived, that's what you taught, that's what I was made for. With the love of your heart, inflame my heart...

Questions for SMALL-GROUP DISCUSSION

1. What struck you most in this passage? What did you notice that you hadn't noticed before?
2. The tone of this discourse seems to be "negative." How do you think it sounded when Christ himself was giving it?
3. Why do you suppose Christ spoke so "threateningly" about salvation, when God is supposed to be "merciful"?
4. What can we do to make sure everyone around us gets to heaven? What will we have to sacrifice in order to do that?

Cf. Catechism of the Catholic Church, 668-679 *on the end of history and Christ's final judgment;* 1023-1037 *on heaven, hell, and purgatory;* 1021-1022 *and* 1038-1041 *on the particular and universal judgment*

THE GOSPEL OF LUKE
Chapter 14

"Lord, who can grasp all the wealth of just one of your words? What we understand is much less than what we leave behind, like thirsty people who drink from a fountain. For your word, Lord, has many shades of meaning, just as those who study it have many different points of view. The Lord has colored his words with many hues so that each person who studies it can see in it what he loves. He has hidden many treasures in his word so that each of us is enriched as we meditate on it. The word of God is a tree of life that from all its parts offers you fruits that are blessed. It is like that rock opened in the desert that from all its parts gave forth a spiritual drink.... The thirsty man rejoices when he drinks and he is not downcast because he cannot empty the fountain. Rather let the fountain quench your thirst than have your thirst quench the fountain. Because if your thirst is quenched and the fountain is not exhausted, you can drink from it again whenever you are thirsty."

– ST. EPHRAEM

201. Aiming Really High (Lk 14:1-14)

"Only when we meet the living God in Christ do we know what life is. We are not some casual and meaningless product of evolution. Each of us is the result of a thought of God. Each of us is willed, each of us is loved, each of us is necessary." – Pope Benedict XVI

LUKE 14:1-14

Now on a sabbath day he had gone for a meal to the house of one of the leading Pharisees; and they watched him closely. There in front of him was a man with dropsy, and Jesus addressed the lawyers and Pharisees. "Is it against the law," he asked, "to cure a man on the sabbath, or not?" But they remained silent, so he took the man and cured him and sent him away. Then he said to them, "Which of you here, if his son falls into a well, or his ox, will not pull him out on a sabbath day without hesitation?" And to this they could find no answer.

He then told the guests a parable, because he had noticed how they picked the places of honour. He said this, "When someone invites you to a wedding feast, do not take your seat in the place of honour. A more distinguished person than you may have been invited, and the person who invited you both may come and say, 'Give up your place to this man.' And then, to your embarrassment, you would have to go and take the lowest place. No; when you are a guest, make your way to the lowest place and sit there, so that, when your host comes, he may say, 'My friend, move up higher.' In that way, everyone with you at the table will see you honoured. For everyone who exalts himself will be humbled, and the man who humbles himself will be exalted." Then he said to his host, "When you give a lunch or a dinner, do not ask your friends, brothers, relations or rich neighbours, for fear they repay your courtesy by inviting you in return. No; when you have a party, invite the poor, the crippled, the lame, the blind; that they cannot pay you back means that you are fortunate, because repayment will be made to you when the virtuous rise again."

CHRIST THE LORD Jesus addresses himself to the leading Pharisees (Israel's religious and intellectual elite) and other high-class personnel as their superior. No earthly power can intimidate him; nothing can deter him from announcing the truths of the Kingdom. That he was even invited in the first place shows that he was as comfortable interacting with Palestine's leaders as he was tending to their poor and lame. That he seized the opportunity of the invitation to sow the seeds of the gospel shows that the glitz of power, wealth, and fame held no sway over his heart. Such is our Lord; so he would have his followers be.

Viewed in light of Christ's passion, the advice he gives these Pharisees takes on a deeper meaning. He followed this advice—radically. He took the lowest place here on earth, that of a criminal. He took on the most humiliating form of death, that of crucifixion. He was stripped of every honor, even the honor of his reputation, which was defamed and dragged through the mire by his enemies' lies and corruption. And yet, because he humbled himself, the Lord was glorified; this is the law of his Kingdom.

CHRIST THE TEACHER At first glance, the lessons of this passage seem simple and straightforward; at second glance, they are shocking. On the surface, they advocate humility and generosity: don't assume your importance by sitting in the seat of honor on your own initiative; don't give your hospitality just to people who can pay you back. Certainly Jesus intends to teach these lessons, and certainly the pompous and vain, hoity-toity Pharisees needed to learn them. But isn't it curious that Jesus doesn't say, "You should not want to be honored at all," and "You should seek no reward for your good deeds"?

That is what the modern secular humanist would tell us: true charity means absolute selflessness; they would fault us even for doing right, if it makes us happy. But Christ doesn't condemn the natural desire for honor and reward; he elevates it. We should seek our reward in heaven—the reward of lasting happiness that comes from living in friendship with God. And we should put ourselves in "the lowest place" now, serving others while we can, so that we can be lifted higher later. Christ is the ultimate realist; he knows the human heart (after all, he made it), and he doesn't want to stifle it—he wants to set it free.

CHRIST THE FRIEND Christ's method of teaching reveals how sincerely he cares for us. By telling the parable to the dinner party, he exposes everyone's vanity without embarrassing anyone. He teaches and corrects us not to humiliate us, but to gently lead us toward the freedom of truth. When he instructs the host on how to win eternal favors, he doesn't condemn him for doing something bad (inviting one's friends to a banquet is hardly an evil deed), but he invites him to do something even better. Every word of Christ, every gesture and deed, has our good as its aim. He is the ever-faithful Friend.

Perhaps it was this unblemished goodness of God that the Pharisees most needed to perceive. Their objections to Christ's Sabbath miracles reflect a very different idea of God. The Sabbath was the Lord's Day, and honoring the Lord, from their perspective, meant a strict, harsh, cold obedience to the letter of the law—as if God were a stern judge who was just waiting to pounce on anyone who stepped out of place. For Jesus, on the other hand, honoring the Lord on the Lord's Day meant relieving people of their sufferings and sorrows, giving them a glimpse and a taste of the Father's omnipotent love, emphasizing that the highest place of honor in every heart should belong to the Giver of all good gifts. Two different ideas of God produced two different ways of relating to God. We should make sure our idea is as close to Christ's as possible, so we can live as he wants us to live.

CHRIST IN MY LIFE I know you planted the desire for happiness in my heart for a reason. I know you want my happiness. Untangle all the complicated ideas linked to the meaning of life that bombard me from here and there. You are my Lord. Your gospel is my plan of action. Help me to know you better each day, so I can follow you more closely and love you more deeply...

Sometimes I still doubt your care and concern for me. Not in my mind, but in my heart. Part of me still recoils at your tenderness. Heal my wounded heart, Lord. Let me love you more by trusting you completely. Let me glorify you by confiding in you wholly...

I am your ambassador—you made it so on the day of my confirmation. I should have the same purposeful but humble confidence in all my encounters as you did. Why don't I? Why do I get nervous, hesitant, uncertain? I still have a divided heart. Make your will into my only desire, and teach me to walk in your ways...

Questions for *SMALL-GROUP DISCUSSION*

1. What struck you most in this passage? What did you notice that you hadn't noticed before?
2. In what ways can we fall into seeking "the places of honor" in opposition to the humility of heart that the gospel calls for?
3. Why do you think Christ accepts an invitation to a dinner party given by one of the leading Pharisees, when they had already openly declared their opposition to him?
4. Christ is at home with the rich and the poor, with the leaders of society and the large crowds of ordinary citizens. How was he able to be so universal? How can we follow in his footsteps?

Cf. Catechism of the Catholic Church, 22 and 1718-1719 on the natural human desire for happiness; 2544-2547 on humility

202. RSVP (Lk 14:15-24)

"If we let Christ into our lives, we lose nothing, nothing, absolutely nothing of what makes life free, beautiful, and great.... Only in this friendship are the doors of life opened wide. Only in this friendship is the great potential of human existence truly revealed. Only in this friendship do we experience beauty and liberation." – Pope Benedict XVI

LUKE 14:15-24

On hearing this, one of those gathered round the table said to him, "Happy the man who will be at the feast in the kingdom of God!" But he said to him, "There was a man who gave a great banquet, and he invited a large number of people. When the time for the banquet came, he sent his servant to say to those who had been invited, 'Come along: everything is ready now.' But all alike started to make excuses. The first said, 'I have bought a piece of land and must go and see it. Please accept my apologies.' Another said, 'I have bought five yoke of oxen and am on my way to try them out. Please accept my apologies.' Yet another said, 'I have just got married and so am unable to come.' The servant returned and reported this to his master. Then the householder, in a rage, said to his servant, 'Go out quickly into the streets and alleys of the town and bring in here the poor, the crippled, the blind and the lame.' 'Sir,' said the servant, 'your orders have been carried out and there is still room.' Then the master said to his servant, 'Go to the open roads and the hedgerows and force people to come in to make sure my house is full; because, I tell you, not one of those who were invited shall have a taste of my banquet.'"

CHRIST THE LORD One of the guests at the dinner responds to Jesus' previous comment about giving feasts and inviting the poor, and about taking the last seat when you're invited to a feast, by calling to mind the great Jewish idea of the Messianic Feast. The Jews believed that when the Messiah finally came, he would organize a huge feast for all of the faithful Jews. Jesus' response must have been sobering. He acknowledges the man's comment and explains that those who were originally invited to the Messianic feast were already in the process of declining to come—the very Pharisees and other exteriorly righteous Jews were the ones who rejected Jesus. And so Jesus invites the poor and indigent of the town—the tax collectors, the ignorant, and the public sinners of Palestine who welcomed Christ's message. But there is still room for more, so Jesus sends messengers outside of the town, into the highways and byways, and the Gentiles too are brought into the banquet. In short, those who were supposed to be the guests of honor ended up missing the event entirely, while those who didn't even know about the feast were the ones who enjoyed it.

Jesus tells this parable to the Pharisees hoping it will wake them up to Christ's truth. But it tells us a lot about the Lord as well. It tells us that he considers himself incomplete unless his subjects come and celebrate with him. He is the antithesis of a lone ranger. (Here is the root of the Church's admonition that all her children faithfully attend Sunday Mass.) It tells us that he respects our freedom—the line about forcing people to come in alludes to the compulsion of love, not to injustice. It tells us that he desires to bring as many people as possible into his Kingdom. This is our Lord, and as his ambassadors, we should be the same.

CHRIST THE TEACHER The Pharisees' rejection of Jesus is mysterious. Why were they so blind? Why did they persist in their blindness? Maybe many more than we realize eventually became believers and followers of Christ, but many of them held out against him to the bitter end. How could that be? The three refusals in the parable explain.

One man was occupied with his business deals—he's the man of power. Another was excited about his new purchase—he's the man of possessions. And a third was engrossed in the raptures of a newlywed—he's the man of pleasure. To understand their situations completely, it's important to realize how these ancient banquets worked. When a banquet was to be held, two invitations went out. The first merely announced the host's intention of throwing the party; it didn't give the details of date and time. When those were arranged, servants would be sent out to announce the actual hour of the banquet, and those who had accepted the first invitation would now come and enjoy the feast. To say yes to the first invitation and then decline the second was considered a grave insult. All three of these men had accepted the original invitation. They valued the host enough to commit to coming to his banquet. But then the weeks went by, and they became absorbed in their own affairs. By the time the second invitation arrives, their own preoccupations—whether power, possessions, or pleasure—have crowded out their allegiance to the host.

From this perspective, the Pharisees' failure to welcome Jesus makes sense. It was God who had chosen the Chosen People; his call and covenant came out of his initiative. Therefore, following through on it necessarily involves putting God's plans ahead of one's personal plans. And who of us hasn't experienced the difficulty in that? Put in those terms, the parable applies to all of us. The first invitation is our baptism, by which we are put on the roster of God's family. But later in life, the Lord comes and asks each one of us to follow through, and unless we have kept in touch with God, with his wisdom and goodness, we too can easily ignore his voice in favor of self-absorption. The tragedy is double: we not only miss out on the feast, but if we simply trusted in God, we could have both the feast and our personal interests—the businessman didn't have to lose his land in order to come to the feast, he only had to delay his appointment, and likewise with the others. So the Pharisees' rejection of Christ is not so mysterious after all—it was just like ours.

CHRIST THE FRIEND Jesus' favorite image for his Kingdom is the banquet, the feast. Not just a little dinner party, but a huge festival, worthy of the kind of King he is. Banquets are full of enjoyment, communion, conversation, and delight; they are icons of fulfillment. This is what Jesus has in store for his friends. We would do well to contemplate this image so that it sinks deeply into our hearts and minds, especially because we know that his banquet lasts forever, whereas our little earthly plans and pleasures are quickly coming to an end. Contemplating this image will help us begin to value our friendship with Christ the way it deserves to be valued—and cherish and nourish it as we ought.

Jesus: The banquet I am preparing for you is beyond what you can imagine. Remember all of the most beautiful sunsets, landscapes, and night skies that you have enjoyed? They are a dim, colorless shadow compared to heaven. Remember the most satisfying discoveries you have made through your books, travels, hobbies, and education? They are just a title page compared to all that you still have to discover. Remember your greatest and purest pleasures: the summer sun warming your shoulders, a glass of cool lemonade after a long afternoon's work, the hard-fought victory won by a dramatic comeback, the embrace of a loved one after a long time apart? These are just whiffs of the pleasures to come. Remember the more substantial joys of friendship, of forgiveness, of loving and being loved in return, of knowing and being known by the one you love? All these are my gifts to you here on earth, and they are but a prelude to their fulfillment in heaven. I promised to go and prepare a place for you in my Father's house. It is almost ready. I am looking forward to showing it to you. I hope you are looking forward to coming.

CHRIST IN MY LIFE You invite me to your banquet every day: the Eucharist. What more could I desire than to enter into such intimate communion with you? You are all I need. The troubles and sufferings of life can't take you away from me; you are faithful. Teach me to live as you lived, to love as you love, and to think as you think. Make me a channel of your peace…

I shake my head at those three men in the parable who foolishly miss their chance to come to the banquet. But you know that I too decline your invitations many, many times. You are always inviting me to follow you more closely, to be more like you. Yet I decline. I am so slow to reach out to those who rub me the wrong way, so reluctant to forgive, so quick to criticize, so swift to pass judgment. Forgive me, Lord. Never let me be separated from you…

I am that servant you sent out to gather people for your banquet. Teach me what to say. Teach me how to bring others closer to you. Show me how to use my talents and opportunities to give you glory and to benefit my neighbor as much as possible. Make me more aware of the mission you have given me, so I can throw myself into it with all the love of my heart…

Questions for SMALL-GROUP DISCUSSION

1. What struck you most in this passage? What did you notice that you hadn't noticed before?
2. Which of the three excuses is commonly heard today?

3. What are some of the most common excuses people make for not going to Mass, the banquet of the Eucharist? How do they hold up in light of this parable?
4. Why do you think it's so easy for us to discard God's invitations?

Cf. Catechism of the Catholic Church, 1023-1029 on what heaven will be like; 2794-2796 on the significance of heaven; 1720-1724 on Christian beatitude

203. Christian Conditions (Lk 14:25-35)

"But above all things maintain peace of heart which surpasses every treasure. For maintaining this peace, nothing is more effective than to renounce one's own will and to set in its place the will of the Sacred Heart..." – St. Margaret Mary Alacoque

LUKE 14:25-35
Great crowds accompanied him on his way and he turned and spoke to them. "If any man comes to me without hating his father, mother, wife, children, brothers, sisters, yes and his own life too, he cannot be my disciple. Anyone who does not carry his cross and come after me cannot be my disciple. And indeed, which of you here, intending to build a tower, would not first sit down and work out the cost to see if he had enough to complete it? Otherwise, if he laid the foundation and then found himself unable to finish the work, the onlookers would all start making fun of him and saying, 'Here is a man who started to build and was unable to finish.' Or again, what king marching to war against another king would not first sit down and consider whether with ten thousand men he could stand up to the other who advanced against him with twenty thousand? If not, then while the other king was still a long way off, he would send envoys to sue for peace. So in the same way, none of you can be my disciple unless he gives up all his possessions. Salt is a useful thing. But if the salt itself loses its taste, how can it be seasoned again? It is good for neither soil nor manure heap. People throw it out. Listen, anyone who has ears to hear!"

CHRIST THE LORD We easily become familiar with Christ; we lose our sense of wonder and amazement of him. But the people of his time knew that it was no ordinary man who walked among them—rather, they knew that he was an ordinary man who at the same time was extraordinary. Thus we run into brief phrases like "great crowds accompanied him on his way" strewn throughout the Gospels. Try to picture that. A rabbi walking the dusty streets of Palestine, drawing thousands of people in his wake.... Even if later some of the people in these crowds were also in the crowd that convinced Pilate to crucify him on Good Friday, we should credit them with recognizing that Christ was more than a name in one of Western culture's great books—indeed, he was and is the Lord.

CHRIST THE TEACHER At this point in Luke's Gospel, Jesus is steadfastly making his way to Jerusalem, where he knows that he can expect nothing but betrayal, condemnation, humiliation, torture, and death, but he knows that on the third day he will rise again. He also knows that everyone who wants to be his follower, everyone who has tasted the incomparable meaning and deep joy of his Kingdom and wants its fullness, will have to follow the same path: every Christian has to die with Christ in order to rise with him (cf. Rom 6:8). Death in this sense will not necessarily take the form of physical crucifixion, although for many of his closest followers (the martyrs) it did. But whatever form the cross takes in a particular Christian's life, it will require a painful renunciation of things dear to us. Like a good surgeon, Christ has to cut away whatever holds us back from him, and that can hurt. The Church has always understood that Christ's exhortation to hate father and mother and brothers and sisters simply points out that a true Christian can prefer nothing to Christ.

Jesus also teaches us that following him involves more than feelings and inspirations. We are meant to use our minds. The builder and the warring king had to channel their enthusiasm through the cool filter of reason. Christians must do the same. The emotional excitement that comes from a retreat or a pilgrimage or a special grace-filled encounter with the Lord is like the blossoms on a cherry tree. They bloom quickly and fill our souls with a sweet aroma, but then the long summer comes, and we have to persevere patiently, following an intelligent plan of spiritual and apostolic work, before the fruit matures. Love is often born amidst intense emotions, but it matures through suffering and sweat, and these are only endured through the aid of reason and conviction. Following Christ is more than following a whim; it is a long-term project that engages the whole person.

CHRIST THE FRIEND Jesus didn't want his followers to be under any illusions. Perhaps some people in that crowd were hoping for a sweeping political victory to overthrow the hated Roman yoke as soon as they would arrive in Jerusalem. Perhaps some were entertaining fanciful illusions about effortless prosperity—after all, hadn't Jesus multiplied five loaves so as to feed more than five thousand people? Jesus knew that his Kingdom was of a different stripe. He knew that it was much greater, much better than anything they could imagine, but he also knew that attaining it would be more demanding than they thought. If they would be his friends, then, he would tell them right from the outset what such a friendship would entail. "None of you can be my disciple unless he gives up all his possessions. . . ." Jesus isn't advocating delay or hesitation in following him, but he is advocating firm resolution. Salt that loses its flavor is good for nothing, just so a disciple who loses his fervor when fidelity to Christ gets tough. Jesus is no fair-weather friend, and he's looking for more than fair-weather followers.

St. Luke doesn't tell us what tone of voice our Lord used when speaking these words, nor does he say how the crowds reacted, but we don't really need him to. As always, Jesus was inviting these people to trust in him, and in his eyes was the fire of love and the warm hope of a heart that longs to give.

CHRIST IN MY LIFE Open my eyes, Lord. I want to know you better. I fall into routine so easily. Grant me the grace to perceive your majesty, your goodness, and your wisdom. If you don't let me see your beauty, I will be turned aside by the passing fancies of this world. Open my eyes, Lord; increase my faith...

I want to be your follower, cross and all. But it's hard for me to recognize my crosses. The contradictions and struggles of every day seem so petty—where is the redemption in them, Lord? I know it's there somewhere, but where? Teach me to see my crosses, so that I can bear them, united to yours, with faith, hope, and love...

I know that following you will be costly. It's much easier to go with what's popular, easy, and pleasurable. But as long as you walk beside me, I would never desire another path. What would life be like without you? A tumbleweed, a passing cloud, a firecracker. You plug my life into eternity, and I know in my heart that's where I belong...

Questions for *SMALL-GROUP DISCUSSION*

1. What struck you most in this passage? What did you notice that you hadn't noticed before?
2. What are the hardest sacrifices we face in following Christ on a day-to-day basis? Why are they hard?
3. If God really wants us to follow Christ, why doesn't he make it easier?
4. In the Gospel of Matthew, Jesus says, "My yoke is easy and my burden is light" (Mt 11:30). How can we reconcile that statement with, "Whoever does not carry his own cross and come after me cannot be my disciple"? After all, crosses are not exactly easy and light.

Cf. Catechism of the Catholic Church, 409 and 2015 on the difficulties of Christian discipleship

THE GOSPEL OF LUKE

Chapter 15

"What greater proof could he have given of his mercy than by taking upon himself that which needed mercy? Where is there such fullness of loving-kindness as in the fact that the Word of God became perishable like the grass for our sakes?… Let man infer from this how much God cares for him. Let him know from this what God thinks of him, what he feels about him. Man, do not ask about your own sufferings, but about what he suffered. Learn from what he was made for you, how much he makes of you, so that his kindness may show itself to you from his humanity. The lesser he has made himself in his humanity, the greater has he shown himself in kindness. The more he humbles himself on my account, the more powerfully he engages my love."

– ST. BERNARD OF CLAIRVAUX

204. WHAT GOD THINKS OF SINNERS (LK 15:1-10)

"The Word spoke, and by these words he turned man away from disobedience, not enslaving him by force or necessity, but inviting him to choose freedom of his own accord." – St. Hippolytus

LUKE 15:1-10

The tax collectors and the sinners, meanwhile, were all seeking his company to hear what he had to say, and the Pharisees and the scribes complained. "This man," they said, "welcomes sinners and eats with them." So he spoke this parable to them: "What man among you with a hundred sheep, losing one, would not leave the ninety-nine in the wilderness and go after the missing one till he found it? And when he found it, would he not joyfully take it on his shoulders and then, when he got home, call together his friends and neighbours? 'Rejoice with me,' he would say, 'I have found my sheep that was lost.' In the same way, I tell you, there will be more rejoicing in heaven over one repentant sinner than over ninety-nine virtuous men who have no need of repentance. Or again, what woman with ten drachmas would not, if she lost one, light a lamp and sweep out the house and search thoroughly till she found it? And then, when she had found it, call together

her friends and neighbours? 'Rejoice with me,' she would say, 'I have found the drachma I lost.' In the same way, I tell you, there is rejoicing among the angels of God over one repentant sinner."

CHRIST THE LORD If one of the self-righteous Pharisees had possessed the power and authority of Christ, he would have destroyed all the "sinners." But Christ deploys all his power and authority to bring them back into communion with God. Once again we see that the Pharisees' idea of God is off base. They see God as harsh and judgmental, when the truth is that God is a dedicated shepherd. The return of a sinner actually makes God rejoice—as the shepherd rejoices upon retrieving his sheep, and as the woman rejoices upon recovering her coin. The parables show us that God feels anxiousness in regards to sinners, not anger; he wants them back, he doesn't want to condemn them. The Pharisees can't understand this because they have painted their image of God in their own likeness. They enjoy condemning others for being less perfect than themselves because it feeds their vanity, making them feel superior. But the Lord has no vanity, only love. If we are to be his followers, we need to see him as he really is and work to become more like him.

The Pharisees were impossible to please. They found fault with everything Jesus did. But he never gave up trying to win them over. Here, when they complain about his rubbing shoulders with tax collectors and sinners, he responds by telling them some of the most beautiful stories in all of Scripture—pleading with them to soften their hearts and accept God's mercy. The Lord rules, but he rules wisely and mercifully, and his patience never wears thin, no matter how sorely we try it.

CHRIST THE TEACHER The parables always teach us about ourselves. The lost sheep is helpless and vulnerable; it needs the flock and the shepherd to protect and guide it. Just so, every person is created to find meaning and fulfillment in communion with God and others—thus the two great commandments of loving God and loving neighbor. The lost coin is completely without value unless it is possessed by its owner. Even if it had been a gold piece worth one thousand drachmas, it would be completely worthless buried in the dust under the sofa—of absolutely no use to anyone. Likewise, each of us has a mission in life, a purpose and a task, but its proper place is within Christ's Kingdom. Outside of the Kingdom we can do wonderful things and have exciting adventures, but everything we do is utterly unsubstantial, like a puff of smoke, unless it's plugged into eternity through God's saving grace. Our lives only have real meaning through Christ, with Christ, and in Christ—otherwise they're just tasteless wafers of unleavened bread.

These parables also show the truth about the sacrament of confession. Far from a drudgery or manipulative coercion, this sacrament is God's way of making it as simple and direct as possible for us to come back into the fold and set the bells of his heart ringing.

CHRIST THE FRIEND These two parables teach us more about the heart of God than a whole library full of theological treatises. God cares about each one of us (he will not rest if only one sheep is missing or one coin is lost). He cares deeply enough to go out of his way to save us when we are lost. (It was certainly an inconvenience to go bushwhacking after the foolish stray sheep, and to light the lamp and sweep the dirt-floored house trying to find the lost coin.) He rejoices when we return to him—he actually rejoices. Every sinner who returns to God causes joyful celebration in the halls of heaven and in the heart of the Father.

A shepherd counts his sheep after a long day of grazing, as the sun goes down. One is missing. He counts again. Yes, one sheep has wandered away from the flock. High on the mountainside pasture, the air is already getting cold as daylight fades. The flock huddles together. The shepherd leads them into a natural hollow under an overhanging cliff. He turns around and retraces his steps; he sets out to find the lost sheep. He stumbles over sharp rocks in the lengthening shadows. He has to climb off the path, pushing through brambles and thorns. He pulls his cloak tighter around him to keep out the chill. It starts to drizzle. Will the wolves come out in the rain? There is no moon tonight, and the clouds block out the stars. Maybe he should turn back while he can still find his way. He will come and search for the lost sheep in the morning. A wolf howls. The morning may be too late. He trudges on. The mud is slippery. The wind picks up. Water drips down the back of his neck. Soon he is soaked to the skin. The night crawls on. He will find his sheep. That's what matters. He is a good shepherd.

CHRIST IN MY LIFE Unless you make my heart more like yours, I will continue judging my neighbor just like the Pharisees. Unless you give me a deeper experience of your goodness, I will keep slipping into the wrong idea about you. I see the Pharisee in myself, Lord, and I don't want him to win out. I want to be your ambassador, not your adversary...

I was that lost coin, and you found me. I have been the lost sheep many times, and you have always come after me. Thank you, Lord. I don't thank you as often as I should. I am glad you haven't given up on me. Now, please teach me to be like you, to seek and find lost coins and lost sheep, so I can repay your love to me by bringing joy to your heart…

How patient you were with the stubborn, self-righteous Pharisees! Pour some of that patience into my heart, Lord. I have too short a fuse. I know I'm acting like a fool when I harp on others and become exasperated with them—as if I were perfect. Help me to think more about the good of my neighbor than the satisfaction of my own desires. Teach me to love as you love…

Questions for *SMALL-GROUP DISCUSSION*

1. What struck you most in this passage? What did you notice that you hadn't noticed before?
2. In what areas of your life do you tend to try God's patience?
3. As faithful followers of Christ, we should do our best to go after the lost sheep and look for the lost coins on his behalf. In what ways can we improve our imitation of Christ the Good Shepherd?
4. What does popular culture tell us to base our self-esteem on? How does that compare with Christ's message in these parables?

Cf. Catechism of the Catholic Church, 1468-1470 on the effects of sacramental confession; 210-227 on God's mercy and other qualities

205. Coming Home (Lk 15:11-32)

"On the basis of this way of manifesting the presence of God who is Father, love, and mercy, Jesus makes mercy one of the principal themes of his preaching." – St. John Paul II

LUKE 15:11-32

He also said, "A man had two sons. The younger said to his father, 'Father, let me have the share of the estate that would come to me.' So the father divided the property between them. A few days later, the younger son got together everything he had and left for a distant country where he squandered his money on a life of debauchery. When he had spent it all, that country experienced a severe famine, and now he began to feel the pinch, so he hired himself out to one of the local inhabitants who put him on his farm to feed the pigs. And he would willingly have filled his belly with the husks the pigs were eating but no one offered him anything. Then he came to his senses and said, 'How many of my father's paid servants have more food than they want, and here am I dying of hunger! I will leave this place and go to my father and say: Father, I have sinned against heaven and against you; I no longer deserve to be called your son; treat me as one of your paid servants.' So he left the place and went back to his father. While he was still a long way off, his father saw him and was moved with pity. He ran to the boy, clasped him in his arms and kissed him tenderly. Then his son said, 'Father, I have sinned against heaven and against you. I no longer deserve to be called your son.' But the father said to his servants, 'Quick! Bring out the best robe and put it on him; put a ring on his finger and sandals on his feet. Bring the calf we have been fattening, and kill it; we are going to have a feast, a celebration, because this son of mine was dead and has come back to life; he was lost and is found.' And they began to celebrate.

"Now the elder son was out in the fields, and on his way back, as he drew near the house, he could hear music and dancing. Calling one of the servants he asked what it was all about. 'Your brother has come,' replied the servant, 'and your father has killed the calf we had fattened because he has got him back safe and sound.' He was angry then and refused to go in, and his father came out to plead with him; but he answered his father, 'Look, all these years I have slaved for you and never once disobeyed your orders, yet you never offered me so much as a kid for me to celebrate with my friends. But, for this son of yours, when he comes back after swallowing up your property—he and his women—you kill the calf we had been fattening.' The father said, 'My son, you are with me always and all I have is yours. But it was only right we should celebrate and rejoice, because your brother here was dead and has come to life; he was lost and is found.'"

CHRIST THE LORD Many leaders in the world are "in it for themselves." Christ isn't. His greatest glory is winning people's hearts for God, which also happens to be the best thing for them. When the Pharisees complained about his generosity to sinners, he made the most of their attention to try and teach them a lesson. He didn't have to—they certainly didn't deserve his mercy—but he chose to. Then, within the parable itself, Christ profiles his own heart—the heart of God—in the behavior of the father, who lived only for his sons' well-being. "All I have is yours" is no empty rhetoric: in Christ, in the Church, in the Eucharist, God has held absolutely nothing back from us. Jesus is Lord, but he is the Lord of love, longing for hearts that will submit to his gentle and life-giving reign.

CHRIST THE TEACHER This parable teaches us that it is possible to live "in the father's house" without really getting to know the Father. If the younger son had truly known how much his father loved him, how generous his father was, how eagerly he wanted to bequeath to him prosperity and joy, he would never have paid him the insult of asking for his share of the inheritance while his father was still alive. That was equivalent to saying that his father would be of more use to him if he were dead. And if the older son (the dutiful one who seemed to do everything just right) had known how much his father cared for him, he would not have resented the celebration at this brother's return. So although they had lived their entire lives under the same roof, they had not opened their hearts to their father; instead they had closed themselves into the little world of their egoism.

We can easily do the same—spend our whole lives as "practicing" Catholics, going through all the right motions and looking great on the outside, but not opening our hearts to the grace and love of God, not getting to know him on a personal, intimate level. If we operate this way, we run the risk of some day abandoning the Father, convinced that he is treating us unjustly, when the truth is that he is giving us everything he owns.

CHRIST THE FRIEND "While he was still a long way off, his father caught sight of him..." God never stops hoping that we will come to him. He has his eyes on us all the time—not to pounce on us when we mess up, but to run to us, embrace us, kiss us, and clothe us with the robe of his grace and the sandals of divine sonship (servants went barefoot in ancient households, but family members wore sandals). The devil likes to make us forget about this—especially when we most need to remember it; let's not give him that pleasure.

We can also please the Father by going in search of our prodigal brothers and sisters. The rebellious son abandons his father, and his father respects that—he won't go out and try to force his son to come back home. But if the older brother had really cared for both his father and his younger sibling, he could have made a trek or two in search of the unfortunate youth. We can imagine the conversation they would have had at the pig farm. The older brother, "We miss you and we would love for you to come back." The younger brother, "But how can I, what I did was so horrible?" "Don't worry, just come back—trust me, we'll work it out. You don't have to stay here eating corn husks..."

How many lost and sorrowful younger brothers are all around us, if only we would open the eyes of our hearts to see them! And how easy it would be to invite them back to the Father's house, if only we could see beyond our self-centered preoccupations!

CHRIST IN MY LIFE While the Pharisees needed to understand your goodness and mercy, I think that at times I need to be more aware of the evil of sin. I have been infected by the prevailing mentality that forgets about personal responsibility and about the wounds selfishness causes to others. Lord, why do I act as if self-centeredness were okay? Free me, Lord, to love...

Something made that younger son come back to his senses. You are working in mysterious, hidden ways in every heart. I have placed my hope in you,because I believe that you are the way, the truth, and the life. But sometimes I have less confidence in your ability to help others, who seem so far from the truth, to come to their senses. Increase my hope, Lord...

I don't have to go far to find people who are in trouble, who are sad, who need to come back to you and don't know the way. Open my heart so I can reach out to them. Will you not use my slightest effort, even if it's clumsy, as a channel of grace? I don't want to hoard the treasure you have given me—knowing your love. The more I give away, the more you will give to me...

Questions for *SMALL-GROUP DISCUSSION*

1. What struck you most in this passage? What did you notice that you hadn't noticed before?
2. Which son do you think caused the father more sorrow? Which son do you tend to resemble more?
3. In what ways does our society encourage us to fall into a merely exterior, routine living out of our faith, instead of a heartfelt, loving relationship with God?
4. What do you think made the younger son "come to his senses"? Does that apply to us in any way?

Cf. Catechism of the Catholic Church, 1461-1470 on God's forgiveness in the sacrament of confession; 2084-2100 on what it means to love God

THE GOSPEL OF LUKE
Chapter 16

"Despite all the mysteries and wonders which have been discovered by holy doctors and understood by holy souls in this state of life, there still remains more for them to say and to understand. There are depths to be fathomed in Christ. He is like a rich mine with many recesses containing treasures, and no matter how men try to fathom them the end is never reached. Rather, in each recess, men keep on finding here and there new veins of new riches."

- ST. JOHN OF THE CROSS

206. Serving One Master (Lk 16:1-13)

"Christian charity ought not to be content with not hating our enemies and loving them as brothers; it also demands that we treat them with kindness." – Pope Benedict XV

LUKE 16:1-13

He also said to his disciples, "There was a rich man and he had a steward denounced to him for being wasteful with his property. He called for the man and said, 'What is this I hear about you? Draw me up an account of your stewardship because you are not to be my steward any longer.' Then the steward said to himself, 'Now that my master is taking the stewardship from me, what am I to do? Dig? I am not strong enough. Go begging? I should be too ashamed. Ah, I know what I will do to make sure that when I am dismissed from office there will be some to welcome me into their homes.' Then he called his master's debtors one by one. To the first he said, 'How much do you owe my master?' One hundred measures of oil was the reply. The steward said, 'Here, take your bond; sit down straight away and write fifty.' To another he said, 'And you, sir, how much do you owe?' One hundred measures of wheat was the reply. The steward said, 'Here, take your bond and write eighty.' The master praised the dishonest steward for his astuteness. For the children of this world are more astute in dealing with their own kind than are the children of light.

Use money wisely

"And so I tell you this: use money, tainted as it is, to win you friends, and thus make sure that when it fails you, they will welcome you into the tents of eternity. The man who can be trusted in little things can be trusted in great; the man who is dishonest in little things will be dishonest in great. If then you cannot be trusted with money, that tainted thing, who will trust you with genuine riches? And if you cannot be trusted with what is not yours, who will give you what is your very own? No servant can be the slave of two masters: he will either hate the first and love the second, or treat the first with respect and the second with scorn. You cannot be the slave both of God and of money."

CHRIST THE LORD "No servant can be the slave of two masters." Jesus doesn't give a third alternative; we have to serve someone. In another place he puts it like this: "He who does not gather with me scatters" (Lk 11:23). We cannot be morally neutral in life. If we live selfishly, we contribute to the culture of selfishness; we extend the kingdom of money and follow the lord of selfishness, Satan. If we live for Christ, on the other hand, we extend the Kingdom of justice and love, the eternal Kingdom. He doesn't give us any alternative: either we follow a lord, or we follow the Lord.

At the same time, Jesus reminds us that our lives are extended through time; the Christian life consists in an ongoing series of decisions in which we reinforce or undermine our basic choice to follow Christ. How we use money (since it represents power—the ability to do and acquire things) can serve as a trustworthy thermometer of our commitment to Christ. If his Kingdom is our true priority, our checking account will show it, because we will put that power (money) at the service of the Kingdom as much as we can.

CHRIST THE TEACHER "For the children of this world are more astute in dealing with their own kind than are the children of light." We see that every day. The great men and women of the world, the CEOs, the athletes, the movie stars, the political leaders—many of them are exemplary in their tenacity, their determination, and their astuteness. They set a goal and let nothing stop them from achieving it. They turn everything into an opportunity to advance their cause. No sacrifice is too great. Imagine how different the Church (and the world) would be if every Catholic pursued holiness as energetically as most people pursue pleasure, honor, and wealth. Jesus is not rebuking us for striving after excellence in worldly pursuits, but he is rebuking us for not dedicating ourselves with equal conviction to advancing his Kingdom. After all, the former will pass away, but the latter will endure forever—so which is the better investment?

Jesus uses a curious image to instruct us about how to use money. First he says that money is "tainted"—but he doesn't condemn it outright. It's tainted because it is so easily abused by fallen human nature. Then he tells us to use it to win friends, so that when money fails (the moment of death) those friends will welcome us into heaven. In other words, we should marshal our wealth to serve others, not to indulge ourselves. Certainly he doesn't mean that a Christian should abstain from all the world's pleasures and entertainments, but those should be kept under control. The end goal of life is to reach heaven, not to fabricate it here on earth. Using money wisely means investing in the former, not the latter.

CHRIST THE FRIEND Jesus gives this advice so that his disciples might be welcomed into "tents of eternity." The advice may be hard to follow, but the results are worth it.

Nothing Christ demands of us is gratuitous. God doesn't make up rules just for fun. Every word of the Lord is spoken for our benefit, to guide us along the path of eternal life. Every teaching that the Church puts forward is meant to be a beacon of light in a dark and confused world. Unfortunately, we often ignore them as if they were arbitrary no-parking signs. Whenever Christ or the Church seems too demanding, all we need to do is look at a crucifix.

Christ gave everything for our sake, absolutely everything. We are his one love. He became a servant, a criminal, a victim, just for us. That means we can trust him without hesitation, even when he is demanding. He is the friend who will never fail.

CHRIST IN MY LIFE I am glad to be a citizen of your Kingdom, and to have received from you the call to help spread that Kingdom. I can't imagine any other occupation in life that would be more worthwhile. Thank you, Lord. So please help me see all that I do—my normal responsibilities, my apostolic initiatives, my relationships—from this perspective: Thy Kingdom come, thy will be done...

Money is a tough topic, Lord. Everywhere I turn, I am being invited to spend it —and even to spend more than I have. I am part of this culture, Lord, this consumerist culture in which the highest priority is a robust economy. Teach me self-discipline and generosity, so I never fall prey to idols...

Once again you remind me of heaven, of the "tents of eternity." You were always talking about that. O Lord, give me a foretaste of heaven, give me the wisdom that sees this earthly life from the proper perspective. Stir up in my heart a desire for that definitive encounter with you that will take place when my terrestrial pilgrimage reaches its fulfillment. Hallowed be thy name…

Questions for SMALL-GROUP DISCUSSION

1. What struck you most in this passage? What did you notice that you hadn't noticed before?
2. Why do we tend to be more ingenious and proactive when it comes to worldly pursuits than when it comes to spiritual things?
3. What has helped you most in keeping your financial life as Christian as possible? What has hindered you? How can we know where to draw the line between responsibility and generosity?
4. We call ourselves Christians, followers of Christ. If someone were to follow us around for a day, what evidence would there be that this is truly the case? What evidence might they find that could prove the opposite—that we serve some other lord?

Cf. Catechism of the Catholic Church, 50-67 and 2822-2827 on what God wants; 2850-2854 on the Prince of this World; 2401-2418 on a Christian's proper relationship to "mammon"

207. God Sees the Heart (Lk 16:14-18)

"It is for love of him that I do not spare myself in preaching him." – Pope St. Gregory the Great

LUKE 16:14-18

The Pharisees, who loved money, heard all this and laughed at him. He said to them, "You are the very ones who pass yourselves off as virtuous in people's sight, but God knows your hearts. For what is thought highly of by men is loathsome in the sight of God. Up to the time of John it was the Law and the Prophets; since then, the kingdom of God has been preached, and by violence everyone is getting in. It is easier for heaven and earth to disappear than for one little stroke to drop out of the Law. Everyone who divorces his wife and marries another is guilty of adultery, and the man who marries a woman divorced by her husband commits adultery."

CHRIST THE LORD Imagine Jesus being laughed at. Imagine God being laughed at—the Creator of the oceans, the earth, the solar system, the sculptor of mountains, volcanoes, and daffodils, the fashioner of the Pharisees themselves. And why did the Pharisees laugh at him? Because they loved money, St. Luke tells us, and Jesus had just put money in its place, which was not a very high one.

How does Jesus respond to this scorn? He takes no offense; rather he warns his interlocutors that they are dangerously wrong. They have one set of priorities: reputation, influence, wealth; but these coveted goods are "loathsome" in the sight of God. The literal translation of the Greek at that point is "stinks in God's face." It's as if Jesus were saying that they may laugh at God's standards, but in so doing they separate themselves from the God they claim to serve. God has a different set of priorities: moral integrity (thus his comment about the endurance of the law), fidelity (thus his reminder about the evil of divorce), and self-forgetfulness (thus the reference to getting into the Kingdom of God by violence—by the self-mastery and renunciation exemplified by John the Baptist, not the self-indulgent prosperity exemplified by the money-loving Pharisees).

Few passages make so clear the clash between the values promoted by a worldly society and those promoted by the Lord. Since we live both in the world and in Christ, we have to make a point of setting our sights on God so that this world's standards won't blind us to the truth, as they did with the Pharisees.

CHRIST THE TEACHER The Pharisees would have held the Old Covenant view that economic prosperity was necessarily a sign of God's favor and poverty a sign of his disfavor. They drew this conclusion from the many promises in the Old Testament where God encourages Israel to look forward to fruitful vines and bountiful harvests. But the Pharisees' interpretation of this imagery went off track. They used it as an excuse to justify hoarding, indulgence, and even injustice—the more wealth they could accumulate, the more they would appear blessed by God. Thus they used the Law and the Prophets (the Old Testament) to legitimate their self-aggrandizement.

Jesus corrects their misinterpretation. Now that the Kingdom of God is being preached, the Old Testament can be understood in its fullness (thus the extension of Moses' limits on divorce to a complete exclusion of divorce, for example). Just as John the Baptist, who was a bridge between the Old and New Covenants, lived a life of austerity and self-mastery, so the true prosperity that indicates God's favor is that of virtue. The virtuous, those who do what is right and true even when it is costly to their worldly tendencies, those whose hearts are pleasing to God, experience interior peace and vigor; they enter God's Kingdom (a Kingdom of the heart) by doing violence to their selfish tendencies, not by indulging them.

The world today is still obsessed with appearances. Today's Pharisees still laugh at Jesus and call his followers weaklings. Yet God still looks to the heart, hoping to find good soil where he can raise a bumper crop of authentic joy, peace, and spiritual prosperity. At times it is painful to live in the world without giving in to the world's standards, but in the end it is well worth it. There is nothing in this world that can satisfy us as much as the love of Christ.

CHRIST THE FRIEND It was impossible for the Pharisees who rejected Jesus to be true friends to anyone because they were self-centered. Jesus, on the other hand, was completely self-forgetful. What interested him was the mission he had received from his Father to lay the foundation of his Kingdom, which would bring light into darkened souls until the end of time. He preaches about selflessness, and he exemplifies it in every detail of his life. He continues to exemplify it in the Church, in his saints, and especially in the Eucharist. He patiently waits in every Tabernacle across the globe, glad to be able to adore the Father in our name, and willing to put up with hours and hours of loneliness in order to still be there when one of his followers needs to talk.

Surely it is more beautiful and fulfilling to be a true friend than to be a Pharisee. If we let Christ be the friend he wants to be, maybe we will learn to be that kind of friend for others.

CHRIST IN MY LIFE When I look into my soul, I find a clash. I do love you and want to follow you, but I also love my comfort and the praise of my peers. It's so hard to strike the right balance between giving the good things of this world their due and keeping on the high road to holiness. Thank you for walking this path at my side. I know you will guide me; you have guided me so faithfully already…

Help me to want what you want, Lord. Help me to do what you want. Help me to want what you do. I don't want to deceive myself the way the Pharisees did. I want to hear your word and obey it. I don't care what other people say about me—only you have the words of eternal life. You are the Lord, my Savior and Guide. Thy will be done…

You are more interested in how I treat my colleague down the hall than in the biggest headlines of the biggest newspaper in the world. You are more interested in my heart than in wars and disasters. Everything here is passing away, but every human soul will live forever, either in light or darkness. Lord, make me a lantern and a flame to spread your light…

Questions for
SMALL-GROUP DISCUSSION

1. What struck you most in this passage? What did you notice that you hadn't noticed before?
2. Which aspects of our popular culture reflect Christ's scale of values? Which reflect the Pharisees' scale of values?
3. In what way is it easiest for us to fall into hypocrisy, to look virtuous on the outside but actually be selfish on the inside at the same time?
4. Why do you think God doesn't always reward holiness with earthly prosperity?

Cf. Catechism of the Catholic Church, 1750-1761 on the morality of human acts; 1804-1811 on the moral virtues

208. Money and Fire (Lk 16:19-31)

"Girding our loins then with faith and the observance of good deeds let us so follow his paths under the guidance of the gospel that we may be worthy to see him who has called us into his kingdom." – St. Benedict

LUKE 16:19-31

"There was a rich man who used to dress in purple and fine linen and feast magnificently every day. And at his gate there lay a poor man called Lazarus, covered with sores, who longed to fill himself with the scraps that fell from the rich man's table. Dogs even came and licked his sores. Now the poor man died and was carried away by the angels to the bosom of Abraham. The rich man also died and was buried. In his torment in Hades he looked up and saw Abraham a long way off with Lazarus in his bosom. So he cried out, 'Father Abraham, pity me and send Lazarus to dip the tip of his finger in water and cool my tongue, for I am in agony in these flames.' 'My son, 'Abraham replied, 'remember that during your life good things came your way, just as bad things came the way of Lazarus. Now he is being comforted here while you are in agony. But that is not all: between us and you a great gulf has been fixed, to stop anyone, if he wanted to, crossing from our side to yours, and to stop any crossing from your side to ours.' The rich man replied, 'Father, I beg you then to send Lazarus to my father's house, since I have five brothers, to give them warning so that they do not come to this place of torment too.' 'They have Moses and the prophets,' said Abraham, 'let them listen to them.' 'Ah no, father Abraham,' said the rich man, 'but if someone comes to them from the dead, they will repent.' Then Abraham said to him, 'If they will not listen either to Moses or to the prophets, they will not be convinced even if someone should rise from the dead.'"

CHRIST THE LORD Jesus knew what was going to happen to him. He knew that he would suffer, die, and "rise from the dead." And he knew that even then many would not believe in him. He is like a King who is determined to free a captive people from slavery, knowing that once he does, many of them will go off and enslave themselves again. So why go to all the trouble? For the few who will not leave him. Even if one person—you—could be reunited to God through his Passion, death, and Resurrection, it would be worth it. The value of one soul is a concept that eludes the modern mind, affected so profoundly by polls and percentages, but it is at the center of God's heart. Because his love is not limited by time and space, he is able to love each person with a personal, intimate, determined attention.

This simultaneous universality and individuality of God's love is mirrored in the two great vocations of the Church: marriage and celibacy. Marriage establishes the deep and almost unbreakable bond of family love, highly personal and intimate. Celibacy shows forth the universal extension of God's love, which plays no favorites and excludes no one.

"Yes, God loved the world so much that he gave his only Son, so that everyone who believes in him may not be lost but may have eternal life" (Jn 3:16). Love moves our Lord, and love never gives up. If we are faithful followers, we should faithfully follow in his steps of self-forgetful love.

CHRIST THE TEACHER Jesus told this parable to the Pharisees. A few verses earlier, St. Luke points out that they "loved money, heard all this, and laughed at him." They were the religious and intellectual elite of Palestine. Everyone respected them; everyone revered them. They were sought after as teachers and leaders of synagogues—they were the ones who had all the right degrees, had gone to all the right schools, got all the top jobs.... They had it made. And Christ reminds them of a lesson that the successful of this world too easily forget: this world is not all there is. In fact, it is bound to disappear, giving way to either eternal reward or regret. The purpose of this world is to prepare us for heaven, but if we get attached to it, we may never make it to heaven.

And that would be the real tragedy, because heaven is where the soul lives in perfect communion with God—which is what the soul was created for. Outside of heaven, there is only the frustration of unfulfilled longings—more painful than even the most parched physical thirst. Christ could not have been clearer about this, and yet so many still refuse to listen.

CHRIST THE FRIEND Perhaps Christ's greatest act of charity was his patient effort to win over the hearts of the self-satisfied Pharisees. Many of them showed no sign of respect or even mild interest in the truth of his claims, and yet he kept buffeting them with parables and miracles, desperately hoping that they would let in the light of his grace. Christ commanded his disciples to love their enemies, to forgive those who persecuted them, and he shows them how—by being a true friend to his most vicious antagonists.

He continues this conquest of love. Yesterday, today, and tomorrow, Jesus continues to go after every single soul. He wants to hold each one close to his heart, just as Lazarus was held close in Abraham's bosom. It is God's will that none be lost. His mission is to draw all men to himself. This is the desire in the heart of our Friend, and if we are to be faithful, it should become our desire too, for he has given us a share in this same mission of gathering souls to the bosom of the Father.

CHRIST IN MY LIFE Because you love me, you created me. Because you love me, you gave me the gift of faith. Because you love me, you surround me with innumerable gifts of love, you involve me in your own mission of building up the eternal Kingdom, and you never tire of guiding me to a more fruitful, virtuous life. Open my eyes, Lord, so that I can see the beauty of your love...

So many people live as if this life were all there is. Why? Why don't we believe in heaven and hell? I admit, it's possible to get obsessed with the afterlife, but it would be a foolish traveler who kept moving ahead every day without ever thinking about his destination. Keep me in tune with the truth, Lord, and teach me to bear witness with courage and love...

Who are my enemies, my antagonists? Do I love them as you loved yours? The Pharisees didn't give you warm, fuzzy feelings, but you loved them all the same. You went out of your way to give them what they most needed—a vision of your love and truth. Teach me to love as you love and to give as you give...

Questions for *SMALL-GROUP DISCUSSION*

1. What struck you most in this passage? What did you notice that you hadn't noticed before?

2. How do you think Jesus was hoping the Pharisees would react to this parable? How is he hoping we will react to it?
3. Why do you think inordinate love for money makes it so hard for the Pharisees to receive Christ's message?
4. How should the reality of heaven, hell, and purgatory (all revealed doctrines of the Church) impact our day-to-day lives?

Cf. Catechism of the Catholic Church, 2443-2449 *on love for the poor;* 2405-2418 *on a Christian's use of material goods;* 2534-2550 *on love for money;* 1020-1050 *on death, judgment, hell, purgatory, and heaven*

THE GOSPEL OF LUKE
Chapter 17

"Our king, though he is most high, came for our sake in great humility, but he could not come empty-handed. He brought with him, as it were, a great bonus for his soldiers, which not only made them abundantly rich, but also gave them strength to fight and conquer. The gift he brought was love, and which brings men into fellowship with the Godhead.... Love, therefore, is the origin and source of all good things; it is a most excellent defense, the road that leads to heaven. Whoever walks in love can neither stray nor be afraid. Love guides, love protects, love leads to the end. Christ our Lord, brethren, set up for us this ladder of love, and by it every Christian can climb to heaven. You must, therefore, keep a firm hold on love, you must show it to one another, and by progress in it climb up to heaven."

- ST. FULGENTIUS OF RUSPE

209. Real Humility (Lk 17:1-10)

"Wherever we find ourselves we not only may, but should, seek perfection." – St. Francis de Sales

LUKE 17:1-10

He said to his disciples, "Obstacles are sure to come, but alas for the one who provides them! It would be better for him to be thrown into the Sea with a millstone put round his neck than that he should lead astray a single one of these little ones. Watch yourselves! And if he wrongs you seven times a day and seven times comes back to you and says, 'I am sorry,' you must forgive him." The apostles said to the Lord, "Increase our faith." The Lord replied, "Were your faith the size of a mustard seed you could say to this mulberry tree, 'Be uprooted and planted in the sea,' and it would obey you. Which of you, with a servant ploughing or minding sheep, would say to him when he returned from the fields, 'Come and have your meal immediately'? Would he not be more likely to say, 'Get my supper laid; make yourself tidy and wait on me while I eat and drink. You can eat and drink yourself afterwards'? Must he be grateful to the servant for doing what he was told? So with you: when you have done all you have been told to do, say, 'We are merely servants: we have done no more than our duty.'"

CHRIST THE LORD The easiest thing for us to do is forget that we are not God. When we achieve something great, when we receive applause, we let it go to our heads. One of the very first prayers we all learn is: "Glory be to the Father, and to the Son, and to the Holy Spirit, as it was in the beginning, is now, and ever shall be, world without end. Amen." All good things come from God, so ultimately all praise should go to him as well. Even our talents and our opportunities are gifts of God, so if we bear fruit because of them, very little of the credit should go to us. When we start to take more credit than is our due, we are forgetting who really is Lord. That was Satan's mistake; let's not repeat it.

This kind of humility can sound harsh to us. Isn't Jesus being a bit hard on that servant of the parable? The servant works hard, obeys, submits, and Jesus says he should look for no recompense; he's just doing his duty. It seems rather cold. But in fact, it's just the opposite. Imagine how unstable our lives would be if the intensity of God's love for us depended on the efficiency of our service in his Kingdom. If we could increase or decrease God's love for us just by our performance rating, what would be the difference between God's Kingdom and this world? We would be just as anxious, ambitious, and self-centered working for Christ as we tend to be working for money and promotions.

In the Lord's Kingdom, the opposite is true. God's love for each of us is already so total, so personal, so unconditional, and so untiring that nothing we do can increase or decrease it. And so the servant in God's Kingdom does his work energetically, joyfully, and peacefully as a response to that gratuitous love of God. God's love doesn't depend on our achievements; our achievements flow from knowing how much God loves us and from wanting to thank him. This is true humility; this is what the Lord wants us to learn.

CHRIST THE TEACHER The two lessons of the passage are unrelated, except that St. Luke reports them together in a section of his Gospel where he summarizes several of Jesus' lessons. The first lesson stresses the power and importance of faith. Faith unleashes God's power in our lives. When we let ourselves be won over by God, he can do wonders with us; when we doubt him, trusting ourselves and our ideas more than his infinite wisdom and love (e.g., filtering out Church teaching that we find uncomfortable), we cut ourselves off from his grace. He won't force his way in; he respects us too much for that. But if we invite him in, and give him full control over our lives, amazing things begin to happen.

The second lesson is the hardest one to learn: the lesson of humility. Simply put, all we have comes from God; it is all a gift. So strictly speaking, we deserve nothing (except recompense for our sins). And yet we think we deserve everything. Even our basic human rights stem from our existence, which is a gift of God and not a personal achievement. Our duty is not to rule the universe, but to serve God, to get to know him, and discover his plan for us. If we do that, we will experience the peace and meaning we long for—just as flowers achieve their beauty only when they grow as God designed them to.

CHRIST THE FRIEND The apostles did the right thing. When they detected a flaw in their spiritual life (a lack of faith), they humbly approached the Lord and asked him to take care of it. They trusted him. They knew that he was sincerely interested in making them men of his Kingdom, so they did not hesitate to come to him with their needs. The answer he gives is indirect, and somewhat unsatisfying, which probably means that they weren't ready for the full answer yet, but we can be sure that it only drew them closer to him. Whenever we come to Christ in sincerity and humility, he draws us closer to him—which is why we should come to him more often.

The warning against scandal—putting obstacles in the way of others' faith and trust in God—couldn't be more frightening. This too shows how intensely Jesus is interested in each one of us. In the first place, he gives us a chance to help build his Kingdom, to bring others to Christ. In the second place, he vehemently warns us against abusing that privilege. This shows that our friendship is real—Jesus takes a risk with us. All real friendship involves risk, the risk of having one's trust betrayed. And it also gives us a glimpse of heaven, where our friendship with Christ will have automatically made us into friends with everyone else he has befriended.

CHRIST IN MY LIFE The default position of my self-conception is still me-centered, Lord. I don't like considering myself a mere servant. But it's true. You didn't have to create me, you didn't have to redeem me, you didn't have to give me the talents and gifts you gave me—in short, everything I am and everything I have depends on you. Jesus, teach me the joy and freedom of humility...

Increase my faith, Lord. I want to do great things for your Kingdom. You have put in my heart a burning desire to make a difference in the world, to bring others into your friendship. But I am so clumsy, so blind. Increase my faith, Lord. Teach me to do your will...

Because you have made me a free person, I am equally capable of both good and evil. I know that my impatience and self-centeredness offends you and pushes others away from you. But I also know that the power of your grace is infinite. You are working in my soul, recreating me in your own image. Make me more attentive to your words, Lord...

Questions for SMALL-GROUP DISCUSSION

1. What struck you most in this passage? What did you notice that you hadn't noticed before?
2. How should a Christian react to praise? How can we learn to do that?
3. What hinders us from having a stronger faith?
4. How would our lives be different if we really, truly believed that we were just "mere servants," that God doesn't really need us in the way we need him, but that he passionately desires us to come into his Kingdom?

Cf. Catechism of the Catholic Church, 142-184 on faith; 2083-2141 on the proper relationship between God and the human person

210. A Rare Flower (Lk 17:11-19)

"Compelled by his great love, or rather, as the apostle says, by the excess of his love for us, he sent his beloved Son that he might make satisfaction for us, and recall us to the life which sin had taken away." – St. Alphonsus Liguori

LUKE 17:11-19
Now on the way to Jerusalem he travelled along the border between Samaria and Galilee. As he entered one of the villages, ten lepers came to meet him. They stood some way off and called to him, "Jesus! Master! Take pity on us." When he saw them he said, "Go and show yourselves to the priests." Now as they were going away they were cleansed. Finding himself cured, one of them turned back praising God at the top of his voice and threw himself at the feet of Jesus and thanked him. The man was a Samaritan. This made Jesus say, "Were not all ten made clean? The other nine, where are they? It seems that no one has come back to give praise to God, except this foreigner." And he said to the man, "Stand up and go on your way. Your faith has saved you."

CHRIST THE LORD To this day, leprosy is an incurable disease. It can be controlled preventively, through proper hygiene, but it can't be cured. (Leprosy is a bacterial infection that causes loss of sensation and eventual paralysis, along with the grotesque disintegration of a person's extremities—fingers, facial features, etc.) Yet Christ cures these ten lepers with a mere command. Showing oneself to the priest was a requirement of Old Testament law for anyone who claimed to have been cured from leprosy. This law had been instituted in order to ensure a full cure. They took this precaution because leprosy is thought to be highly contagious, and a miscalculation in an individual case could cause a severe outbreak among a whole village or city. Christ's Lordship rarely appears so clearly and nobly as when he commands the powers of nature for the benefit (never for the harm) of the people he came to save—Jews and foreigners alike.

This encounter stands in sharp contrast, however, to the ongoing verbal fencing between Jesus and the stubborn Pharisees. They refused to call Jesus "Master"; they refused to accept his grace—simply put, they refused him. Why? Because the Pharisees were successful, strong, healthy, and talented, so it was easy for them to consider themselves self-sufficient. The lepers, on the other hand, had no alternative but to acknowledge their utter helplessness. Those who think they can make something truly worthy of their lives depending only on their own resources shut out the authentically transforming grace of God. What's more, the Pharisees didn't even see their error; they thought they were in communion with God. That kind of tragic self-deception should make each one us take a closer look at our own relationship with the Lord.

CHRIST THE TEACHER At the end of his Gospel, St. John tells us that if everything Christ did during his brief earthly life were written down, the entire world would not contain the books. We can infer, therefore, that many of Christ's miracles were not recorded in the New Testament. Why did St. Luke include this one? Clearly because of the lesson that Christ teaches us by it: the ugliness of ingratitude and the beauty of gratitude.

The ten lepers had no hope but Christ. Even their closest relatives dared not come near them. They were required to live in isolated colonies, and if they had to travel, the law obliged them to ring a bell wherever they went, shouting out, "Unclean! Unclean!" to warn people of their approach (which is why they addressed Christ from a distance). On top of that, they had to live with the repulsion of their own decaying bodies—the pain and the stench of leprosy are almost unbearable. Leprosy was a long, humiliating, and dismal agony, the most horrible of ancient diseases. Jesus frees these ten lepers entirely from their hopelessness and dread, and only one comes back to thank him for it—and that one happens to be a Samaritan (the Samaritans were archenemies of the Jews, racially and religiously).

We are all moral lepers. The human race was infected with mortal selfishness by original sin. Christ saved us, not with a mere command, but by his Incarnation, life, suffering, and painful death on a cross. How many of us render him sincere, heartfelt thanks for all he has done for us? Not to live with an attitude of gratitude toward God is more than being impolite—ingratitude is ugly because it's positively unjust. Gratitude, on the other hand, is one of the most beautiful flowers in the whole garden of virtue. It directly contradicts self-centeredness, self-indulgence, and self-absorption. It builds bridges, unites communities, and softens hearts. It encourages and inspires. It cuts through discouragement and counteracts depression. It opens the soul to the truth and releases anxiety. It brings smiles and gladness wherever it blooms. What a pity that it is as rare as it is lovely!

CHRIST THE FRIEND Jesus cannot resist a cry for pity. For him, a soul in need is an obligation to help. He needed no convincing, no cajolery—these lepers cried out to him from the depths of their hearts and automatically his heart was moved. We see it over and over again in the Gospels—his heart being moved to miraculous action by the needs of those around him. Of course, that same sensitivity was the motive for his coming to earth in the first place; love simply can't hold back when it sees others in need. This truth about Jesus can be the source of our confidence in him, but it should also be the source of our own activity in the world. We who feast on Christ's very own Body and Blood in the Eucharist need to share also the beatings of his heart, his desire to do as much good as possible; otherwise, our hearts will beat in vain.

CHRIST IN MY LIFE It's easy for me to forget about my sins, my sinfulness, and my need for you. The slightest success puts me into a preening mode. Lord, never let me forget that all that I have and all that I am is a gift of your goodness. Teach me to live with the attitude of humble wonder and gratitude that you praised in the Samaritan. For all those people who never thank you, I thank you now…

It is a mystery to me that I am still nervous about exposing my "leprosy" to you in the sacrament of confession—you wouldn't have instituted the sacrament if we didn't need it. I can't help feeling ashamed at my egoism, but I ask you to always use that shame to drive me closer to you, my hope and my salvation…

It doesn't take much to detect the moral leprosy affecting our world; it only exacerbates the poverty and sickness that afflict so many people. It moves your heart so much; why does it move mine so little? What more would you have me do, Lord, to relieve my neighbors' suffering? Jesus, meek and humble of heart, make my heart more like yours...

Questions for SMALL-GROUP DISCUSSION

1. What struck you most in this passage? What did you notice that you hadn't noticed before?
2. Gratitude has been called "the rarest flower in the garden of the virtues." Why do you think that is? What can we do to increase this beautiful virtue in our lives?
3. Why do you think the other nine lepers didn't come back to thank Jesus?
4. People who have grown up Catholic often take the beauty and greatness of the Church for granted, or don't even recognize it, whereas converts to the Church are some of its most avid fans. Why is this? Is there any relationship between this phenomenon and the fact that the one leper who thanked Jesus was not a Jew?

Cf. Catechism of the Catholic Church, 1359-1361 the Eucharist and gratitude; 2097, 2099, and 2637-2638 on gratitude owed to God; 396-412 on original sin and God's response to it

211. Thy Kingdom Come! (Lk 17:20-37)

"He is the man of sorrows and of hope. It is he who will come and who one day will be our judge and—we hope—the everlasting fullness of our existence, our happiness." – Pope Paul VI

LUKE 17:20-37

Asked by the Pharisees when the kingdom of God was to come, he gave them this answer, "The coming of the kingdom of God does not admit of observation and there will be no one to say, 'Look here! Look there! 'For, you must know, the kingdom of God is among you." He said to the disciples, "A time will come when you will long to see one of the days of the Son of Man and will not see it. They will say to you, 'Look there!' or, 'Look here!' Make no move; do not set off in pursuit; for as the lightning flashing from one part of heaven lights up the other, so will be the Son of Man when his day comes. But first he must suffer grievously and be rejected by this generation.

"As it was in Noah's day, so will it also be in the days of the Son of Man. People were eating and drinking, marrying wives and husbands, right up to the day Noah went into the ark, and the flood came and destroyed them all. It will be the same as it was in Lot's day: people were eating and drinking, buying and selling, planting and building, but the day Lot left Sodom, God rained fire and brimstone from heaven and it destroyed them all. It will be the same when the day comes for the Son of Man to be revealed. When that day comes, anyone on the housetop, with his possessions in the house, must not come down to collect them, nor must anyone in the fields turn back either. Remember Lot's wife. Anyone who tries to preserve his life will lose it; and anyone who loses it will keep it safe. I tell you, on that night two will be in one bed: one will be taken, the other left; two women will be grinding corn together: one will be taken, the other left." The disciples interrupted. "Where, Lord?" they asked. He said, "Where the body is, there too will the vultures gather."

CHRIST THE LORD "The Kingdom of God is among you," Jesus tells the inquiring Pharisees. Obviously, he didn't mean that they had already entered the Kingdom, because they hadn't believed in him or accepted his rule. So what does Jesus mean? He means that in the epoch of the Son of Man—the New Covenant—God's grace is at work in the midst of our everyday life. Just as through the Incarnation, Jesus—the King—came to dwell among the people of Palestine, among the Pharisees, so throughout the whole of the Church's era, God will be inviting and inspiring and knocking on the doors of people's hearts from within. This is the Lord's methodology throughout his Palestinian ministry, and through the Church, it will continue to be his methodology. When will the Kingdom come? Whenever we care to listen. Praying for the coming of the Kingdom, then, means praying for hearts to be docile to the Lord.

CHRIST THE TEACHER The Pharisees ask a question we all long to ask: When will the Kingdom come? And Jesus answers: it already has come. Where Jesus is accepted, believed in, and obeyed, there he reigns; there the Kingdom can be found. But then he goes on to explain to his disciples that although it is primarily a Kingdom of the heart, it will have a visible manifestation as well.

Many Jews at the time of Jesus were expecting a Messiah to come and restore a highly visible Kingdom, a political and social arrangement in which the Jews would once again have independence and international influence, as they did in the time of David. From their perspective, these were key ingredients for the beginning of the Messianic era, what Jesus calls the "days of the Son of man." But Jesus corrects their mistaken conception. He describes in this passage the symbolic end of the Old Covenant, the fall of Jerusalem, which took place in A.D. 70 after a horrific siege of the city left more than a million Jews dead. Jesus warns his disciples to leave the city as soon as the enemy appears to avoid suffering in this siege. And that's exactly what the Christian community in Jerusalem did when the Roman legions appeared on the horizon; they fled to a town across the Jordan, and they survived. The Roman legions were the vultures bent on tearing apart the city of Jerusalem, which by its official rejection of Jesus had become a spiritual corpse. The Church then took up the baton and continued to embody and spread Christ's reign.

But this discourse has a lesson for us as well. The end of the Old Covenant and the destruction of Jerusalem foreshadowed the end of history, just as the end of Sodom and Noah's flood foreshadowed the end of Jerusalem. Then, all of creation will "wear out like a garment" (Heb 1:11). It will be destroyed just as Jerusalem was, and in its place Jesus will establish the new heaven and the new earth, in which the interior Kingdom of his reign will be perfectly manifested on the outside as well. That ending will come as swiftly and surprisingly and definitively as the ending of the Old Covenant, so we too should be ready, and we should let nothing distract us from following the Lord in the meantime.

CHRIST THE FRIEND Jesus knows what we need to know, and he knows what we don't need to know. He answers these thorny questions, therefore, without giving all the details. Dates and times won't help the disciples to be more faithful, so he doesn't reveal them.

Jesus: Sometimes you wonder why I don't show you my master plan for your life. I do have one. I have a dream for you. I know what will satisfy you and how you can achieve it. If it would help to tell you everything at once, do you think I would hesitate for the slightest instant to do so? You need to live out my plan for your life one day and one decision at a time. In my wisdom and love, I can tell you that what matters most is that you learn to trust me more and more. Your acts of trust, your obedience to my will, your docility–that is your contribution in making my plan a reality. I know that sometimes you feel frustrated because you can't figure out what I am up to. That's when you need to remember that good friends know how to administer the right medicine one dose at a time, and I am the very best of friends.

CHRIST IN MY LIFE How many times I pray this prayer, "Thy Kingdom come!" O Lord, I want to pray it from my heart. I want everyone, starting with me, to be docile to your will, to respond generously and trustingly to the nudges and invitations you constantly give. Teach me to make this the real motto of my life: Thy Kingdom come, thy will be done...

So often I want to be able to put everything into a nice little package, to be able to understand everything and live placidly with all the answers. You don't want that. You want me to exercise virtue, trust, and faith. Somehow, you prefer to work that way. Life is an adventure, a journey. Keep me on the right path, going at the right pace...

I trust in you, Lord. When a cathedral is being built, it looks like a mess, but a master plan is guiding that mess and turning it into something beautiful, something magnificent. I know you are the master architect of my life and my efforts to build your Kingdom. Teach me to trust in you at all times and never doubt your wisdom...

Questions for *SMALL-GROUP DISCUSSION*

1. What struck you most in this passage? What did you notice that you hadn't noticed before?
2. If a non-believing friend were to ask you the same question the Pharisees asked Jesus, "When will the Kingdom come?"—how would you answer them?
3. Why do you think Jesus described all these horrible things that would happen at the fall of Jerusalem? When these events actually occurred and some of the Pharisees who had heard Jesus' explanation saw them, what might they have thought?
4. What has been hard for you to trust Jesus about? What has helped you most to trust in difficult moments?

Cf. Catechism of the Catholic Church, 667-677 on Christ already reigning in the Church; 2816-2821 on what the petition "Thy Kingdom come!" really means

THE GOSPEL OF LUKE
Chapter 18

"For he who will reward us on judgment day for our works and alms will even in this life listen mercifully to those who come to him in prayer combined with good works."

- ST. CYPRIAN OF CARTHAGE

212. Never Losing Heart (Lk 18:1-8)

LUKE 18:1-8

Then he told them a parable about the need to pray continually and never lose heart. "There was a judge in a certain town," he said, "who had neither fear of God nor respect for man. In the same town there was a widow who kept on coming to him and saying, I want justice from you against my enemy! For a long time he refused, but at last he said to himself, 'Maybe I have neither fear of God nor respect for man, but since she keeps pestering me I must give this widow her just rights, or she will persist in coming and worry me to death.'" And the Lord said, "You notice what the unjust judge has to say? Now will not God see justice done to his chosen who cry to him day and night even when he delays to help them? I promise you, he will see justice done to them, and done speedily. But when the Son of Man comes, will he find any faith on earth?"

CHRIST THE LORD The judge in the parable, although an unworthy fellow, has real authority. He can issue a decision that will have actual repercussions both for the widow and for her adversary. Christ also has real authority—"all authority in heaven and earth," as a matter of fact (Mt 28:18). He is able to influence our lives and history, and he has chosen to put this influence at our disposal. Just as the judge would not have given the widow a fair decision if she had not pleaded with him to do so, God also has decided to make his graces depend (at least in part) upon our initiative. "Ask, and it will be given to you," our Lord pointed out earlier (Lk 11:9); "Search and you will find. . . ." It seems that Christ refuses to be a dictator, but delights in being a generous and responsive King.

CHRIST THE TEACHER Jesus is politely telling us that we are weak petitioners. He probably detected impatience behind the Pharisees' question about when the Kingdom would come, an impatience we too are familiar with. We give up too easily; we approach God with less confidence than this determined widow had in approaching a crooked judge. We doubt God. We think that just because he doesn't answer us in the way we expect him to, he isn't answering us at all. That shows a lack of faith, a truncated vision of God. No prayer that we utter goes unheard. God is never out of his office; he's never on vacation. He is longing for us to bombard him with our prayers. He is eagerly searching for hearts that trust him enough to ask him unceasingly for everything they need. He always answers our prayers, even when the answer is "no."

On judgment day, one of our greatest regrets will be how little we prayed. Prayer costs us nothing and can be done anywhere and any time; it's an investment that simply can't go wrong, and yet we relegate it to a few minutes here and there. It's like refusing to turn on the lights because we're afraid they might not work, or because we have become oddly attached to the dark.

CHRIST THE FRIEND In Jesus' last sentence, we detect a tinge of sadness. It is a rhetorical question: When he comes again, will he find any faith? Will he find anyone who recognizes him and is glad to welcome him? He certainly hopes so. He wants to be able to grant us the intense joy of eternal life, but he knows that not everyone will accept the gift, and it pains him.

Jesus: Love is always a risk. I risked it when I came to find you and invite you to follow me in my Kingdom. I knew that in order to offer myself in friendship, I had to become vulnerable; it had to be possible for you to reject me. Look at me hanging from the cross. Look at my side, pierced to my heart with the soldier's lance. This is what love risks; this is love's vulnerability. I am willing to take the risk, because I long for your friendship; I long for you to follow me, day after day. If you accept my invitation, you will have nothing to fear. When it comes to friendship with me, the vulnerability only goes in one direction: you may hurt me by preferring your own will and being unfaithful to me, but I will never be unfaithful to you.

CHRIST IN MY LIFE Thank you for the gift of prayer, Lord. Thank you for giving me a share in your work, for not doing it all yourself. Now my life can have eternal repercussions as you want it to. Dear Lord, teach me to use my freedom well. I don't want to live at the mercy of passing fancies or stock market fluctuations. I want to live grounded in you, grounded in your love and truth…

Teach me to pray, Lord. My faith is so weak. Teach me to pray at all times, to never tire of conversing with you about everything. Help me to develop the habit of lifting my heart and mind to you in the midst of a meeting, a traffic jam, or a chore. Help me to confide in you with all my heart, as you want me to, so that you can work through me to bring many souls into your Kingdom...

I believe in you, Lord. I have put my hopes in you. I love you, though my love is weak and scrawny. If thousands ignore you, I at least want to stay close to you. Guide me, lead me along the path of your wisdom and your peace, and make me a channel of your grace...

Questions for SMALL-GROUP DISCUSSION

1. What struck you most in this passage? What did you notice that you hadn't noticed before?
2. What experience or conversation might have prompted Jesus to tell this parable?
3. Why are we less persistent in our prayers than the widow was with her case?
4. What things tend to hold us back from being perfectly docile to God's will? Jesus lived his whole life for us, for the Kingdom. How can we better follow his example?

Cf. Catechism of the Catholic Church, 2742-2745 on the need for perseverance in prayer; 2725-2737 on difficulties in prayer and the "battle" of prayer

213. The ABCs of Success (Lk 18:9-17)

"Confession heals, confession justifies, confession grants pardon of sin. All hope consists in confession." – St. Isidore of Seville

LUKE 18:9-17

He spoke the following parable to some people who prided themselves on being virtuous and despised everyone else, "Two men went up to the Temple to pray, one a Pharisee, the other a tax collector. The Pharisee stood there and said this prayer to himself, 'I thank you, God, that I am not grasping, unjust, adulterous like the rest of mankind, and particularly that I am not like this tax collector here. I fast twice a week; I pay tithes on all I get.' The tax collector stood some distance away, not daring even to raise his eyes to heaven; but he beat his breast and said, 'God, be merciful to me, a sinner.' This man, I tell you, went home again at rights with God; the other did not. For everyone who exalts himself will be humbled, but

> the man who humbles himself will be exalted." People even brought little children to him, for him to touch them; but when the disciples saw this they turned them away. But Jesus called the children to him and said, "Let the little children come to me, and do not stop them; for it is to such as these that the kingdom of God belongs. I tell you solemnly, anyone who does not welcome the kingdom of God like a little child will never enter it."

CHRIST THE LORD God has the right to be Lord. He is eternal, all-powerful, all-knowing, all-good, and all-loving. He created all things, and he keeps all things in existence. Everything (and everyone) else owes everything to him. Without God, we would not even be able to sin—because to sin, first of all we have to exist, and second of all, we have to possess free will. Without God, who supplies both of these requisites, we are nothing. When we address Christ as "Lord," we acknowledge this utter dependence on him, and we express our trust that he will continue showering his blessings upon us—not because we deserve them, but because of who he is: abounding in generosity and loving-kindness.

When we address Christ as "Lord," we also acknowledge that he deserves our complete fidelity and obedience. And since we are not completely obedient to God (even the just man falls "seven times" a day, cf. Prv 24:16), addressing him as Lord needs to include a confident plea for his mercy. This is the bedrock of all true prayer, because it is the bedrock of the truth about us and about God. In this light, the Pharisee's sin was much greater than "greed, dishonesty, or adultery"; it was the sin of thinking he didn't need God, that he was independent of the Lord.

By this standard, the Pharisee was not going to make it into the Kingdom of God, because that requires being like children—serenely aware of our dependence. Children aren't angels, but they certainly are dependent on their parents, and they know it. This is basic humility, and without it we can never live in communion with the Lord.

CHRIST THE TEACHER Through the centuries, the prayer of the publican (i.e., tax collector: a Jew who collaborated with the occupying Roman forces by collecting taxes from fellow Jews, often looked upon as the epitome of infidelity to God and a betrayer of the Covenant) has been described as a complete summary of Christian spirituality. There are even cases of monks who made this prayer the only words that they spoke, and who reached the heights of sanctity by means of it.

First of all, it recognizes God's greatest quality—in relation to fallen mankind, that is: his mercy. Mercy is the form love takes in the face of suffering.

The word "mercy" comes from the Latin *misericors*: *miser* (wretched, miserable) plus *cor* (heart)—to take someone else's wretchedness into one's heart. Because of original sin, and because of our personal sins, we are miserable creatures, and when we bring our misery to God, he takes it up into his heart. Second, the publican's prayer recognizes his own need: he accuses himself for being a sinner, someone who has abused the gifts of God, someone who has given into selfishness.

The Pharisee's prayer shows no knowledge either of God's mercy or of his own need for God. In truth, it is no prayer at all—there is no connection between God and the one who is praying: it is just an exercise in narcissism, in self-admiration. God wants to connect with us, but he can only do so if we let him.

CHRIST THE FRIEND Jesus went after the big sinners—you don't get much bigger than "people who prided themselves on being virtuous and despised everyone else." He didn't just preach to the choir (which, in fact, is why his enemies had to have him killed; his influence was simply becoming too widespread). This shows how much he cared about others, and how little he worried about himself. If he had been after comfortable self-satisfaction, he would never have gone after big sinners. This is confirmed by our own experience: When we don't go after those who need Christ most, isn't it because we care more about our own comfortable self-satisfaction than about expanding Christ's Kingdom?

His concern for big sinners also gives us another reason to trust him without limits. No sinner is too big for Christ's mercy. His mercy is infinite, like an ocean; even the greatest sins are finite, like a thimble. How foolish we would be to think our thimble was too deep for his ocean!

CHRIST IN MY LIFE You are my Lord. I understand what that means: I owe everything to you. You hold my entire existence in the palm of your hand. You never cease thinking of me and drawing me closer to you. You are my Lord, but you are also my Father, my Brother, and my Friend. Jesus, I trust in you...

I ask you to have mercy on me, for all the selfishness I know about, and for all the selfishness I'm unaware of. And I ask you to have mercy on all sinners. It is your mercy that makes your glory shine! Teach me to confide in your mercy no matter what, and to be merciful, forgiving, gentle, and meek—especially with those who don't deserve it...

Pour your courage into my heart, Lord. I am hampered in my apostolate and my testimony because I still care too much about what other people will think. I'm glad you didn't give in to those temptations. Teach me to be adventurous in building your Kingdom and spreading it, even to the "big sinners" who seem so hopeless...

Questions for *SMALL-GROUP DISCUSSION*

1. What struck you most in this passage? What did you notice that you hadn't noticed before?
2. How would you describe the proper basic attitude that should be used when we approach God in prayer? What does this parable teach us about God's attitude toward us when we pray?
3. How can we become less like the Pharisee and more like the publican in our prayer? Why should we want to?
4. If an open-minded non-believing friend asked you how to pray, what would you say?

Cf. Catechism of the Catholic Church, 2558-2565 on the prerequisites for prayer; 2568-2589 on models of prayer from the Old Testament; 2779-2785 on how we should approach God in prayer; 1846-1851 on mercy and sin

214. Right Question—Tough Answer (Lk 18:18-30)

"It is not those who commit the least faults who are most holy, but those who have the greatest courage, the greatest generosity, the greatest love, who make the boldest efforts to overcome themselves, and are not immoderately apprehensive of tripping." – St. Francis de Sales

LUKE 18:18-30

A member of one of the leading families put this question to him, "Good Master, what have I to do to inherit eternal life?" Jesus said to him, "Why do you call me good? No one is good but God alone. You know the commandments: You must not commit adultery; You must not kill; You must not steal; You must not bring false witness; Honour your father and mother." He replied, "I have kept all these from my earliest days till now." And when Jesus heard this he said, "There is still one thing you lack. Sell all that you own and distribute the money to the poor, and you will have treasure in heaven; then come, follow me." But when he heard this he was filled with sadness, for he was very rich. Jesus looked at him and said, "How hard it is for those who have riches to make their way into the kingdom of God! Yes, it is easier for a camel to pass through the eye of a needle than for a rich man to enter the kingdom of God." "In that case," said the listeners, "who can be saved?" "Things that are impossible for men," he replied, "are possible for God." Then Peter said, "What about us? We left all we had to follow you." He said to them, "I tell you solemnly, there is no one who has left house, wife, brothers, parents or children for the sake of the kingdom of God who will not be given repayment many times over in this present time and, in the world to come, eternal life."

CHRIST THE LORD Throughout the Gospels Jesus repeats the phrase, "I tell you solemnly" (often translated as "Amen, amen, I say to you"). It is another sign of Christ's incomparable stature. Others could use the phrase for rhetorical emphasis, but Christ can speak it with utter exactitude. He is the very Word of God made man—the idea God has of himself, so vibrant and unique that it shares the divine nature and is eternally begotten as the Son. Christ can make solemn declarations, indubitable statements about things inscrutable to even the most illustrious, but still only human, intellects.

When Jesus prefaces statements with this phrase, he is preparing his listeners for a flash of divine revelation. In this case, he makes the unambiguous claim that a life devoted entirely to him is both more fruitful and more fulfilling than a life devoted to anything else, no matter how good and noble it may be. He doesn't disdain prosperity ("house") and family, but he puts them in their proper context. They are gifts from God meant to provide us with arenas for choices where we can exercise virtue and learn to live in communion with God. But too often they become rivals for our hearts, and we become so attached to them that they usurp the place God ought to have—as was the case for this rich young man. Those who trust God, obeying and following him even under the shadow of the cross and self-sacrifice, will find that all the yearnings of the human heart will be abundantly fulfilled, starting in this life and overflowing in the next. It has to be that way, because that's the way of our Lord.

CHRIST THE TEACHER Jesus recognizes the man's sincerity and openheartedness, and he immediately teaches him a preliminary lesson: the question of life's meaning, of eternal life, what every heart knowingly or unknowingly longs for, can only be resolved by God: "Only God is good." Who has not asked this question in their heart? Who has not gazed on a moonrise or a sunset and felt that plaintive ache in their soul, that yearning to reach out and touch the source of all that beauty? This is the burden Jesus' interlocutor lays at the Lord's feet.

How wise he was to lay it there! How foolish so many others have been through the ages (and how foolish many still are today), seeking the answer to this question anywhere else but in the Word of God! But even though this rich young man asked the right question of the right Master, he ended up making the same mistake as those who ask it of the wrong masters. This young man thought he could achieve meaning and fulfillment by some formula, by some action of his own, by his own natural powers. He had faithfully obeyed the commandments Jesus lists, all having to do with how he treated his neighbor, but it seems he was still depending on his own resources. He had neglected the very first commandment, to love God with all his heart, soul, and mind. He was still in the driver's seat of his life. And when Jesus asks him to give us his false sense of security and self-sufficiency—symbolized by his money—he simply can't do it. He won't let God drive.

Jesus draws out the lesson after this saddening refusal: those who are rich in this world's goods easily fall into the deception that they can achieve life's meaning on their own, without God's help. But when they buy into this deception, they sabotage their chance at fulfillment, because "man is made to live in communion with God, in whom he finds happiness" (CCC, 45). Only God satisfies.

CHRIST THE FRIEND *Jesus: My child, if only you knew how much I want to give you. I created the whole universe just to show you a little bit of what I want you to have. I am glad you are here with me now, taking time to consider what I came to earth in order to teach you. But do you really believe it with all your heart? The more you follow me and trust me, the more space you give me to lavish my gifts upon you. How it pains me when people prefer passing wealth to the everlasting wealth I created them to enjoy! You trust in me, I know. Never let the desire for the good things of this world sway you from the path of my will. I will always let you know which way to turn on your journey through life, and if you trust me, you will always recognize my voice, because you will know I am always at your side. You belong to my Kingdom, and I am your Shepherd; stay close to me.*

CHRIST IN MY LIFE Lord, thank you for giving me the Gospels. I am so thirsty to know the truth. I have asked this question about life's meaning so many times. And now I know that I am on the right path, because it is your path. O Lord, grant me the gift of wisdom, so that I can always taste the sweetness of your truth and prefer it to every false deception of this fallen world...

I know that money tempts me, and you know it too. You know that I love the good things of this world, all the pleasures and comforts that money can buy. Sometimes I think it would be easier to just live with absolutely nothing, but I know that you want me to live the virtue of detachment while still using these good things. Help me, Lord, to do your will...

I love the phrase you say to St. Peter, "Things that are impossible for men are possible for God." Oh Jesus, burn that into my mind and my heart! Never let me forget it! I am so easily daunted and discouraged, but how can I be when I know that you are my Lord, my champion? I want to give my whole heart to you through doing your will today. Be my strength, Lord Jesus...

Questions for SMALL-GROUP DISCUSSION

1. What struck you most in this passage? What did you notice that you hadn't noticed before?
2. What has helped you most as you strive to live the spirit of Christian poverty and detachment in the midst of a consumer-crazed world?
3. What light does this passage shed on the first beatitude, "How happy are the poor in spirit; theirs is the Kingdom of Heaven"?
4. Besides wealth, what are some of the other most common obstacles to following God's will in our lives?

Cf. Catechism of the Catholic Church, 2112-2114, 2172, 2424, and 2536 on idolatry and the divinizing of what is not God; 2402-2406 on the universal destination of all earthly goods; 2426-2436 on economic activity and social justice

215. Things Are Not as They Seem (Lk 18:31-43)

"Everyone – whether kings, nobles, tradesmen, or peasants – must do all things for the glory of God and under the inspiration of Christ's example." – St. Francis Borgia

LUKE 18:31-43

Then taking the Twelve aside he said to them, "Now we are going up to Jerusalem, and everything that is written by the prophets about the Son of Man is to come true. For he will be handed over to the pagans and will be mocked, maltreated and spat on, and when they have scourged him they will put him to death; and on the third day he will rise again." But they could make nothing of this; what he said was quite obscure to them, they had no idea what it meant. Now as he drew near to Jericho there was a blind man sitting at the side of the road begging. When he heard the crowd going past he asked what it was all about, and they told him that Jesus the

> Nazarene was passing by. So he called out, "Jesus, Son of David, have pity on me." The people in front scolded him and told him to keep quiet, but he shouted all the louder, "Son of David, have pity on me." Jesus stopped and ordered them to bring the man to him, and when he came up, asked him, "What do you want me to do for you?" "Sir," he replied, "let me see again." Jesus said to him, "Receive your sight. Your faith has saved you." And instantly his sight returned and he followed him praising God, and all the people who saw it gave praise to God for what had happened.

CHRIST THE LORD Jesus predicts his passion yet again, instructing his apostles in even more detail than before, mentioning the Roman ("pagan") involvement this time. St. Luke makes it painfully clear, however, that the apostles still understood absolutely nothing of this. Why does Jesus keep repeating it when it's clear they simply can't grasp what he's telling them?

He was arming them for the crisis they would face in the aftermath of the event. At that moment (which is just around the corner), in the midst of their fear and confusion, they would remember that Jesus went to Jerusalem with full knowledge of what was going to befall him. Reflecting on Jesus' prior knowledge and his willingness to suffer will prepare them to accept the Resurrection and to understand the sacrificial meaning of his death. It will also help them appreciate more fully the great truth that will make such an impact on St. Paul—that Jesus took the punishment for our sins upon himself while we were still sinners, before we had asked for forgiveness or repented. This is the mightiest proof that the Lord's love and saving mercy are entirely dependable and always accessible, because they are entirely independent of our worthiness. The Lord loves us madly simply because we are.

CHRIST THE TEACHER This last miracle before his Passion is particularly eloquent. St. Luke has just emphatically explained that Jesus' predictions were "quite obscure" to the apostles—they couldn't see what he meant; they were blind to the coming storm. And upon Christ's entry into Jerusalem, St. Luke will go on to describe a series of encounters with the leaders of the city in which they continually refuse to see the glaring credentials of the Messiah; they too are blind, unable to recognize Jesus for who he is. And in the middle of all this spiritual darkness, we find a man who is physically blind but spiritually brilliant. He believes in Jesus whom he has never seen. He has never seen any of his miracles and has probably never heard him preach before; if he had, he would have asked for his cure then.

How is it that the blind man of Jericho can see so clearly? What illuminates for him the priceless lamp of faith? He alone recognizes his need for Christ's grace. The leaders of Jerusalem don't recognize their need for anything—the status quo is profitable and under their complete control. Even the apostles don't recognize their real need for Christ's grace, because they don't yet recognize the true, supernatural essence of their mission. They will soon profess their undying loyalty, basing it on their natural strength, only to fall away and abandon him when things get uncomfortable. The Gospels never tire of telling us that humility alone frees God to do miracles in our lives. And maybe that's because God knows we are ceaselessly tempted to think we know better than he does.

CHRIST THE FRIEND *Jesus: My child, the hour of my passion is drawing near. I am eager for it to come. Too many hearts will never trust me unless I show them that nothing they can do can diminish even a nanometer of my love for them. But we will talk more of that later.*

Look at this blind man who moved my heart. He had once been able to see, but now all was dark to him. He is like the whole human race, which had seen my goodness and wisdom in all its beauty at the dawn of creation but had fallen into darkness at the rebellion of original sin. Every heart still harbors a memory of that intimacy we enjoyed before the Fall, because I made every heart for that intimacy. Why do so many hearts seek the light they long for in the shadows? Why don't they come to me, who came to bring it to them? I will open their eyes, as I opened this man's eyes. Ask me to give you back more and more of that original light. I will fulfill your deepest desires, because you believe in me.

CHRIST IN MY LIFE I am sometimes afraid that I am just like the apostles, Lord. You told them the same thing over and over again—about your Passion and Resurrection—and they were still shocked when it happened. You keep telling me the same things over and over again too, and I think I am just as slow a learner. But you didn't give up on them, and I know you will never give up on me...

Why is humility so hard, Lord? I want to depend on you, to be like a little child in his mother's arms. I know that your grace can give me that trust, confidence, and littleness. How full of peace and joy is the humble heart! That's what you want for me. Jesus, meek and humble of heart, make my heart more like yours...

Send me to bring your torch into the darkness, Lord. I don't have to be the light; I just have to carry it. You are the light. I want to spread your light to the farthest corners of the world—geographically and spiritually. Fill me with your light, and then send me to those of your children who are in darkness. Make me generous and docile, and I will go wherever you want me to go…

Questions for *SMALL-GROUP DISCUSSION*

1. What struck you most in this passage? What did you notice that you hadn't noticed before?
2. What does popular culture think about the virtue of humility, and how does it compare to Christ's view? How can we make sure to keep Christ's vision fresh in our minds?
3. Do you think Christ's foreknowledge of his Passion diminished or increased his suffering when it actually began? Why and in what way?
4. Why do you think the crowd tried to keep the blind man away from Jesus? Is there a lesson here for us?

Cf. Catechism of the Catholic Church, 27-30 on man's desire for God; 153-165 on the nature of faith

The Gospel of Luke
Chapter 19

"Why, dearest daughter, do you waste time in sadness when time is so precious for the salvation of poor sinners? Get rid of your melancholy immediately. Don't think any more about yourself. Do not indulge in so many useless and dangerous reflections. Look ahead always without ever looking back. Keep your gaze fixed on the summit of perfection where Christ awaits you. He wants you despoiled of all things, intent only on procuring his greater glory during this brief time of your existence. For the short time that remains, is it worthwhile to lose yourself in melancholy like those who think only of themselves, as if all were to end with this life? Ah no. We must not even desire that our pilgrimage on this earth be a short one because we do not yet know the infinite value of every minute employed for the glory of God. Carry your cross then but carry it joyfully, my daughter. Think that Jesus loves you very much. And in return for such love, don't lose yourself in so many desires, but accept daily with serenity whatever comes your way. May the heart of Jesus bless you and make you holy not as you want but as he desires."

– ST. FRANCES XAVIER CABRINI

216. Seek and You Will Find (Lk 19:1-10)

"Help me, O Lord, that my eyes may be merciful, so that I may never suspect or judge from appearances, but look for what is beautiful in my neighbors' souls and come to their rescue." – St. Faustina Kowalska

LUKE 19:1-10

He entered Jericho and was going through the town when a man whose name was Zacchaeus made his appearance; he was one of the senior tax collectors and a wealthy man. He was anxious to see what kind of man Jesus was, but he was too short and could not see him for the crowd; so he ran ahead and climbed a sycamore tree to catch a glimpse of Jesus who was to pass that way. When Jesus reached the spot he looked up and spoke to him: "Zacchaeus, come down. Hurry, because I must stay at your house today." And he hurried down and welcomed him joyfully. They all complained when they saw what was happening. "He has gone to stay at a sinner's house," they said. But Zacchaeus stood his ground and said to the Lord, "Look, sir, I am going to give half my property to the poor, and if I have cheated anybody I will pay him back four times the amount." And Jesus said to him, "Today salvation has come to this house, because this man too is a son of Abraham; for the Son of Man has come to seek out and save what was lost."

CHRIST THE LORD Leaders, to be effective, need to base their leadership on something deeper than opinion polls and popularity ratings. Jesus had attracted a crowd as he made his way to Jerusalem (previous passages call it a "great crowd"). Perhaps it was a member of this crowd who pointed Zacchaeus out to Jesus and mentioned what an evil man he was. (Tax collectors made their handsome livings by requiring the people to pay more taxes than Rome demanded and then skimming off the excess for themselves—that's how the Roman authorities kept the tax collectors in tow.) In any case, when Jesus decided to go over to Zacchaeus' house, the crowd was appalled. They all "began to grumble, saying, 'He has gone to stay at a sinner's house.'" If Jesus had cared more for what people said about him than for what God was asking of him, Zacchaeus would have continued in his sin, and the countryside would have continued to suffer from his injustice. But Jesus knew his mission, and he didn't let vain gossip and opposition deter him from it. He is the Lord, and he will rule his Kingdom according to his own standards, whether or not everyone else is comfortable with it. True Christians will do likewise.

But truly effective leadership, from Christ's perspective, also requires truly caring for others, a trait Jesus exemplifies here yet again. Zacchaeus didn't know that he was in dire need of a spiritual renewal (or perhaps he did know, deep down), but Christ recognized it immediately. And even though he had intended to pass through the town, Christ changes his plans and invites himself over for dinner at the unpopular tax collector's house. "...Come down. Hurry..." he told Zacchaeus, expressing his eager desire to bring "salvation" to this man's house. And Zacchaeus "hurried down and welcomed him joyfully." Jesus continues to do the same thing with us, going out of his way to bring us the light and strength we need to live in accordance with God's hopes for us—and if we, like Zacchaeus, come quickly and receive God's advances with joy, salvation will come to our house too.

CHRIST THE TEACHER In this passage Jesus teaches us about himself. He provides a living parable that illustrates the entire meaning of the Incarnation, and then, just in case we didn't get the message, he summarizes it for us: "The Son of Man has come to seek out and save what was lost."

Christ's whole life while he was on earth was dedicated to bringing people back into friendship with God and to establishing his Church to continue that mission throughout history. If that is the mission of Christ, and if that is the mission of the Church, than it also ought to be the mission of every Christian, of every member of the Church. And when we make it the mission of our lives, we, like Christ, will become messengers of deep and lasting peace, both for the hearts of troubled souls and for the hearts of troubled societies. Zacchaeus's conversion affected not only himself, but also the entire region—all the poor and all those who "grumbled" when Jesus went to stay at his house. The path to social justice follows the path of one-on-one reconciliation with God.

CHRIST THE FRIEND *Zacchaeus: I wanted to see this man that everyone was talking about. At first, it felt like normal curiosity. But then, when I went out into the streets and saw the crowds, when I felt the intensity of emotion and expectation, it became more than curiosity. Something inside of me pushed me, drove me, propelled me to find a way to see this rabbi from Nazareth. One of the soldiers helped me climb up into the crook of that tree—and it was just in time, too. As soon as Jesus came into sight, I couldn't take my eyes off him. It was as if the rest of the world receded and only he existed. I watched him make his way slowly through the throngs. He was coming closer. I could feel my heart beating. Suddenly a voice seemed to tell me to get down from the tree, to hide before he saw me. I don't know why I didn't do that. I only know that something even deeper in my heart kept me riveted to him. Then he stopped, right beside the tree. He looked up. Even before he said my name, I could sense his goodness rising up to me. I know it sounds strange.... It was—the whole encounter was strange. But it was real; it was true. I spent the day with him. He brought my soul back to life. He freed my heart from chains that I didn't even know were there. That's how he was.*

Jesus: My child, do you see what happens whenever you make even a little effort to find me, to see me more clearly, like Zacchaeus? He was joyful because salvation came to his heart, but I think I was even more joyful, because the shepherd loves the sheep more than the sheep can ever love the shepherd. You bring joy to my heart whenever you welcome me into your home, your soul, and your mind. When you receive me in Holy Communion, I bring all my grace to strengthen your soul for doing good and living in the light, just as when Zacchaeus took me into his household. How I long for more souls who would receive me in Holy Communion! So many don't even know I'm there, and many who do know don't take full advantage of this gift. I am glad that you do. Now, speak to me of your plans, your hopes, and your struggles.

CHRIST IN MY LIFE I am vulnerable to other people's opinions—a bit too vulnerable. If I loved you more and if my faith were stronger, I would care less about what they think and more about what you think. That's what I want, Lord. Increase my faith! Increase my love! Make me passionate about the mission you have given me, as you were passionate about the mission the Father gave you...

You know I want to bring many souls into your friendship; I want to go out and find the Zacchaeuses, the ones everyone else has given up on. I want to speak to them about your goodness and your love, your forgiveness, and the meaning you give to life. But I am clumsy and inconsistent; you knew that when you made me your disciple. You can be my strength, Lord...

What did you create me for? You made me to live in communion with you. You want me to get to know you, more and more, for all eternity, as best friends keep getting to know each other better—and the more they do, the more enjoyable the friendship becomes. I want that too. I want to share in your work. Whatever you want me to do, I want to do, because I want to follow you...

Questions for *SMALL-GROUP DISCUSSION*

1. What struck you most in this passage? What did you notice that you hadn't noticed before?
2. Why do you think Christ was able to resist popular trends and "peer pressure"? Why do we often find it difficult to do so?
3. If Christ were with us now, how would he be fulfilling his mission to "seek and save what was lost"? In other words, how does that essential mission translate into the "here and now" for us? Who are the Zacchaeuses in our lives?
4. Christ went out of his way—changed his plans even—to take advantage of an opportunity to bring Zacchaeus back to God. How can we become more sensitive to such opportunities and take better advantage of them?

Cf. Catechism of the Catholic Church, 456-460 on Christ's mission; 976-983 on Christ and the forgiveness of sins; 1886-1889 on conversion and society

217. Lord of History, Lord of Hearts (Lk 19:11-27)

"That man is your best servant who is not so much concerned to hear from you what he wills as to will what he hears from you." – St. Augustine

LUKE 19:11-27

While the people were listening to this he went on to tell a parable, because he was near Jerusalem and they imagined that the kingdom of God was going to show itself then and there. Accordingly he said, "A man of noble birth went to a distant country to be appointed king and afterwards return. He summoned ten of his servants and gave them ten pounds. 'Do business with these,' he told them, 'until I get back.' But his compatriots detested him and sent a delegation to follow him with this message, 'We do not want this man to be our king.' Now on his return, having received his appointment as king, he sent for those servants to whom he had given the money, to find out what profit each had made. The first came in and said, 'Sir, your one pound has brought in ten.' 'Well done, my good servant!' he replied. 'Since you have proved yourself faithful in a very small thing, you shall have the government of ten cities.' Then came the second and said, 'Sir, your one pound has made five.' To this one also he said, 'And you shall be in charge of five cities.' Next came the other and said, 'Sir, here is your pound. I put it away safely in a piece of linen because I was afraid of you; for you are an exacting man: you pick up what you have not put down and reap what you have not sown.' 'You wicked servant!' he said. 'Out of your own mouth I condemn you. So you knew I was an exacting man, picking up what I have not put down and reaping what I have not sown? Then why did you not put my money in the bank? On my return I could have drawn it out with interest.' And he said to those standing by, 'Take the pound from him and give it to the man who has ten pounds.' And they said to him, 'But, sir, he has ten pounds' . . . 'I tell you, to everyone who has will be given more; but from the man who has not, even what he has will be taken away. But as for my enemies who did not want me for their king, bring them here and execute them in my presence.'"

CHRIST THE LORD Up to the very end, St. Luke tells us, Jesus' followers still mistakenly thought that Jesus was going to take possession of Israel like the return of an Old Testament political leader. You can't blame them. Even though Jesus had been predicting his fate—betrayal, Passion, and death in Jerusalem—for a while now, the immense crowds, the festive atmosphere (it is estimated that several million pilgrims were in and around Jerusalem for the Passover festival), and the crescendo of miracles and verbal defeats of the Pharisees all seemed to indicate an impending, dramatic, glorious emergence of Jesus as the new David. But Christ has his sights set on something even greater.

His Kingdom, of which David's was but a shadowy forerunner, will include all people, and it will last forever. It won't be a Kingdom of military might and political prudence, but one of deep, definitive renewal of the human spirit by plugging it back into communion with God. It is the Kingdom of grace, the New Covenant community, the Church, which will spread through every land for all of history until Jesus comes again to inaugurate its fullness. Its foundation, therefore, must go deeper than merely political maneuverings. Jesus is going up to Jerusalem to lay that foundation by performing his own redemptive sacrifice on Calvary. By suffering, dying, and rising from the dead in perfect love and obedience to the Father, Jesus—the second Adam—will conquer not merely political enemies, but the archenemy of the human race, Satan himself, who instituted the reign of death by instigating the first Adam to mistrust and disobey the Father.

Christ is Lord of life and history because he makes himself Lord of human hearts, which, by their choices, lead lives and history either to their fulfillment or to their frustration. As we walk with Jesus from Jericho to Jerusalem, up the dusty roads of Judea, we should thank him for setting his sights so high, renew our allegiance to his Kingdom, and ask for the grace to have the same priorities in our lives that he had in his.

CHRIST THE TEACHER Jesus, always patient and understanding, explains to his misconstruing followers yet again the Kingdom that they continue to confuse. Since it is a Kingdom of hearts, they themselves will be primary players in it. Jesus will give them the three tools they will need to perform their role in the Kingdom.

First, Jesus will give them the grace of redemption, an interior renewal of their souls, a fresh start in their relationship with God and their fellow men. This is the sanctifying grace that comes to us from his Passion, death, and Resurrection through the sacraments of his Church. The "pound" that the king in the parable gives his servants represents this grace, the same gift received by all. Second, Jesus gives them an unspecified period of time in which to make this grace grow by living out his teachings and his commandments—most especially the commandments of love and evangelization. This corresponds to the time in the parable during which the new king is traveling to be invested with his kingship, the period after Christ's ascension. Third, Jesus gives his disciples the knowledge that he will come again at the end of history in order to reward his faithful followers, but those who have been selfish and wicked, sticking to their old way of life in spite of the gift of grace, will have forfeited their membership in his Kingdom.

This parable should be one of the most highly prized treasures of every Christian. It brings all of the human condition into sharp, refreshing, unmistakable focus. We are here to receive God's gifts and make them bear fruit for his Kingdom, to invest our lives in giving witness to Christ in our thoughts, words, deeds, and manner. This life is brief and only has meaning in relation to the life to come. How clear our Lord makes it for us! How eager he is for us to use our freedom wisely, so that he can reward us richly when the time comes!

CHRIST THE FRIEND *Jesus: My child, many people, like the third servant in the parable, think I am angry, irrational, unpredictable, selfish, and irascible. But what evidence have I given for such a characterization? Is my creation not a beautiful abode? Do I not maintain the laws of physics and chemistry and biology, so that humanity can continue to live without descending into chaos? And when my children rebelled against me and lost the harmony I had given them at first, did I not continue to care for them and then come and teach them with my gospel the meaning of life, suffering, and death? Am I not willing to forgive them at any moment, no matter how horrendous their offenses? Did I myself, all-powerful and all-knowing, not suffer humiliation, rejection, betrayal, scourging, beating, and crucifixion just to prove to them that I am not an evil, selfish King, but their brother as well as their Lord?*

When they accuse me of being harsh and unyielding, they accuse themselves; they continue living in the self-destruction of self-centeredness and self-indulgence. I will wait as long as possible for them to become disenchanted with that life and turn again to the light. I will send my messengers to them over and over, in myriad ways. But I will not force them to trust me. No, I gave them freedom, the capacity to love, and I will never take it away.

CHRIST IN MY LIFE Lord Jesus, I have placed all my hopes in you. I have confessed my faith in you and I have committed myself to doing your will and living as you would have me live. And I am glad I have! You are a generous Lord—you are generosity itself! Whatever you ask of me, I will give you, because all I have, you have given to me…

I have precious few things, but they are all I need. I have the grace you have given me, my faith, my friendship with you, the pearl of great price. I have my life, however long or short it may be—only you know, Lord. And I have the knowledge that you have given me a mission to accomplish. I need nothing more, except the strength to say each day, "Thy will be done…"

I will go to those who are hiding their pound because they are lazy and self-absorbed. I will be your goodness to them. I will be your voice to them. Teach me what to say, what to do, what to write, how to act—so that your Kingdom will triumph in the hardest of hearts…

Questions for SMALL-GROUP DISCUSSION

1. What struck you most in this passage? What did you notice that you hadn't noticed before?
2. Why do you think his followers still misunderstood the nature of his Kingdom? Do you think we are really as free from this error as we think we are?
3. Jesus is basically instructing his followers to live diligently and responsibly in this earthly life, but to focus on the life that is to come. Why do you think so many contemporaries make fun of this view of reality? How can we respond to their objections?
4. If an agnostic friend came up to you and asked how to get to heaven, what would you tell them?

Cf. Catechism of the Catholic Church, 678-679 on Jesus' judgment at the end of history; 668-677 on Christ's second coming in glory

218. Palms and Stones (Lk 19:28-40)

"Sing with your voices, sing with your hearts, sing with your lips, sing with your lives."
– St. Augustine

Luke 19:28-40
When he had said this he went on ahead, going up to Jerusalem. Now when he was near Bethphage and Bethany, close by the Mount of Olives as it is called, he sent two of the disciples, telling them, "Go off to the village opposite, and as you enter it you will find a tethered colt that no one has yet ridden. Untie it and bring it here. If anyone asks you, 'Why are you untying it?' you are to say this, 'The Master needs it.'" The messengers went off and found everything just as he had told them. As they were untying the colt, its owner said, "Why are you untying that colt?" and they answered, "The Master needs it." So they took the colt to Jesus, and throwing their garments over its back they helped Jesus on to it. As he moved off, people spread their cloaks in the road, and now, as he was approaching the downward slope of the Mount of Olives, the whole group of disciples joyfully began to praise God at the top of their voices for all the miracles they had seen. They cried out: "Blessings on the King who comes, in the name of the Lord! Peace in heaven and glory in the highest heavens!" Some Pharisees

in the crowd said to him, "Master, check your disciples," but he answered, "I tell you, if these keep silence the stones will cry out."

CHRIST THE LORD The King is coming to take possession of his Kingdom. The King happens to be God's only Son, the Anointed One, the Messiah, and the Kingdom happens to be the eternal Kingdom of God himself. It is the first act of the sacred drama of Christ's greatest work: his Passion, death, and Resurrection. That drama is the crux of all history: everything that came before was leading up to it, preparing for it; everything that has come since has flowed from it. If Christ had not obeyed the Father by loving his disciples "to the end" (Jn 13:1), mankind would still be alienated from God. The salvation of the universe was at stake, and though the King's throne would be a cross and his crown would be of thorns, even so, that throne and that crown would outlast every other earthly king's and be glorified even into eternity. Indeed, as much as the Pharisees were disturbed by talk of kings and heavenly glory, if they had been silent, the stones would surely have had to cry out.

Yet, were the crowds shouting and singing in recognition of this eternal Kingdom, the Kingdom of grace, redemption, and spiritual renewal? They were hoping for a different kind of prosperity, unfortunately, as would become evident when they all abandoned Jesus in fear and confusion later in the week. They looked at Christ and knew that he was their King, their Deliverer, but they looked at him through the filter of their own narrow, mundane expectations. Jesus had something much greater that he wanted to give them. As he scanned their ecstatic faces, did his own expression betray a hint of sadness? The Lord was being misunderstood by the people he came to save. Is he perhaps still being misunderstood by us?

CHRIST THE TEACHER When we were baptized, we became sharers in Christ's Kingship; we became "coheirs" with Christ the King, as St. Paul would put it (Rom 8:17). In his royal entry into Jerusalem, Jesus gives us a model for the kind of kings we are to be. First, we are to be faithful to God's will. It was Zechariah who prophesied in God's name that the Messiah would enter Jerusalem riding on a colt, so Christ made sure to do so. Second, we are to be bearers of peace. When kings in the ancient near East rode on donkeys (which were considered much nobler animals there than they were in the West), it was a sign that they traveled in times of peace and came in peace; when they rode on horses, they rode to war. Third, we are to pay attention to the little things. Perhaps Christ had previously arranged a "password" with the owners of the colt; perhaps he simply knew that they would understand when his disciples said "The Master has need of it." In any case, he had planned ahead; he had done his homework. We should strive to be worthy of such a Master, showing our Christian love in the little things, where love matters most.

CHRIST THE FRIEND *Jesus: My child, notice how I had it recorded exactly where this great event occurred: "near Bethphage and Bethany, close by the Mount of Olives." I am not the abstract deity that so many make me out to be. I am not just a divine architect who holds creation at arm's length. I am present in the real, day-to-day flow of your life. That's where I want to bring my victory. What good would it do if I were to stay far away from you? How would I be able to convince you of my love, of the offer of my friendship? I want to walk with you through life. I want to share your joys and sorrows and have you share mine. You can find me always at your side; this is the whole reason behind my Incarnation. I am with you, loving you, guiding you, teaching you. Even when you forget about me, I never forget about you: in the library, on the racquetball courts, in the nursery, at the office. I told you my name because I already knew yours, even before you were born. Thank you for letting me walk with you. Let me accompany you in your daily life.*

CHRIST IN MY LIFE I believe in you, Lord. I believe that you are the Savior sent by the Father to lead us home to heaven. You know that this is not the most popular belief these days. But I don't care about what's popular; I care about what's true. I believe in you, and I want to follow you. Thank you for the gift of faith, Lord. Teach me to live it radically, totally, like the saints…

You knew your mission so thoroughly. Is it possible for me to know mine as thoroughly? Sometimes it seems so vague to me. Maybe it will always have that layer of mystery, but I know that it can't be too mystical, because then I wouldn't be able to carry it out. Help me to understand my mission better, Lord, so that I can fulfill it more energetically and completely…

I know you walk with me every step of my life. What would I do without you? But what about all my neighbors, and what about the thousands of others who don't even know your name? They need your presence and your strength and wisdom just as much as I do. Reach out to them, Lord. Make me your messenger. I give you my feet to follow your path…

Questions for SMALL-GROUP DISCUSSION

1. What struck you most in this passage? What did you notice that you hadn't noticed before?

2. The "Holy, holy, holy..." that we pray every Mass is taken from this Gospel event. Considering its original context, why do you think the Church inserted it into the Mass in the place we find it today? What should the attitude of our hearts be when we pray it?
3. What could have been in Christ's heart and mind during this procession—knowing, as he did, that soon some of these same people would clamor for his crucifixion?
4. How can we avoid treating Jesus as an abstract deity? In other words, how can we learn to find him near the "Bethphage and Bethany" of our everyday lives?

Cf. Catechism of the Catholic Church, 557-560, 569, and 570 on the meaning of Palm Sunday

219. The Sacred Heart Unfurled (Lk 19:41-48)

"Do not be afraid of Christ! He takes nothing away, and he gives you everything. When we give ourselves to him, we receive a hundredfold in return. Yes, open, open wide the doors to Christ—and you will find true life." – Pope Benedict XVI

LUKE 19:41-48

As he drew near and came in sight of the city he shed tears over it and said, "If you in your turn had only understood on this day the message of peace! But, alas, it is hidden from your eyes! Yes, a time is coming when your enemies will raise fortifications all round you, when they will encircle you and hem you in on every side; they will dash you and the children inside your walls to the ground; they will leave not one stone standing on another within you—and all because you did not recognise your opportunity when God offered it!" Then he went into the Temple and began driving out those who were selling. "According to scripture," he said, "my house will be a house of prayer. But you have turned it into a robbers' den." He taught in the Temple every day. The chief priests and the scribes, with the support of the leading citizens, tried to do away with him, but they did not see how they could carry this out because the people as a whole hung on his words.

CHRIST THE LORD Some kings wish destruction on their enemies; the Lord desires his enemies' salvation. Few passages of the Gospels reveal so emphatically the love Christ bore the people he came to save: "As he drew near... he shed tears..." Amidst the jubilation of the crowds, Jesus weeps. He looks down upon this city, chosen by God to be a lantern for the world, whose vocation is to be frustrated by the stubborn refusal of its leaders to admit God's sovereignty. Jesus weeps not because his pride is wounded, but because he knows that those who reject God's rule and the peace it brings simultaneously submit themselves to Satan's (we only have two options), and that means destruction. The devastation he describes here will eventually take place just as he predicted it, in A.D. 70 under the merciless siege engines of the Roman army.

The all-powerful King weeps over his rebellious subjects because he is unwilling to force them into subjection and freely accepts their rejection of him, drinking it to the bitterest dregs, just to show forth the extent of his love. If we truly contemplated this portrait of our Lord, it would change our hearts forever.

As his followers, our hearts too should resonate with the needs of the world. If Jesus wept over ancient Jerusalem, how would he react upon coming to modern New York, or Paris, or Tokyo? We should know, because our hearts are one with his, and the concerns and desires of our Lord should be reflected in those who love him.

CHRIST THE TEACHER Shrewd businessmen bent the rules of Temple purity during Passover time, and the Temple officials let them. To take advantage of the huge amount of pilgrims coming from all over the Mediterranean world, all of whom had to change money so they could buy sacrificial animals for the worship ceremonies, they set up commerce booths inside the outermost courtyard of the sacred precincts—the only place where Gentile pilgrims were allowed to pray. Jesus scatters them. His action prefigures the approaching scattering of the Temple itself that will happen at the end of the siege of Jerusalem—that too will be the result of the leaders of Jerusalem preferring worldly desires to God's plans.

But the action has a deeper lesson as well. Every Christian soul is a temple of the Holy Spirit (1 Cor 6:19). We too can defile ourselves by letting habits of self-indulgence and self-centeredness disrupt the communion with God we are called to enjoy. We can even transform our religious actions into subtle tactics for self-aggrandizement, seeking profit in the eyes of others instead of the eyes of God. When our friendship with Christ becomes one more item on our to-do list instead of the motivation behind all we do, it's a sign that we have set up money changer booths in our hearts. When we ignore the voice of our conscience, treat the apostolate as a favor we do for Jesus, and start blaming the faults of others for our own shortcomings, we can be sure that the temple of our soul is being defiled.

Few times in the Gospels does Jesus act so forcefully and angrily as in this scene. We should take the lesson to heart now and do regular spring-cleaning willingly, lest we suffer worse consequences unwillingly later on.

CHRIST THE FRIEND *Jesus: When I saw the city of Jerusalem, gleaming in the sunlight as I descended Mount Olivet, I saw all its history and all its future. How could I not weep? Certainly it pained my heart to be rejected by so many of my Chosen People, but many of them also recognized their Messiah and welcomed me – Mary did, and Peter, James, the other apostles, Nicodemus, and many others. But this city meant so much more. It was the symbol of my Father's fidelity and love for all mankind, the symbol of his untiring effort to lead the stray sheep back home to the sheepfold, of his eternal plan of salvation. And just as so many in Jerusalem turned a deaf or fearful ear to my words that week, spurning my Father's generosity, just so many others would do the same all along the centuries in many other cities throughout the world.*

That is why you should never doubt my commitment to you, my joy at your yes to my invitations. If I wept so openly at others' rejections, do you not think I rejoice even more at your trusting acceptance? Follow me, and I will show you the way to the life you long to live.

CHRIST IN MY LIFE Lord Jesus, why do I not weep for those souls who reject you? Why do I not burn with a desire to bring them closer to you? You know why. My heart is still stained and tainted with too much selfishness. But you knew that when you called me to follow you. You can work with that. You are all powerful. I put my heart in your hands. Teach me to love as you love…

It is hard to keep first things first in this world, Lord. I think a few money changers have sneaked their way into the Temple of my heart. But you know that I want to follow you. You know I want to be the saint you created me to be. So let's get to work, Lord. Show me what has to change, and give me the strength to change it…

Thank you, Lord, for your persistent love. Thank you, Father, for sending your Son to walk with me. Look me in the eye and teach me about your greatness and your mercy. Thank you for giving me the Church through which I can still see Christ's eyes and hear his voice. How you must love me to give me so much! Blessed be your name forever…

Questions for SMALL-GROUP DISCUSSION

1. What struck you most in this passage? What did you notice that you hadn't noticed before?
2. How do you think the apostles reacted when Jesus was cleansing the Temple?
3. What are some of the common "money changers" that we let set up shop in our hearts these days?

4. Jesus' cleansing of the Temple is an image of what happens in the individual soul during confession. Does it help explain in any way why going to confession is always difficult? How can we make the most of this sacrament?

Cf. Catechism of the Catholic Church, 583-586 on Jesus and the Temple; 2083-2094 on keeping the First Commandment in the Era of the Church; 1763-1770 on passions (like anger and sadness) and the moral life; 2302 on the sin of anger

The Gospel of Luke
Chapter 20

"Prayer, then, and penance are the two potent inspirations sent to us at this time by God, that we may lead back to him mankind that has gone astray and wanders about without a guide: they are the inspirations that will dispel and remedy the first and principal cause of every form of disturbance and rebellion, the revolt of man against God."

– POPE PIUS XI

220. Fruitful Vines and Shriveled Hearts (Lk 20:1-19)

"The Lord said to me, 'I want to give myself to souls and to fill them with my love, but few there are who want to accept all the graces my love has intended for them.'" – St. Faustina Kowalska

LUKE 20:1-19

Now one day while he was teaching the people in the Temple and proclaiming the Good News, the chief priests and the scribes came up, together with the elders, and spoke to him. "Tell us," they said, "what authority have you for acting like this? Or who is it that gave you this authority?" "And I," replied Jesus, "will ask you a question. Tell me: John's baptism: did it come from heaven, or from man?" And they argued it out this way among themselves, "If we say from heaven, he will say, 'Why did you refuse to believe him?'; and if we say from man, the people will all stone us, for they are convinced that John was a prophet." So their reply was that they did not know where it came from. And Jesus said to them, "Nor will I tell you my authority for acting like this."

And he went on to tell the people this parable: "A man planted a vineyard and leased it to tenants, and went abroad for a long while. When the time came, he sent a servant to the tenants to get his share of the produce of the vineyard from them. But the tenants thrashed him, and sent him away empty-handed. But he persevered and sent a second servant; they thrashed him too and treated him shamefully and sent him away empty-handed. He still persevered and sent a third; they wounded this one also,

> and threw him out. Then the owner of the vineyard said, 'What am I to do? I will send them my dear son. Perhaps they will respect him.' But when the tenants saw him they put their heads together. 'This is the heir,' they said, 'let us kill him so that the inheritance will be ours.' So they threw him out of the vineyard and killed him. Now what will the owner of the vineyard do to them? He will come and make an end of these tenants and give the vineyard to others." Hearing this they said, "God forbid!" But he looked hard at them and said, "Then what does this text in the scriptures mean: It was the stone rejected by the builders that became the keystone? Anyone who falls on that stone will be dashed to pieces; anyone it falls on will be crushed." But for their fear of the people, the scribes and the chief priests would have liked to lay hands on him that very moment, because they realised that this parable was aimed at them.

CHRIST THE LORD Picture Jesus at the end of telling this parable, when, as St. Luke writes, "he looked hard at them..." What does that mean? What did that look contain? The full fire of Christ's burning love! He has put up with his opponents since the very start of his ministry. Now that his time is running out, he is becoming more and more explicit in exposing the true, and truly heinous, state of their souls. Just when they try to discredit him in the eyes of the crowd with their shrewd question about authority, Jesus tells this parable to that same crowd, while his adversaries sit listening in. The parable unmistakably identifies Jesus as the Son of God in a unique sense (this is the very claim that his enemies had latched onto as grounds for blasphemy) and also paints a sad picture of the history of Israel. Generation after generation of Israelite leaders (the tenants in the parable) have refused to respond to God's goodness with gratitude and fidelity, or even with basic justice. Now, when God (the vineyard owner in the parable) sends his own Son, the current generation of leaders goes even one step further, murdering him in hopes of being able to usurp complete power over the nation.

That hard look of Jesus was meant to shake up those closed-hearted listeners into not only understanding the parable—it was impossible to avoid that—but also into letting it sink in. The warm-up was over, and the final clash was about to begin. Even at such a moment—especially at such a moment—Jesus makes yet another effort to win his enemies over to the truth.

CHRIST THE TEACHER This parable teaches us valuable lessons about God and about man. God goes beyond the demands of justice in order to give all people the chance of salvation. The owner of the vineyard had every right to get rid of the greedy and rebellious tenants after their first refusal to pay what they owed their master. But the owner waits patiently and then sends another messenger, and then finally a third. At that point, who would have blamed him for throwing the tenants out, or even for putting them in prison? But he waits yet another amount of time, and then he sends his very own son to plead with them, hoping beyond all hope that they will come to their senses, realize that the master is generous and longsuffering, not harsh and intransigent, and put things to rights. This is how God was with Israel, how he has been with all mankind, and how he never ceases to be with each soul. Whoever ends up spending eternity without Christ as his Friend will have only himself to blame—that much we know for sure.

Regarding the human person, this parable illustrates (but fails to explain fully) the great mystery of freedom. Why did the tenants consistently and deliberately refuse to do the right, fair, and just plain sensible thing? Why did the Pharisees refuse to welcome Jesus? Why do so many Christians refuse to follow Christ's teachings? How can anyone who has received life—and all the good things that go with it as a pure gift from on high—turn their back on God as if he didn't even exist? Jesus offers no explicit answer, but the bottom line remains clear: the end of the story, for each person, isn't determined by fate, destiny, or some incontrovertible, meta-historical force; the end of our story is up to each one of us.

CHRIST THE FRIEND *Jesus: My child, I only want one thing. I only want you to flourish, to become the saint I created you to be. Your life is like the vineyard, and the fruit I ask from you is the fruit of the Spirit: love, joy, peace, patience, kindness, goodness, faithfulness, gentleness, and self-control. The more you seek and follow my will for you, the more abundant your harvest will be, and the more fulfilled and fulfilling your life will become. The leaders of Jerusalem who resisted my grace were afraid of losing the passing things of this world that they had spent so much time and energy acquiring: wealth, position, reputation, power. But those fruits are bitter unless they are seasoned with the fruits of the Spirit.*

I set up my vineyard in your heart when you were baptized. I have tended it faithfully through the rest of the sacraments and through the teaching of my Gospels. Often I have come and requested a harvest by asking you to act in accordance with my will. Many times you have treated me just as the tenants in the parable treated the owner of the vineyard. You have squandered my grace. But I haven't given up on you. Many other times you welcome my inspirations and commands, and you have experienced the joy of doing so. You always know what I am asking of you—my will is no great enigma. Be courageous, be generous, continue trusting me, one step at a time, and we will enjoy your eternal harvest together.

CHRIST IN MY LIFE Lord, I don't understand how so many people reject you. I don't understand why I sometimes refuse to follow your will, disobey my conscience, skirt along the edges of Church teaching. I don't so much ask you to help me understand it; I ask you to help me overcome it. Let me know you so clearly that I can't help loving you with all my heart, mind, and strength...

Thank you for your patience and mercy. You never give up on me—you never have, and you never will. You have adopted me into your own family. Now you are my brother, my friend, my companion! Thank you, Lord. Now teach me to be generous and strong and merciful, just like you...

When I see how little you are loved, and when I see how they treat your representatives and how they lead your faithful astray, my heart sinks. Then it burns with desire to react. I want to do something! I love you, and I want to show you my love. I want to do your will, Lord. I can only do a little bit, here and now, today, of what you ask of me, but I want to put in all the love I can...

Questions for SMALL-GROUP DISCUSSION

1. What struck you most in this passage? What did you notice that you hadn't noticed before?
2. In your experience, what is the real reason behind the disbelief of those people who refuse to accept Christ?
3. Why would Jesus answer these leaders' question about his authority with another question, instead of giving them the real answer?
4. What has been the one thing that has helped your friendship with Christ most in the last six months?

Cf. Catechism of the Catholic Church, 1846-1848 on mercy and sin; 1854-1864 on the different kinds of sins (especially the sin against the Holy Spirit, 1864)

221. Cunning Doves (Lk 20:20-26)

"Each of you will stand in the presence of God, before countless hosts of angels. The Holy Spirit will set a seal upon your souls, and you will be enlisted into the service of the great King." – St. Cyril of Jerusalem

LUKE 20:20-26

So they waited their opportunity and sent agents to pose as men devoted to the Law, and to fasten on something he might say and so enable them to hand him over to the jurisdiction and authority of the governor. They put to him this question, "Master, we know that you say and teach what is right; you favor no one, but teach the way of God in all honesty. Is it permissible for us to pay taxes to Caesar or not?" But he was aware of their cunning and said, "Show me a denarius. Whose head and name are on it?" "Caesar's," they said. "Well then," he said to them, "give back to Caesar what belongs to Caesar—and to God what belongs to God." As a result, they were unable to find fault with anything he had to say in public; his answer took them by surprise and they were silenced.

CHRIST THE LORD Jesus' enemies try to trap Jesus with an astute ploy. About twenty years prior to this conversation, a dispute about whether or not the Jews should pay taxes to Rome erupted in a rebellion, ending with the crucifixion of two thousand Jews. Some Jews thought such taxes impeded efforts to achieve Israel's independence. Others thought that evading these taxes would bring down an even harsher Roman rule. By presenting the question to Jesus, therefore, the scribes were showing their acumen.

Jesus' answer, in addition to confounding his enemies, reveals a central characteristic of his Kingdom: it is not of this world. Christianity consists in renewing the human heart through Christ's grace. This is the work of the Church. In turn, this interior renewal gradually overflows into a hidden renewal of every arena of human endeavor, as leaven gradually works its way into the whole loaf as its being kneaded. (The energetic kneading of human culture is performed by the seemingly inscrutable flow of history, guided by Providence.)

Christians sometimes fail to make this distinction, and they can fall into committing injustices in the name of Christ when they do, but the distinction is there, in Christ's teaching and that of the Church. The Lord cannot be pigeonholed into a single political party or agenda; instead, he sends his disciples to rectify and edify them all.

CHRIST THE TEACHER Jesus provides both a negative and a positive lesson about how to deal with hypocrites. First, we are to avoid being naïve. The Christian life and mission is not a walk in the park. The devil cares infinitely more about what the Christian is doing to spread the faith than about whatever else he's doing, and he continually throws up opposition. The experience of two millennia leaves no room for doubt: If you would like to start a tennis club, you won't find any out-of-the-ordinary obstacles popping up every step of the way; if, however, you try to start a Catholic kids club, or an apostolate dedicated to retrieving fallen-away Catholic businessmen, watch out.

The dynamics of human history, on the small scale and the large scale, really are what Hollywood tells us they are: the forces of good (Christ, his angels, his followers) pitted against the forces of evil (the devil, his angels, fallen human nature and the culture it produces). Christians who take their mission seriously automatically become threats to men and women who have set their hearts on manipulating their sphere of influence towards their own self-aggrandizement—just as Christ posed a threat to the leaders of Jerusalem.

So we should expect attacks from duplicitous people—we should not be naïve—but how should we respond to them? Shrewdly. Jesus used his wits. He never lowered himself to the lying and deceptive tactics of his enemies, but he crossed verbal swords with them, outdoing them in their own canniness. He doesn't answer their question directly, because he sees that they don't care about the truth anyway. He answers it in a way that will make them think and maybe open their minds and hearts to his message. Jesus is following his own advice to "be cunning as snakes" with hypocrites, but "innocent as doves" by not adopting their sinful ways (Mt 10:16). He is neither intimidated nor distracted by obstacles and opposition; he forges ahead, continuing to do good, to find creative ways to communicate his message. As his disciples, we should do the same.

CHRIST THE FRIEND God created us in his own image. He created us to be able to live in friendship with him, to know truth, goodness, and beauty, and to be able create our own expressions of them. Unfortunately, we often see the sinful side of human nature so clearly that we forget how noble the human soul really is. We need the reminder that Christ gives us in this conversation with the Pharisees; we need to make an effort to call to mind repeatedly that every man, woman, and child is created in God's image, noble beyond description and destined for eternal life. The most beautiful and magnificent parts of creation will all pass away, but the human person will live forever. Each one will be resurrected, either to eternal life or eternal death.

Jesus: When I look at you, I see the true you—I can see how you will be when I have purified you from all your selfishness and you have let my grace renew each corner of your soul. Little babies have no idea how wonderful it will be when they grow up and come into full possession of all their faculties, but their mothers do, and they delight in the thought of it and care for their children with that in mind. Your soul is like that little child, and I am as attentive and delighted in you as the most tender of mothers.

CHRIST IN MY LIFE I am a citizen of two kingdoms, Lord—this world and your everlasting reign. You want me here, like leaven, influencing my circle of activity with your grace. I am your ambassador. Lord Jesus, make me a good one. I want to bring you to many hearts. I want to be a light to those around me. May your light shine through me…

Sometimes the challenges of being faithful to your will and to your mission intimidate me. Sometimes they tire me out. Sometimes they rile me up. Lord, whatever my reaction, you know that the only way I can persevere is if you fill me with your wisdom and strength in each challenge. I don't care how I feel; I care only about being faithful to what you are asking of me…

Why do I so easily forget the bigger picture? Lord Jesus, I get so discouraged, so distracted. Be patient with me, Lord, and teach me to be patient with those around me. You have designed things to take time, and your design is wise. Teach me to be docile, to do your will…

Questions for SMALL-GROUP DISCUSSION

1. What struck you most in this passage? What did you notice that you hadn't noticed before?
2. What difference should there be between a Christian and a non-Christian when it comes to political opinions and activity? Why?
3. What has helped you in the past to be shrewd with hypocrites while at the same time extending Christian charity and justice?
4. If a non-believing acquaintance were to come up to you with the following question, how would you respond: "Why should I follow Christ? He's supposed to be all about a nice afterlife, but he hasn't even been able to fix this earthly life."

Cf. Catechism of the Catholic Church, 1897-1904 *on legitimate political authority;* 1905-1912 *on the common good;* 356-361 *on man being created in the image of God*

222. Saving the Sadducees (Lk 20:27-47)

"Living faith working through love—this is what leads mean to put aside the goods of the present in the hope of those of the future, and to look to the future rather than to the present." – Pope Benedict XIV

LUKE 20:27-47

Some Sadducees—those who say that there is no resurrection—approached him and they put this question to him, "Master, we have it from Moses in writing, that if a man's married brother dies childless, the man must marry the widow to raise up children for his brother. Well then, there were seven brothers. The first, having married a wife, died childless. The second and then the third married the widow. And the same with all seven, they died leaving no children. Finally the woman herself died. Now, at the resurrection, to which of them will she be wife since she had been married to all seven?" Jesus replied, "The children of this world take wives and husbands, but those who are judged worthy of a place in the other world and of the resurrection from the dead do not marry because they can no longer die, for they are the same as the angels, and being children of the resurrection they are sons of God. And Moses himself implies that the dead rise again, in the passage about the bush where he calls the Lord the God of Abraham, the God of Isaac and the God of Jacob. Now he is God, not of the dead, but of the living; for to him all men are in fact alive." Some scribes then spoke up. "Well put, Master," they said because they would not dare to ask him any more questions.

He then said to them, "How can people maintain that the Christ is son of David? Why, David himself says in the Book of Psalms: The Lord said to my Lord: Sit at my right hand and I will make your enemies a footstool for you. David here calls him Lord; how then can he be his son?" While all the people were listening he said to the disciples, "Beware of the scribes who like to walk about in long robes and love to be greeted obsequiously in the market squares, to take the front seats in the synagogues and the places of honour at banquets, who swallow the property of widows, while making a show of lengthy prayers. The more severe will be the sentence they receive."

CHRIST THE LORD Imagine the scene. We are in the Temple courtyards, where rabbis continuously discuss, instruct, and debate with peers and public alike. Jesus has been spending the last few days there, teaching the people and gallantly repelling crafty attacks from envious Pharisees, the religious leaders of contemporary Jewry. Worn out and exasperated, the Pharisees bring in reinforcements, the Sadducees, to continue trying to discredit this incorrigible young Galilean rabbi. (Usually the Sadducees and Pharisees were rivals, but the common threat posed by Christ's new teaching brings them together.) The Sadducees slip into the circle of disciples gathered around Jesus. They are Israel's political leaders, eager collaborators with their Roman overlords; they are in love with the pleasures of this present world and disdain many of the common Jewish beliefs and practices, like the resurrection of the dead. At just the right moment, one of them steps forward to issue the challenge, posing a previously unanswerable theological conundrum. With a rhetorical flourish he finishes stating his case, certain that everyone there now clearly perceives how ridiculous the resurrection doctrine really is. A hush ensues as the crowd now turns to Jesus. Will he be able to respond? He is gazing steadily at the self-satisfied Sadducee, but he offers no reprimand, as he did to the Pharisees. Rather, he takes up the challenge directly and points out their mistake.

St. Luke's concise description of this dramatic encounter brings to light the weight of Christ's authority, the incomparable power of Christ's presence and words, which in this case silences Israel's most accomplished sophists. Why else would St. Luke include a discussion about Jewish doctrinal nitpickings when his primary readership was non-Jewish? Once again, the Gospel gives us a glimpse of the magnificent but munificent Lordship of Christ.

CHRIST THE TEACHER The lesson Jesus teaches his attackers strikes home as much for us as for them. They were conceiving of heaven in earthly terms and applying human restrictions to God. The doctrine of eternal life and the resurrection of the dead threatened the worldly lifestyle of the Sadducees; if there really is life after death, then they would have to adjust their pattern of life on earth to be ready for it—something they were reluctant to do. Christ's answer points out both their theological and their moral blunders.

God has revealed himself as the living God, powerful enough to give eternal life and raise us from the dead, just as Christ's own Resurrection would prove definitively. Furthermore, the pleasures and obligations of this life will be transformed in the life to come. Even marriage, one of the most sacred of human institutions, will fall away in the newness of heaven, where the love we practiced on earth will be caught up into a higher love, bringing our longing for union with God and one another to its utter fulfillment.

Christianity is not a mass of restrictions and rules, but the true path to peace, joy, life, and fulfillment. If only we had more strength to trust in the God who shaped the mountains and carved out the seas instead of trying all the time to avoid his wise law, we would find the peace we long for but vainly search for everywhere else.

CHRIST THE FRIEND *Jesus: My child, if I didn't love you with all the strength of my heart, I wouldn't challenge you. I wouldn't push you to grow, expand your views, and go beyond your limited understanding and assumptions. Some think of me as a weakling, a starry-eyed dreamer – I know. It is because my mercy is boundless, and they mistake mercy for weakness. But my mercy is the elemental building block of the universe. Look into my eyes. You will see my love—I will show it to you. And you will see that it is burning and determined. Listen to my voice. Is it wavering and noncommittal and superficial? It is compassionate, but my compassion grips your heart and demands that you change. You* *know this, because you have had the courage to listen. You know that when you follow my footsteps, you feel hope and joy, but the kind that flourishes in the shadow of the cross. I am the Lamb of God, but I am also the Lion of Judah. And the only reason you should let me into your life more deeply each day is because I love you even more than you love yourself.*

CHRIST IN MY LIFE I am bewildered and frustrated by the resistance the leaders of Jerusalem showed you, Lord, but even more than that, I am mesmerized by your wisdom and your majesty. Lord, teach me to be wise. Attract me to your heart. I want my words to reflect your goodness. I know I will not be able to open every heart to your gospel, because even you didn't open every heart, but I want to give you my mouth to speak your words...

I know you want me to be faithful to my daily responsibilities. You are not some strange guru with weird, otherworldly practices—you are Jesus of Nazareth, and you know what it means to work and sweat. But you also want me to think of the Resurrection. This life has a purpose. I believe it, Lord. Increase my faith...

Challenge me, Lord. Lead me forward. Why do I want to stay comfortable when there is so much for me to do for you, so many ways for me to give myself to you by giving myself to those around me? Challenge me, Lord, and never let me forget that you are with me, that you are the very strength you demand of me...

Questions for SMALL-GROUP REFLECTION

1. What struck you most in this passage? What did you notice that you hadn't noticed before?
2. What factors in popular culture tend to reduce Jesus Christ to an abstract concept or historical artifact instead of a living person? How can we minimize their influence in our lives?
3. How should our reverence for Christ's authority as exercised through the Church's teaching manifest itself? What are some telltale signs that we might be falling into subjectivism, preferring our own version of the gospel (maybe one that fits well with our personal likes and dislikes, our personal "comfort zones")?
4. How should the doctrine of the resurrection from the dead, which we profess to believe every Sunday when we recite the Creed at Mass, impact our lives, our decisions, and our perception of what is important?

Cf. Catechism of the Catholic Church, 638-658 on Christ's Resurrection; 988-1004 on Christians' resurrection; 577-582 on Jesus and the Law

THE GOSPEL OF LUKE
Chapter 21

223. A WIDOW'S MIGHT (LK 21:1-7)

"We cannot all do great things, but we can do small things with great love." – St. Teresa of Calcutta

> *LUKE 21:1-7*
> As he looked up he saw rich people putting their offerings into the treasury; then he happened to notice a poverty-stricken widow putting in two small coins, and he said, "I tell you truly, this poor widow has put in more than any of them; for these have all contributed money they had over, but she from the little she had has put in all she had to live on." When some were talking about the Temple, remarking how it was adorned with fine stonework and votive offerings, he said, "All these things you are staring at now—the time will come when not a single stone will be left on another: everything will be destroyed." And they put to him this question: "Master," they said, "when will this happen, then, and what sign will there be that this is about to take place?"

CHRIST THE LORD The widow who depends entirely on God throws into sharp relief the lesson Jesus has just been teaching—that his Kingdom transcends this world, and only those who recognize their need for God will enter into it. Jesus' prediction of the destruction of the Temple, the symbol of the earthly Kingdom of Israel, which Jesus' enemies mistakenly thought would last forever, calls to mind this contrast between Christ's Kingdom and all earthly kingdoms. The things of the earth will pass away, but the things of God will remain.

This is why Jesus can say that the widow put more into the treasury than the rich people, even though her gift was only a small sum of money. Jesus saw into her heart. She was a widow, alone in the world, having lost the husband she had loved and cherished. She was poverty-stricken, with nothing to attract the attention of a possible future husband. She had experienced the loss of what was most precious to her as well as the fragility of her own existence, and this had led her to abandon herself completely to God. As she dropped her last two pennies into the treasury box, Jesus saw both the tears of sorrow and helplessness in her eyes, and also the trust and gratitude in her heart. Her monetary gift was the embodiment of her gift of self. It expresses the wisdom her suffering had taught her, the wisdom God wants all of us to acquire through our own suffering: only the Lord's love endures, so only his Kingdom is worth living for.

CHRIST THE TEACHER Jesus wants to make sure we are never deceived by the appearances of this world. Certainly it is filled with good and beautiful things, and human culture adorns it even more magnificently. The Temple of Jerusalem was known throughout the ancient world as a towering artistic achievement, even this reconstructed Temple. However, the rightful pleasure taken in good worldly achievements can lead us astray, because it can make us start looking for heaven on earth. But heaven is heaven, and earth is earth, and the glories of the former will not last, "not a single stone will be left on another; everything will be destroyed." This prediction applies both to the Temple at Jerusalem and to the earth itself and all the achievements of human hands. What will last forever, on the other hand, is what we do for God and what we do for our neighbor—these are the two coins the widow puts into the treasury.

In contrast to the well-educated, well-respected, well-to-do people who ostentatiously pour into the coffers objectively large amounts of money that are subjectively worthless to them, she puts in an objectively minuscule amount (two "lepta" coins, the lowest value coin in circulation at the time), in which consists, subjectively, her whole entire livelihood. In other words, she gives her whole self to God. Jesus says this is the worthy and lasting gift. To give ourselves to God by seeking and fulfilling his will (summed up by the commandment to love) is the only investment we can make that will bring in everlasting dividends.

CHRIST THE FRIEND *Jesus: Do you see this widow? She is alone in the world, and she is poor, and yet she has more wisdom and strength than the rich, the powerful, and the popular. She gives all she has to me in humble gratitude, knowing that since she has received everything from me, I will take care of her. The only worries in her heart are worries about others' needs. I want you to learn from her. I want you to trust me as she trusted me. She is the model of all my saints, who have realized that the good things of this world pass quickly. They all know that what pleases my heart and enriches the treasury of my Kingdom are the two seemingly tiny little coins: love for God and love for neighbor. These coins are looked down upon by the powerful of this world, those who think they can bring heaven to earth with their great projects and programs. But without self-forgetful love, what good is any organization or any political platform? I want you* *to look at this widow, look into her heart. Learn to see the world and the people in the world as I do, and you will discover the wisdom I want to give you.*

CHRIST IN MY LIFE Thank you for giving me enough of your eternal wisdom, Lord, to know that nothing beautiful on this earth will last forever. All the toys and trinkets and achievements are like flowers; they bloom and wither. But your grace bears fruit that never dies. Thank you for the gift of life and faith, and thank you for giving me a mission in life that really matters, the mission of love...

I love the scene of this destitute widow dropping everything she has into the treasury. She doesn't care about the greedy chief priests who will probably steal from the collection—she cares only about you. She wants to give everything she has to you. What a noble soul! Teach me to give you everything I have by throwing myself into your will for me here and now...

I feel in my heart the desire to make a difference in the world. Where did that desire come from if it didn't come from you? You put it there, Lord, and then you taught me how to fulfill it: Love God and love my neighbor. Yes, Lord, this is what I want. Show me the way to go; I will follow you, and you will make my life bear fruit...

Questions for *SMALL-GROUP DISCUSSION*

1. What struck you most in this passage? What did you notice that you hadn't noticed before?
2. What helps you to keep in mind the passing nature of the things of this world?
3. In what ways do we tend to follow in the footsteps of the rich people Jesus observes in this passage—appearing to give a lot to God, but really holding back the only thing he wants us to give?
4. If everything in the world is going to pass away, why does the Church still encourage us to be fully engaged in society and culture?

Cf. Catechism of the Catholic Church, 1913-1917 on responsibility and participation in society; 2095-2103 on giving worship to God; 1052-1074 on a summary of the two great commandments

224. Staying Faithful in the Fray (Lk 21:8-24)

"The charms of prosperity must not lead us astray; for only a foolish traveler, when he sees pleasant fields on his way, forgets to go on towards his destination." – St. Gregory the Great

LUKE 21:8-24
"Take care not to be deceived," he said, "because many will come using my name and saying, 'I am he' and, 'The time is near at hand.' Refuse to join them. And when you hear of wars and revolutions, do not be frightened, for this is something that must happen but the end is not so soon." Then he said to them, "Nation will fight against nation, and kingdom against kingdom. There will be great earthquakes and plagues and famines here and there; there will be fearful sights and great signs from heaven. But before all this happens, men will seize you and persecute you; they will hand you over to the synagogues and to imprisonment, and bring you before kings and governors because of my name and that will be your opportunity to bear witness. Keep this carefully in mind: you are not to prepare your defence, because I myself shall give you an eloquence and a wisdom that none of your opponents will be able to resist or contradict. You will be betrayed even by parents and brothers, relations and friends; and some of you will be put to death. You will be hated by all men on account of my name, but not a hair of your head will be lost. Your endurance will win you your lives.

"When you see Jerusalem surrounded by armies, you must realise that she will soon be laid desolate. Then those in Judaea must escape to the mountains, those inside the city must leave it, and those in country districts must not take refuge in it. For this is the time of vengeance when all that scripture says must be fulfilled. Alas for those with child, or with babies at the breast, when those days come! They will fall by the edge of the sword and be led captive to every pagan country; and Jerusalem will be trampled down by the pagans until the age of the pagans is completely over."

CHRIST THE LORD Imagine the tone of this conversation. One of the bystanders makes an offhand comment, a little bit of small talk about the beauty of the Temple. Christ takes up the theme as a chance to voice what has been on his heart. He describes the coming destruction of the Temple by the Roman army (this was to occur in 70 A.D.), which will mark the definitive end of the former age, the Old Covenant epoch. And then, in response to that description, one of the disciples asks him when this will occur. That question is what immediately precedes this speech of the Lord. He tells them that other claimants to his Messianic title will appear—and they did appear. He tells them that wars and natural disasters will occur—and they did occur between the years of his death and the destruction of Jerusalem, all over the Mediterranean basin (e.g., the Parthians moved against the eastern border of the Roman Empire; Laodicaea was devastated by an earthquake in 60 A.D.; a famine ravaged Rome during the reign of Claudius, etc.). He tells them that foreign armies will surround Jerusalem and lay a horrible siege to it, and he tells them that they should get out before the siege begins. And then he tells them that before Jerusalem is destroyed, they themselves will suffer fierce persecution from all sides, but that very persecution will afford them an opportunity to spread the Good News.

Maybe his listeners didn't grasp the whole meaning of his prediction until the events began to play themselves out, but as Jesus spoke they would have had no doubt that Christ was declaring himself to be the lynchpin of time and eternity. With the completion of his earthly mission, human history takes its final turn; the Old Covenant is being brought to its definitive end ("Jerusalem will be trampled down by the pagans until the age of the pagans is completely over"), and the New, Everlasting Covenant is about to be inaugurated by the Lord.

CHRIST THE TEACHER Although this speech was the response to a question about when the Temple would be destroyed, Jesus doesn't really give a specific date and time. He is more interested in explaining the pattern of events so that his disciples will have reference points as they experience life in the era of the Church. He's interested in pointing out the three most critical facts about the future: 1) He is going back to the Father's house, but he will return to bring to fruition the eternal Kingdom that he founded through the Church (thus the reference to the "age of the pagans" being "completely over"); 2) In the meantime, he is sending his disciples to announce that Kingdom to all peoples; and 3) Although this mission will bring with it a crescendo of suffering and humiliation and opposition of all kinds, he will be with his Church always, working in and through his followers by the power of the Holy Spirit.

CHRIST THE FRIEND Christ's mission is much greater than many people think. It isn't only to make life on earth a bit easier; it is cosmic and eternal. His bottom line is not measured in dollars and cents, but in salvation itself—in everlasting life for real people like our neighbors, our family members, and us. He calls all his followers to share in this mission, to make it their priority, and to persevere in it by leaning on him and not on themselves as they weather storms of pain and violent rejection. They may even suffer rejection at the hands of their closest relatives, but he assures them that if he permits that to happen, it's only because it will redound in the end for a greater good. Consciously, actively sharing in Christ's mission grows our friendship with him, because it leads us to continue seeking his will and trusting in him. And when all the battles are over, the victory will come. He is looking forward to sharing that victory with us. After all, that's why he came.

CHRIST IN MY LIFE I am struck by how vivid these future events were to you, long before they occurred. All knowledge of the universe is yours by divine right. And yet, the teaching you left us was so simple, understandable, and straightforward—above all, your commandment of love. I want to know your teaching better, Lord. I want to follow it. You are the Lord of history; be also the Lord of my life...

What do the petty concerns of my typical day matter in light of the great events of history? Sometimes I let myself listen to the seductive gospel of the news programs, and I think that my petty concerns don't matter at all. But I know better. What matters to you is that I choose in each moment of the day to love you by doing your will. If I do, I will be a true revolutionary...

Persecution isn't my favorite thing, Lord, but you promised it would come. Sometimes I think it would be easier if it came in the form of a sword or a gun—for being talked about behind my back, laughed at, and criticized wounds my vanity and self-love so deeply. Teach me to overcome evil by doing good, and to love even my enemies as you have loved me...

Questions for SMALL-GROUP DISCUSSION

1. What struck you most in this passage? What did you notice that you hadn't noticed before?
2. "He will come again in glory to judge the living and the dead, and his Kingdom will have no end." What impact do you think this doctrine should have on our daily lives?
3. Knowing that fidelity to Christ and his Church will bring with it persecution, misunderstanding, and opposition, how should we prepare ourselves for these eventualities? What form will they take in our current life situation?
4. How can we avoid falling into the frustrating trap of trying to tackle the difficulties and challenges of life all by ourselves, forgetting that Christ is always with us, working in our hearts and in others through us?

Cf. Catechism of the Catholic Church, 780 on the Church as the sign and instrument of salvation; 668-682 on the Second Coming and the Day of Judgment

225. Endgame (Lk 21:25-38)

"He hid the time from us so that we would be on the watch and so that each of us might think that the coming will happen in his own lifetime." – St. Ephraem

LUKE 21:25-38

"There will be signs in the sun and moon and stars; on earth nations in agony, bewildered by the clamour of the ocean and its waves; men dying of fear as they await what menaces the world, for the powers of heaven will be shaken. And then they will see the Son of Man coming in a cloud with power and great glory. When these things begin to take place, stand erect, hold your heads high, because your liberation is near at hand." And he told them a parable, "Think of the fig tree and indeed every tree. As soon as you see them bud, you know that summer is now near. So with you when you see these things happening: know that the kingdom of God is near. I tell you solemnly, before this generation has passed away all will have taken place. Heaven and earth will pass away, but my words will never pass away. Watch yourselves, or your hearts will be coarsened with debauchery and drunkenness and the cares of life, and that day will be sprung on you suddenly, like a trap. For it will come down on every living man on the face of the earth. Stay awake, praying at all times for the strength to survive all that is going to happen, and to stand with confidence before the Son of Man."

In the daytime he would be in the Temple teaching, but would spend the night on the hill called the Mount of Olives. And from early morning the people would gather round him in the Temple to listen to him.

CHRIST THE LORD In this second half of Jesus' speech answering the question about when the destruction of the Temple would occur Jesus changes his imagery. He employs phrases and allusions that all of his Jewish listeners would have recognized as referring to the Day of the Lord that the Old Testament prophets had predicted. The Day of the Lord referred to the coming of the Messiah and the inauguration of the new Messianic Kingdom, which also included the end of the Old Covenant. From the Jewish perspective, this would be the line of demarcation for all human history. By making these allusions, therefore, Jesus associates the events that will occur in the first Christian generation ("Before this generation has passed away all will have taken place") and conclude with the destruction of Jerusalem as that fateful Day of the Lord. But the Day of the Lord doesn't end with the fall of the Temple; it is extended throughout the rest of human history. During that time, the experience of the first generations of Christians—persecution, growth, conversions of whole cities and cultures, wars and disasters—will be repeated by successive generations until Jesus comes again. So Jesus' comments about those days apply to every age of the Church, and the destruction of Jerusalem and the Temple at the end of Old Covenant history is a foreshadowing of the destruction of heaven and earth at the end of New Covenant history.

Jesus Christ is the Lord of history. When we read the history books and watch the daily news it may not seem so, but in reality he is. At some point in the future, the story that mankind has been putting together since the dawn of time will come to an end; the way things are will be radically changed. Thus the imagery Jesus provides of "signs" in the sun, the moon, and the waves of the sea indicate that the stable order of the universe in which we make history will be uprooted and history will end. When that happens, Christ's Lordship will be fully manifest to everyone (he will come again in "a cloud with power and great glory") and will bring to fruition his eternal reign. All human history is moving towards that final, climactic moment. Everyone's personal contribution to the human story will be made known to all at the end, when the Lord renews heaven and earth and takes his place on the everlasting throne.

CHRIST THE TEACHER Jesus doesn't tell us the exact day and hour of his second coming. He prefers for us to stay ready for it at every moment; this is the lesson of the fig tree. If we keep our hearts awake, resisting the sweet lullaby of earthly pleasures and concerns, we will recognize the signs of his approach and be prepared to greet him when he comes. He also warns us that we will have to face tribulations before we are able to stand before him in glory; it will not be easy to stay faithful to God throughout the trials of life. (Otherwise, why would he tell us to pray for "strength to survive all that is going to happen"?)

Though millennia have already passed without his appearance, his warnings are as urgent as ever. For even if another millennium or two unfold before history as a whole concludes, our personal histories have a much more predictable endpoint. As individuals, we could find ourselves standing before him any day. It is up to each one of us to heed his warnings now, before "that day is sprung on [us] suddenly, like a trap." Every year the Church reminds us of this as the Solemnity of Christ the King concludes the liturgical year. We will have no one to blame but ourselves if we don't take the reminders to heart—and that doesn't mean shivering with fright and terror, but simply staying faithful to God's will for our lives, the true source of joy and meaning both in time and in eternity.

CHRIST THE FRIEND *Jesus: Do you think I had fire and brimstone in my eyes when I spoke these warnings? Do you think I spoke them quietly, in intimate conversation with my disciples? You know that I never take pleasure in the destruction of sinners. I only seek their salvation, as I have sought yours. I wanted you to know what the human heart has always wondered about—the end of history will come, and I will make a new creation, and the justice that was not given during the course of your earthly life will be given, and my mercy will shine out in all of its infinite glory. I want you to know that, so that you are able to stand up to the trials that following me always brings with it. I know you trust me, but now you have one more reason to do so. You don't have to fear the future; you already know what it holds. You can be ready, and be at peace, and you can dedicate yourself to loving me and loving those I give you to love. And even though I am with you all the time now, you can already start looking forward to that day when we will be together without the veil of faith.*

CHRIST IN MY LIFE I have to thank you again for the gift of these Gospels. Here you speak to me directly—you who created me and love me more than I love myself. And you nourish my soul with the truth of your words and examples. Lord, I want to become an expert in the Gospels—not an academic expert, but a loving expert in knowing and following you, my Lord and my God...

It isn't easy to stay ready, Lord. Why do you delay your coming? You don't need to tell me—I already know. In your love and your wisdom you are waiting until the right moment. I want to live faithfully while my life lasts. I want to experience your love and your joy, and I want to spread it to those around me. Fill my heart with your grace and my mind with your truth...

I know that being faithful to you, to what is true and right and good, will bring trouble upon me, just as it brought trouble upon you. But you will never let me be tempted beyond my power to endure, and you will always give me whatever strength I need. I am not afraid, Lord. I keep seeing you on the cross, gazing down at me, telling me not to fear, telling me just to be faithful, courageous...

Questions for SMALL-GROUP DISCUSSION

1. What struck you most in this passage? What did you notice that you hadn't noticed before?

2. What influences around us tend to "make our hearts coarsened"? In other words, how do Christ's examples of "debauchery, drunkenness, and the cares of life" apply to us?
3. How can we better follow Christ's advice about "staying awake, praying at all times"?
4. At the risk of scaring us off, Christ has told us about the seriousness of our life decisions in light of his second coming. We should be equally charitable in telling those around us about these fundamental truths. What are some good ways and appropriate times to do so?

Cf. Catechism of the Catholic Church, 673-674 and 1040 on the uncertainty of the time of the Lord's coming; 522-526 on the meaning of Advent and Christmas

THE GOSPEL OF LUKE
Chapter 22

"Thus the passion of the Saviour is salvation for mankind. This was why he willed to die for us, that we should believe in him, and live forever. He willed to become for a time what we are, so that we should receive the promise of his eternity and live with him forever. This is the feast of the year for which we long, the beginnings of life-giving realities. Here is given us the grace of the heavenly mysteries, the gift of the Pasch."

- HOMILY OF AN ANCIENT AUTHOR

226. The Passion Begins (Lk 22:1-13)

"Let us fix our thoughts on the blood of Christ; and reflect how precious that blood is in God's eyes, inasmuch as its outpouring for our salvation has opened the grace of repentance to all mankind." – Pope St. Clement I

LUKE 22:1-13

The feast of Unleavened Bread, called the Passover, was now drawing near, and the chief priests and the scribes were looking for some way of doing away with him, because they mistrusted the people. Then Satan entered into Judas, surnamed Iscariot, who was numbered among the Twelve. He went to the chief priests and the officers of the guard to discuss a scheme for handing Jesus over to them. They were delighted and agreed to give him money. He accepted, and looked for an opportunity to betray him to them without the people knowing. The day of Unleavened Bread came round, the day on which the passover had to be sacrificed, and he sent Peter and John, saying, "Go and make the preparations for us to eat the Passover." "Where do you want us to prepare it?" they asked. "Listen," he said, "as you go into the city you will meet a man carrying a pitcher of water. Follow him into the house he enters and tell the owner of the house, 'The Master has this to say to you: Where is the dining room in which I can eat the passover with my disciples?' The man will show you a large upper room furnished with couches. Make the preparations there." They set off and found everything as he had told them, and prepared the Passover.

CHRIST THE LORD St. Luke points out that Satan "entered into Judas" and crowned Judas' decision to betray Jesus. All that follows, therefore, will be orchestrated by the evil one. As such, it will reveal to us what Satan desires—destruction, suffering, dissension, dishonesty, selfishness. He stirs up all that is evil in the human heart in order to bring sorrow and pain. At the same time, however, St. Luke describes Jesus' minute knowledge of everything that is going to take place. Isn't this a contradiction? If Jesus is in control of each detail, if God is really guiding the events of history and especially these events of history's fulcrum moment, why does Satan have free rein? Only because God's omnipotence embraces even the freedom of his creatures; so powerful and wise is our Lord, that while Satan freely enters Judas and Judas freely decides to betray his Master and Peter and John freely decide to obey him, all four of them equally "prepared the Passover" in accordance with God's will.

The kingdom of evil is not on par with the Kingdom of Christ. The forces are not even; the battle does not hang in the balance. Christ is Lord, and those who follow him triumph.

CHRIST THE TEACHER Peter and John provide a beautiful example of Christian obedience, thrown into special relief by Judas' disobedience immediately preceding it. Jesus gives them a simple task, and they ask for some specific clarifications—"Where do you want us to prepare the meal?" Jesus answers them with a cryptic prediction of an encounter with an unnamed man. Did it strike them as odd that Jesus wouldn't simply tell them where the house was? Maybe he wanted to keep it secret from Judas so as to ensure a peaceful Last Supper, but he doesn't give any such explanation. He simply expects his two closest disciples to trust him and carry out the task. They have no idea that this is going to be the famous Last Supper, during which they will be ordained priests and the Old Covenant will give way to the New Covenant with its new, redemptive sacrifice. No, they don't know any of the details or the greater meaning. Yet, it is enough for them to know that this is what the Master wants them to do. And so they go off, trusting simply in their Lord like children, waiting for what he said to come to pass. And it does—they "found everything as he had told them."

Sometimes it is vain and selfish to ask for complete explanations of why God wants us to do things his way or the Church's way. Sometimes we just need to trust in him and in his chosen instruments (his bishops and priests, the spiritual directors his providence provides for us...) so he can be free to make salvation history.

CHRIST THE FRIEND *Jesus: I knew what was going on in Judas' heart... how he had lost faith in me and was using his intelligence to arrange a profitable way to* *manipulate events in accordance with what he thought were his own plans. But what he didn't know was that as soon as he started to live a double life–appearing to be a faithful disciple on the outside, but really scheming deceptively on the inside–he opened his soul to the influence of the evil one. If only he had come to me with his frustrations, anger, and disappointment! The others had come at different times. They had opened their hearts to me, admitting their weakness and accepting my grace. But he wanted to work everything out himself, and he wanted solutions right away.*

Many others through the years have done the same. Even many of my priests and religious have run into difficulties and tried to resolve them all by themselves, keeping up false appearances on the outside and nurturing rebellion in their hearts. Why didn't they come to me and open their hearts? I know how weak the human heart can be. You will never give up on me, I hope. You know I will never give up on you. Keep your heart crystal clear. Never live a double life. Come to me in confession, in prayer. Stay close to me, as I am always close to you.

CHRIST IN MY LIFE When I try to understand the mystery of evil, Lord, it is so hard to fathom. But I know that it's more important to relish your goodness, spreading it and making it known. How can I ever understand everything that you understand? It is enough for me to follow you each day, to let you teach me at the pace you want me to go. Make me a channel of your peace...

You know, Lord, that obedience is not considered a virtue by anyone in the world today. And yet, you achieved our salvation by obeying your Father's will, and Mary won her crown through her faith-filled obedience. I want to obey you because I know that you are trustworthy. Align my will with yours...

Jesus, never let me fall into the hypocrisy that Judas fell into. Never let me be one thing on the outside and another thing on the inside. I want to be wholly yours, consistent, a Christian with integrity. I don't have to tell everyone about all my interior struggles and temptations, but yes, I do have to live in complete sincerity with you and with myself. Teach me to follow your path...

Questions for SMALL-GROUP DISCUSSION

1. What struck you most in this passage? What did you notice that you hadn't noticed before?
2. If Jesus knew what Judas was up to, why didn't he pull him aside and confront him about it? Is there a lesson in this for us?
3. In what areas of life does popular culture make it hard to be authentic, to be sincere?

4. What do you think the apostles (besides Judas) were thinking as this Passover drew near?

Cf. Catechism of the Catholic Church, 144-149 on the obedience of faith; 2465-2470 on living in the truth; 1790-1794 on erroneous conscience

227. Given for You (Lk 22:14-27)

"In the Eucharist we receive something that we cannot do, but instead enter something greater that becomes our own, precisely when we give ourselves to this thing that is greater, truly seeking to celebrate the Liturgy as the Church's Liturgy." – Pope Benedict XVI

LUKE 22:14-27

When the hour came he took his place at table, and the apostles with him. And he said to them, "I have longed to eat this passover with you before I suffer; because, I tell you, I shall not eat it again until it is fulfilled in the kingdom of God." Then, taking a cup, he gave thanks and said, "Take this and share it among you, because from now on, I tell you, I shall not drink wine until the kingdom of God comes." Then he took some bread, and when he had given thanks, broke it and gave it to them, saying, "This is my body which will be given for you; do this as a memorial of me." He did the same with the cup after supper, and said, "This cup is the new covenant in my blood which will be poured out for you. And yet, here with me on the table is the hand of the man who betrays me. The Son of Man does indeed go to his fate even as it has been decreed, but alas for that man by whom he is betrayed!" And they began to ask one another which of them it could be who was to do this thing. A dispute arose also between them about which should be reckoned the greatest, but he said to them, "Among pagans it is the kings who lord it over them, and those who have authority over them are given the title Benefactor. This must not happen with you. No; the greatest among you must behave as if he were the youngest, the leader as if he were the one who serves. For who is the greater: the one at table or the one who serves? The one at table, surely? Yet here am I among you as one who serves!"

CHRIST THE LORD The Passover meal was a ritual commemorating God's liberation of his people from Egyptian slavery through the ministry of Moses. God had initiated and accomplished the liberation, and he had established the way of celebrating it, so that the Israelites would never forget all that God had done for them. The blood of the lamb sacrificed at Passover was the mark by which God's favor was shown to Israel and by which the Old Covenant would come to be established. Now, during the Last Supper, Jesus reshapes the ritual, reveals the true meaning behind the old symbols (he is the Lamb; he is the Savior), and establishes a new ceremony that will commemorate his own immolation on Calvary until the end of time. If this were the only passage of the Gospels that history had preserved, it would be enough to corroborate Jesus' claim to be divine—only God had the authority to alter the most sacred Passover ritual that God himself had established.

It is the culminating moment of history. Now communion between God and man—the only source of authentic human happiness—is to be reestablished, because from now on men will be able to partake of the Body and Blood of God. Whenever we approach the Lord in this sacrament, he wants to deepen this communion, drawing us closer to his heart, uniting us more firmly with the rest of the Church, and activating our own vocation to become bridges between him and those who still don't know him. He is uniting the scattered and divided human family in himself through the breaking of his body and the pouring out of his blood. When we receive and adore him with this in mind, we help his Kingdom come.

CHRIST THE TEACHER St. Luke mentions that Jesus "gave thanks" before he consecrated the bread. From this Greek term we derive the name Eucharist. On the eve of Christ's passing over to death he leaves us the gift of the Eucharist, a gift that will enable him to enter into intimate communion with each one of his followers throughout human history, to be their strength, their comfort, and their joy. This is why he says, "I have longed to eat this Passover with you before I suffer." He has longed to leave us the sacrament of his love, the guarantee of his presence and forgiveness and fidelity. What more could he have given us?

And yet, even in that solemn moment, the apostles are still bickering about their privileges. We should be glad they did, because it gave Jesus a chance to explain once again the fundamental law of his Kingdom, a law embodied perfectly in the Eucharist, the law of self-giving. Greatness for the Christian means giving oneself for the good of the other, just as Christ has given himself, literally and heroically, in the sacrament of the Eucharist. It is a lesson we should never tire of hearing, because it is a lesson we should never stop striving to learn.

CHRIST THE FRIEND Peter: *How could we have been so oblivious? We all felt that it was a special night, but none of us guessed what was really at stake. Jesus seemed* *pensive, but he was still our familiar leader, our teacher and friend. I was just glad to be sitting beside him. It never occurred to me that this would be our last dinner together. He knew, and that's why he said what he said and did what he did. How could I have been so slow to recognize the importance of what was going on? It was always like that. I was always so preoccupied with my own things that I missed the Lord's hints. And he was so gentle, so patient.*

Jesus: How eagerly I had been looking forward to that supper! When we had the sacrificial lamb on our plates, I thought of my own imminent sacrifice, my own suffering that would remove once and for all any shadow of doubt about my love. How my heart overflowed when I was finally able to give to my first priests and followers the Sacrament of intimate communion–all of the sufferings that had already happened and all that were still to come were worth suffering a thousand times more so that I could leave for you this New Testament, this New Covenant, this bridge between time and eternity.

Do you know that I still look forward just as eagerly to each sacramental celebration of that Supper, to each Holy Communion? I long to give myself to you in this Sacrament. I am wholly present in it, and I bring all my grace and all my wisdom and all my love when you receive me. You can't see all of this, because your faith is still small, still growing. But as you come to know me better, I will show you more and more, and you will see how every Tabernacle in the world shines more brightly than the sun, spreading goodness and hope and redemption all around it.

CHRIST IN MY LIFE Sometimes I think you should have given me a more dramatic way to commemorate your suffering and redemption, Lord. But then I remember that you don't want to impress me; you want to walk with me. You want to be my strength and life. You want to be my daily bread, my daily companion. There, in the midst of the normal daily dramas, you teach and guide me…

I want to be able to give myself to others as completely and generously as you give yourself to me. But I am so hampered by all my selfish tendencies, my oversensitivity, and my complexes and fears! You are my only hope, Lord. Only you can renew my heart and give me whatever it is I need in order to become your true, faithful, persevering disciple…

I want to appreciate your gift of the Eucharist more, Lord. Draw me to your Tabernacles and altars. Increase my faith! You come in such simplicity, such silence, such gentleness! Like the sunshine and the drizzling rain, you come into my heart, and I barely know you're there. Open my eyes of faith, so that I can see more clearly your goodness and love and power and proclaim it more wisely and boldly…

Questions for SMALL-GROUP DISCUSSION

1. What struck you most in this passage? What did you notice that you hadn't noticed before?
2. The Church teaches that Jesus is truly present in the Sacrament of the Eucharist, not just symbolically present. How would you explain that difference to a child preparing for First Communion?
3. If a stranger were to gauge your Eucharistic life during a typical week (your visits to the Lord in the Eucharist, your Communions—their frequency and their fervor—and your spiritual communions...), what kind of a conclusion would they make about the importance of the Eucharist in your life?
4. What more can we do to promote Eucharistic life among our peers?

Cf. Catechism of the Catholic Church, 1333-1344 on the Eucharist in the economy of salvation; 1345-1355 on the Mass as the celebration of the Eucharist

228. The Bestowal of Thrones (Lk 22:28-38)

"As for me, my spirit is now all humble devotion to the cross: the cross which so greatly offends the unbelievers, but is salvation and eternal life to us." – St. Ignatius of Antioch

LUKE 22:28-38

"You are the men who have stood by me faithfully in my trials; and now I confer a kingdom on you, just as my Father conferred one on me: you will eat and drink at my table in my kingdom, and you will sit on thrones to judge the twelve tribes of Israel. Simon, Simon! Satan, you must know, has got his wish to sift you all like wheat; but I have prayed for you, Simon, that your faith may not fail, and once you have recovered, you in your turn must strengthen your brothers." "Lord," he answered, "I would be ready to go to prison with you, and to death." Jesus replied, "I tell you, Peter, by the time the cock crows today you will have denied three times that you know me." He said to them, "When I sent you out without purse or haversack or sandals, were you short of anything?" "No," they said. He said to them, "But now if you have a purse, take it; if you have a haversack, do the same; if you have no sword, sell your cloak and buy one, because I tell you these words of scripture have to be fulfilled in me: He let himself be taken for a criminal. Yes, what scripture says about me is even now reaching its fulfilment." "Lord," they said, "there are two swords here now." He said to them, "That is enough!"

CHRIST THE LORD Jesus is troubled by Judas' betrayal, but he is also encouraged by the others' fidelity and loyalty, in spite of their clumsiness and slowness to understand. In his gratitude, he reminds his apostles that he has promised them a Kingdom, and he assures them that he is conferring it on them even now. And his promise is literally fulfilled in the establishment of the Church, which can only take place at the conclusion of the atoning sacrifice of Calvary. When the spear is thrust through his heart as he hangs dead on the cross, the blood and water that flow out are the blood and water of the Church's birth. The Church is the start of Christ's Kingdom, and he bestows it upon his apostles by making them its first leaders, the overseers and rulers of this new people of God—and once again in his discourse, at this solemn moment, he gives special attention to Peter, entrusting him with the role of confirming the others. Just as King David had thrones in his palace for the ministers who assisted him in ruling his Kingdom, so Jesus will rule through the ministry of his bishops. Just as the Davidic Kingdom had a prime minister who bore the keys in the king's absence, so also would the Church.

Thus, the apostles truly do become the judges (an Old Testament term used for rulers in general, not only court justices as we understand them today) of all the tribes of the new Israel, the Church. And they eat and drink at the Lord's table there, in that Kingdom, by celebrating the sacrament of the Eucharist.

Once again, Jesus reminds us that every step of his Passion is meaningful—part of the Father's plan to redeem fallen humanity through his everlasting Church. We are the heirs of this immensely beautiful, richly mysterious plan, and as heirs, it is up to us to carry forward and carry high its banner.

CHRIST THE TEACHER With this final discourse before his suffering begins, he is once again providing his apostles with what they will need to brave the coming storm—advice about how to understand what will come to pass in the next few hours. When he sent them on mission trips without supplies, he gave them instructions to depend on the goodwill of the people to whom he was sending them. But tonight is different. Tonight they will not be able to depend on the goodwill of anyone, because their Master will be taken away as a criminal. In telling them this, he did not mean for them to gather swords, he simply meant for them to understand that he knew beforehand what was going to happen. When they reflected back on it as the crisis was unfolding, his foreknowledge and willing acceptance would provide enough assurance to give them at least a glimmer of hope during the dark three days to come.

Just so, the memory of Jesus' passion should give us the amount of strength we need to persevere in fidelity and in doing what's right even in the face of trials, persecution, and suffering. All that Jesus did, he did for our sake to encourage us to stay the course. It remains up to us to take advantage of our inheritance and make it bear fruit by keeping it always in mind along the twists and turns of our own journey through life.

CHRIST THE FRIEND *James: We still didn't understand what was going to happen, even though he had told us so many times. We didn't want to believe him, and so we simply failed to understand. At least, that's how it was with me. I still had my hopes on an easy victory and a taste of worldly glory. I still thought we would be able to fulfill our mission as his disciples with our own natural strengths and talents. I thought I could stay faithful to him by depending on myself. We were all like that—so attached to our own ideas that we weren't listening to him. That's when we were most vulnerable. That's always when his followers are most vulnerable, when they lean on their own strength and forget that without him we can do nothing.*

Jesus: I created you to need me, so that you would feel drawn to the eternal life that I can give you. I want you to enjoy my friendship for all eternity, and that's something you can't achieve with your own talents. (I know, I gave those to you too.) Sometimes I have to remind you that you need me, as I had to remind Peter. You never need to be ashamed of your weakness; it's no surprise to me. I am always ready to come to your aid. It's never too late to call my name—but it's even better if you just let me keep walking by your side all the time.

CHRIST IN MY LIFE Thank you for the gift of the Church. Maybe because I'm inside it, I sometimes forget how remarkable and how wonderful it really is. Thank you for all your sacraments. Thank you for the pure, crystalline teaching where I can always relieve my thirst for truth. Are you happy with how I treat the Church? Bless your Church, Lord, and make us all her faithful children...

In the same breath, Lord, you promised to give your apostles the Kingdom, and then you told them they would be shaken and scattered like wheat by the onslaught of evil. You rejoice to give me good gifts, in spite of my faults and sins and failings! Your love doesn't depend on my perfection—how many times must you remind me! My happiness depends solely on your love...

I know that without you I can do nothing. But I also know that you have given me a role in your mission of salvation. You don't want me to just sit back and enjoy the ride. Thank you for this gift. I am glad to have something to do, some way I can grow in my love and serve my neighbor. Keep me faithful, Lord...

Questions for SMALL-GROUP DISCUSSION

1. What struck you most in this passage? What did you notice that you hadn't noticed before?
2. How can we foster, in ourselves and in those around us, a more vibrant and supernatural love and respect for the pope and our bishops?
3. What should be the immediate reaction of Christians when they fall or fail, as Peter is about to do?
4. Why do you think Jesus doesn't protect us from every fall and failure?

Cf. Catechism of the Catholic Church, 551-553 on Jesus' establishment of the Church hierarchy; 874-896 on the hierarchical structure of the Church; 1430-1433 on interior penance

229. A Dark Garden (Lk 22:39-54)

"I've had these temptations for forty-one years now – do you think I'm going to give up after all this time? Absolutely not. I'll never stop hoping in God, though he kill me, though he grind me in the dust of eternity." – St. Jane de Chantal

LUKE 22:39-54

He then left to make his way as usual to the Mount of Olives, with the disciples following. When they reached the place he said to them, "Pray not to be put to the test." Then he withdrew from them, about a stone's throw away, and knelt down and prayed. "Father," he said, "if you are willing, take this cup away from me. Nevertheless, let your will be done, not mine." Then an angel appeared to him, coming from heaven to give him strength. In his anguish he prayed even more earnestly, and his sweat fell to the ground like great drops of blood. When he rose from prayer he went to the disciples and found them sleeping for sheer grief. "Why are you asleep?" he said to them. "Get up and pray not to be put to the test." He was still speaking when a number of men appeared, and at the head of them the man called Judas, one of the Twelve, who went up to Jesus to kiss him. Jesus said, "Judas, are you betraying the son of Man with a kiss?" His followers, seeing what was happening, said, "Lord, shall we use our swords?" And one of them struck out at the high priest's servant, and cut off his right ear. But at this Jesus spoke. "Leave off!" he said. "That will do!" And touching the man's ear he healed him. Then Jesus spoke to the chief priests and captains of the Temple guard and elders who had come for him. "Am I a brigand," he said, "that you had to set out with swords and clubs? When I was among you in the Temple day after day you never moved to lay hands on me. But this is your hour; this is the reign of darkness." They seized him then and led him away, and they took him to the high priest's house.

CHRIST THE LORD One of the most remarkable things about the Passion narratives is how Jesus remains composed and in control the whole time. As the petty wrath and duplicity of his enemies break against him, his fidelity and assurance, his love and self-mastery are completely undiminished, while their hatred surges and splatters and gathers for more and more useless assaults. His betrayer acts so nonchalant and unassuming, but the words of the Master lay bare his heart: "Is it with a kiss you betray me, Judas?" His disciples lash out with their swords, stirred to a worldly fury, but Jesus calms them with a word and restores order, healing his maimed and panicking enemy with a miracle. Faced with the gang of hirelings sent to arrest him, he reminds them that he has not been hiding in caves like an outlaw and thus exposes what they had not wanted to face up to—that something dishonorable and even despicable hovers all around this late-night, secret arrest. Even when he prays in the Garden, while every fiber of his human nature is pulling him away from the Father's will, even then the earnestness and force of his will presides, bringing every emotion and fear and doubt under the sweet yoke of loving obedience.

Jesus lived his Passion this way because he lived it with love and purpose, as he lived every moment of his earthly life. We have received the same love and purpose through his grace, and as a result, as the countless martyrs have shown, we can find the same strength and nobility in the midst of our own passions simply by exercising our faith in him.

CHRIST THE TEACHER Our Lord's sweat pouring out in great drops of blood is more than St. Luke waxing poetic. In extreme states of anxiety, clinical studies have shown that the capillaries near the surface of the skin will burst, and blood will mingle with the perspiration exuded by the sweat glands. What is Jesus teaching us by suffering this kind of anxiety? One simple lesson: fulfilling God's will in a fallen world will require self-sacrifice. It did for him, it did for his mother the Blessed Virgin Mary, and it did for every one of his followers who has been courageous enough to persevere in seeking and carrying out God's will. If it isn't demanding, it isn't the gospel.

Jesus wants us to know that, but he also wants us to know how to endure the suffering: by prayer. This is what he does, and this is what he tells his disciples to do, "Get up and pray not to be put to the test." If we pray, we will receive whatever grace we need to continue along the right path—just as Jesus here in Gethsemane received comfort from the angel.

Suffering and prayer—these are two of the three weapons available to us for spreading Christ's Kingdom. The third is a Christlike love for our neighbor.

CHRIST THE FRIEND *Jesus: I was thinking of you when I prayed in the Garden. I was thinking of what would happen to you if I were to reject the Father's will. You would have never discovered my love for you. You would have been stuck in those sins, hopelessly, for the rest of your life. You would have suffered interior remorse with no hope of forgiveness. You would have had to harden your heart so much just in order to survive that you would have lost the ability to love and let yourself be loved. None of your wounds that I have started to heal would have ever healed. None of the hopes that shine so brightly in your heart would be shining at all. I was glad to say yes to my Father so that you wouldn't have to suffer the darkness of everlasting regret and despair.*

I was also thinking of all the times you would to say yes to me. That was how the angel comforted me. He showed me the times you would confess your sins and accept my forgiveness. He showed me the times you would trust me enough to follow the voice of your conscience, even when the easier, more popular thing was to ignore it. He showed me all your prayers, your Holy Communions, your deeds of selflessness, fidelity, and generosity. He showed me your room in my Father's house, still waiting there for you. How much it thrilled me to see those things! I was glad to go to the cross for you. I would do it again a thousand times.

CHRIST IN MY LIFE If you are for me, Lord, who can be against me? Jesus, give me your courage and your wisdom. This world I live in is in such need of your grace, and by myself I am such a weak grace-dispenser. But you have called me into your Kingdom. And you can work through me. With the zeal of your heart, inflame my heart, and with the fortitude of your heart, make my heart strong…

You suffered and you prayed. Teach me to suffer and to pray. I am afraid of suffering; I run from it. You didn't. You ran towards it. How can I understand these mysteries without the light of your Holy Spirit? How can I learn to pray as I ought without your help? Jesus, I trust in you; let your will be done, not mine…

I can't help thinking about all the people who have to suffer without the comfort of your friendship. Jesus, come to their aid. Some suffer physically, others only in the secret of their souls. Send your messengers to them. Send me to them. Who can I bring your friendship to today, Lord? Show me how to be a better instrument of your grace today...

Questions for SMALL-GROUP DISCUSSION

1. What struck you most in this passage? What did you notice that you hadn't noticed before?
2. What tone of voice do you think Jesus used to address Judas? What did he mean by his question?
3. The Church teaches that Jesus suffered, died, and rose for us. What different ways can you think of for interpreting what "for us" really means?
4. If an agnostic acquaintance asked you why Jesus, if he was really God, had so much trouble accepting the Father's will in the Garden of Gethsemane, what would you say?

Cf. Catechism of the Catholic Church, 609-61 on Jesus' self-offering at the Last Supper and in Gethsemane; 2824-2827 on the meaning of Jesus' prayer in Gethsemane

230. Myriad Sins, Multifaceted Love (Lk 22:55-71)

"Therefore let no one presume on his own powers when he speaks; let no one trust in his own strength when he undergoes temptation, since in order to speak well and prudently, we must have wisdom from the Lord; and in order to bear misfortune bravely, we must receive the gift of endurance from him." – St. Augustine

LUKE 22:55-71

Peter followed at a distance. They had lit a fire in the middle of the courtyard and Peter sat down among them, and as he was sitting there by the blaze a servant-girl saw him, peered at him, and said, "This person was with him too." But he denied it. "Woman," he said, "I do not know him." Shortly afterwards someone else saw him and said, "You are another of them. But Peter replied, "I am not, my friend." About an hour later another man insisted, saying, "This fellow was certainly with him. Why, he is a Galilean." "My friend," said Peter, "I do not know what you are talking about." At that instant, while he was still speaking, the cock crew, and the Lord turned and looked straight at Peter, and Peter remembered what the Lord had said to him, "Before the cock crows today, you will have disowned me three times." And he went outside and wept bitterly. Meanwhile the men who guarded Jesus were mocking and beating him. They blindfolded him and questioned him. "Play the prophet," they said. "Who hit you then?" And they continued heaping insults on him. When day broke there was a meeting of the elders of the people, attended by the chief priests and scribes. He was brought before their council, and they said to him, "If you are the Christ, tell us." "If I tell you," he replied "you will not believe me, and if I question you, you will not answer. But from now on, the Son of Man will be seated at the right hand of the Power of God." Then they all said, "So you are the Son of God then?" He answered, "It is you who say I am." "What need of witnesses have we now?" they said. "We have heard it for ourselves from his own lips."

CHRIST THE LORD During his Passion, Jesus seems to make a point of suffering in every way possible, just so we will never have to suffer alone, no matter what brand of hardship life throws at us. By letting evil have free rein with him, and by persevering in love through it all, he shows his Lordship over the kingdom of darkness. And even in this final battle of his earthly life, he has us in mind, so that the revelation of his love exposes the face of sin as well. Every type of suffering that Jesus undergoes is caused by its own type of sin. As we contemplate his sorrows, then, he purifies our multifaceted selfishness, so that we who get a chance to share his sorrows here in this fallen world can also share his victories.

In this passage Peter causes Christ the immense sorrow of being abandoned by his closest friend. Peter, Jesus' privileged disciple, disowns his Master. Why did Peter do it? Unlike Judas, Peter didn't premeditate his betrayal. He hadn't fondled and coddled and nourished his feelings of self-righteousness and self-pity to the point where he thought turning Christ in was a justifiable and even, perhaps, virtuous act. No, Peter's sin was simple weakness. Disoriented by the arrest in the Garden, intimidated by the Sanhedrin's show of force, and surprised by the aggressive accusations made at him around the fire, he unthinkingly falls back into a self-centered self-defense mode. His true self was still caked with egoism, in spite of his acclamations to the contrary just hours before and his authentic desire to be faithful to Christ. We all share this weakness, and when we lean on our own strength as if we didn't, our inevitable falls grieve the heart of the Lord.

CHRIST THE TEACHER The guards were "mocking and beating him." We should not overlook the raw physical suffering this treatment caused our Lord. Just because the suffering of his heart was deeper and more painful, that doesn't mean that the suffering of the body ought to be minimized. Jesus had come to save these very men who were beating him; he came to pay the price for their sins and give them the light and grace that would renew their spirits and lead them to the happiness they yearn for. But they treated him cruelly. Theirs is the sin against charity, against the love we ought to have for our neighbors. Perhaps they had no way to recognize Christ as Lord, but they still had before them a fellow man, and yet they treated him like an animal, sporting with him. How often we do the same to our fellow men! Our careless words and pointed criticisms, our unforgiving judgments and arrogant gossip—these are cruel blows leveled against Christ himself, because "I tell you solemnly, in so far as you did this to one of the least of these brothers of mine, you did it to me" (Mt 25:40).

The leaders of the Sanhedrin, the Jewish governing body in Palestine at the time, simply refused to listen to him. "If I tell you, you will not believe me, and if I question you, you will not answer." By far, this caused Jesus the greatest suffering, that of unrequited love. Jesus is the pure love of the Father who has come to dwell among us. He is the Father's final and definitive declaration of love, and yet "his own people did not accept him" (Jn 1:11). Whenever we sin, in little things or big, we echo the Sanhedrin's proud refusal to accept their Savior. Whenever we say no to the voice of conscience, whenever we set ourselves up as judges of the Church's teaching, we join the ranks of "his own people, who did not accept him."

CHRIST THE FRIEND *Jesus: Many people think I must have been angry as my enemies destroyed me piece by piece. But how could I be angry? I was sad. I knew each one of my persecutors; I had created them, I was holding them in existence even as they rejected me. I knew that in destroying me, they were working their own destruction. Have you ever watched a loved one work his own destruction? Then you can feel a tinge of the sadness that drowned my heart during my Passion. But even as they crushed me, body and soul, underneath the sadness I was still able to rejoice because I knew that the supreme witness of my love on the cross would break open some of those tightly closed hearts, and at the very culmination of their colossal crimes, they would feel remorse and turn to me in repentance, and all would be well.*

You were with me then too. Your sins were raining down upon me, but your repentance gave me joy. It was all worth it, because my sacrifice would convince you of my love, and it would bring you onto my team and into my heart. Stay close to me, and offer your sufferings for the conversion of the many hearts that remained closed, and let us rejoice together in the victory of love.

CHRIST IN MY LIFE I don't want to forget about my sins, Lord, because your love shines brightest in your mercy. I believe in your mercy, and I am sorry for my sins. But if your mercy has overcome my sins, and if the sun of your mercy still shines even after my many attempts to blot it out with my sins, then what could ever steal my peace of soul? In your love I find all that my heart desires…

Why is it so hard for me to control my words, Lord? I am like those brutal soldiers, completely oblivious to the effect my criticisms and jibes have on those around me. What would we talk about all the time if we didn't criticize people? I want to know, Lord; I want to discover how to spread peace and light with the precious gift of speech, not bitterness and darkness…

Mary, you know I believe in Jesus. I have put my hopes in him. I don't want to cause him any suffering. Teach me to please him with my faith, my hope, and my efforts to build his Kingdom. Mother of mercy, pray for the many people who still refuse to believe in him. Help me to make his goodness visible to them, as you made it visible by standing by him at Calvary, so that his grace will win over their hearts…

Questions for *SMALL-GROUP DISCUSSION*

1. What struck you most in this passage? What did you notice that you hadn't noticed before?
2. Why is speaking badly of others such an easy sin to fall into, and why is speaking well of others such a hard habit to form? How can we help each other to make the switch?
3. Why do you think Jesus purposely turned to look at Peter right after his third denial and the crowing of the rooster?
4. If you had to explain the evil of sin to an agnostic acquaintance who asked you about it, what would you tell them?

Cf. Catechism of the Catholic Church, 1846-1848 on mercy and sin; 1849-1853 on sin; 1865-1869 on the proliferation of sin; 2839-2841 on asking God's forgiveness

THE GOSPEL OF LUKE
Chapter 23

"How precious is the gift of the cross! See, how beautiful it is to behold! It shows no sign of evil mixed with good, like the tree of old in Eden; it is all beautiful and comely to see and to taste. For it is a tree which brings forth life, not death. It is the source of light, not darkness. It offers you a home in Eden; it does not cast you out. It is the tree which Christ mounted as a king his chariot, and so destroyed the devil, the lord of death, and rescued the human race from slavery to the tyrant. It is the tree on which the Lord, like a great warrior with his hands and feet and his divine side pierced in battle, healed the wounds of our sins, healed our nature that had been wounded by the evil serpent."

- ST. THEODORE THE STUDITE

231. Unruly Rulers (Lk 23:1-12)

"O man, rouse yourself! Learn to know the dignity of your nature. Remember that image of God in which you were created, which, though defaced in Adam, is now restored in Christ." – Pope St. Leo the Great

LUKE 23:1-12

The whole assembly then rose, and they brought him before Pilate. They began their accusation by saying, "We found this man inciting our people to revolt, opposing payment of the tribute to Caesar, and claiming to be Christ, a king." Pilate put to him this question, "Are you the king of the Jews?" "It is you who say it," he replied. Pilate then said to the chief priests and the crowd, "I find no case against this man." But they persisted, "He is inflaming the people with his teaching all over Judaea; it has come all the way from Galilee, where he started, down to here." When Pilate heard this, he asked if the man were a Galilean; and finding that he came under Herod's jurisdiction he passed him over to Herod who was also in Jerusalem at that time. Herod was delighted to see Jesus; he had heard about him and had been wanting for a long time to set eyes on him; moreover, he was hoping to see some miracle worked by him. So he questioned him at some length; but without getting any reply. Meanwhile the chief priests and the scribes were there, violently pressing their accusations. Then Herod, together with his guards, treated him with contempt and made fun of him; he put a rich cloak on him and sent him back to Pilate. And though Herod and Pilate had been enemies before, they were reconciled that same day.

CHRIST THE LORD We too often doubt God's powerful action in the course of human events simply because it is hidden. This passage gives us one of the great examples of the omnipotence of Providence. Pilate and Herod were rivals. Galilee and Judea were under different Roman jurisdictions; Judea was part of a procuratorship directly under Roman rule, while several of the neighboring areas, including Galilee, were under the rule of Herod, an semi-independent king allied with Rome. Because of the proximity of these territories and the constant flow of commerce and culture between them, the people often took advantage of Herod's policies to wheedle out of complying with Pilate's, and vice versa. You can imagine how doubly glad Pilate must have been to be able to slough off this tough case onto Herod's shoulders, taking advantage of a jurisdictional detail.

On the great day of Christ's Passion, however, this rivalry ends. St. Luke doesn't explain the reason behind Pilate and Herod's reconciliation; he just says it happened as a result of their both being involved with Christ in his Passion. Already, even before the consummation of his sacrifice, the leaven of redemption is bringing together the peoples (Pilate was Roman; Herod was part Jew and part Samaritan) and the hearts that original sin had antagonized. How great should the confidence of the Christian be in the face of the greatness of the power of Christ! No challenge is too great for him; only his followers can imbue the frustrated world with the real, fruitful hope of lasting progress.

CHRIST THE TEACHER Jesus is faced with false charges. He is given two opportunities to defend himself, and he doesn't use them to his advantage. He humbly accepts the injustice (from Pilate) and the mockery (from Herod). Reflect a moment on the strength of soul that this requires. Think about how hard it is for us to enact this virtue in much smaller things. How quickly we justify ourselves in the eyes of others! How deftly we shift the responsibility for failures onto other shoulders! We take such delicate care of what other people think of us, and here our Lord, for the good of the Kingdom, lets his enemies annihilate his reputation in a dozen different ways and says nary a word in his own defense.

Often our determined demands for justice or recognition are really desperate attempts to save face. We would have more peace in our hearts, and we would be freer to do more for the Kingdom, if we cared less about the opinions of others and about getting the credit for doing good. What should matter to the Christian is God's opinion.

CHRIST THE FRIEND When Jesus spoke with Pilate, he saw a man whose soul had been starved by his ambition. Pilate was no longer able to defend truth and justice, because he had sold his heart to the idol of success. So many Pilates still walk the halls of government today. Christ longs for his faithful disciples to take the truth and light of virtue into the midst of the world's rulers! With his grace in their hearts and his teachings giving light to their minds, they will be able to do so much good for the human family. But many of them lack courage. God has doled out to plenty of his children the talents for government, but too many of them have preferred a comfortable life.

He has given talents to each one of us. We know what some of them are; others are still waiting to be discovered. They are meant to be put at the service of the Kingdom. Christ's true friends know they are never alone, and so they never lack the courage to rejoice in the talents he has given to others and to use generously those they have received. The time is short. There is no time to be afraid. We should tirelessly forge ahead with whatever he inspires us to do for the good of the Church and of our neighbor. He is close beside us, guiding our every step.

CHRIST IN MY LIFE I believe in your Providence, Lord. I believe that you are guiding all things to their glorious conclusion in your Kingdom. Sometimes I am discouraged by the lack of visible progress, but I know that's only a temptation. Help me to do my part. Help me to give my best in everything I do, and to do only what I know you want me to do. Jesus, I trust in you…

This world is an expert at enticing me, Lord. How attractive it makes everything look! The pull of ambition, pleasure, popularity—it's constant, it's strong, it's seductive. I guess I still need a lot of help to keep things in proper perspective. Increase my virtue, Lord, so that I can do the right thing better, faster, more often, and with greater satisfaction…

I believe that you care about the course this world is taking. Raise up more leaders after your own heart, Lord. Remember how much you suffered for us, how much you love us, and don't abandon us to the whims of selfish and dishonest rulers. Thy Kingdom come…

Questions for SMALL-GROUP DISCUSSION

1. What struck you most in this passage? What did you notice that you hadn't noticed before?
2. Why do you think we don't find more virtuous Catholics in leadership positions throughout the world?
3. Herod was interested in a good show and Pilate wanted to climb the ladder of success, while Christ was focused on the mission he had received from the Father. Which of the three approaches to life do you think resonates most with popular culture? Why?
4. What are some of the most common ways we can fall into the sin of wasting time? How can we help ourselves make better use of this precious commodity?

Cf. Catechism of the Catholic Church, 302-314 on God's Providence and how it works; 898-900 and 2442 on Catholics' intervention in political life; 2520 on purity of intention

232. Carrying the Cross (Lk 23:13-32)

"Throughout history the most wonderful events have been only the symbols and foreshadowings of this cross." – St. Theodore the Studite

LUKE 23:13-32

Pilate then summoned the chief priests and the leading men and the people. "You brought this man before me," he said, "as a political agitator. Now I have gone into the matter myself in your presence and found no case against the man in respect of all the charges you bring against him. Nor has Herod either, since he has sent him back to us. As you can see, the man has done nothing that deserves death, So I shall have him flogged and then let him go." But as one man they howled, "Away with him! Give us Barabbas!" (This man had been thrown into prison for causing a riot in the city and for murder.) Pilate was anxious to set Jesus free and addressed them again, but they shouted back, "Crucify him! Crucify him!" And for the third time he spoke to them, "Why? What harm has this man done? I have found no case against him that deserves death, so I shall have him punished and then let him go." But they kept on shouting at the top of their voices, demanding that he should be crucified. And their shouts were growing louder. Pilate then gave his verdict: their demand was to be granted. He released the man they asked for, who had been imprisoned for rioting and murder, and handed Jesus over to them to deal with as they pleased. As they were leading him away they seized on a man, Simon from Cyrene, who was coming in from the country, and made him shoulder the cross and carry it behind Jesus. Large numbers of people followed him, and of women too, who mourned and lamented for him. But Jesus turned to them and said, "Daughters of Jerusalem, do not weep for me; weep rather for yourselves and for your children. For the days will surely come when people will say, 'Happy are those who are barren, the wombs that have never borne, the breasts that have never suckled!' Then they will begin to say to the mountains, 'Fall on us!' to the hills, 'Cover us.' For if men use the green wood like this, what will happen when it is dry?" Now with him they were also leading out two other criminals to be executed.

CHRIST THE LORD Jesus is the Word of God made flesh. As the Word of God, he is the creator of all that exists, including the moral order of human nature. That very moral order is what makes Pilate hesitate to condemn Jesus to death, because it is wrong to punish the innocent and even worse to kill the innocent. Pilate holds out against the crowd for a little while, but in the end he gives in. He violates his conscience, and in so doing condemns Christ to be crucified.

This is a snapshot of the whole moral life. Our conscience, formed and informed by Church teaching and the just laws and traditions of human society, indicates the right thing to do. It is one of God's great gifts, an internal chip that tells us his will and how we can live our lives in communion with him. When we disobey it, we are doing exactly what Pilate did—crucifying Christ, executing God, and banishing him in order to eliminate the discomfort his presence can cause. The same factors that influenced Pilate's decision influence ours: he was afraid to lose his position, his reputation, his livelihood, his hopes for promotion, and his cushy retirement. The shouts of the crowds—like the shouts of our passions and emotions—inflated the value of his temporal welfare, so much so that he was willing to sacrifice his own moral integrity to protect it.

Where was Christ in the midst of the battle? Why didn't he rescue Pilate? Jesus was right there. Pilate was looking at him the whole time. He knew exactly what he was doing. Just so, Jesus is with us every time we are faced with a moral decision, big or small. And when we are honest with ourselves, we know very well that we are fully responsible for each one of those decisions. This is why it is so important to reflect and pray about why we should stay faithful to God's will, to what is right, before the moments of conflict. Only then will we be able to resist the violent pressure of our emotions and fears in order to stay faithful to the Lord.

CHRIST THE TEACHER What is going on in Jesus' mind as he shoulders the cross and begins the long, excruciating, humiliating march to Calvary? Thanks to his encounter with the compassionate women who were walking beside him, we know the answer. He was thinking of us, of his beloved brothers and sisters for whom he was offering his life as an atoning sacrifice. Amazingly, even in a furious hurricane of personal suffering, his mind is not on himself, but on those whom he loves. He tells these women not to weep for him. He tells them to think of those who are rejecting him, and what will happen as a result of their rejection. Once again he uses language reminiscent of the Old Testament prophets, language used by those prophets to predict the fall of Jerusalem to the Babylon armies in 586 B.C. and the fall of the Northern Kingdom of Israel to the Assyrian armies in 733 B.C. Those who refuse God's grace are cutting themselves off from the source of existence itself, and only one result can ensue.

This conversation teaches us how to carry our crosses—and Jesus promised that his followers will have crosses to carry, every day. We are to remember that our acceptance of God's will when it's costly is the only way to exercise the virtues of faith, hope, and love that will restore our souls to health and holiness. We are to remember that when God sends us crosses, they too can be redemptive—just as Christ won grace by carrying and dying on his cross. We can win graces for the lives of those around us, the lives of those who need them most, through carrying and dying on our crosses with Christ, uniting our imperfect fidelity and trust to his perfect surrender. Jesus wanted to teach us that salvation comes not in spite of or instead of suffering, but through suffering. And he wanted to give us a chance not only to be saved ourselves, but to become agents of salvation for others, to become other Christs.

CHRIST THE FRIEND *Jesus: Do you realize what Barabbas was in prison for? He had rebelled against the Roman authority. Do you remember what crime my enemies accused me of in front of Pilate? Of raising up anti-Roman rebellions. Barabbas had committed the crime that I was accused of but had not committed, and he went free while I suffered his just punishment. Now do you see how my justice and mercy go together? I take upon myself the just punishments that others deserve, so that I can forgive their sins and give them a fresh start. I did the same with your sins—every one of them. The disorder they caused had to be set right—I did that during my Passion, and I do it at every Mass. I am the Lamb of God who takes away the sins of the world.*

Would you be willing to do the same? Are you willing to suffer what others deserve to suffer, so that they can go free and have a fresh start? I know that you love me and want to show me your love. I also know that the more you show me your love, the happier you will be. Here is a vast arena where you can love. Every time I permit a small suffering to come your way, if you accept it the way I accepted mine, you can offer it to the Father in reparation for the sin of someone who is still imprisoned in sin, and if you do this in my name, you will help set that person free. I have put the power of my Kingship in your hands.

CHRIST IN MY LIFE If I don't follow your will, Lord, who else's can I follow? There's mine, but I know how ignorant and selfish I am. There are other people's, but who is a wiser guide than you? There's the trend of popular culture, or any of the sub-cultures, but who's behind those trends if not some other self-proclaimed guru, or maybe even the devil? I want to follow your will, Lord; show me the way...

I see you carrying your cross, thinking about the mission the Father has entrusted to you. You are engrossed in the needs of others. You are glad to sacrifice yourself for me. O Jesus, give me a heart like that! Make me love as you love! I tend to turn in on myself when the going gets rough. Help me, Lord. Teach me to embrace my crosses as you embraced yours...

Mary, your love and fidelity helped Jesus redeem the world. Jesus wanted you to help. I know he wants me to help too. I know that my own prayer and fidelity can really help undo the evil of sin—mine as well as others'. I am not only an adopted child of God, but a real child of God. His life, nurtured in your womb, is my life. You are my mother too. Teach me to understand the dignity of being a Christian, and teach me to live in accordance with that dignity...

Questions for SMALL-GROUP DISCUSSION

1. What struck you most in this passage? What did you notice that you hadn't noticed before?
2. How can we better help each other carry our crosses?
3. Why do you think we resist suffering even though we know that it's an essential ingredient of human life?
4. How can we strengthen our consciences so that we make fewer and fewer sinful choices and more and more virtuous choices?

Cf. Catechism of the Catholic Church, 1750-1756 on the morality of our actions; 1776-1789 on the conscience; 602-605 on Christ's atoning sacrifice; 901-903 and 2099-2100 on offering sacrifices to God in union with Christ

233. The King's Pardon (Lk 23:33-43)

"O wonderful cross, upon whose branches hung the treasure and redemption of captive men, through you the world is redeemed by the blood of the Lord." – Liturgy of the Hours

LUKE 23:33-43

When they reached the place called The Skull, they crucified him there and the two criminals also, one on the right, the other on the left. Jesus said, "Father, forgive them; they do not know what they are doing." Then they cast lots to share out his clothing. The people stayed there watching him. As for the leaders, they jeered at him. "He saved others," they said, "let him save himself if he is the Christ of God, the Chosen One." The soldiers mocked him too, and when they approached to offer vinegar they said, "If you are the king of the Jews, save yourself." Above him there was an inscription: "This is the King of the Jews." One of the criminals hanging there abused him. "Are you not the Christ?" he said. "Save yourself and us as well." But the other spoke up and rebuked him. "Have you no fear of God at all?" he said. "You got the same sentence as he did, but in our case we deserved it: we are paying for what we did. But this man has done nothing wrong. Jesus," he said, "remember me when you come into your kingdom." "Indeed, I promise you," he replied, "today you will be with me in paradise."

CHRIST THE LORD We are gazing at the pivotal moment of human history: Jesus Christ being crucified on the hill of Calvary. In the Church's liturgy, this passage is read on the Solemnity of Christ the King at the end of liturgical year C. It's as if the Church directs our gaze to this pitiful man, wounded, dying, and rejected, and says to us: "Behold your King." A King enthroned upon a cross? Yes. Christ reigns from the cross. What is a King but the one responsible for bringing peace and prosperity, justice and order to a people? On the cross, Christ does just that for us. The human family had fallen from grace when our first parents gave in to temptation and rebelled against God. Thereafter the proliferation of sin demolished the order, the peace, and the joy of God's original design for creation. Jesus Christ came to earth to put things right, to "undo the work of the Devil" (1 Jn 3:8). His obedience "unto death, and death on a cross" (Phil 2:8) reversed the disobedience of Adam and Eve and closed the breach opened by man's rebellion against God, making possible once again intimate friendship between them, the friendship which alone can produce true peace and order in the heart of men and human societies.

One of the thieves detected this somehow. He watched as Christ carried his cross to Calvary. He saw the Lord nailed to the wood and lifted up from the earth. And through it all, he saw how differently Jesus suffered. There was pain and humiliation, but no fear, no panic, no hatred. The Lord bore it all with purpose, determination, and serenity; he bore it like the King he truly is. And the good thief recognized this. Hope kindled in his heart, even at that darkest hour. He looked into Christ's eyes and made an act of faith, a promise of loyalty, and he did not go unrewarded.

Indeed, Christ the King does reign from the cross, the perfect expression of his unconditional yes to the Father, the yes that conquered sin, death, and the devil, the yes of unconditional forgiveness that opened for us the gates of Heaven: "Father, forgive them.... Today you will be with me in Paradise."

CHRIST THE TEACHER At Calvary, Christ teaches us what he meant when he proclaimed, "Mine is not a Kingdom of this world" (John 18:36) and "If anyone wants to be a follower of mine, let him renounce himself and take up his cross every day and follow me" (Lk 9:23). Jesus faithfully obeyed the Father's will. In this fallen world, such obedience led him to experience physical torture, abandonment by his friends, mockery and misunderstanding from his peers, humiliation, sorrow, and death.

When we decide to follow Christ, we can expect much of the same. Only through death to ourselves, to our selfishness and vanity, can the new life of Christ take root in us: "If then we have died with Christ, we believe we will also live with him" (Rom 6:8). Each time we see a crucifix, not only do we see our King enthroned, but we see the path we must follow to enter his Kingdom.

CHRIST THE FRIEND *Jesus: The people watched and stared at me hanging and dying on the cross; do you see them? I saw them so clearly. The rulers sneered at me; the soldiers mocked me; one of the thieves abused me.... You were there too, along with all of those who have called themselves Christians. Every time my followers fail to come to their neighbor's aid, they join Calvary's passive spectators; when they disdain the teachings of the Church, they join the sneering rulers and mocking soldiers; when they give up their faith or let it smolder because they prefer the passing kingdoms of this world, they join the abusive thief.*

I saw your face looking up at me as I hung upon the cross. At first you laughed and mocked; you were distracted and careless, just like the others. Then you saw that I was looking at you, waiting for you, hoping in you, and your expression changed. A flash of recognition flitted across your eyes. I knew that you had glimpsed my love and that you were sorry. And even then, in my agony, I smiled. As soon as you repent, as soon as you come to me in your need and ask me to be your King, I take you by the hand and rejoice in leading you to Paradise.

CHRIST IN MY LIFE If you reign from a cross, why do I still look for earthly glory and pleasure? Am I not your follower? I only have a short time to work for you here on earth, Lord. Help me to spend it well. Help me to love and rejoice in you and to help as many others as possible to do the same. With the Kingdom of your heart, reign in my heart…

Please purify my heart, Lord. I still desire fruitfulness and fulfillment without self-mastery and self-sacrifice. How many times I make the sign of the cross! And yet I still run from so many of the crosses that you send me. Teach me to embrace my cross. Teach me to trust in your truth, to do what is right, to put you first, my neighbor second, and myself third…

My sins crucified you, Lord. When I sin, I banish you from my world, just as the Pharisees tried to banish you from theirs. I hate sin, Lord. Even as I say it, I know that I will be tempted, but you know that my heart is yours. I am still full of selfishness, which holds me back from loving you, but I trust in you. You can renew me…

Questions for SMALL-GROUP DISCUSSION

1. What struck you most in this passage? What did you notice that you hadn't noticed before?
2. What can we do to avoid getting so used to seeing the crucifix that we become oblivious to the inexhaustible lessons Christ has to teach us from the cross?
3. What has helped you the most in your efforts to imitate Christ by accepting and responding ingeniously to difficulties, persecution, ridicule, or resistance, without getting frustrated or discouraged? What tends to encourage you to adopt the mentality of those who will serve Christ only if he comes down from the cross and does things "my way"?
4. What most inhibits us from trusting Christ enough to regularly bring our sins and sinfulness to him in the sacrament of reconciliation, instead of making him wait for us while we continue rejecting his grace?

Cf. Catechism of the Catholic Church, 606-618, 550, 853, and 440 on the meaning of Christ's sacrifice at Calvary; 1430-1433 on the importance of repentance; 2015, 1816, and2427 on the role of sacrifice and self-denial in the Christian walk

234. The Perfect Death (Lk 23:44-56)

"We are celebrating the feast of the cross, and with the crucified one we are raised up, leaving behind us the earth and sins so that we may possess what is above."
– St. Andrew of Crete

LUKE 23:44-56
It was now about the sixth hour and, with the sun eclipsed, a darkness came over the whole land until the ninth hour. The veil of the Temple was torn right down the middle; and when Jesus had cried out in a loud voice, he said, "Father, into your hands I commit my spirit." With these words he breathed his last. When the centurion saw what had taken place, he gave praise to God and said, "This was a great and good man." And when all the people who had gathered for the spectacle saw what had happened, they went home beating their breasts. All his friends stood at a distance; so also did the women who had accompanied him from Galilee, and they saw all this happen. Then a member of the council arrived, an upright and virtuous man named Joseph. He had not consented to what the others had planned and carried out. He came from Arimathaea, a Jewish town, and he lived in the hope of seeing the kingdom of God. This man went to Pilate and asked for the body of Jesus. He then took it down, wrapped it in a shroud and put him in a tomb which was hewn in stone in which no one had yet been laid. It was Preparation Day and the sabbath was imminent. Meanwhile the women who had come from Galilee with Jesus were following behind. They took note of the tomb and of the position of the body. Then they returned and prepared spices and ointments. And on the sabbath day they rested, as the Law required.

CHRIST THE LORD At the very moment of his apparent defeat, our King begins to enjoy the abundant spoils of his eternal victory—the allegiance of loving hearts. The centurion, who had overseen Christ's whole condemnation, torture, mockery, and expiration, opens his heart with an act of faith; he becomes a soldier of Christ. The bystanders, who minutes before had been laughing and berating, repent as they stumble home. His friends and followers stand gazing at their Lord, unable to turn away from this horrendous scene, which has become beautiful to them and has changed their hearts forever. Joseph of Arimathea, a member of the Sanhedrin, risks his own reputation as he publicly defies the enemies of Christ and pays homage to his crucified Lord. The women of Galilee show their fierce and constant fidelity, obeying the Law while they also obey the law of love by preparing spices to anoint their beloved

Jesus. As much as the powers of darkness tried to shatter once and for all the Kingdom of Christ, his followers continue to serve him, like iron filings that just keep converging on a magnet.

Love—Christ's love—is stronger than death.

CHRIST THE TEACHER Jesus taught us how to live, seeking and fulfilling God's will in all things, loving God and loving our neighbor. Now he teaches us how to die. He dies so well that in the very moment of death he wins a convert: "When the centurion saw what had taken place, he gave praise to God…."

Death will come for each of us. It is one of the few things the future holds that we can be absolutely sure of. And yet we spend precious little time considering it and preparing for it. Christians are not meant to be obsessed with death, but neither should they join the swelling ranks of those who frantically distract themselves from this simple truth.

Jesus dies well because he dies in perfect communion with the Father. At the end of his earthly mission, as he feels his life slipping away from him, he is able to pray, "Father, into your hands I commit my spirit." It is a phrase from the Psalms (Ps 31:5). It shows us the two qualities of a good death. First, Jesus was close to the Father. In the moment of final crisis, God is not a stranger to him. God is not someone Jesus has been trying to deceive, avoid, or play games with. God is his Father. Second, it shows Jesus' total trust in God's goodness. Few realities instill fear like death, when our very lives, our very selves seem to be drifting outside our grasp. Panic and despair often take over, but not for Jesus. Quietly, confidently, surely, he commits his soul and all that will come after into the Father's hands.

Staying close to God through daily prayer and frequent sacramental life, especially frequent confession, is the best preparation we can make for this all-important event. And spending at least as much time filling our minds with thoughts of God's goodness (drawn from reflection, readings, and conversations) as we do filling it with the flotsam and jetsam of news and useless chatter will help store up inner peace and strength for our final battle. But if death comes and finds us unprepared, we need not fear. If we say with Jesus his own last prayer, how could the Father not honor it?

CHRIST THE FRIEND *Mary: It is over. He has done it. He has revealed everything. The world now knows that God is not a tyrant, not a cold architect, not a fickle force. Now they know that he is a Lover. Lovers give their lives for the ones they love. He has given his life. He has given it in such a way that anyone who sees him will be attracted by his meekness and mercy, just as you have been. His mercy is more powerful* *than all the greatness of this passing world. Now you know that you can trust him. He seeks nothing for himself—do you see him on the cross? He cares nothing for himself; all his teaching and all his will is for your good, for your happiness. Now you don't have to be suspicious. Trust him. Tell others that they can trust him. And you will see that this cross, erected to deal out death, has become the new and everlasting Tree of Life.*

CHRIST IN MY LIFE I am one of your followers, Lord, and I want to follow you to the end. Who else is there to follow? Who else has done so much for me? Thank you for being completely faithful. How I have longed for someone who will be faithful! Teach me to be faithful—faithful to my family and friends, faithful to my conscience, faithful to my mission in life, just like you...

When will my death come, Lord? What will it be like? You know. I don't need to know. I only need to know that it will come. Of course I am afraid of it a little bit. But you have gone before me, and you have shown me how to go there. Help me to remember that this life is only a journey. Jesus, I hope in you...

Love is more than feelings—it is self-giving; it is the cross. I want to learn to love the way you created me to love, and I want to experience the immense joy and meaning that come from a life given to loving. I can't receive you in Communion right now, but come at least spiritually into my heart as I unite myself to your sacrifice of love. Teach me to love...

Questions for SMALL-GROUP DISCUSSION

1. What struck you most in this passage? What did you notice that you hadn't noticed before?
2. What is the significance of the sky going dark during the last hours of Christ's agony? Of the Temple veil being torn in two at the moment of his death?
3. Why do you think St. Luke makes a point of twice mentioning the women from Galilee in this passage?
4. What is your favorite artistic depiction of the crucifixion and why?

Cf. Catechism of the Catholic Church, 440, 550, 617, 813, 1505, 1741, 1992, and 2305 on the effects of the sacrifice of the cross; 1323, 1364-66, and 1382 on the Eucharist as the ever-present sacrifice of the cross; 1005-1014 on the Christian vision of death; 1684-1690 on the celebration of funerals

THE GOSPEL OF LUKE
Chapter 24

"Though Lord, he became man; he suffered for those who were suffering, he was bound for the captive, judged for the condemned, buried for the one who was buried; he rose from the dead and cried out: 'Who shall contend with me? Let him stand up to face me. I have freed the condemned, brought the dead to life, raised up the buried. Who will speak against me?' 'I am the Christ,' he says, 'It is I who destroyed death, who triumphed over the enemy, who trampled Hades underfoot, who bound the strong one and snatched man away to the heights of heaven; I am the Christ."

– ST. MELITO OF SARDIS

235. Love and Life (Lk 24:1-12)

"You are alive! Your murderers handled your life like farmers: they sowed it like grain deep in the earth, for it to spring up and raise with itself a multitude of men." – St. Ephraem

LUKE 24:1-12

On the first day of the week, at the first sign of dawn, they went to the tomb with the spices they had prepared. They found that the stone had been rolled away from the tomb, but on entering discovered that the body of the Lord Jesus was not there. As they stood there not knowing what to think, two men in brilliant clothes suddenly appeared at their side. Terrified, the women lowered their eyes. But the two men said to them, "Why look among the dead for someone who is alive? He is not here; he has risen. Remember what he told you when he was still in Galilee: that the Son of Man had to be handed over into the power of sinful men and be crucified, and rise again on the third day?" And they remembered his words. When the women returned from the tomb they told all this to the Eleven and to all the others. The women were Mary of Magdala, Joanna, and Mary the mother of James. The other women with them also told the apostles, but this story of theirs seemed pure nonsense, and they did not believe them. Peter, however, went running to the tomb. He bent down and saw the binding cloths but nothing else; he then went back home, amazed at what had happened.

CHRIST THE LORD No one escapes death. Emperors die, geniuses die, business tycoons die—death is the great equalizer, the great reminder that we are not gods. But Christ rose from the dead; he conquered the grave. He died, yet he is still alive. He lives and reigns now, in this very moment. He is as alive as anyone walking the earth today, even though he truly died. No other historical figure has even made such a claim, let alone given proof, century after century (through the otherwise inexplicable vitality of the Church), to substantiate the claim. The Resurrection is Christ's trump card, Christian life's unshakable foundation. This is our Lord, the definitive conqueror of sin and death. We, like Peter, should be "amazed." If we are not, we don't really know our Lord.

CHRIST THE TEACHER The Resurrection validates all of Christ's other lessons. Without it, they would be nice pieces of advice, beautiful ones even, but ultimately impractical. If his doctrine doesn't lead to true life, why make the sacrifices necessary to follow it? By rising from the dead, he confirms that his doctrine does lead to life. The Resurrection is his "most marvelous work," as St. Augustine put it. The odd thing is that he entrusts the announcement of this all-important message to his weak and fragile followers. Unless we spread the news, it won't get spread at all.

The news of this most marvelous work doesn't come from his own lips. He entrusts the message first to the angels, then to the women who came to his tomb. Only after the women hear the news from the angels does he appear to them (cf. St. Matthew's version); and only after the women have announced the news to the apostles does he appear to them. This is the pattern of evangelization in all times and places: a personal, life-changing encounter with the living Lord is always mediated by Christian witness. We who have met the risen Jesus through the gift of faith have to announce the good news to those who have not. As St. Paul put it: "But how can they call on him in whom they have not believed? And how can they believe in him of whom they have not heard? And how can they hear without someone to preach?" (Rom 10:14).

CHRIST THE FRIEND *Joanna: When the angels spoke to us, they called Jesus "someone who is alive." The words struck me, though I only had time to reflect on them later. At the time, we were so exhausted by our sadness and shocked by the bright angels and the open tomb that we couldn't think at all. I am sure we were quite incoherent when we went to tell the apostles. How beautiful are the angel's words! Jesus truly is the one most alive, because he is the one who loves the most. The cross was the testament to his immense love; the Resurrection is the testament to his overflowing life. God is love, and God is also the source of all life. True life and true love are inextricably intertwined.*

When Jesus offered me his friendship, he was inviting me to share in his life. That meant experiencing his love so that I could learn to love as he does, which is the path to the indescribable life he wishes to give us.

Jesus: I want my life to be your life. Imagine an iron rod being thrust into a blazing fire. Just as the cold, hard rod becomes red-hot and supple, taking on the characteristics of the fire, so your life, united in friendship to mine, will take on the intensity of my life. I came for this, that you might have life and have it in all its abundance.

CHRIST IN MY LIFE How little I think about your Resurrection, Lord! And yet, you really did rise from the dead. Only you have done it. I believe in your goodness, and I believe in your power. And so I will continue to seek your will for my life, because your will is both your goodness and your power custom-fitted to the needs and yearnings of my soul. Teach me to do your will...

Sometimes I am intimidated by the commission you have given me to spread your Kingdom. But you don't ask me to convert the world, you just ask me to bear witness right here and right now, with my life, and when necessary with words, to all that you have done for me. All I need to do is make myself available, and you will take care of the rest. Jesus, I trust in you...

Mary, your heart still beats with Christ's. I want to burn with the love that consumes your heart. I want to live the life of overflowing abundance, unlimited surrender, and uncontainable joy that Jesus gave to you and gives to all his saints, to everyone who trusts in him unconditionally. Let it be done to me according to his word...

Questions for SMALL-GROUP DISCUSSION

1. What struck you most in this passage? What did you notice that you hadn't noticed before?
2. Why do you think the reality of the Resurrection doesn't have a bigger impact on our lives? Why don't we think it about it more often?
3. How concerned should we be about spreading the good news of Christ's Resurrection (and all that it implies)? How should we show that concern?
4. How can we deepen our friendship with Christ this week—allowing him to be more alive in our daily lives?

Cf. Catechism of the Catholic Church, 638-655 on the meaning of Christ's Resurrection; 599-618 on the meaning of Christ's death

236. The Lord Draws Near (Lk 24:13-35)

"This glorious son of the carpenter, who set up his cross above the all-consuming world of the dead, led the human race into the abode of life." – St. Ephraem

LUKE 24:13-35

That very same day, two of them were on their way to a village called Emmaus, seven miles from Jerusalem, and they were talking together about all that had happened. Now as they talked this over, Jesus himself came up and walked by their side; but something prevented them from recognising him. He said to them, "What matters are you discussing as you walk along?" They stopped short, their faces downcast. Then one of them, called Cleopas, answered him, "You must be the only person staying in Jerusalem who does not know the things that have been happening there these last few days." "What things?" he asked. "All about Jesus of Nazareth," they answered, "who proved he was a great prophet by the things he said and did in the sight of God and of the whole people; and how our chief priests and our leaders handed him over to be sentenced to death, and had him crucified. Our own hope had been that he would be the one to set Israel free. And this is not all: two whole days have gone by since it all happened; and some women from our group have astounded us: they went to the tomb in the early morning, and when they did not find the body, they came back to tell us they had seen a vision of angels who declared he was alive. Some of our friends went to the tomb and found everything exactly as the women had reported, but of him they saw nothing."

Then he said to them, "You foolish men! So slow to believe the full message of the prophets! Was it not ordained that the Christ should suffer and so enter into his glory?" Then, starting with Moses and going through all the prophets, he explained to them the passages throughout the scriptures that were about himself. When they drew near to the village to which they were going, he made as if to go on; but they pressed him to stay with them. "It is nearly evening," they said, "and the day is almost over." So he went in to stay with them. Now while he was with them at table, he took the bread and said the blessing; then he broke it and handed it to them. And their eyes were opened and they recognised him; but he had vanished from their sight. Then they said to each other, "Did not our hearts burn within us as he talked to us on the road and explained the scriptures to us?" They set out that instant and returned to Jerusalem. There they found the Eleven assembled together with their companions, who said to them, "Yes, it is true. The Lord has risen and has appeared to Simon." Then they told their story of what had happened on the road and how they had recognised him at the breaking of bread.

CHRIST THE LORD Leaders know how to motivate, how to inspire. The greater their leadership capacity, the deeper the motivations they stir up. A great teacher not only knows the subject well, but also spreads a passion for it among the students. A great statesman buoys up the hopes of citizens in times of trouble and inspires them to self-sacrifice for the common good. How much more in the case of Christ the Lord! These downcast disciples had given up. They had left everything to follow Jesus, but the events of Good Friday had dashed their hopes, and they were walking sadly back to their old lives. A few words from their Leader, however, an opening of their eyes to share his vision, and suddenly their heavy hearts were "burning" again, so much so that they retraced their seven-mile trek in the dark without complaint.

If we truly wish to follow Christ, he will lead us as no one ever could; if we attentively listen to him, he will stir up our hearts with a wisdom this world can never give.

CHRIST THE TEACHER The Risen One was recognized "at the breaking of the bread." That was one of the names the early Church used to refer to the celebration of the Eucharist. The gestures of Christ at supper with these two disciples mirror those of the Last Supper and have been perpetuated in those of the Mass: "He took the bread and said the blessing; then he broke it and handed it to them. And their eyes were opened and they recognized him." Do you want to find the Lord? Do you want to know him? Do you want to discover the inexhaustible riches of life in communion with him? He teaches us how: come to him in the Eucharist.

Our primary encounter with Christ in the Eucharist takes place through the sacrifice of the Mass, which makes Christ's unique sacrifice offered on the cross at Calvary present for us in the here-and-now of our lives. Notice how closely the structure of the Mass follows the structure of this encounter between Christ and the disciples on the road to Emmaus: Christ comes to meet them on the road; through the priest, Christ comes to meet us right where we are. In the midst of our sorrows and joys he is present, veiled behind the personality of the priest, but really there through the sacrament of Holy Orders. Christ then explains the scriptures to them, showing how they point to him, and relating them to the disciples' present needs; and what is the first part of Mass (the readings and the homily) if not a reenactment of this walk to Emmaus? Finally, Christ joins them for the evening meal and breaks bread with them; here is the second part of Mass, the Eucharistic prayers, the consecration of the bread and wine into Christ's Body and Blood, and the reception of Holy Communion. To have the privilege of participating in the celebration of the Eucharist is to encounter the Crucified and Risen One, and to let him set our hearts on fire.

CHRIST THE FRIEND "Jesus himself came up and walked by their side." Christ continues to do this every day in the Blessed Sacrament. In every Mass, in every Tabernacle, he draws near to us and walks by our side. In Holy Communion, he continues to share his life with us. He is truly present, reaching out to us, speaking to our hearts, behind the thin veil of faith. If only we, like these two disciples, are honest and courageous enough to open our hearts to him and invite him into the secret places of our souls, we will see him anew, and his love will burn within us.

Jesus: I know when you are downcast and sad. I know when the shadow of the cross and Good Friday make you turn away from Jerusalem and head back to your old ways. I know, and I care, more than you can imagine. I am always drawing near to you. I speak in the quiet voice of your conscience, where only you can hear me. Sometimes I speak to you through the words of a friend or a verse from the Bible. Whenever you hear my voice, and you know when you do, you have only to welcome it, to make your prayer the same as these two disciples who pressed me to stay with them. Will I ever deny such a request, I who came all the way down from heaven just because I couldn't stand being far away from you? This is why I came; this is why I died; this is why I rose again—to stay with you.

CHRIST IN MY LIFE I have chosen to follow you, Lord, and no one else. I know it's only because you called me, but I have made the choice. You didn't force me. And I want to be true to that choice. You are the Lord. You are the fount of wisdom, forgiveness, love, and life that fills the world with whatever goodness it has. Make me a channel of your grace, a riverbed for your flowing fountain...

The struggles of my life seem so irrelevant sometimes when I go to Mass. But how could they be? Do you not care about them? Dear Lord, it's a mystery to me, this passing life, so busy but so out of focus. Help me to know in each moment what I should do and how I should be. I have only this life to live, and I want to live it well...

Stay with me, Lord. How I need a friend who knows me through and through and doesn't judge me! How I need a coach who knows my strengths and weaknesses and who knows how to profit from the former and shore up the latter!

I feel such a burning desire to do something worthwhile, to do more—you put that desire in my heart. Now show me what to do with it...

Questions for SMALL-GROUP DISCUSSION

1. What struck you most in this passage? What did you notice that you hadn't noticed before?
2. Why do you think Christ appeared to these two disciples but didn't reveal his identity until the end of the encounter? Why did he disappear at that point?
3. What was the real reason that these two disciples were "downcast"?
4. Why did Christ give the impression that he was going on further ("He made as if to go on...")? What lesson is there in that for us?

Cf. Catechism of the Catholic Church, 1322-1405 on the meaning of the Eucharist

237. Amazing Peace (Lk 24:36-48)

"He submitted to death and endured it of his own free will, in order to destroy death against death's will." – St. Ephraem

LUKE 24:36-48
They were still talking about all this when he himself stood among them and said to them, "Peace be with you!" In a state of alarm and fright, they thought they were seeing a ghost. But he said, "Why are you so agitated, and why are these doubts rising in your hearts? Look at my hands and feet; yes, it is I indeed. Touch me and see for yourselves; a ghost has no flesh and bones as you can see I have." And as he said this he showed them his hands and feet. Their joy was so great that they still could not believe it, and they stood there dumbfounded; so he said to them, "Have you anything here to eat?" And they offered him a piece of grilled fish, which he took and ate before their eyes. Then he told them, "This is what I meant when I said, while I was still with you, that everything written about me in the Law of Moses, in the Prophets and in the Psalms has to be fulfilled." He then opened their minds to understand the scriptures, and he said to them, "So you see how it is written that the Christ would suffer and on the third day rise from the dead, and that, in his name, repentance for the forgiveness of sins would be preached to all the nations, beginning from Jerusalem. You are witnesses to this."

CHRIST THE LORD In describing this appearance to his disciples, St. Luke emphasizes the reality of Christ's resurrected body. They were not seeing a ghost; it was not a mass hallucination; it was far too shocking to be wishful thinking—Jesus makes all of this abundantly clear by his gestures and actions. As the reality of his complete, physical, personal presence sinks in, the disciples are overcome with joy and amazement. Their Lord had turned the worst of defeats into a definitive victory; he had conquered injustice, violence, hatred, rejection, and death itself by taking them all upon himself and then dissolving them in the Resurrection. If such an unparalleled event had failed to elicit joy and amazement on behalf of those who love him and put his trust in him, something would have been very wrong.

The level of our spiritual joy and amazement when we contemplate these same realities can in turn give us an inkling of the level of our love and trust. We cheer with gusto when our favorite team wins the championship; how enthusiastically do our hearts cheer at the Resurrection of our Lord, the pledge of our own resurrection?

CHRIST THE TEACHER Christ's glorified body suffers none of the limitations of our natural body, but it still bears the marks of his sacrifice on the cross. He shows his wounds to the disciples to prove to them that it really is he. To this day, as he reigns in heaven, he still bears those wounds; he will bear them throughout all eternity. They are God's remarkable answer to the perennial question of human suffering. He doesn't explain the mystery with a syllogism or a philosophical discourse; he explains it by taking it upon himself and bathing it in everlasting glory. If we unite our sufferings to those of Christ, if we attach our crosses to his, then all of our wounds will be found in his, and they all will share in his eternal splendor. The hardship of following Christ—the cross—is only half the story; the joy and glory of following Christ—the Resurrection—is the other half. If we accept the one, it's only because we believe firmly in the other.

CHRIST THE FRIEND *Jesus: Do you remember what I said most often after my Resurrection? "Peace be with you." Peace. Peace is my antidote to modern man's most endemic diseases: stress, depression, and anxiety—and I know you have been affected by those diseases. If you trust in me, I will give you all the peace you need: peace for your mind, because when you look at my wounds that are now sharing my everlasting life, you can know for certain that my unbounded forgiveness lasts forever; peace for your heart, because when you see those nail marks and my pierced side, you know for certain that I love you with an undying, unconditional, personal, determined love—and that too will never change; peace for your soul, because I who am your King reign now and always,* *and I have given you a task worthy of the restlessness that stirs your will. You are to be my witness, both among those close at hand in your own Jerusalem, and to all peoples everywhere through your surrender to my will, your prayers, your example, and your apostolic activity. I want to give you my peace. Trust me, and you will be able to accept it.*

CHRIST IN MY LIFE I am like your disciples, Lord: reluctant to believe. I see the bad side, the hard side, the problems. These come easily to mind. But at times it seems almost impossible for me to smile, to laugh, to rejoice in the victory that I know you have shared with me. Teach me, Lord. Train me. Open my eyes. Fill me with your light. With the joy of your heart, expand my heart...

You are in heaven right now, body and soul. And you are preparing a place for me there. You want me to come and spend eternity in the adventure of your friendship. You will resurrect my body too and will give me a share in your glory. Help me to taste the joy and amazement that your goodness and power should stir up in my mind. Blessed be your name in all the earth...

Not only do I want to experience your peace, the peace that goes deeper than emotions and passing moods, but I want to be a channel of your peace. Fill me with your abundant fullness of life, Lord; fill me so much that I overflow with it, spreading it to everyone I meet, work, and live with. With the Kingdom of your heart, reign in my heart...

Questions for SMALL-GROUP DISCUSSION

1. What struck you most in this passage? What did you notice that you hadn't noticed before?
2. If a non-believing acquaintance were to challenge you by claiming that Christ's Resurrection was just a hoax, how would you respond?
3. What can we do to live more fully the steady, deep, consistent peace that comes from a solid and vibrant friendship with Jesus Christ?
4. Spiritual writers often tell us to unite our sufferings to Christ's. What has helped you to do that? What difference does this make in your life?

Cf. Catechism of the Catholic Church, 631-658 on the nature and meaning of the Resurrection; 1047, 1468, 1784, and 2302 on peace of heart and the Christian life; 609, 440, 601, 1505 and 1521 on the meaning of suffering

238. Anchored in Heaven (Lk 24:49-53)

"Let us keep ever before our eyes this great thought—everything in this world comes to an end, whether it be prosperity or adversity. Eternity alone never ends." – St. Alphonsus Ligouri

LUKE 24:49-53

"And now I am sending down to you what the Father has promised. Stay in the city then, until you are clothed with the power from on high." Then he took them out as far as the outskirts of Bethany, and lifting up his hands he blessed them. Now as he blessed them, he withdrew from them and was carried up to heaven. They worshipped him and then went back to Jerusalem full of joy; and they were continually in the Temple praising God.

CHRIST THE LORD In Luke's Gospel, this scene takes place immediately after Jesus appeared to his apostles, showed them his wounds, and ate with them in order to assure them that he was no mere ghost. Thus, his Ascension into heaven shares in the earthly reality of the rest of his Resurrection appearances. It is not an ethereal dissipation into some shadowy realm of vague symbols; it is the establishment of his Kingship on unshakable ground. Earthly kings and emperors always remain vulnerable; if their enemies don't usurp them, death surely will. But Christ's reign will never come to an end. Because he has ascended into heaven, his Kingdom is firm; his Church will never be destroyed. If we stay faithful to this King, our victory over sin, evil, and injustice (and the happiness that such a victory implies) is assured. Christ's Ascension should fill us with joy, as it did his disciples, because now we know for certain that the Christian cause is unassailable and that Christ's Lordship is imperturbable.

CHRIST THE TEACHER Christ's entire life—his words and works, and above all his suffering, death, and Resurrection—is a lesson. It teaches us the way to repentance for the forgiveness of sins. Nothing is more important, since sin separates us from God, the only source of lasting happiness. This lesson must be preached in his name to all nations, as Christ instructed his apostles before this parting scene. For that reason, the apostles were called upon to be witness of these things. Of course, they would not be able to carry out their witness all by themselves; they would need the Holy Spirit. They would need to be "clothed with power from on high," which happened at Pentecost. Thus, in the Ascension of our Lord, we come face-to-face with the core of the entire Gospel: Christ's saving message being transmitted to all people through the ministry of the Church.

Sometimes we become so involved in related but secondary issues (theological squabbles, new projects and ministries...) that we forget about this core. We shouldn't need to wait for the annual liturgical Solemnity of the Ascension to return to it—to focus once again on the essentials and cut away any superfluities that might have been accumulating in the décor of our Christian life.

CHRIST THE FRIEND *Jesus: Before I left them, I blessed them. Do you realize that the same blessing continues to radiate throughout the world today? What is my Church, if not the extension of my blessing, my life-giving love and grace, into every time and place, to all the nations? Isn't that how you discovered my love for you, through my Church? How I long to bless you even more! How I long to draw you closer and closer to my heart. My fullness of life is no good to me alone. I want to share it with you, to fill you to overflowing with my abundant, fruitful life. I have no hidden agendas, no second, selfish intentions. What more could I desire than what I already have, unless it is your heart, the full flourishing of your soul? I want to bless you, and I want the blessing of your friendship...*

CHRIST IN MY LIFE Who else can say, "My Kingdom will last forever"? No one. Absolutely no one else can say that. Only you. And you are mine, and I am yours. Dear Lord, thank you for giving me the gift of faith. Never let me take it for granted. Never let me be discouraged by the trials of life. You are reigning right now from a throne that will never pass away...

I am your messenger, Lord. Your triumph over sin and evil is my message. But so often, I really have no idea how to get the message across. I want to spread your Kingdom; I want to bear witness boldly, with words of truth and deeds of love. Be my strength, Lord, be my help; be my hands and feet and mouth. I give myself wholly to you—do with me as you please...

You know that I want to follow you. You know that the burdens and troubles of my life sometimes make me forget about that. Aren't you here in the midst of them? I know you are, but I need help to find you. You have given me so much, but I need even more, Lord. I need you to open my eyes so I can discover and embrace your will and love in every moment of every day...

Questions for *SMALL-GROUP DISCUSSION*

1. What struck you most in this passage? What did you notice that you hadn't noticed before?
2. What impact should this great mystery of the Ascension have on our lives?

3. How can we help each other stay focused on the important things in life—most especially defending and spreading Christ's Kingdom in our own hearts and in the hearts of those around us—and not be distracted by lesser concerns?
4. Why do you think Christ took his apostles out of Jerusalem before blessing them and ascending into heaven?

Cf. Catechism of the Catholic Church, 659-667 on the meaning of our Lord's Ascension; 748-750 and 758-769 on the Church's origin, foundation, and mission; 802-810 on Christ's presence in the Church

APPENDIX 1

UNITS LINKED TO PARTICULAR POINTS OF SPIRITUAL WORK

APOSTOLIC ZEAL: 149, 155, 156, 158, 159, 160, 162, 163, 165, 166, 167, 168, 169, 177, 178, 180, 181, 184, 185, 186, 187, 188, 190, 193, 196, 197, 198, 204, 205, 206, 208, 209, 214, 215, 216, 219, 221, 224, 225, 235, 236, 237, 238

CHARITY/LOVE FOR NEIGHBOR: 149, 158, 159, 162, 164, 169, 170, 171, 172, 173, 183, 187, 192, 196, 197, 199, 201, 204, 205, 206, 207, 208, 209, 216, 227, 230, 232

CONFIDENCE IN GOD (FAITH, HOPE, LOVE) (This point of spiritual work is the bedrock of Christianity. Almost every passage in the Bible can be read as a revelation of God's trustworthiness): 149, 150, 151, 152, 153, 154, 155, 156, 157, 159, 160, 161, 162, 163, 164, 165, 166, 167, 168, 169, 170, 171, 172, 173, 174, 175, 176, 177, 178, 179, 180, 181, 182, 183, 184, 185, 186, 187, 188, 189, 190, 191, 193, 194, 195, 196, 199, 201, 202, 203, 204, 205, 206, 207, 208, 209, 210, 212, 213, 214, 215, 216, 217, 218, 220, 221, 222, 223, 224, 226, 227, 228, 229, 230, 231, 232, 233, 234, 235, 236, 237, 238

DEATH/HEAVEN/HELL/JUDGMENT: 159, 170, 178, 186, 190, 194, 196, 198, 200, 202, 206, 211, 217, 220, 222, 224, 225, 226, 234, 235, 238

EUCHARIST: 150, 155, 172, 173, 180, 210, 227, 236

FORGIVENESS/MERCY/REPENTANCE/CONFESSION: 166, 170, 171, 173, 175, 187, 198, 204, 205, 210, 213, 216, 229, 233

HUMAN RESPECT/VANITY: 161, 163, 168, 169, 171, 175, 179, 180, 181, 188, 192, 193, 197, 201, 203, 204, 207, 213, 215, 221, 223, 224, 230, 231

HUMILITY/OBEDIENCE: 149, 151, 152, 153, 154, 157, 158, 159, 160, 161, 163, 165, 167, 169, 171, 172, 174, 175, 176, 177, 179, 180, 181, 183, 184, 186, 190, 191, 192, 196, 198, 200, 201, 203, 207, 209, 210, 211, 213, 214, 217, 218, 220, 226, 227, 228, 230, 231, 234

LOVE FOR THE CHURCH AND THE POPE: 149, 150, 157, 162, 168, 185, 186, 187, 196, 198, 227, 228, 238

MARY: 151, 152, 154, 155, 156, 157, 173, 177, 191, 230, 232, 234, 235

PATIENCE/FORTITUDE/PERSEVERANCE: 149, 150, 161, 169, 171, 179, 181, 182, 183, 184, 185, 189, 193, 196, 198, 199, 203, 207, 211, 212, 217, 219, 224, 225, 230, 232, 233

POVERTY/DETACHMENT: 151, 154, 155, 156, 161, 167, 170, 184, 185, 186, 187, 194, 195, 196, 202, 203, 206, 207, 208, 214, 216, 220, 223, 232

PRAYER: 150, 152, 153, 154, 155, 161, 164, 165, 166, 176, 177, 182, 185, 188, 189, 210, 211, 212, 225, 228, 229

PURITY/CHASTITY: 207, 222

PURITY OF INTENTION/SPIRITUAL SIMPLICITY: 149, 152, 161, 162, 166, 169, 175, 186, 187, 188, 192, 195, 196, 201, 205, 207, 209, 221, 223, 231

SIN/TEMPTATION: 158, 161, 166, 168, 171, 174, 175, 187, 190, 192, 198, 207, 208, 210, 213, 214, 217, 219, 225, 226, 229, 230, 232, 233

APPENDIX 2

Books on Prayer and the Spiritual Life

Navigating the Interior Life, Daniel Burke
This Tremendous Lover, Eugene Boylan
The Secrets of the Interior Life, Luis Martinez
Difficulties in Mental Prayer, Eugene Boylan
Talking with God, Francois Fenelon
How to Pray Always, Raoul Plus
Spiritual Combat, Lorenzo Scupoli
Weeds among the Wheat, Thomas H. Green, SJ
When the Well Runs Dry, Thomas H. Green, SJ
Opening to God, Thomas H. Green, SJ
A Vacation with the Lord, Thomas H. Green, SJ
Darkness in the Marketplace, Thomas H. Green, SJ
Prayer and Common Sense, Thomas H. Green, SJ

Sophia Institute

Sophia Institute is a nonprofit institution that seeks to nurture the spiritual, moral, and cultural life of souls and to spread the Gospel of Christ in conformity with the authentic teachings of the Roman Catholic Church.

Sophia Institute Press fulfills this mission by offering translations, reprints, and new publications that afford readers a rich source of the enduring wisdom of mankind.

Sophia Institute also operates the popular online resource CatholicExchange.com. *Catholic Exchange* provides world news from a Catholic perspective as well as daily devotionals and articles that will help readers to grow in holiness and live a life consistent with the teachings of the Church.

In 2013, Sophia Institute launched Sophia Institute for Teachers to renew and rebuild Catholic culture through service to Catholic education. With the goal of nurturing the spiritual, moral, and cultural life of souls, and an abiding respect for the role and work of teachers, we strive to provide materials and programs that are at once enlightening to the mind and ennobling to the heart; faithful and complete, as well as useful and practical.

Sophia Institute gratefully recognizes the Solidarity Association for preserving and encouraging the growth of our apostolate over the course of many years. Without their generous and timely support, this book would not be in your hands.

www.SophiaInstitute.com
www.CatholicExchange.com
www.SophiaInstituteforTeachers.org

Sophia Institute Press® is a registered trademark of Sophia Institute.
Sophia Institute is a tax-exempt institution as defined by the Internal Revenue Code, Section 501(c)(3). Tax I.D. 22-2548708.